IN SEARCH OF THE IRISH DREAMTIME

J. P. Mallory

IN SEARCH OF THE IRISH DREAMTIME

Archaeology & Early Irish Literature

 Thames & Hudson

For all my Machas

Frontispiece: The mound at Emain Macha, Co. Armagh.

First published in the United Kingdom in 2016 by Thames & Hudson Ltd,
181A High Holborn, London WC1V 7QX

In Search of the Irish Dreamtime
© 2016 Thames & Hudson Ltd, London

British Library Cataloguing-in-Publication Data
A catalogue record for this book is available from the British Library

ISBN 978-0-500-05184-9

Printed and bound in China by Everbest Printing Co. Ltd

To find out about all our publications,
please visit **www.thamesandhudson.com**.
There you can subscribe to our e-newsletter,
browse or download our current catalogue,
and buy any titles that are in print.

Contents

Preface

I t all started in the summer of 1968 when I walked into a Galway pub and met an Irishman who had fought with Alfred the Great. I still recall how I fell in with two drinkers, one a retired soldier in the Irish army who was quite unimpressed that an archaeologist could not write out Cleopatra's name in hieroglyphics (he could and did so to show me up). The other drinker was much younger, an Irish soldier whose hands were bandaged from a recent boxing match, and claiming that he had fought with Alfred the Great. I knew I looked gaunt but I didn't think I looked that simple minded until he explained that he really had fought with Alfred. The film *Alfred the Great* had recently been shot around Galway and, I presume, he and other members of his unit had either been banging their swords on shields under the command of Michael York's Viking Guthrum or making up numbers in David Hemmings's Anglo-Saxon *caput porcinum* or flying wedge.

The following day, a Sunday as I recall since there seemed to be no public transport, I attempted to hitch my way eastwards. As chance would have it, I had the incredible good fortune to be given a lift by kind-hearted Paddy Healy who was on his way to the Castlestrange stone in Roscommon, one of the few decorated La Tène stones known in Ireland. There we met up with Michael Duignan and his wife who were studying the stone. Michael was Professor of Celtic Archaeology in the National University in Galway and had already undertaken a study of the more famous (and larger) Turoe stone. Later that afternoon I went on my way and did not meet Michael again for nearly ten years, when I was invited to Galway to give a lecture. Only then did I discover that Michael had served as a technical advisor on *Alfred the Great* (though I hardly think he was responsible for putting an Irish round tower in the Wessex landscape).

In 1978 I was invited to contribute a paper to Michael Duignan's festschrift. As I had recently reread Kenneth Jackson's *The Oldest Irish Tradition*, this stimulated me to pour through every reference to swords in the Ulster cycle of tales to see how well they accorded with Jackson's passing statement that they reflected the type of swords employed in the Iron Age. For the festschrift, I published my paper on 'The sword of the Ulster cycle'. During the following year when I was desperately seeking some topic to convince the Institute of Irish Studies at Queen's University to appoint me their Senior Research Fellow, I proposed to make a thorough examination of the material culture of the Ulster tales. After my appointment, I found myself daily pouring through the tales, writing down information on 3 × 5 index cards, then transferring them onto sheets of paper, and eventually (with help from a graduate student who is now Professor Gregory Toner) inputting them onto my brand new Amstrad.

Since then I have occasionally published or edited work on the archaeology of early Irish literature, largely as a release valve from other research. Escaping into the worlds of Lug, Nuadu, the Dagda, Cú Chulainn, Emer, Fergus, Medb, Conchobar, Deirdre, Conall, Fintan and the others has always provided welcome displacement activities. But the Ulster cycle also managed to penetrate my more professional duties and I was fortunate enough to direct excavations at Haughey's Fort, the Late Bronze Age hillfort nearly adjacent to the centre of the Ulster tales and, finally in 1998, to excavate the ditch that surrounded Emain Macha, the ancient capital of Ulster.

This book, written in retirement, was initially intended to bring together many of the things that I had written about earlier. But once I began reviewing and updating the literature I realized that I would need to expand my view, incorporating much more recent research and also re-thinking earlier conclusions. I also discovered that there were still far more problems to deal with than I had earlier imagined and, I am afraid, enough of them still remain to keep another generation busy.

In a way, this book is a companion to my earlier *The Origins of the Irish* (2013) that attempted to examine the various origins of the land, people and language of Ireland up until the early Middle Ages when we can talk with certainty that we are dealing with a population that is recognizably Irish. In that book I set aside a short chapter, briefly summarizing (and dismissing) the native Irish account of their own origins as a series of invasions. This book is an attempt to revisit the native account in much greater detail but from a very different perspective. It should be emphasized that this book is not an attempt to recover or examine the mythology of the Celts across the Irish landscape. John Waddell has recently tackled this very subject.[1] Nor does this book dwell on the ancient tales of Ireland as works of literature as one might encounter, for example, in the excellent monographs of Anne Dooley[2] or Ralph O'Connor.[3] Rather, this is an exploration into the actual reality of the traditional Irish version of their earliest history that, at least since the Middle Ages, has claimed to offer the longest account of any nation in Europe.

In writing this book I wish to thank John Koch and my long-time academic sparring partner Richard Warner, for reading an earlier draft and attempting to reduce the number of outright howlers that I might have perpetrated on the public. Also, a very big thanks to Libby Mulqueeny of the School of Geography, Archaeology and Palaeoecology at Queen's University, Belfast, for preparing the illustrations. And thanks also to those whom I have pestered to supply me with essential reading material, information and illustrations (Finbar McCormick, Mark Gardiner, John Waddell, Paul Gosling, Phil Macdonald, Noel Ross, Raimund Karl, Chris Lynn and Jackie McDowell). A special thanks to Colin Ridler for encouraging me to complete this project and, especially, Ben Plumridge, who both edited my far from perfect manuscript and oversaw the layout of this book. And a final thanks to Tom Gordon Mallory who has had to endure countless treks to the graves of people who never existed.

Introduction

On 17 May 2011 Queen Elizabeth II, beginning her three-day tour of Ireland, visited the Garden of Remembrance in Parnell Square, Dublin. Established to commemorate those who had died in the cause of Irish freedom between 1798 and 1922, the garden depicts the disposal of the weapons of war, with images of shields, swords, scabbards and spears lying at the bottom of a long cruciform pool. At the head of the pool one encounters a large sculpture depicting a scene from one of the most iconic of the tales of early Ireland, the Children of Lir, who were turned into swans by a jealous stepmother (PL. XV).

Most nations would be content to consign such a story to a timeless mythological past. But not the Irish whose chroniclers set the tale to the generation after the reign of Eochaid Ollathar who died in 1740 BC.[1] Eochaid was the twelfth named king in Ireland's history and the medieval Irish have left us records of the events that occurred on the island since its first occupation. The account of the colonizations of Ireland describes not only the sequence of successful and unsuccessful attempts at settlement but also the making of the Irish landscape, the formation of its major rivers and lakes. It describes how kings and heroes introduced innovations to Irish culture, cleared forests, established fortifications and developed new symbols of power, wealth and technology. And once the land was fully settled by populations directly ancestral to the present population of Ireland (c. 1700 BC), manuscripts relate the events surrounding the reigns of kings whose dates can be determined to the precise year extending from what other nations would describe as deep prehistory to the 12th century AD. In short, the Irish possess a written account of their Dreamtime.

The concept of a Dreamtime is, of course, derived from the aboriginal peoples of Australia who recognize a sacred time in which both the natural world and human culture and traditions originated and that these beginnings still resonate in the spiritual life of people today. With apologies to the native peoples of Australia for appropriation or even misappropriation, I have employed this same term in the title of this

0.1. Statue of Macha by F. E. McWilliam at Altnagelvin Hospital, Derry. The unusual selection of an Irish war goddess as the 'patron' of a hospital is prompted by Geoffrey Keating, who claimed that Macha built a house of healing at Emain Macha.

book because of some similarities that can be found in Irish tradition which seem to tick at least some of the boxes of the Australian definition.[2] But does this tradition still have any valence?

We leave the Garden of Remembrance and take a short walk back toward the centre of town. Here we pass the General Post Office, where since 1935 has stood a bronze statue of Ireland's greatest warrior, Cú Chulainn, who reputedly died between 7 BC and AD 2, here symbolizing the blood sacrifice of those who fell during the Easter Rising (PL. XIII, PL. XVII). Cú Chulainn fought for an Ulster whose capital was at Emain Macha. The site is named after its founder, Macha, who reputedly ruled from 661 to 634 BC: F. E. McWilliam's statue of Macha stands today before Altnagelvin Hospital in Derry (FIG. 0.1). While most countries adorn their paper money with the portraits of their reigning monarch or a famous historical figure, before the Irish shed their own currency for the Euro, their one-pound (punt) note depicted Cú Chulainn's nemesis, Queen Medb of Connacht, who died in AD 70 (PL. XVI). A visit to Ardee, Co. Louth, will bring the tourist eye to eye with a more than life-sized statue of Cú Chulainn holding his foster-brother Fer Diad (PL. XIV) whom he tragically slew there during the great cattle-raid of Cooley (19 BC); and in the village of Knockbridge, Co. Louth, one encounters a plaque that informs the visitor, in four languages no less, that only a kilometre away stands the very stone against which, in AD 2, the dying Cú Chulainn bound himself over 2,000 years ago (FIG. 0.2; PL. I). The Irish landscape is littered with monuments that commemorate its Dreamtime.

But unlike the Australian, the Irish past is not only fixed in the landscape, it is also fixed in time and this changes things. Once one abandons *Fada ó shin* ('long ago') or 'Once upon a time...' and applies a precise chronological scale to the earliest accounts of Ireland's Dreamtime, the tales no longer seem so much *fabula*, stories of events that never happened, as *historia*, accounts of what really did happen. Until the mid-19th century this was certainly the attitude of many Irish scholars, who held up and defended a distinctly native historical tradition in the

0.2. Plaque at Knockbridge, Co. Louth, commemorating the death of Cú Chulainn.

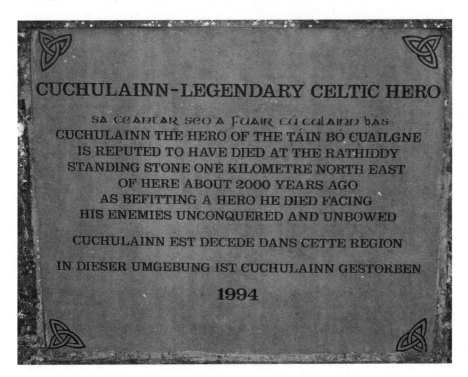

CUCHULAINN-LEGENDARY CELTIC HERO

SA CEANTAR SEO A FUAIR CÚ CULAINN BÁS
CUCHULAINN THE HERO OF THE TÁIN BÓ CUAILGNE
IS REPUTED TO HAVE DIED AT THE RATHIDDY
STANDING STONE ONE KILOMETRE NORTH EAST
OF HERE ABOUT 2000 YEARS AGO
AS BEFITTING A HERO HE DIED FACING
HIS ENEMIES UNCONQUERED AND UNBOWED

CUCHULAINN EST DECEDE DANS CETTE REGION

IN DIESER UMGEBUNG IST CUCHULAINN GESTORBEN

· 1994

face of a British account of Ireland's past that dismissed the local narrative as the product of 'lying bards'.

To put matters into a wider perspective, the early Irish claimed to have had a history that extended beyond that of the Greeks (be it the first Olympiad in 776 BC or the fall of Troy in c. 1184 BC), beyond the Etruscans (968 BC), Romans (753 BC for Rome, otherwise the fall of Troy as Aeneas flees), earlier than the Babylonians (747 BC), the Assyrians (c. 1700 BC), easily earlier than the latecomers of Japan (660 BC) and even earlier than the Chinese (2697 BC). In the Old World only a few such as the Egyptians (1st dynasty, c. 3100 BC) and the Jews (c. 3760 BC) trumped the Irish when it came to the length of their 'traditional' history.[3]

Of course, the past century has been far more critical of the Irish claims to great antiquity, yet there are still those who would argue that the accounts of at least some of these events and even characters may be accurate within certain limits and can still inform us of the general way of life that existed during the Irish Iron Age. This is still a bold claim indeed since it argues that after the classical world of the Greeks and Romans, the Irish retain the longest memory in Europe.

How can we assess such claims to antiquity? In the 19th century scholars such as Eugene O'Curry and W. K. Sullivan began to compare the world depicted in the earliest Irish literary tradition with the evidence then being assembled in the collections of the Royal Irish Academy. Irish archaeology has come a long way since then and after about a century and a half it is time for a fresh look.

CHAPTER ONE

Discovering the
Oldest Irish Tradition

...the Irish date their history from the first aeras of the world...so
that in comparison with them, the antiquity of all other countries
is modern, and almost in its infancy!

Roderic O'Flaherty[1]

In 1188 a 42-year-old prelate, diplomat and scholar spent three days entertaining
the citizens of Oxford with a public reading of his first-hand account of a 'wild
and inhospitable people' who were 'so barbarous that they cannot be said to have
any culture', and 'wallowing in vice' so much so that they contaminated any visitor to
their shores. They were also the 'most deceitful' people in the world although, as we
will soon see, the speaker was not very hard to fool. Their only saving grace was that
they seemed to have a good sense of rhythm. The speaker, Giraldus de Barri, more
commonly known as Giraldus Cambrensis or Gerald of Wales (FIG. 1.1), having
recently finished his fieldwork among this abhorrent people, had just completed a
book about them as he could no longer refrain from 'offering to public view the light
of wisdom burning clearly and carefully trimmed'. It is claimed that the Archbishop
of Canterbury, Baldwin of Forde, never tired of reading it. Needless to say, Giraldus'
work did not enjoy quite such a high reputation among the wild and deceitful subjects of his book, the people of Ireland.[2]

Giraldus divided *The History and Topography of Ireland* (*Topographia*) into three
parts, each of which he read out on separate days.[3] On the first day the poor of Oxford
were invited to hear about the landscape and animals of Ireland, especially the birds
(Giraldus believed that along with gold, birds from Ireland would make a suitable
tribute to Britain);[4] there was even a section on beavers that was just plain padding as
Giraldus well knew that there were no beavers in Ireland[5] (we will be reminded again
of this fact later on). They also got to hear his dismissal of the notion that St Patrick
had driven the snakes out of Ireland; according to Giraldus (and here he was correct),

1.1. Giraldus Cambrensis (1146–1223).

poisonous reptiles had never made it to the island in the first place. As Giraldus' book was in Latin it is difficult to know what an uneducated audience made of it. His friend, Walter Mapes, had written to him lamenting that his 'works, being in Latin, are understood by only a few persons'.[6] Perhaps the audience only turned up for the sandwiches.

On day two Giraldus invited the highest ranks of Oxford academics, who would have had no problem with Latin, to his reading of part two on the wonders and miracles of Ireland. Stories of the miraculous activities of Irish saints would have been common fare for such an assembly but one can only wonder what they made of his account of a fish with gold teeth, a talking wolf (FIG. 1.2), a half-man-half-ox or a wandering church bell.

On the final day it was the turn of the rest of the scholars, the knights and some other citizens to hear his account of the six attempted colonizations of Ireland. As we will need to revisit these in detail later, they are as follows:

1. Cæsara (Irish Cesair), granddaughter of Noah, attempted to colonize Ireland with a party of three men and 50 women but all were drowned in the Flood.

2. Bartholaunus (Partholón) and his people came to Ireland 300 years after the Flood and cleared forests to work the land. In another 300 years the population of Ireland had climbed to 9,000. Bartholaunus' people fought and won a major battle against a race of Giants (Fomorians) but a pestilence induced by their rotting corpses carried away the entire population save Ruan (Tuan) who survived until the time of St Patrick to relate the early history of Ireland.

3. Nemedus (Nemed), a Scythian, arrived with his sons and they too engaged against pirates (Fomorians). The population eventually

covered the entire island but the majority died in battle once again fighting the Giants (Fomorians). Nemed and his descendants held Ireland for 216 years. The survivors abandoned Ireland and returned to either Scythia or Greece.

4. The five brothers and sons of Dela (the Fir Bolg) then arrived in Ireland, which they divided up into its five provinces (the four current provinces with a central province of Meath (the 'middle'). After a time, one of the brothers, Slanius (Sláine) became the sole ruler and first king of Ireland.

5. The descendants of the fourth colonization suffered major losses against another invader from Scythia (that Giraldus does not mention by name but who are known in Irish as the Tuatha Dé Danann). His account of this invasion is subsumed in his treatment of his fifth (our sixth) colonization.

6. Eventually Ireland was colonized by the Sons of Milesius (Míl) who had come from Spain. They divided Ireland into halves under Herimon (Erimon) and Heber (Eber) and after the death of Heber, Herimon became the first king of the Irish 'race'.

Giraldus continued the story up through St Patrick and the coming of Christianity, the raids and settlements of the Norse, and until the barbarous Irish found themselves under the enlightened rule of Henry II, the 'invincible king', who (with some help from Giraldus' relatives) managed to conquer a substantial part of the land. A considerable portion of this section was also given over to the character assassination of the Irish, justifying the civilizing activities of the British crown.

1.2. A talking wolf implores a priest to grant the last rites to his mate.

According to the most ancient histories of the Irish...

So begins Giraldus' account of the six attempts to colonize Ireland undertaken by Cesair, Partholón, Nemed, the Fir Bolg, the Tuatha Dé Danann and, finally, the Sons of Míl from Spain. It appears that this 'most ancient' account was, in fact, a now lost Latin summary of the Irish original, the *Lebor Gabála Érenn* 'Book of the Takings of Ireland' (LG). This account of what John Carey has called the Irish National Origin Legend[7] (INOL) was compiled in the 11th century from various earlier poems that dealt with the initial settlement of Ireland through the coming of the immediate ancestors of the historical Irish. The antiquity of the account of Ireland's first colonists, in a Latin version, must go back to at least the 9th century since a similar account[8] also appears in the *Historia Britonum* (*c.* 829–830), dubiously attributed to another Welshman, Nennius, who is reputed to have gained it from learned men in Ireland.[9] There is evidence that some of the personages mentioned in this account appear in poems dating as far back as the 8th century[10] and incidents from the colonization were probably entered into the Irish annals in *c.* 743–753.[11] It should be recalled that before the Norse 'Troubles', the Irish monasteries were among the most sought after educational institutions in Europe where scholars came to study in both Latin and Old Irish. During the 7th century Aldhelm, the abbot of Malmesbury, described how boatloads of Englishmen came to Ireland to study[12] and even a number of Northumbrian kings learned Irish.[13] After all, the Venerable Bede had described the Irish as 'a harmless race that had always been most friendly to the English'.[14] It is in the 7th and 8th centuries that the most famous of Ireland's illuminated manuscripts such as *The Cathach*, and

1.3. An Irish scribe, after being tutored in calligraphy by an angel, tries his hand.

the books of Durrow and Kells were prepared; Giraldus regarded one such manuscript that he saw in Kildare as the work of angels (FIG. 1.3).[15]

If Giraldus had really wanted to do his homework on understanding the earliest traditions of the Irish, he would have tracked down one of the major compendia of Irish (rather than Latin) learning that were current in the 12th century, some of which still survive.[16] This was a time when the monasteries, who had endured pillaging by both the Norse and rival groups of Irish, were about to face a new threat from the Anglo-Normans, who had begun their conquest of the island in 1167. Gathering earlier books and manuscripts that had survived several centuries of onslaught, major anthologies of these earlier works were prepared and expanded upon in Irish monasteries. The oldest of these that still survives is known as the *Lebor na hUidre* (LU) or 'Book of the Dun Cow' (PL. IX) which had been initially compiled in 1106 since that is the date when one of its principal scribes had been killed during a raid on his monastery of Clonmacnoise in Co. Offaly. If Giraldus had knocked on the door when he was resident in Ireland (1183 and then again in 1185) to get a peek at the book he would probably have received a frosty welcome as the Normans had torched the monastery in 1179, burning over 100 houses. It is believed that by then the manuscript had been taken far to the west (Connacht or Donegal) for safe keeping. Of the original manuscript, only 67 leaves survive today but during Giraldus' time he would probably have been able to view the now missing 66 leaves. These would have been critical to his research because they likely included the *Lebor Gabála Érenn* that was the initial text in a number of other such anthologies and was referred to by later authors.[17] All that remains of this earliest account of the Irish National Origin Legend in the *Lebor na hUidre* today is a section on the children of Noah.[18]

If Giraldus had chosen to do his research at the monastery of Terryglass in north Tipperary he would have had similar luck. This monastery had possessed a much larger compendium which is properly known as the *Lebor na Núachongbála* but, thankfully, far more commonly as the 'Book of Leinster' (LL). This manuscript was closely associated with Dermot Mac Murrough, the king of Leinster who was driven out of his own country in 1166, five years after the initial stage of preparing the text had been completed. The manuscript even laments the king's exile although the later Irish would have prayed that he had never returned for Dermot is the king who sought allies in Britain and returned with Anglo-Norman knights, including two uncles of Giraldus, and who initiated the English conquest of Ireland. Two years before Dermot was forced into exile, the monastery had been destroyed by fire and Giraldus would have had to chase the manuscript up from where it had been taken for safe keeping,

1.4. A page of the *Lebor Gabála* from the *Book of Leinster* outlining the invasions of Ireland.

possibly Co. Laois. Should Giraldus had been lucky enough to find it and an Irishman to translate it for him, he would have found that the first 14 pages opened with the *Lebor Gabála Érenn* whose English translation runs to a little more than 50 pages (one could compress a lot of material onto a page of an Irish manuscript).[19]

A scholar armed with both the 'Book of the Dun Cow' and the 'Book of Leinster' would have possessed enough material to keep the good citizens of Oxford both informed and entertained for many months. The early version of the *Lebor Gabála* (copied into the 'Book of Leinster'; FIG. 1.4) not only presented a historical account of the peopling of Ireland (in addition throwing in a reference to how the British were colonized by the offspring of an Irish ancestor) but also provides the 'back-story' to a series of tales that flesh out many of the characters or events recorded in it, or events that should have happened in about the same period covered by the *Lebor Gabála*.

The cycles

The earliest Irish manuscripts not only contained poems and prose narratives but also partial indices of the various stories. The earliest compendia list 185 or so tales or *scéla* (singular *scél*; the Vikings lost the Battle of Clontarf so let's avoid the use of *saga*, which is more appropriate for Norse tales, and use the Old Irish forms). These were catalogued according to genre: courtships, elopements, battles, destructions, cattle-raids, migrations, deaths and so on.[20] Modern scholarship has tended to group them otherwise, generally into four main groups that can be organized both topically and chronologically into the following sequence:

1. The Mythological cycle. These tales primarily relate to the earliest settlement of Ireland down until about the 1st century BC. The historical core, if you will, is the *Lebor Gabála* and the 'prehistoric' events mentioned in the Irish annals. In addition, we find a series of tales associated with people or events mentioned in the *Lebor Gabála*. Among the most important are those that deal with the last three colonizations, such as the First Battle of Mag Tuired[21] between the Fir Bolg and the Tuatha Dé Danann, the Second Battle of Mag Tuired between the Tuatha Dé Danann and Fomorians, and events surrounding some of the Tuatha Dé Danann and Milesian kings of Ireland. Obviously, as these accounts deal with the initial settlement of Ireland, the time of action of this cycle must precede all other

'historical' events in Ireland. On the other hand, a large number of the tales associated with this earliest cycle only emerge in comparatively late manuscripts or in relatively late versions in terms of their language. The story of the Children of Lir, for example, is really a late medieval romance that appears in a manuscript dating to *c.* 1500.

2. The Ulster cycle. A much larger assemblage of tales is primarily concerned with the battles, duels and cattle-raids that provided a stage for the achievements of Ireland's elite warrior class, set to the first centuries BC and AD. These are assigned to the Ulster cycle as they mainly focus on the deeds of the Ulstermen and their opponents.[22] The central tale of this cycle is the *Táin Bó Cuailnge* ('Cattle-raid of Cooley'), which is an epic account of a cattle-raid led by the queen and king of Connacht with forces from the rest of Ireland against Ulster, which is defended by the cycle's greatest champion, Cú Chulainn. The *Táin* is recorded in three different editions or recensions, the earliest in the *Lebor na hUidre* and the second and much more polished version in the Book of Leinster. The distinction between the Ulster tales and some of the Mythological tales is not absolutely rigid and, occasionally, a character well known in one cycle will make a guest appearance in a tale from the other. Throughout the *Táin* as well as a number of other tales the tradition of recounting changes to the landscape and the names of places, earlier seen in the *Lebor Gabála*, is continued.[23] It might be noted that the Ulster cycle, along with the Mythological cycle, enjoys very broad international popularity and has been translated extensively into German, French, Russian, Croatian and Italian.[24]

3. The Finn or Osiannic cycle. Another warrior tradition, focusing on the warband of the Irish hero Finn mac Cumhail (McCool) and his son, Oisín, comprises the Finn cycle, most of the events of which are set after the Ulster cycle. Although there are some early tales, the main popularity of the Finn cycle did not occur until the 12th century.

4. The Kings cycle. A fourth genre is devoted to the lives of Irish kings, most of whose lives were played out later than the other three cycles, many in a period where we can employ the word 'historical' without having to cross our fingers.[25]

These are by no means the full contents of these books. For a historian such as Giraldus, one of the more useful tools was the extensive lists of the kings of Ireland and the lengths of their reigns. Clonmacnoise had other historical treasures such as the *Annals of Tigernach*, one of a number of Irish annals that recorded, year by year, the reigns of kings, bishops and important political, religious and natural events. Giraldus himself noted that there had been 131 kings in Ireland from the reign of Eremon, the Milesian king who established his capital at Tara, until the arrival of St Patrick. Indeed he could have lain his hands on a list of Irish rulers that would have detailed the reigns of 197 of Ireland's kings from his own time back to the initial colonization of Ireland, complete with the dates of every reign. But why did the medieval Irish believe that they knew the dates of kings that extended so far back into what today we would regard as prehistory?

Irish traditional chronology

Before the 19th century and the emergence of archaeology as an independent means of establishing chronologies, any attempt at narrating the human past was entirely founded upon historical, that is, written documents. For the West, the Bible related human history as far back as Adam and creation, providing a scaffold upon which one could attempt to hang the events of nations that lay beyond the Near Eastern arena of biblical history.[26] Working out the precise chronology of events had been greatly facilitated by the Roman biblical scholar and bishop, Eusebius, who died around AD 340. Eusebius had already assembled lists of the kings of the ancient world (such as Assyrians, Persians, Egyptians and Greeks) that, when coupled with the testimony of the Bible, provided a rundown of dates for human history from his starting point (Abraham) down until AD 325. He even provided summary tables of all the major reigns and events, for example the date of each Olympiad, the activities of Hercules, the Trojan War and the coming of Aeneas to Rome. St Jerome translated Eusebius into Latin and extended the dates of events on to AD 380. The baton was passed further, eventually to Rufinus of Aquileia who took the timeline up to AD 422, and his work served as a major starting point for many others including early scholars in both Britain (including Bede, who also adopted the AD system of reckoning dates) and Ireland.[27] Throughout the Middle Ages Irish monks had recorded notable events in a series of regional annals that were tied into the earlier works of the church fathers. The start dates for most annals and other historical sources were during the historical period but some took their lead from Eusebius and correlated the previous *pre*history of Ireland farther back in time, all the way to Noah. Indeed, Irish tradition claimed that in AD 266 the high king, Cormac mac Airt, assembled the chroniclers to synchronize the lives of the various kings of Ireland against world events.[28]

The problem with utilizing the Bible to provide a chronology of human events was that it was notoriously difficult to recover from it a single coherent set of dates that could take one back to Adam. In preparing his own history of Ireland, the 17th-century Irish historian Geoffrey Keating wrestled with this very problem and summarized the issue by recording the various chronologies known to him, which ranged from the more recent dates of most Jewish scholars (Baalsederhelm set Adam to 3518 BC) to the more ancient dates of Greek and Latin Christian sources that went as early as Alphonsus' date of 5984 BC; thus among biblical scholars the dates for Adam varied by nearly 2,500 years.[29]

In the first half of the 17th century two Irishmen occupied themselves with sorting out the major problems of both biblical and Irish chronology. The more famous, the Dublin born James Ussher (1581–1656), Archbishop of Armagh and Primate of all Ireland, tackled the now centuries' old problem of calculating the age of creation. By this time many of the best minds had attempted to work backwards to sort out the discouraging discrepancies between the reigns of various kings recorded in different manuscripts and traditions. The real prize was a historically accurate chronology that might take one from the present back to *Genesis* 1. This was not seen as an idle undertaking as it had drawn the efforts of such luminaries as Johannes Kepler and Isaac Newton, along with many others. But the last scholar standing was James Ussher who in 1650 published his *Annales Veteris Testamenti...* (*Annals of the Old Testament...*) in Latin from which is drawn probably the most frequently cited piece of marginalia in the history of writing, 'Year before the Common Year of CHRIST 4004', which has graced the first page of the Authorized Version of the Bible.

While Ussher busied himself with the affairs of the Irish church in Armagh another Irish cleric of a different persuasion, Micheál Ó Cléirigh (1590–1643), a Franciscan lay brother, was tackling his own equally daunting Irish chronological projects but unlike Ussher, Ó Cléirigh was also working against time. The traditional repositories of ancient Irish tradition had long passed from the monasteries to the landed elite who funded their own historians, but by the first decade of the 1600s Elizabethan forces had crushed the Gaelic order along with much of their patronage of the arts and learning. The Irish Franciscans, operating from the continent, sought to insure that the Irish past would not entirely disappear and Ó Cléirigh and a team of three other antiquarians worked to assemble documents to this end. Crisscrossing the island, he attempted to acquire or copy as many of the ancient documents as he could (he may even have obtained a look at Ussher's copy of the Book of Lecan in Dublin[30]). Ó Cléirigh's team produced a series of books that included a chronological list of the kings and saints of Ireland and then in 1631 these Four Masters, as they are commonly known, produced their edition of the *Lebor Gabála*. But the project for which they are best known, which began on 22 January 1632 and was signed off on 10 August 1636, was an annalistic compilation of the entire history of Ireland from the Deluge until 1616.

Annals of the Four Masters

Michael Ó Cléirigh and his colleagues had been trained in the traditional Gaelic schools established by the leading families and by the 17th century it was apparent to them that Ireland required a truly national history. To meet this need they adopted the existing format of the earlier medieval annals to produce a summary of the entire recorded history of Ireland, the *Annála Ríoghachta Éireann*, which is more commonly known today as the '*Annals of the Four Masters*' (AFM; PL. x). They not only gathered together the traditional annalistic sources but others as well to fill out the events of Ireland from the Flood down until just before their own time. Ó Cléirigh, following the Greek (Septuagint) version of the Bible rather than the Hebrew one employed by Ussher, reckoned the date of creation as 5200 BC and so the Flood was set to AM (Anno Mundi 'year of the world [since creation]') 2242, which would equate to 2958 BC. They recorded the most important dates and events until AM 3266 (1934 BC), which marked the beginning of the reign of Sláine, the first Fir Bolg king in Ireland. From then on, they had an entry for every single year until AD 1616 although the printed edition, prepared and translated by John O'Donovan, lacks 88 per cent of the prehistoric entries (which are merely lists of the uneventful 2nd, 3rd...nth year of the various king's reigns). We are still left with by far the longest 'annal', the printed version of the AFM weighing in at nearly 400,000 words (to which one could add the missing 1720 prehistoric entries).[31] As Bernadette Cunningham observes, the Four Masters, by stripping away the biblical material to provide an essentially Irish narrative and by detailing the events of an Irish monarchy over thousands of years, both enhanced the credibility and emphasized the enormous antiquity of Ireland's history.[32] On the other hand, their work was hardly a popular element of Irish culture as the annals only first saw print in 1826[33] and the main edition, edited and translated by John O'Donovan, dates to 1851.[34] It was another Irishman who provided a truly national history.

Foras Feasa ar Éirinn

About the same time that the Four Masters were assembling and producing their accounts of early Irish history, the priest Seathrún Céitinn, more commonly known in English as Geoffrey Keating, had also been gathering together as much as he could to prepare his own history of Ireland. A sermon that angered the Lord President of Munster, George Carew, provided him with a four-year sabbatical while he avoided Carew's wrath, during which time he worked on his *Foras Feasa ar Éirinn* 'Foundation of Knowledge on Ireland', which was completed in 1633 or 1634. He set out to write:

> The history of Ireland, and of every name that was given to it, and
> of every division that was made of it, and of every invasion that was
> made of it, and of every people who took it, and of every famous
> deed which was done in it during the time of each high-king who
> was over it at any time from the beginning to this time....[35]

Keating opened his work with a defence of Irish history, indeed civilization, in the face of all the critics who had either preceded Giraldus (for example there were classical authors who had attributed cannibalism and incest to the ancient Irish) or had followed him. He dealt with a representative sample of their errors, with, for example, Giraldus's account of Ireland seeming to Keating to be the product of either a blind man or blockhead who 'gave him such a shower of fabulous information'. In fact, Giraldus was dismissed as being solely interested in doing a hatchet job on the Irish with no real interest in legitimate research, as well as for only being in Ireland for a limited time, dumping the unfinished collection of data on a colleague.[36] Keating, on the other hand, had collected whatever he could of the ancient books of Ireland, determined that the Irish 'should not go into oblivion without mention or narration being left of them'.[37] And to ensure that no one could accuse him of naked chauvinism, Keating reminded the reader that he himself was a member of the 'Old English' stock, the Anglo-Norman invaders of Ireland.

Although Keating's history covers what I have termed the Irish Dreamtime in depth, he was never in doubt that much of this constituted history and not fiction and that one could tell the difference. For example, he made it clear that he regarded the entire story of Cesair as questionable ('the antiquarians do not regard it as for certain as an invasion') and the story of Fintan's millennia-long survival (as a member of Cesair's party Fintan either hibernated in a cave or changed himself into a salmon and avoided being drowned in the Flood) as even less plausible[38] and he lambasted Meredith Hanmer (1543–1604) for regarding the Battle of Ventry as historical along with a series of other tales from the Finn cycle which the antiquarians of Ireland (the *seanchaí*) had dismissed as romances.[39] Among these he included a favourite of children's compendia of Irish folk tales, the story of Labraid Lorc and his horse-ears, which he also dismissed as a romantic tale (*finnscéal fhilidheachta*) and not real history (*stair*).[40] Nor would he accept the rendition of the death of the Ulster king Conchobar who reputedly died the same day as Christ, since Christ should not have been born until long after Conchobar's death.[41] In short, he clearly recognized the classical distinction between *historia*, things that really happened, and *fabula*, things that neither happened nor could happen. In this, he approached his often conflicting material in the same way as the author of the earliest manuscript version of the *Táin*, who assembled different versions of the epic cattle-raid and tried to sort out which was the most likely by comparing the versions before him.[42]

Keating's work was *the* major extensive and popular history of Ireland written in Irish. Copied by hand thousands of times, it became in a sense the 'Peoples history of Ireland' that helped insure continued knowledge of the earliest Irish tradition.

British reception

The assessment of the *Lebor Gabála* version of the settlement of Ireland had already been challenged at least by the time of Giraldus. Although he held his critical tongue through most of his account (after all a good story is a good story), he couldn't help but note that if Cesair and her entire company drowned in the Flood, how could knowledge of this event have been conveyed? He gave this the benefit of a doubt and at least offered what (as we will soon see) was an old escape clause: maybe someone wrote it down on stone. The mechanics of such a solution were not pondered (who in early Ireland could read Hebrew, a language whose script would not be invented until long after the date of the Flood and what would such a message have read? – 'wives drowning like flies…can't tread water much longer'!).[43]

In any event, scepticism was making itself clear through the 16th century. Edmund Campion (1540–1581), on the eve of shifting from Protestant scholar to Jesuit martyr, in his *Historie of Ireland* (1571) totally rejected the Cesair part of the narrative, always regarded the weakest element, as not only false but also impossible. His own reasons were not very convincing since he argued that before the Flood geographical knowledge was confined to the Near East and sailing was unknown in the world at this time (the Ark, built to God's specifications, was the first vessel). As for the written-down-on-stone ploy, Campion dismissed this on the grounds that it had already been used by the Jewish historian Josephus (prescient Adam, wanting to preserve his discoveries from a possible future flood, recorded them on both brick and stone).[44] As for Partholón's settlement we were dealing with 'blinde legends' and 'idle fantasies'.[45] On the other hand, he had no problem repeating absurd legends himself, also rehearsed by Giraldus, to substantiate that by 376 BC the Irish had been 'subjects to the Crowne of Brittaine, before they set foote in Ireland'.[46]

In the same year as Campion's book, Meredith Hanmer published his *Chronicle of Ireland* that similarly discounted the Cesair incident but also conflated and embellished some of the other colonizations. For example, the failure of Partholón's expedition was due to a battle fought with the Fomorians (who he had brought from Egypt) who were destroyed in the fighting and stunk so bad that they mortally infected the offspring of Partholón who all died 'excepting a few silly soules scattered in remote places'.[47] Hanmer also calls attention to major discrepancies in the absolute dates of the events. For example, that various authors had set the creation of the Irish language anywhere from 1,000 years after the Flood to AD 75 certainly should warn his readers of 'the dissonance that I find in the observation of times'.[48]

In the 17th century we find a more famous writer who was very much interested in the Irish claims to great antiquity. Edmund Spenser (1552–1599), author of the *Faerie Queen*, presented his *A View of the State of Ireland* in 1596 and was quite interested in discussing the claim of the Irish 'to be more antiente then moste that I knowe in this eande of the worlde'.[49] Written in the form of a schizophrenic dialogue, Spenser attempted to evaluate traditional Irish history as the product of lying bards with every bit of auxiliary evidence he could utilize to work out the 'probabilitie of thinges'.[50]

Spenser faces the accusation that it seems impossible for us to put any reliance on the accounts of ancient Ireland that describe periods long before there were any written records, our only source being poets who lived many centuries after the events they recount.[51] Yet there are aspects of Irish antiquity that a 'well eyed man' could ferret out. For example, while Spenser may not have bought into all the native tradition, he certainly accepted the notion that the Irish originally came from Scythia and provided a list of Irish traits that continued the barbaric practices of their Scythian ancestors, including pastoralism, dress, hairstyles, battle-cry, their broad swords, short bows, long wicker shields and swearing on their swords.[52] And their transit through Spain was also marked by the adoption of Spanish customs, such as the fact that women had complete charge of the household and deep smock sleeves that hung to the ground.[53] To the question of why the Irish sought to derive themselves from Spain rather than Gaul (whose population was regarded as more ancient and honourable[54]), it might be put down to 'a verye desire of newfainglenes and vanitye'.[55]

Dismissal of the traditional Irish narrative continued from British circles in the following centuries. Writing in the 17th century Richard Cox (1650–1733) claimed it was simply too difficult to sort out the fact from the fiction of native Irish tradition.[56] To be sure, there was a period in the early 18th century when the glories of ancient Ireland did hold some attraction for both Anglo-Irish and even some English (Keating had been translated into English in 1723),[57] but by the later 18th century scepticism had settled in again. In 1784 Thomas Leland (1722–1785) basically dismissed all accounts of Irish history before the reign of Henry II.[58] As Francis Plowden remarked: 'The hour which united the two kingdoms under one crown gave birth to the national contest about the authenticity of the ancient history of Ireland'.[59]

The Irish rebuttal

Irish apologists traced this entire camp of English sceptics back to Giraldus who, in the words of Geoffrey Keating, was to be likened to a beetle rolling around in the dung of a cow or horse[60] or as James Mac-Geoghegan (1702–1763) would have it, was to be compared with asps and vipers.[61] A quote from Thomas Mooney (1845) sums up the attitude of a large number of Irish writers:

> The policy of Britain, since her first invasion of Ireland, in 1169,
> has ever been to disparage the fair character of her sister isle; to
> darken it before the nations of the earth…to pay dishonest writers
> for discrediting its glorious history of civilization, independence,
> and government, which commenced a thousand years before
> England herself had emerged from a state of barbarism, or slavish
> subjection to pagan Rome.[62]

That a blatantly obvious political agenda was driving both sides in the debate regarding Irish antiquity can hardly be denied and the argument raged between the various camps that were sometimes driven primarily by national identity (English, Irish,

Scottish) and sometimes by religion (Catholic, Protestant) or both.[63] During the 19th century debate on the 'Irish Question', Irishmen could claim that they enjoyed an antiquity as a nation that carried them back 260 years before the foundation of Rome and 'at least a thousand years before the arrival of Caesar in Britain, and his discovery that its inhabitants were half-naked savages'.[64] From the other side, the Irish were simply deluding themselves with the fairy tales of their medieval monks.[65] But this is to oversimplify the positions and we should acknowledge that there were two major issues that were frequently debated which indicated that while the Irish might have claimed to be the most ancient people in Europe, they were not also aspiring to be the most gullible. The issues were the chronology of the events recorded in the various sources and the reality of the events themselves.

Chronology

A major attempt at sorting out the chronology of the earliest Irish tradition is found in Roderik O'Flaherty's *Ogygia, or a Chronological Account of Irish Events* (1684). Although O'Flaherty (1629–1718?) bought into the high antiquity of Irish civilization, he found reconciling the different systems of calendar dates harrowing. On the other hand, when the different sources appeared to agree this was regarded as absolute proof: for example, when the king lists and all other sources indicated a date for the foundation and fall of Emain Macha as the Ulster capital over a period of 684 years, the sources 'have infallibly rendered certainty itself still more *certain* if possible, by their unerring and undeviating assertions'.[66]

A century later O'Flaherty's book was translated (from the original Latin) by James Hely, who observed that his author's chronology was far too high and that while the earlier tradition of claiming a high antiquity for events in Ireland had gratified national pride, this has been rejected by 'more learned antiquarians'. For example, while O'Flaherty might set the coming of the Sons of Míl to *c.* 1700 BC, Hely would move it down to 489 BC.[67]

That the veracity of the ancient dates was not accepted on blind faith can be seen most spectacularly in the works of Mary Cusack (1829–1899), the redoubtable 'Nun of Kenmare' who marshalled a series of arguments why one should accept the early dates ascribed to the Irish.[68] The Irish genealogies were preserved by an Irish learned class who were, she argued, forbidden under penalty of law to lie or tamper with the genealogical records. As both property rights and the acquisition of political power in early Ireland depended on one's genealogy the Irish had institutions that guaranteed the integrity of its historical record and the genealogies were publicly announced every third year at a convocation at Tara by *ollams*, the highest ranking of the learned class who had studied 12 years. If one turns to ancient Rome, we have a history that is accepted that extends four centuries before we have contemporary accounts from any classical authors. This could only have been accomplished through an oral tradition very much like that ascribed to the ancient Irish. So if one accepts the earliest accounts of Roman history, why not those of the Irish as well?[69]

The integrity of the genealogies, which provided a chronological spine for the earliest Irish tradition, was still defended at the end of the 19th century on arguments very similar to those advanced by Cusack. While Douglas Hyde (1860–1949) might dispense with many of the earliest dates, he argued that valid dates began with the first centuries BC because too much genealogical importance was riding on them.[70] We should note that the earliest Irish texts, largely from before 1200, provide us with the genealogies of 20,000 individuals and 2,000 dynasties.[71]

Historicity

Although there are abundant arguments to support the idea that the medieval Irish treated their earliest tradition as history rather than fable, we can find evidence that the veracity of the events described was being challenged by the very scribes who copied out the tales. We get a taste of this scepticism in the margins of the second recension of the *Táin* in the Book of Leinster where on 24 occasions the scribes remarked 'Emanuel', perhaps the monkish equivalent to 'bloody hell!', when they would come across an event that strained their credulity.[72] The crowning touch, whose import has been long debated by Irish scholars, is the famous double colophon,[73] the afterword, at the end of Book of Leinster *Táin*.[74] The first, written in Irish, presumably by the author of the tale, reads:

> A blessing on every one who shall faithfully memorise the *Táin*
> as it is written here and shall not add any other form to it.[75]

But then, the scribe who had just copied out the tale inscribes in Latin:

> But I who have written this story, or rather this fable, give no
> credence to the various incidents related in it. For some things
> are the deceptions of demons, others poetic figments; some are
> probable, others improbable; while still others are intended for
> the delectation of foolish men.

It is clear that here in the late 12th century there was already scepticism regarding the historical accuracy of the *Táin* (although at least it was not as harsh as the scribe who copied out the adventures of Saint Brendan the Navigator and thought it was so bad it should be consigned to the fire).[76]

Although Roderick O'Flaherty argued for a great antiquity for the Irish, he was willing to jettison some its contents. Tales of the settlements of Cesair and Partholón had versions that produced impossibly long-lived survivors, Fintan and Tuan respectively, which he dismissed as soul migration myths.[77] The elaborate derivations of the Irish from Scythia, Egypt and Spain were replaced by Camden's argument that migrations into Ireland most likely proceeded from Britain.[78] And in the popular Irish histories of the 19th century there was a frequent recognition that much of the earliest part of the narrative was not history but 'fabulous legends'.[79] But the fabulous legends were also so entertaining and so embedded in the historical sources that one could never simply dismiss them. Hence Mary Cusack regarded the antediluvian settlement of Ireland 'too purely mythical to demand serious notice' but its consistent presence in Irish manuscripts also meant that we cannot totally ignore it.[80] As to the utility of such material, the optimistic Cusack provides us with a good summary of a persistent attitude:

> Ancient writings, even of pure fiction, must always form an important historical element to the nation by which they have been produced. Unless they are founded on fact, so far as customs, localities, and mode of life are concerned, they would possess no interest; and their principal object is to interest. Without some degree of poetic improbabilities as to events, they could scarcely amuse; and their object is also to amuse. Hence, the element of truth is easily separated from the element of fiction, and each is available in its measure for historic research.[81]

These sentiments would be echoed again at the beginning of the 20th century when Patrick Weston Joyce (1827–1914) argued that

> ...though the stories are partly or wholly fictitious, they abound... in incidental pictures of real life, which, speaking generally, are as true, and consequently as valuable for our purposes, as if the main narratives were strictly historical.[82]

The first great synthesis

Eoghan Ó Comhrai (1794–1862), better known as Eugene O'Curry, after a variety of posts that formed a superb background for Irish studies (for example, he transcribed the entire text of the *Annals of the Four Masters* for the printers), was appointed Professor of Irish History and Archaeology at the newly founded (but very short-lived) Catholic University in 1854. There he presented two monumental lecture series. The first (*Lectures on the Manuscript Materials of Ancient Irish History*) was published in 1861 and provided a groundbreaking survey of all that was known then about early Irish manuscripts. He covered in detail the various annals, genealogical works, histories (including the Ulster cycle) and ecclesiastical sources, all coupled with many examples of the different genres and a large appendix of translations and other works. He believed that because the totality of Irish documents had never been exploited 'the history of ancient Erinn is yet entirely unwritten'[83] and that the only three historians of early Ireland who merit attention were Keating, Mac-Geoghegan and Thomas Moore, the last of whom had produced a book, based mainly on English sources, which is 'nowhere to be relied on'.[84] He outlined how he thought the writing of this ultimate history of Ireland should be undertaken. It should be grounded on the annals, especially the *Annals of the Four Masters*, which would serve as a spine from which one could expand with information gleaned from the genealogies and then the historical literature (which would include the literary tales), upon which 'we shall chiefly have to depend for that minute illustration of the details of historic life'.[85] And in presenting an example of what he had in mind, O'Curry provided a summary of the literature concerning the Milesian conquest of Ireland and argued for the authenticity of such events as the battle between Eber and Eremon at Geisill (near Tullamore, Co. Offaly) and the two battles of Mag Tuired.[86]

His second course of lectures was edited posthumously by the polymath W. K. Sullivan (1820–1890) in 1873, where it was titled *On the Manners and Customs of the Ancient Irish*. The massive first volume of this three-volume set was written entirely by Sullivan, who attempted to expand and update many of O'Curry's discussions. The work was an encyclopedic survey of ancient Ireland drawn almost entirely from written sources, many of them comprising the same documents that provide the source of the oldest Irish tradition.

O'Curry's attitude to the veracity of his material was still very much anchored in an acceptance of a chain of evidence that extended back to at least 600 BC.[87] He was not wholly convinced about material relating to the Tuatha Dé Danann, both because of its alleged antiquity and also because we had to depend entirely on the histories of events passed on down by the descendants of Míl, who took little interest in earlier peoples.[88] Sullivan, whose training was in chemistry, was more cautious. The veracity of the whole Irish National Origin Legend, for example, was for him still an open question[89] and he was well aware that the medieval Irish had simply tacked their stories onto the Book of Genesis. As with other writers of the 19th century, Sullivan could remark:

> Scepticism regarding ancient traditions may be carried too far,
> as well as a credulous faith in their truth, and is often more
> dangerous to science. Every legend, every myth, contains
> a kernel of truth, if we could only remove the husk of fable
> which enveloped it.[90]

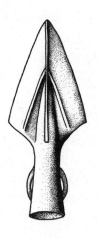

1.5. A Tuatha Dé Danann spear (*sleg*).

But up until the time of O'Curry and Sullivan, the discourse concerning the veracity of events in the deep past had relied exclusively on the evidence of written records. But now a new source of information had become available. Antiquarians had been accumulating antiquities and many of these were gathered into major collections such as those of the Royal Irish Academy, which began amassing objects in 1785.[91] So when O'Curry and Sullivan worked their way through the early Irish nomenclature for spears and their descriptions in the tales, they made recourse to the different spearheads in archaeological collections, attempting to identify the different weapons of the Fir Bog and Tuatha Dé Danann (FIG. 1.5).[92] Archaeology had entered the Dreamtime.

CHAPTER TWO

Impossible Stories and Impertinent Tales

Who were the *Aborigines* or first Inhabitants of *Ireland*, it were in vain
to guess, for the Irish Historians are of no Credit in this Matter, the very
Truths they write do not oblige our Belief, because they are so intermixt
with Impossible Stories and Impertinent Tales, that it is exceeding
difficult to distinguish which is the History and which the Fable.

Sir Richard Cox, 1689[1]

As we will be examining the evidence for the Ireland depicted in the historical
and literary sources it may be useful to review the sequence of events and
main personalities tagged against their traditional historical dates, here following the suggestion of Eugene O'Curry in employing the *Annals of the Four Masters*
as our spine. The basic sequence of the Mythological cycle is primarily anchored to the
Lebor Gabála and the annals to which the Mythological tales have been attached.[2] The
subsequent events portrayed in the Ulster cycle are fixed in absolute time against a few
entries in the annals. Although I have attempted to bring the Ulster tales into some
form of sequence, a considerable number of them are internally so inconsistent (containing characters who should have been separated by many centuries) that even a
medieval *ollam* (the highest ranked poet) would be hard pressed to put them into a
sensible order. The purpose of all this is to provide the reader with a summary of the
sources, events and characters whose world is the subject of the rest of this book.

THE MYTHOLOGICAL CYCLE

Third millennium BC

In 2958 BC[3] the granddaughter of Noah, Cesair, finding no room on the Ark, sailed to
Ireland 40 days before the Deluge.[4] After shipwreck, the surviving company that

arrived consisted of three men and 50 women who came ashore at Dún na mBarc in Corcu Duibne (the Dingle and Iveragh peninsulas in Co. Kerry[5]). Before the Flood, two of the men had already died (one was Cesair's father who was servicing 17 women and was buried under a cairn on Sliab Betha). When the Flood came, the waters drowned everyone[6] but (in some accounts) one male, Fintan,[7] survived for millennia until he was summoned to relate the earlier history of Ireland. Other accounts have Fintan buried in a barrow above Tul Tuinne.[8] Although this is the earliest 'canonical' account there is another version where three fishermen from Spain were blown off-course to Ireland. They returned to Spain and attempted to bring their wives to Ireland but all were drowned in the Flood.[9]

A second larger-scale colonization took place in 2680 BC under the leadership of Partholón, a descendant of Magog, a grandson of Noah. Partholón led his people to Ireland, settled and began the clearance of its forests. During his colonization seven lakes burst forth. Another group of (as we will see recurrent) invaders, the Fomorians, also arrived and were defeated by Partholón's people in Ireland's first battle; the odds should have favoured Partholón as at that time his opponents were reputed to have only one arm and one leg. But in 2380 BC all 9,000 of Partholón's people were wiped out by plague and Ireland was again deserted, this time for 30 years. Later versions again admit a single survivor, Tuan mac Cairill, who also lived to relate the past history of Ireland to an Ulster king in the 6th century AD.[10]

The third colonization, led by Nemed, occurred in 2350 BC. During his reign many more forests were cleared to make fields, lakes burst forth and forts were built. Although Nemed and 3,000 of his followers died of plague, the rest of his people continued to increase and fought with the Fomorians, concluding with a cataclysmic battle at the tower of Conainn in 2134 BC where both sides nearly annihilated each other. The surviving members of Nemed's people scattered to different parts of the world. Many of the refugees settled in Greece where they were forced to serve as slaves, hauling earth in bags, which provides the etymology for their descendants, the next colonists, the Fir Bolg (supposedly 'bag-men').

Second millennium BC

In 1934 BC the Fir Bolg turned their bags into boats and returned to Ireland. The synchronization of Irish rulers in the later annals is very much tied to the sequence of rulers starting with the first Fir Bolg king, Sláine, who reigned 1933–1931 BC. The last Fir Bolg king was Eochaid mac Eirc, who brought in a time of plenty and abolished spears from the land. Also, it was during the reign of the Fir Bolg that Ireland was originally partitioned into five provinces (with the advice of Cesair's Fintan). The Fir Bolg had the island to themselves for 30 years when there arrived a new people.

In 1897 BC, during the tenth year of Eochaid's reign, Ireland was invaded by the Tuatha Dé Danann. The events of this colonization are not only recorded in the LG but also as a separate tale.[11] The Fir Bolg and Tuatha Dé Danann learned of each other's presence and sent spies to reconnoitre: Sreng of the Fir Bolg and Bres of the Tuatha Dé. On meeting each other they discovered that they both spoke the same language as they were both descendants of Nemed. But they also possessed a different array of weapons (see Chapter Seven). The Tuatha Dé demanded that the Fir Bolg either give them half the island or face them in combat. The Fir Bolg chose war and eventually the two sides met in a titanic battle (the First Battle of Mag Tuired) that lasted for days and where the fortune of each side fluctuated as the body count of heroes continued to rise. During one duel Sreng cut off the arm of the Tuatha Dé Danann king, Nuadu, although later he was well enough to meet Sreng in a rematch, but had to be rescued and carried from the field. The druids of the Tuatha Dé Danann cast a spell of thirst on the Fir Bolg king that drove him to the sea where he was killed. In the end, both sides accepted a treaty where the Fir Bolg were banished to Connacht while the Tuatha Dé Danann were free to settle the rest of Ireland.

The year 1829 BC marked the beginning of the 80-year reign of Eochaid Ollathir, also known as the Dagda, who, among other things, fancied the wife of Elcmar of Brug na Bóinne (modern Newgrange) and managed to father a child by her without Elcmar knowing.[12] The child, Oengus, was sent to Midir to be fostered and learned from him that his father was the king of Ireland. The Dagda instructed Oengus on how to gain the Brug na Bóinne for himself[13] from Elcmar (in another tale Manannán mac Lir teaches Oengus an incantation to drive Elcmar out).[14] When Oengus had gained the land, his foster-father Midir came to visit him. Midir asked for gifts and Oengus offered him the most beautiful woman in Ireland, Étaín, who lived in Ulster. Midir went to woo Étaín but to satisfy her father he had to undertake two impossible (at least without the help of his father) landscape projects and pay her father Étaín's weight in gold and silver. She was then given to Midir who brought her back home where his naturally jealous wife Fúamnach, also gifted in the magic arts, turned Étaín into a pool of water that transformed first into a worm and then a large and marvellous scarlet fly that accompanied Midir. Fúamnach continued her revenge against Étaín by creating a wind that blew her about for seven years until she was taken in by Oengus, and then she was blown away again until, now 1,012 years since she had originally been born, she landed in a drink of the wife of the Ulster warrior Étar, was swallowed, and was then reborn as her own daughter. Étaín mark II was then reared as a princess, and was sought out in 129 BC by the newly crowned high king Eochaid Airem whose brother, Ailill, fell madly in love with her as well. Étaín II attempted to minister to Ailill's torturous longing and agreed to meet him several times away from Eochaid's house, but instead she kept encountering a man who looked like Ailill but ultimately revealed himself to be her former husband Midir (I hope you're following all this). She agreed to return to him if Eochaid permitted it. After a year Midir came to Tara and challenged Eochaid to a game of *fidchell* (an Irish board game, see Chapter Nine), with high stakes, which he deliberately lost. Then Eochaid set Midir a series of impossible tasks, among which was the construction of a causeway across the bog Móin Lámraige, which he accomplished (see Chapter Eight). Finally, after another game of *fidchell*, Midir won and claimed as his prize the chance to hold Étaín in his arms once. Although Eochaid surrounded Tara with his troops, Midir ascended with Étaín through the roof and they flew off as swans. Eochaid went in pursuit and began digging up all the *sídhe* (Otherworld mounds) in Ireland until Midir agreed to return Étaín. But he did so only on condition that Eochaid could pick her out of a line-up of 50 girls who all looked like his wife. Eochaid selected one that seemed to be closest and said that he was satisfied, only to learn that he had actually selected (and had a daughter by) Étaín's own daughter who was born in the *síd*. This daughter was then married to Eterscél to whom she bore a son, Conaire Mór (who we will meet below in the 1st millennium BC).

Another tale[15] concerns the marriage problems of Oengus himself, who repeatedly endured a nightly visit from Miss Ireland *c.* 1890 BC which left him sick for love. After much searching the girl was found in Connacht. Again there was an identity parade comprising the girl, Caer, and 150 other girls, none taller than Caer's shoulder. But Oengus could not obtain her without going first to the king and queen of Connacht, Ailill and Medb (who lived nearly 2,000 years later!), who said they also had no power to grant Oengus the girl. But they dug up the *síd* of her father and learnt that the girl spent much of her time as a swan and so Oengus met with her and the two eventually flew off to his place. For assisting Ailill and Medb Oengus brought 300 head of cattle on the *Táin*. This tale, which has chronological elements that are nearly two millennia out of sync, clearly straddles both the Mythological and (as we will soon see) the Ulster cycle.

Also among the Tuatha Dé Danann warriors who distinguished themselves at Mag Tuired were the three sons of Tuirenn Bigrenn. Their fate is recalled both in the *Lebor Gabála*[16] and as an independent tale, one of three sorrows of storytelling.[17] After the First Battle of Mag Tuired, the Tuatha Dé Danann were suppressed by the Fomorians and Lug attempted to raise resistance against them. He sent his father Cian to seek reinforcements but Cian ran into the three sons of Tuirenn who, although counted among the best of the warriors of the Tuatha Dé Danann, were also inveterate enemies of Cian and his brothers. They killed Cian but were then forced to agree to pay Lug a seemingly impossible blood price, collecting a series of marvellous talismans comparable to the trials of Hercules, that took them from Greece and Persia and across the Mediterranean. These talismans were to be employed by the Tuatha Dé Danann in their forthcoming battle with the Fomorians. Accomplishing all the tasks but left mortally wounded, the brothers returned to Ireland and sought a talisman from Lug that would heal them, but he refused and the three brothers died, soon followed by their father.

After the First Battle of Mag Tuired, the king of the Tuatha Dé Danann, Nuadu, having lost his arm, was ineligible to remain as king. He was replaced by Bres, the son of the Tuatha Dé princess Ériu and the king of the Fomorians.[18] Bres ruled poorly and oppressed the Tuatha Dé until he was satirized by an indignant poet and his reign went into freefall. Bres went to his father and assembled an enormous Fomorian fleet to insure that he would retain his throne. The Tuatha Dé had brought back Nuadu with a bionic silver arm to rule them and the Tuatha Dé heroes were joined by Lug, whose father was of the Tuatha Dé but mother was a Fomorian. Nuadu relinquished his rulership to Lug, who led them in the Second Battle of Mag Tuired (1870 BC), the events of which are recounted in its own tale (see Chapter Seven). The army of the Tuatha Dé (18,000 strong) assembled just before *Samain* (Halloween) and after the Dagda's bizarre reconnoitring mission (though the segue between excessive porridge consumption and sex is certainly novel) the battle commenced on a hitherto unparalleled scale until Lug was able to destroy the Fomorian's most formidable warrior, Balor of the evil eye, and the Fomorians were driven from Ireland for good.[19]

The final colonists had worked their way from Scythia across the Mediterranean to conquer Spain. In Spain their leader was Míl with his sons and hence the final wave of invaders are known as the Sons of Míl. From Spain, on Bregon's tower, Íth son of Bregon caught sight of Ireland and led a small band there but was killed by the Tuatha Dé Danann, and so the Sons of Míl (who we can now regard as the Gaels or Irish)

2.1. Offerings left at the Tomb of Scotta, Sliab Mis, Co. Kerry.

came in 1700 BC to avenge Íth and take the island. Arriving in 36 ships the Gaels defeated the Tuatha Dé in the Battle of Sliab Mis. Here, the wife of Míl, Scotta, died and her tomb is still venerated to this day (FIG. 2.1). The Milesian leaders were approached by the three wives of the Tuatha Dé kings, each asking that the island be named after her, and the winner was Ériu (otherwise Ireland would be known today as either Fial or Banba). When the Sons of Míl met the three kings of the Tuatha Dé they were requested to accept a short truce and to sail offshore for three days. Having agreed to do so, the Tuatha Dé cast spells to drive the Sons of Míl away but Amairgen, the Milesian poet, calmed the waves and the Sons of Míl returned to conquer Ireland. The *Lebor Gabála* then provides genealogical lists that tie the regional dynasties of Ireland to the various leaders of the Milesian invasion.

Although the Tuatha Dé Danann had been defeated, they still maintained their own kings to avoid rule by the Milesians. In order to assuage the anger of Lir, the newly elected king, Bodb Derg, gave to Lir his daughter in marriage and she produced four children before dying.[20] A second daughter, Aífe, was then supplied as wife and stepmother but jealousy drove her into transforming the children into swans who spent 300 years on Lough Derravaragh in Co. Westmeath, then another 300 years in the cold waters off the Antrim coast before spending their final 300 years off Co. Mayo. Eventually, in the period after St Patrick, they were transformed back into human form, and baptized before they crumbled from old age.

The events immediately following the Milesian conquest involved a major filling out of both the natural landscape, such as the bursting forth of rivers and lakes, as well as the built landscape, such as the establishment of various forts. In 1698 BC, for example, Tea requested as her marriage dowry the hill of Drum Caein, which would be named after her and serve as her final resting place. It still carries her name as Tea-múr 'Tea's rampart' – Irish Temair, which is anglicized as Tara. The succession of kings served as culture heroes, introducing various items of material (gold-working, gilded cups, dyeing, silver shields; see Chapter Four) or spiritual culture (the establishment of the Feast of Tara).

First millennium BC

From 724 BC Irish kingship involved a primitive form of power-sharing where rule was rotated among three men, each for seven years, until 668 BC when one of the claimants died and his daughter, Macha Mongruad, claimed the kingship. The other two claimants (Dithorba and Cimbaeth) refused to share power with a woman but Macha defeated them in battle, married one of them (Cimbaeth) and forced Dithorba's sons to build Emain Macha, the capital of Ulster, with Cimbaeth as its first king. According to this tale she marked out the precinct of the capital with her *eó-muin* 'neck-brooch', which allegedly explains the name of the Ulster capital (Emain)

Alternatively, there was a woman who came to live with a widowed landlord named Crunniuc in Ulster.[21] While she stayed with him, his household flourished. One day he attended the *oenach* ('fair') and made passing comment on the king's chariot team that although the king's horses were fast, his wife could run faster. His wife was then forced to run a race against the king's chariot despite the fact that she was pregnant and begged the Ulstermen for a delay. When she crossed the finishing line she gave birth to twins and as her name was Macha, the place became known as Emain Macha, 'the twin(s) of Macha'. She also cursed the Ulstermen for forcing her to run the race and for the next nine generations the Ulstermen in times of their greatest difficulty would be laid up in bed as weak as a woman in labour.

In 592 BC King Lóegaire Lorc was treacherously killed by his brother, Cobthach Cóel.[22] Feigning death while laid out in his chariot, Cobthach stabbed his brother, who had come to pay him his last farewell. Cobthach then went on to have Lóegaire's son poisoned. But Lóegaire's grandson, Labraid Loingsech, was able to return from exile and with the assistance of men from Munster he sacked the fortress of Dind Ríg and assumed the kingship of Leinster. There he built a house of iron, fronted and backed by timber to disguise it, and invited King Cobthach and 30 kings to a feast where they were burnt in the house. Labraid then assumed the kingship of Ireland. Labraid is also credited with bringing 2,200 foreigners to Ireland who bore broad spears (*lagin*) from whence the Laigin, i.e. Leinstermen, gain their name.

THE ULSTER CYCLE[23]

Before the Táin

At a time when Fachtna Fáthach was high king (143–131 BC), he made a journey around Ulster.[24] At the same time Eochaid Feidlech raided Ulster with a great army and took hostages. Hearing of this, Fachtna assembled an army of Ulstermen and foreigners and they made their way to Dún Láegaire where they set up camp, and we are introduced to the main Ulster heroes. Eventually, Leitir Ruide was agreed to serve as the place of battle. During the course of the battle, after many had fallen, Eochaid perceived that he was on the point of losing and so he led a direct assault on the high king himself, killed him and took his head. The Ulstermen were forced to retreat and Eochaid assumed the kingship (131–116 BC) while Fergus mac Róich became king of Ulster.

In 109 BC[25] Conaire Mór (grandson of the long-lived and reborn Étaín, see above) succeeded Eterscel when he appeared at Tara and demonstrated his right to the kingship by passing a series of tests with the chariot of kingship.[26] He presided over a charmed reign that ended in 40 BC.[27] His foster-brothers had raided through-out Ireland and rather than properly punishing them as a king was required, he ban-ished them to Britain where they continued their plundering until they met up with a British pirate, Ingcel, who proposed that they join forces and first attack Britain and then Ireland. The raiders came to Ireland at the same time that King Conaire was caught in a series of circumstances whereby all of his *gessa* (taboos) were inadvert-ently being broken as he came to spend the night at the Hostel of Dá Derga. The raiders attacked the hostel and after epic carnage (of the raiders) Conaire died due to a spell of thirst cast on him that could not be quenched. Of his own retinue, only four survived: his own bodyguard, Mac Cecht, who had been sent for water and three heroes known from the Ulster cycle, most notably Conall Cernach.[28]

One day the Ulster king, Fergus mac Léti,[29] rested by the sea. While asleep, his sword was stolen and he was carried off by the *Lúchorpan* (the earliest reference we have to what are later called Leprechauns) who got him to the sea before he awoke, managing to grab three of them. To spare their lives, they granted him three wishes, one of which gave him the power to travel below the sea, except for Loch Rudraige (Dundrum Bay), in his own territory. One day while in Loch Rudraige, Fergus encountered a *muirdris*, a sea monster, that was so frightening that Fergus's face became frozen in rictus. Although now blemished and, consequently, unsuitable to serve as king, the elders of Emain Macha arranged it that Fergus would not know his own appearance and so this remained for seven years until a chastised servant vented her anger at the king about his disfigurement. He cut her in half with his sword (the same sword later used by Fergus mac Róich) and then plunged into the lake where he battled the *muirdris*. He killed the monster but died himself immediately on emerging from the sea.

A different version[30] of Fergus's death involves the capture of the king of the *Lúchorpan* (after falling into a bowl of porridge at Emain). This king was held in ransom, ultimately yielding his magic shoes to Fergus who donned them when he went to fight the sea monster (here a *sinech*) where, as in the previous version, he was disfigured. Here it is an altercation with his wife that led to his discovery of his distorted face. He defeated the sea monster in the rematch with his sword, the *caladcholg*, but died of his wounds, although before his death he bequeathed his sword to Fergus mac Róich. This tale concludes by explaining the name 'Ulster' (Irish *Uladh*) as deriving from the stones (*uladh*) that comprised the cairn over Fergus's grave.

Assa ('gentle'), the daughter of the Ulster king, Eochaid Yellow-heel, was a pliant, docile girl who was traumatized by the slaughter of all her tutors by a druid, Cathbad.[31] She changed into a woman-warrior with an appropriate change in name to Nessa (i.e. *ni-assa* 'un-gentle'). She raided across Ireland but once, when bathing in a spring, Cathbad confronted her with his sword, standing between the dripping woman and both her clothes and weapons. She pleaded for her life and was granted it on condition of becoming Cathbad's wife. She did so and eventually bore him a son, Conchobar, who came into the world at the same hour as Christ. When Conchobar was seven years old, Fergus sued for Nessa's hand in marriage but she required as a bride-price that her son rule for one year. She then instructed Conchobar to win friends by distributing gold and silver and when the year was up the Ulstermen would not consent that Fergus return as king but handed the kingship to Conchobar.[32] Conchobar maintained a household of 365 attendants and arranged and presided over enormous feasts at *Samain*. He was both a great warrior and a wise judge (he also enjoyed not only the right of the first night but also the right to the wife of any of his men who granted him hospitality). His capital at Emain Macha comprised three buildings: the Cróeb-ruad (the king's residence), the Téite Brecc (the armoury and where the table services were stored) and the Cróeb-derg (where the heads and spoils of the Ulstermen's victims were kept).[33]

Conchobar's first wife was Medb, the daughter of Eochaid Feidlech, the high king of Tara, and she was given to him in blood payment for the fact that Eochaid had killed Conchobar's father in the Battle of Leitir Ruide.[34] Medb, however, deserted Conchobar and returned to Tara, which helps explain the later animosity between the two. To make matters worse, at an assembly at Tara Conchobar came upon Medb bathing in the Boyne and he raped her. The king of Tara led the men of Ireland against the Ulster king but they were defeated and Medb was brought to Cruachain, the capital of Connacht, by Eochaid Dála whom she married and he became the king of Connacht. Then Ailill mac Máta came to Cruachain as a youngster to be raised and he developed into a fine warrior and Medb fell in love with him. Her husband became jealous and challenged Ailill to a duel but lost and Ailill married Medb and became the king. It was by Ailill that Medb gave birth to seven sons whose names were all changed to Maine when Medb mistakenly understood from a druid that a son named Maine would kill Conchobar (a son did but the druid meant a different Conchobar).

At one time the fields around the Ulster capital at Emain Macha were being repeatedly ravaged by birds and the major Ulster heroes mounted their chariots and pursued the birds as far south as the Boyne.[35] Conchobar's daughter, Deichtine, served as her father's charioteer. During a snowy night lodging was found for the company in a strange house near the Brug na Bóinne and there Deichtine assisted a woman in labour who gave birth to a son. The next day the house had vanished, leaving only the baby and two colts that had been born at the same time. The infant was brought by Deichtine to Emain Macha where he eventually took ill and died. While Deichtine was mourning the loss of her foster-child a small 'creature' crawled into a goblet that Deichtine drank from and she had a vision of Lug who said that she would bear his child and she should name him Sétanta. While pregnant, her father gave her to Sualtaim to be her husband and she bore a son.[36] A major dispute broke out among all the Ulster leaders as to who should raise the child and it was settled that each one would assist in his upbringing according to their special skills. The young Sétanta was then taken to Muirthemne (north Co. Louth) to be raised.

When Sétanta was five years old he set off for Emain Macha to be trained as a warrior.[37] He arrived without the protection of a warrior and was assaulted by the 150-strong boy-troop who were playing ball. He defeated them all and forced them to accept his protection. When Sétanta was six he was invited to a feast at the fort of Culann the smith but arrived late after the smith had closed the gates and released a ferocious guard dog. Sétanta came upon the guard dog and when it attacked him he launched a ball clear through the hound and splattered it against a pillar-stone. While the Ulstermen were relieved to see that the boy had survived, Culann lamented the loss of his guard dog and so it was decided that Sétanta would serve as his guard until another hound could be raised. For this reason Sétanta was called the hound of Culann, or Cú Chulainn. One day in the following year Cú Chulainn learned that he who took up arms on that day would have a short life but his fame would last in Ireland forever. Cú Chulainn demanded weapons and a chariot and set off south where he killed three of the main enemies of Ulster (the three sons of Nechtan Scéne). Returning to Emain Macha, Cú Chulainn not only had their three heads mounted on the chariot but also a captured deer and a flock of swans, and he arrived in a state of warrior-madness. He was subdued only when the women of Emain exposed their breasts, and while the young boy averted his eyes he was plunged into three vats of cold water.

There are several versions of Cú Chulainn's training in arms.[38] As Cú Chulainn grew, he became the object of attention of all the girls of Emain Macha and the men of Ulster decided that he needed to marry, both to end the competition for his affection and also to secure an heir for him in case he died young. After they failed to find a suitable partner, Cú Chulainn set out on his own to see Emer, the daughter of Forgall Manach, a wealthy landowner. He arrived to find Emer with her handmaids and the two had a long discussion, much of which was in riddles to disguise the fact that Cú Chulainn was courting her. Still, when the maids related the visit to her father, Forgall was determined that his daughter would not marry the 'mad-man' from Emain. He journeyed to Emain Macha disguised as a Gaulish emissary and let it be known how much greater Cú Chulainn's ability would be if he went to Scotland for training (in the hope that he would be killed by his fierce instructor, the woman-warrior Scáthach).

Cú Chulainn was separated from his companions on the way to Scotland. His journey involved riding the back of a ferocious beast for four days and crossing an extremely difficult plain with the help of a wheel and an apple, and negotiating the treacherous Bridge of Leaps, a major training obstacle that required for all others long instruction from Scáthach. Scáthach's daughter, Uathach, saw him attempting the bridge and fell in love with him. Cú Chulainn managed the bridge within an hour and was then brought to lodge in the house of a group of deadly barbers who attacked him with spears. Cú Chulainn warded them off and beheaded all of his attackers. He then challenged Scáthach but her son Cuar took Cú Chulainn on and was killed. He at first repulsed the advances of Uathach, injuring her, but when she offered him a way to gain instruction in three feats not taught to the other students, he allowed the girl to spend the night with him. The next day Cú Chulainn caught Scáthach with her guard down and she secured her freedom by teaching him the three feats (as well as providing him with the 'friendship of her thighs' and her daughter!). After another year Cú Chulainn took up with a third woman-warrior, Aífe, the most deadly woman-warrior in the world and major opponent of Scáthach, from whom he learnt three more feats. He also left Aífe pregnant. Returning to Scáthach he first killed an old hag who threatened him on the Bridge of Leaps. He then spent another year with Scáthach along with a new shipment of students from Ireland including Fer Diad, Fráech and Noíse, son of Uisnech. These become his foster-brothers (two of whom he would subsequently have to kill). By now he had learned all the necessary feats, including the *gae bolga*, the deadliest feat that no other of his companions was taught. He bid farewell to Scáthach who recited a poem[39] indicating how during the *táin* (cattle-raid) he would face innumerable enemies, slay many and find himself alone and injured and how his life would not exceed 30 years.

Cú Chulainn journeyed onwards to the country of the men of Catt and there he befriended a woman who was being offered to the Fomorians and he killed their lead warrior (his first official kill after training). He continued on with his companions to the house of the king, who was mourning the loss of his daughter to the Fomorians but then rewarded Cú Chulainn when he learned that he had already rescued her. Then Cú Chulainn and his companions returned to Ulster. Cú Chulainn made his way to the well-guarded fort of Forgall Manach, whom he killed, and ran off with Emer and Forgall's treasure. Hundreds were killed by Cú Chulainn in the ensuing pursuit until he arrived at Emain Macha. Then the arch-troublemaker, Briccriu, enraged Cú Chulainn when he reminded him that Conchobar must exercise the right of the first night. The upset groom was given the task of assembling a herd of wild animals from Sliab Fúait as a form of anger management. The situation was finally resolved when Conchobar went to bed with Emer but had to share the bed with Fergus and Cathbad as chaperones.

On one occasion Cú Chulainn set out with his charioteer, Láeg, early one morning from Emain Macha, intending to make a circuit of his home territory of Muirthemne.[40] Cú Chulainn, who could not return to Emain without slaying an enemy, took a nap while Láeg scanned the sea and saw an enormous ship approaching, carrying a giant so large that he thought that the entire force of Ulster heroes could not stand against him. The giant introduced himself as Goll mac Carbad from northern Germany. He had come with his two brothers to conquer Denmark, Britain and, in Goll's case, Ireland. Cú Chulainn challenged Goll and after several failed attempts he managed to kill the giant and strike off his head. Meanwhile, Conchobar and the rest of the Ulstermen were invited to Dún Colptha by Conall the son of Gleo Glas. The Ulstermen chose a short but rough road that took them past the two-headed Garb of Glenn Rige, who destroyed 50 men of the rearguard. The Ulstermen arrived at Dún Colptha and enjoyed a feast while their host released Conbél, his savage watchdog. By this time Cú Chulainn and Láeg had returned to Emain Macha with the head of Goll. They arrived to find the fort abandoned and were told that everyone had gone on to Conall's fort. At first Cú Chulainn was enraged that he was not invited but he eventually calmed down and set off for the feast, but then he encountered Garb. After a fight, Cú Chulainn killed Garb and cut off his two heads, placing them in the chariot, and they continued onwards. Cú Chulainn then confronted the watchdog and killed it. When he arrived at Conall's he concealed his true identity but asked for admission. The scene turned ugly when Cú Chulainn was not admitted but Fergus and Conall Cernach eventually welcomed him and the three heads were displayed. Cú Chulainn was congratulated over his kills but in the case of the watchdog, Conall Cernach stepped in to offer a replacement and Conchobar offered recompense for the loss. All returned to Emain Macha and the question of Cú Chulainn's insult (not being invited to the feast) was rectified.

On another occasion Cú Chulainn was with his charioteer on the banks of the Boyne when he captured a small man, Senbecc,[41] in a bronze boat who ransomed his life with a series of wondrous gifts. These included a one-size-fits-all protective cloak, weapons and a harp which when played shifted Cú Chulainn's mood until he fell asleep. Then Senbecc went off (the end of the story has not survived).

Briccriu Neimthenga ('poison-tongue') built a magnificent hall and invited the Ulstermen to a feast in order to foment as much discord as he could.[42] The Ulstermen reluctantly came and Briccriu succeeded in driving three of the Ulster champions, Lóegaire Búadach, Conall Cernach and Cú Chulainn, into vying with each other for the champion's portion of the feast, with their respective wives competing to be the first who should enter the mead hall. The Ulstermen attempted to outsource the decision as to who was the rightful champion to several parties, resulting in a series of contests that Cú Chulainn invariably won but which his opponents refused to accept. Finally, the championship was decided by a contest where each was allowed to cut off the head of a giant (Cú Roí in disguise) provided that he could return the favour the following night. Of the contestants, only Cú Chulainn had the courage to face death and was awarded the undisputed championship.

At another feast Briccriu suggested that before enjoying the food and drink the warriors of Ulster should raid across Ireland and give a victory shout regarding their deeds.[43] Cú Chulainn led a party to Connacht and they came across Findchóem, daughter of Eochu Rond, who expressed an enormous crush on Cú Chulainn. They decided that bringing the daughter of a king of the Uí Maine (a major tribe of Galway-Roscommon) back to Emain Macha would be enough of a raid. Along the way they encountered a group of warriors and Cú Chulainn killed and beheaded 12 of them, and the Ulstermen moved on to Cruachain where they were greeted by Medb. Here the heads, which apparently belonged to plunderers, were mounted on the palisade. The next morning the Uí Maine arrived with Eochu Rond seeking his daughter. He hurled a spear at Cú Chulainn who turned it back against the man's horse and then carried the girl's father into the fort. Medb demanded that the two make peace with one another but Eochu placed Cú Chulainn under an injunction to determine why the three sons of Dóel Dermait left the land or he would find no peace. Cú Chulainn then set off, beheading a variety of craftsmen who had made the mistake of confusing him with a porter, until he acquired a boat that would carry him to a place where he could determine what happened to the sons of Dóel Dermait. He sailed to an island where he was offered hospitality of food, drink and a woman. He then rowed to the next island where he met Achtland, the daughter of Dóel Dermait, who explained that there was a prophesy that Cú Chulainn would come and save the three sons. They sailed to another island where Cú Chulainn fought a duel with Cairbre Cundail who only surrendered when Cú Chulainn threatened to use the *gae bolga*. The next day Cairbre was to fight Eochaid Glas but the combat shifts to Cú Chulainn and Eochaid, who thrice blew Cú Chulainn away before Cú Chulainn succeeded in killing him with a vertical spear throw. Everyone kept captive by Eochaid was freed, including the sons of Dóel Dermait, and Cú Chulainn, after receiving presents from the various people he visited, returned to Emain Macha where he finally made his peace with Eochu and Findchóem stayed with him.

After hearing stories about Cú Chulainn, Derbforgaill, the daughter of the king of Norway, fell in love with him and flew to Ireland in the shape of a bird, only to be knocked out of the sky by a stone thrown by Cú Chulainn.[44] She resumed her human shape and Cú Chulainn sucked the stone out. She explained that she had come to see him but agreed to Cú Chulainn's suggestion that she be given to his best friend, Lugaid Riab nderg (of the red stripes).[45] She agreed and the couple have children. But one day in winter the local men made pillars of snow which the women mounted in a pissing contest under the understanding that whoever could urinate the deepest, she would be the 'hottest'. Derbforgaill unwillingly joined in and won the contest and the jealous women maimed her face horribly. She fled into her house as Cú Chulainn and Lugaid approached and was dead by the time they entered. Seeing her, Lugaid also dropped dead. In vengence, Cú Chulainn killed all of the women and then buried Derbforgaill.

Athairne, the sociopath chief-poet of Ulster, made a circuit of Ireland, demanding extravagant gifts or the right to sleep with the wives of the provincial kings under threat of his ridicule.[46] Leaving Leinster with great spoils and 150 of the wives of the local leaders, he sent to Ulster for help after he realized the Leinstermen were not going to tolerate his behaviour any more. Conchobar arrived with his forces but was defeated, taking refuge in the fort of Howth. After his foster-son was killed, Cú Chulainn entered the field and shattered the Leinster army, which was routed by the Ulstermen. Conall Cernach took up the pursuit of the Leinstermen who had killed two of his brothers. He overtook the Leinster king, Mesgegra, who had just lost a hand in an altercation with his own charioteer. In the ensuing duel, which Conall fought with one hand bound to ensure fair play, Mesgegra was defeated and beheaded. Conall and his charioteer took Mesgegra's chariot and horse as well as his head and when confronted with her husband's head, Buan, the wife of Mesgegra, dropped dead. Conall had Mesgegra's brain removed and calcified with lime (see p. 56 for its subsequent use) and then returned to Ulster.

Both Connacht and Ulster desired to acquire a famous hound, Ailbe, that belonged to Mac Dathó, who was in charge of one of the great hostels of Leinster.[47] To avoid insulting one of the parties, Mac Dathó invited the leaders of both provinces to his hostel to gain the hound. On arrival the two groups were offered a feast and an enormous pig was served from which the champion's portion was to be carved. Both sides disputed who should claim the champion's portion until the Connacht champion, Cet mac Mágach, managed to verbally humiliate each of the Ulster claimants. Just before he was to carve the pig, Conall Cernach burst in. Cet reluctantly yielded his place to Conall, remarking that things would be otherwise if his brother Anluan were there. At this point Conall brandished the head of Anluan and established himself as the champion. Eventually the feast turned into a slaughter that spread from the mead hall into the courtyard. The hound was turned loose, taking the side of the Ulstermen. Ailill and Medb fled in their chariot but their charioteer slew the attacking hound and then managed to overpower Conchobar, who had to yield treasures to him to spare his life.

The Ulstermen were once in the house of the king's storyteller, Feidlimid, and they heard a cry from the womb of his pregnant wife.[48] Cathbad was consulted and he prophesied that the child born would be the most beautiful woman in Ireland but also the cause of the death of many of Ulster's warriors and the exile of many more. Although the Ulstermen were all for having the infant killed, Conchobar ordered that she be raised apart from all other men until she came of age to be his consort. But this was not to be as the girl, Deirdre, heard of a young man named Noíse and then she encountered him on the rampart of Emain and shamed him into running off with her along with his two brothers. The four were harried through Ireland and then fled to Scotland where again they found their lives in peril. The Ulstermen convinced Conchobar to allow the sons of Uisnech to return with Fergus serving as guarantor of their safety. But Conchobar had Fergus separated from the party (invited to a feast as there was a *geis* (taboo) on him, prohibiting him from refusing such an invitation). The party arrived at Emain, apparently under the protection of Fergus's son, Fiachu. But the king had Eógan mac Durthacht kill both Noíse and Fiachu and then the other brothers were killed and Deirdre brought to Conchobar. When Fergus and the other guarantors arrived they set out to avenge this violation of their protection until there was full-scale war. Eventually, Fergus led 3,000 Ulster warriors away with him to serve Ailill and Medb in Connacht. After a year had passed, Deirdre committed suicide rather than be shared between Conchobar and Eógan.

After Fergus had gone into exile he was invited to Tara by Eochaid Feidlech, who gave him his daughter, Clothra, in marriage.[49] Fergus led 700 warriors on a raid into Ulster, capturing a fort and raiding a series of sites, and then returned to Tara with his booty as a bride-price for Clothra. Conchobar retaliated with his own raids and Fergus returned with a large army that slaughtered and burnt its way through Ulster. Finally, messengers were sent to negotiate a peace, with Conchobar receiving wergild for the death of his father, and Fergus granted a portion of land and other privileges.

Seven years before the *táin*, Maine, one of the sons of Ailill and Medb, set out with 150 companions from Cruachain to the fort of Gerg, an Ulsterman whose daughter, Ferb, was to marry Maine.[50] Ulster was hostile territory for any Connachtman and when Maine arrived at Gerg's fort there were omens of a disastrous battle. Signs of slaughter also appeared at Emain Macha, where Conchobar heard a prophecy of the *táin* and also that Maine had entered Ulster. He assembled a warband, largely of foreigners, many of whom were Fomorians, and made his way to Gerg's fort, which he immediately attacked at night. Gerg and his sons were killed in the attack although Maine put up a strong defence. Medb was informed in a vision that her son was on the point of being overwhelmed, and dispatched a series of warriors to aid Maine. But by morning Conchobar renewed his attack and in a ferocious duel managed to kill Maine, although he and his charioteer were severely wounded and were the only two attackers to escape. Only then did the first of Medb's reinforcements, led by Finnamail, Maine's foster-brother, arrive to learn of the fate of Maine. Finnamail sought out Conchobar but by this time more Ulstermen had arrived seeking their king and in the ensuing battle Finnamail and his men were killed. A similar thing happened to a second relief detachment and, finally, Medb arrived with her army to fight against Conchobar at the head of his men. In the battle Medb managed to kill two of Conchobar's sons before being defeated and driven into flight. Conchobar then returned to destroy Gerg's fort. After slaying Gerg's remaining son, Conchobar stripped the fort of its treasures and its women (although these all died of grief). Conchobar returned to Emain Macha where he related all the events to Ferchertne, his poet, who prepared a great poem so that the events would be recalled in future days.

Upon the death of Adnae, the chief poet of Ireland, there were two claimants to the position: Adnae's son, Nede, who was then resident in Scotland and Ferchertne, the poet of Ulster.[51] They met at Emain Macha where Briccriu, as usual, helped inflame the situation by placing Nede on the poet's throne and giving him the signs of the office. The older Ferchertne and much younger Nede then engaged in a poetic duel that ultimately wandered into clearly Christian motifs, including the Antichrist and the end of the world, before Nede yielded to Ferchertne, who then graciously praised Nede's wisdom.

In preparation for the great cattle-raid, Medb and Ailill gathered assurances of support from a number of different chieftains. Fráech mac Idath,[52] whose mother (Bé Find) was from the Otherworld, journeyed to Cruachain with his men in order to woo Medb's daughter, Findabair. While he established an understanding with the girl, her father set too high a bride-price which Fráech refused to pay and Medb and Ailill then attempted to have the rejected suitor killed. The attempt was unsuccessful and the king and queen relented and reached an agreement that Fráech should come on the cattle-raid with his troops and cattle and would gain the hand of Findabair in exchange. But upon leaving Cruachain the story slips into a parallel universe worthy of a David Lynch film and we find that Fráech's cattle, his wife and children have all been stolen and carried off by the king of the Lombards whose realm, a very unfriendly place for Irishmen, lay north of the Alps. Fráech journeyed there in the company of the Ulster champion Conall Cernach, defeating the king and his wonder snake, and recovering Fráech's wife and children; the cattle were retrieved from the land of the Picts on the way back. In another tale,[53] however, it is Treblann, who was fostered at Tara by Cairbre Nia Fer, who fell in love with Fráech and sent a messenger to Cruachain to fetch Fráech to her as Cairbre had forbade such a union and claimed he could find a more skilful warrior for her. Fráech set out with his men, urged on by Medb, Ailill and Fergus to avenge the insult. Fráech took Treblann away with him after giving battle to the son of Cairbre but on returning home he found that his cattle had been driven away and that he must fetch them back as they had been promised to Medb for the *táin*. After Fráech had set off with Conall Cernach, Cairbre enlisted the aid of Midir to convince Treblann that Fráech had died on his raid and she then died of grief. Fráech returned from his raid against the Picts and, learning of what Midir had done, he went to his fort and challenged him. Midir sent another warrior against Fráech, disguised as Midir, and in the duel Fráech was victorious. Midir then paid a blood-price for Treblann and he also gained the (miraculously restored?) Treblann who remained with him until he was himself killed by Cú Chulainn.

Ailill and Medb also summoned a Munster king, Eochu Bec, to Cruachain in order to ask for cattle for provisioning the troops for the *táin*.[54] Eochu agreed to provide a cow from each farmer under his rule. On his return home Eochu was attacked by the Sons of Glaschu (from Mayo) and his retinue of fosterlings was killed. Ailill then had a vision to send his son Orlam to wed Dartaid, the daughter of Eochu Bec, and thereby gain her cattle. Dartaid agreed to the proposal but when she and Orlam and her cattle were returning, a defender of Munster attacked and most of Orlam's men were killed along with Dartaid, although Orlam made it home with 40 milch cows and 50 heifers.

Ailill and Medb also sought to acquire cattle from a Connacht warrior, Regamon, who had seven daughters.[55] These were the objects of affection of the seven sons of Ailill and Medb (all named Maine), who sent them on a quest for the cattle. They cornered several of the girls and explained their quest and, after consulting with their sisters, the girls all agreed to go off with the seven Maine's and bring their cattle. On the way home Regamon pursued them but was held off by a thorn-hurdle erected across a river while the girls sought help in Cruachain. Troops from Connacht arrived and a treaty was made where Regamon was offered restitution and he granted the cattle as a dowry for his daughters.

On the feast of *Samain*, Ailill and Medb were at Cruachain having recently hung two captives.[56] They offered a prize to anyone with the courage to go to the corpses that night and hang a withy on the foot of one of the bodies. After others had failed Nera went and repeatedly tried to hang a withy that kept falling off. The corpse told him he would have to fix the withy with a peg and asked Nera to carry him on his back to find a drink. After dismissing two houses they arrived at a third where the corpse got a drink and killed all the occupants of the house by spitting the last of his drink at them. Nera carried him back to the gallows and returned towards Cruachain, which (in a vision) he saw having been burnt and strewn with the heads of its occupants. He followed the warriors responsible for the destruction into the cave at Cruachain and then on into the *síd* (mound) where he met the king of the *síd*. The king directed him to go to a house where he was welcomed by a woman. He daily brought firewood to the king and also discovered that the king's golden crown was stored in a well. The woman (now his wife) explained to him that he has had a vision of the future destruction of Cruachain which would happen unless he warned his people before next *Samain* and they destroyed the *síd*. In order to convince Medb and Ailill of the truth of this prophecy, his wife told him to bring summer fruits from the *síd*. She also bore a son by him. Nera then returned to Cruachain to find that no time had passed since he had left, seemingly days before, and he remained at Cruachain for the year. This is the same year that Fergus led the Ulster exiles to Cruachain. Nera was rewarded with a golden sword and headed back to the *síd* to bring out his wife, son and cows before Ailill and Medb attacked it. The Mórrígan came and stole a cow given to Nera's son and brought it to Cuailnge (Cooley) to be sired by the Donn Cuailgne but Cú Chulainn attempted to stop her as she tried to drive the cow back to Connacht.[57] Nevertheless it did arrive. Nera returned once again to Cruachain and then returned to the *síd* three days before *Samain* and brought his herd out, including the bull sired by the Donn Cuailgne. The bull encountered the Finnbennach (white-horned) bull of Ailill and the two fought each other until the Finnbennach won. The bellowing was interpreted as a threat that if its father (the Donn Cuailgne) came the Finnbennach would be defeated. Medb swore that she would not rest until she saw this fight. The Connachta and Ulster exiles then destroyed the *síd* and carried off its treasures, but Nera stayed with his own people in the *síd* and would not come out again.

The *táin*, as we will soon see, was ostensibly about a contest between Ailill and Medb to possess the best bull in Ireland. Years before the *táin* there were two pig-keepers, one from Munster and one from Connacht, who were good friends but were goaded by others into competing with one another so that they ultimately fell out.[58] As they served the respective *síd* of their provinces, they were also shape-changers and in their struggle with one another they assumed the forms of various animals (birds of prey, stags, sea creatures) and even warriors before becoming small creatures. One was ingested by a cow in Cuailnge belonging to Dáire mac Fiachna that then gave birth to the Brown Bull of Cuailnge, while the other impregnated a cow in

Connacht that bore the Finnbennach (white-horned) bull of Connacht. These then became the objects of a competition between Ailill, who possessed the Finnbennach, and his wife Medb, who did not have a bull of equal quality but learned that there was a match in the Donn Cuailgne.

The Táin Bó Cuailgne[59]

In 19 BC[60] Queen Medb of Connacht, having failed to obtain the Brown Bull of Cuailnge by diplomatic means, assembled an enormous army to invade Ulster on a cattle-raid for the bull. The leader of the army was Fergus, the former king of Ulster, who had led a third of the Ulstermen into exile in the service of Connacht after the Deirdre incident. Fergus sent advance word to Cú Chulainn, the champion of Ulster and the only Ulster warrior fit for combat service (the rest were in their debility from the curse of Macha), who first delayed the invading army by setting a series of challenges. Medb asked who was obstructing their way and Fergus and Conall Cernach related the boyhood deeds of Cú Chulainn (his prowess on both the playing field and in combat, how he achieved his name, his first raid, as recounted above). As the army attempted to make its way it was frequently stymied by Cú Chulainn who killed one warrior after another until an agreement was made whereby Medb sent one man each day to duel with Cú Chulainn. The series of duels against a wide variety of different warriors is described, Medb occasionally offering her daughter Findabair to any hero who would face Cú Chulainn. The boy-troop from the Ulster capital came to help Cú Chulainn but they were all killed. Cú Chulainn avenged them when he attacked Medb's army with his 'scythed' chariot.[61] More duels were fought as Medb moved closer to her goal and carried off a variety of spoils. In desperation Fergus, who was the foster-father of Cú Chulainn, was sent against him but neither he nor Cú Chulainn would fight each other. Cú Chulainn agreed to run away if Fergus promised to yield to Cú Chulainn at a later date. Eventually, Cú Chulainn's foster-brother, Fer Diad, was talked into challenging Cú Chulainn and the two nearly evenly matched warriors fought over three days until Cú Chulainn employed his special weapon, the *gae bolga* (see Chapter Seven), and killed Fer Diad. Severely wounded, Cú Chulainn was out of action as a series of Ulster warriors arrived one-by-one to attack Medb's army until the debility was entirely lifted and the Ulstermen were able to attack the retreating army of Medb. In the major battle Fergus was finally coaxed into fighting against his fellow countrymen but was stopped by Cú Chulainn who arose from his sickbed to confront his foster-father to force him to retreat from the battle. Medb's allies withdrew leaving only the Connachta to endure the vengeance of the Ulstermen, who defeated Medb's army. In the end, the two bulls fought each other and the Ulster beast killed and dismembered the Connacht one, throwing its parts over Ireland until it finally returned to County Down to die. Peace was then concluded between Connacht and Ulster.

After the Táin

Although peace had been made, Conchobar fell into massive depression over the fact that his province had been pillaged and the Brown Bull taken and was advised to seek redress or military victory in the coming summer (the end of winter and spring being quite unsuitable for putting his army into the field).[62] He sent messengers to Conall Cernach, who was in Scotland, to come, and Conall arrived with a fleet of foreign allies, including Norwegians. After feasting, the Ulstermen journeyed south and sent out envoys to Leinster and Connacht demanding full restitution. The king of Leinster, Cairbre Nia Fer, and Ailill and Medb of Connacht made a defensive pact and rejected Conchobar's demands; Medb, however, left the Leinster king to deal with the Ulster forces. The two armies collided at Ross na Ree on the Boyne and the Ulster forces initially broke until rallied by Conall Cernach who turned the tide (his foreign mercenaries nowhere in sight). Also, Cú Chulainn advanced to defeat the Leinster king. Following the Ulster victory, peace, including marriage alliances, was made between Ulster and Leinster.

During the feast of *Samain* Cú Chulainn attempted to capture a flock of marvellous birds to please the women of Ulster but failed and then fell into a stupor.[63] He had been charmed by visitors from the Otherworld who sought to lead him to the recently rejected wife of Manannán (the Irish sea god), Fand, who would give herself to him if he assisted her people in a coming battle. Cú Chulainn's aid decided the outcome of the battle and he lived with Fand for a month, but when they planned another tryst, Cú Chulainn's wife, Emer, ambushed Fann and after discussion, Cú Chulainn returned to his wife while Fann was taken in again by Manannán.

While Cú Chulainn was away on another bird hunt, he left his wife at their home in Dún Dealgan. The territory was raided by Tuir Glesta, a Norwegian prince, with whom Emer fell in love and she ran off with him to Anglesey. Cú Chulainn caught up with them and slew Tuir Glesta in a duel and carried back the spoils and his wife.[64]

Again while celebrating *Samain*, the Ulstermen were to split their feast between the north coast and Dundalk, the home of Cú Chulainn.[65] But leaving the first feast they lost their way and ultimately arrived in Munster at the fort of Cú Roí, who was then entertaining Medb and Ailill of Connacht, the major opponents of the Ulstermen. The hosts lured the Ulstermen into an iron building that was disguised between wooden planks on both the inside and outside (as at Dind Rig above, p. 39). Below the house a fire was set to roast the Ulstermen but led by Cú Chulainn they managed to break out and slaughter their attackers and the site, Temair Luchra, has been left uninhabited since that time. The Ulstermen returned to Cú Chulainn's place to finish their feast.

About seven years after Cú Chulainn had been trained in Scotland by the warrior woman, Aífe, she sent their son, Connla, back to meet his father, enjoining on him that he should neither give his name nor give way to any warrior until he met his father.[66] The boy arrived and demonstrated to the Ulstermen that he was a formidable opponent who bested the Ulster champion Conall, and so Cú Chulainn was sent for. Despite warnings from his wife, Cú Chulainn fought the boy and eventually killed him with the *gae bolga*, his son dying in his arms. For killing his own son, although unknowingly, he was required to pay half-wergild to Conchobar who was his next of kin.[67]

Deaths

Cú Roí mac Dari, who had settled Cú Chulainn's claim to the championship of Ulster, accompanied Cú Chulainn to a siege of the Men of Falga[68] where he was incognito, disguised as the 'man in the grey mantle'.[69] Although he had accomplished half of all the killings, the Ulstermen did not give him his share of the spoils and so he carried off several treasures, including the woman Bláthnait, humiliating Cú Chulainn when he attempted to stop him. Cú Chulainn eventually tracked him down and hatched a plan with Bláthnait whom he had also fancied. She asked her now husband to build a fortress and the Ulstermen approached him under the guise of labourers carrying material for the fort. Bláthnait then took Cú Roí inside to wash him but bound his hair to the bedposts and let the Ulstermen into the fortress where there was mutual slaughter between Cú Roí and his men and the attacking Ulstermen. Bláthnait beheaded Cú Roí (or he was killed by Cú Chulainn[70]). Cú Roí's poet, Ferchertne, recited a eulogy in his honour, including a list of obscure terms for the gifts he had received,[71] and grabbed Bláthnait while she was on top of a cliff so that the two fell to their deaths.

Lugaid, the son of Cú Roí, had plotted vengeance against Cú Chulainn along with the sons and daughters of Cailitin, another victim.[72] The offspring of Cailitin were adept in magic and in AD 2[73] they summoned up an illusion that deceived Cú Chulainn into abandoning Emain Macha and journeying south where he was deliberately set up by his opponents into breaking a number of his *gessa* (such as consuming the meat of a dog). On three occasions he was asked for his spear and each time Lugaid retrieved it to kill first Láeg, Cú Chulainn's charioteer, then one of his horses, and, finally, Cú Chulainn himself was pierced by his own spear. He staggered to a lake to obtain a drink and then lashed himself to a pillar-stone so that he would die standing up. His surviving horse, the Liath Macha, stood defending him while a scald crow descended onto his shoulder, providing the iconic image of Oliver Sheppard's sculpture in the General Post Office in Dublin (PL. XIII). Lugaid finally beheaded Cú Chulainn but at the same time Cú Chulainn's arm came down and his sword cut off Lugaid's right hand. The attackers then carried off Cú Chulainn's head to Tara where it was buried. They split up and Lugaid went to the Liffey to bathe. At the same time Conall Cernach, who had sworn to avenge Cú Chulainn on the day of his death, first found the Liath Macha and the remains of Cú Chulainn and then caught up with Lugaid and they agreed to fight at Airgetros. The now one-handed Lugaid requested that Conall give him a fair fight and tie an arm to his side. The two duelled for hours until Conall's horse entered the action and Lugaid was defeated, his head taken by Conall (though when he placed it on a stone it melted through it). Afterwards Cú Chulainn appeared in a ghostly chariot over Emain Macha and prophesied the coming of Christianity. The Liath Macha came to Emer, Cú Chulainn's wife, and bid farewell and Emer lamented for her lost husband.

Brig Brethach, the wife of Celtchair mac Uithechair, came alone to the hostel of Blaí, who was required to sleep with any woman who arrived without the company of her husband.[74] Fearing the consequences of bedding the wife of one of Ulster's roughest warriors, he begged her to leave but was shamed by the woman into sleeping with her. Afterwards, Celtchair learned of this and slew Blaí in the royal house and then fled to Munster. The Ulstermen intervened with Conchobar and it was arranged that Celtchair could pay off the fine for his act of murder by ridding Ulster of its three worst pests. The first was the nearly invulnerable Conganchnes mac Dedad, who was protected by a skin of horn. By subterfuge Celtchair learned how to kill Conganchnes: he and his men heated two large iron spits and drove them through the soles of Conganchnes's feet and then cut off his head. The second pest was a ferocious hound that ravaged the province. Celtchair prepared a hollowed-out log and baited it so that the dog sank its teeth into one end while Celtchair reached his arm through the log down the dog's gullet and ripped out its heart. The third pest was another hound, the

Dóelchú, whose two brothers were the hounds of Culann the smith and of Mac Dathó. The hound responded only to Celtchair but it began ravaging the province and Celtchair had to put it down. He did so with his spear but a drop of blood from the dog fell on him and went right through him, killing Celtchair.

The poet Aed mac Ainninne was caught dallying with the wife of Conchobar and was sentenced to death by drowning. When they tried to drown him in the lake before the house of Lóegaire Búadach, the hero rushed to Aed's defence but critically injured himself on his own door lintel (see Chapter Six).[75]

Earlier Cú Chulainn, Lóegaire and Conall Cernach had once been contending among themselves as to who was the champion of Ulster.[76] Conall won the contest when he exhibited the calcified brain-ball of Mesgegra. But the brain-ball fell into the hands of Cet mac Mágach, the Connacht champion. Later, on a cattle-raid, Cet was chased by the Ulstermen led by Conchobar. Before the battle the women of Connacht begged Conchobar to display himself before them while Cet lurked in their midst and when he came within range, Cet launched the brain-ball at Conchobar and it lodged in his head. The doctors could not remove the ball without killing Conchobar and he was ordered to refrain from any exertion or physical activity that might dislodge it. Seven years of inactivity passed when one day (in AD 33)[77] when heaven and earth shook, a druid explained to Conchobar that Christ, who had been born on the same night as the Ulster king, had been put to death by the Jews. Conchobar excitedly jumped up claiming that had he been there Christ would not have been killed and in a fury he re-enacted what he would have done by attacking a forest with his sword.[78] This pious act (of anti-semitic deforestation?) impelled the brain-ball to jump out and Conchobar became the first Irishman to suffer red martyrdom (a bloody death for Christ) and the first pagan Irishman to go to heaven.

Following the death of Conchobar's son, Cormac, the Ulstermen asked Conall Cernach to serve as king but he deferred to his foster-son, Conchobar's son Cúscraid, who apportioned the province among its leaders and attempted to reconcile Fergus by inviting him back.[79] Fergus returned, accepting Cú Chulainn's former territory but after his wife, Flidais, died he returned to Medb and Ailill in Connacht. A dispute between the Ulstermen and the Connachta over ownership of Crich Maland (near Athlone) degenerated into a major battle in the territory of Airtech Uchtlethan which the Ulstermen won, destroying, among others, the Fir Domnainn, one of the ancient tribes associated with the colonization of the Fir Bolg.

Fergus mac Róich led his 3,000 Ulster exiles in the service of Connacht for 14 years.[80] One day while bathing in Findloch on Mag Aí, Fergus was joined by Medb who mounted Fergus's chest and locked her legs around him. Ailill saw this and after Medb had left, he had his brother (and a good friend of Fergus) cast his javelin at Fergus. It passed through his chest and out of his back. Ailill fled in a chariot as Fergus attempted to hurl the javelin back at him. Finally, Fergus emerged from the lake, lay down and died.

Cet mac Mágach was once raiding Ulster when he was tracked to a house in Connacht.[81] After being prodded by his charioteer into facing Cet in combat, Conall and Cet fought it out at Cet's ford. Cet was killed and Conall collapsed from his wounds. He was rescued by Belchú, who initially believed Conall dead. Belchú dragged Conall to his own house and had physicians restore his health but was alarmed at setting such a ferocious warrior lose again so he planned to have his sons murder Conall in his bed. But Conall knew what was coming and he forced Belchú to take his place in the same bed; mistakenly, Belchú's sons murdered their own father in the bed and were then killed by Conall who took all their heads back to his own house.

Conall Cernach, after a long career of slaughtering the men of Connacht, decided in his decrepitude to retire to Connacht to be looked after at Cruachain.[82] Here Medb and Ailill had a house built for him and they fed him for a year while he entertained the Connachta by recounting how he had killed their relations and setting their spears for them. Although Medb was constantly entertained by a horde of suitors, she resented any infidelity by her husband Ailill, and she charged Conall to keep an eye out for any of his escapades. On one occasion they both caught sight of Ailill with a woman behind a hazel bush and Medb goaded Conall into casting his spear at the bush where it mortally wounded Ailill (Conall also regarded such an act as revenge for Fergus, who Ailill had killed). Dying, Ailill warned Conall that the Connachtmen would kill him for what he had done and he granted Conall a head start by not dying until Conall had reached his chariot. Conall cut a path through the Connachtmen until he reached a river that had been polluted by miners washing ore (which violated Conall's *geis* not to go into a ford without it having been strained). The waters held him fast and he was killed and beheaded by the three Red-wolves of Martine, who had sought revenge for the Ulstermen's slaying of Cú Roí.

As for Medb, according to some accounts she had killed her sister Clothra, who had been Queen of Connacht.[83] At the time Clothra was pregnant by Conchobar, and the son, Furbaide, was born by a fairly primitive form of Caesarean section on the death of his mother. There was a *geis* on Medb that required her to take a bath in a well at the edge of Lough Rí. Furbaide set up a stake and rope at the place where Medb took her daily bath and practiced his sling at an apple on top of the stake. One day Medb was taking her customary bath when she was pointed out to Furbaide, who launched a piece of cheese at her (he was in too much a hurry to seek out a stone). It struck Medb in the head and killed her in revenge for having killed his mother.

After Patrick

During the reign of Lóegaire (AD 462–484), son of Niall of the Nine Hostages, Patrick came to Tara in order to convert the king, but he rejected Christianity unless Patrick could summon up the spirit of Cú Chulainn.[84] This was done on two occasions and during the latter one, Cú Chulainn related some of his heroic deeds, including a raid on Dún Scaith. He told Lóegaire that his companions were in hell and that Lóegaire should embrace Patrick and God, which the king then did.

When Diarmait mac Cerbaill (AD 553–565) was high king he was required to arrange how Tara should articulate with the five provinces, and so he asked the advice of one wise man after another, including Tuan mac Cairill, the survivor of the colonization by Partholón.[85] But he deferred to the ultimate authority, Fintan mac Bochra, the sole survivor of Cesair's original attempted colonization of Ireland, who was able to relate the entire history of colonizations, and demonstrate his own antiquity and the history of wise biblical and Irish judgments. Fintan passed on the earlier pronouncements of Trefuingid Tre-eochair on the geopolitical ideology of Ireland with Connacht possessing knowledge, Ulster – warfare, Leinster – prosperity, Munster – music, and kingship housed at the centre in Meath. He also set up the pillar-stone at the heart of Ireland on the hill of Uisnech, where all the provinces joined. Finally, he returned to his home at Dún Tulcha to die.

In the 7th century the chief poet of Ireland, Senchán Torpéist, gathered the other poets together to see if anyone could recite the *Táin Bó Cualinge* in its entirety, but none could do it as it had been exchanged for the Cuilmen, the *Etymologiae* of Isidore of Seville.[86] Several poets, along with possibly Senchán himself, set out to recover the full text. One of them, the son of Senchán, rested before the gravestone of Fergus mac Róich. After chanting a poem, Fergus appeared in a mist and recited the entire text of the *Táin*, which was then carried back to Senchán himself.

CHAPTER THREE

Excavating the Dreamtime

Preserved in mediaeval manuscripts in Ireland is this
extraordinary picture of a way of life that had disappeared
from the European continent in the second century BC.

Terence Powell, 1950[1]

Medieval monks have left us an account of Irish history that allegedly
extends back to nearly 3000 BC. In the 17th century much of this *historia*
might have been accepted as a generally accurate account of past events;
in the 21st century this same account, at least that part depicting events before the
5th or 6th centuries AD, had been almost entirely dismissed as *fabula*, the product of
a wild Irish imagination. In terms of testing one's gullibility, there is obviously some
correlation between antiquity and veracity: the older the supposed event, the more
likely that it is entirely fictitious. We have already seen that even the medieval Irish
had trouble swallowing the story of Cesair, and even had doubts about the invasion
of Partholón and the long-lived Tuan. In fact, almost the entire temporal remit of the
Mythological cycle (2958 BC to about the 1st century BC) would usually be rejected
today as obvious fiction although, as we will later see, there are occasionally pieces of
hard evidence that may disturb our natural scepticism.

The Ulster cycle, on the other hand, occupies a much more disputed territory.
There have always been those who claim that even if the specific events described
in the tales may be dismissed, the social structure, political situation, behaviour
and material culture depicted were rooted in Iron Age Ireland. While this would
not support the most extreme claims of the antiquity of Irish tradition, it would still
award Ireland with the earliest 'cultural history' in Europe after that of the Greeks
and Romans. To investigate this proposition we need to compare the evidence of
the earliest Irish literary tradition with archaeology. In short, we need to be literary
archaeologists.

Literary archaeology

Archaeology is the study of the human past through its material remains and one commonly distinguishes between prehistoric and historic archaeology. The latter comprises the practice of archaeology applied to historical societies, those possessing written records. An example of historical text-based archaeology in Ireland might be a medievalist pouring over the Pipe rolls of the English treasury describing the initial allocation of building materials for an Irish castle. Here, the written evidence is administrative which, if the supplier were not engaged in misappropriation of Crown funds, could be regarded as a reasonably firm source. It is the context of the document, dry administrative records, that plays a critical part in assessing its utility to an archaeologist. But once we change the context of the written document, its archaeological utility becomes more problematic. For example, we probably slip a fair few notches in terms of reliability when we engage with body counts from battles reported in the Irish annals. Beyond what we would recognize today as historical accounts we may stray even farther from *historia* deep into the world of *fabula* where archaeologists have tried to recover the time and place of the material culture of imagined worlds. Good examples of this elsewhere in northwest Europe would be the use of the Norse sagas or *Beowulf* in the reconstruction of the early medieval past. But the best example for our purposes is the massive amount of archaeological research and debate concerning the *realia* of Homer's *Iliad* and *Odyssey*. Taking my cue from the Irish monks of the Middle Ages who attempted to enhance their reconstruction of their own deep past by kitting it out with biblical correlations, I will try to carry the more sceptical reader along by slip-streaming the Irish material on the tails of far more respectable Homeric scholarship. At least this has some precedence, for as Gerald Murphy argued:

> the Irish Heroic cycle is unique in being the only branch of
> European literature which has preserved something of the warrior
> spirit and tradition of the ancient Celts as known to writers of
> classical antiquity. It is in Greek epic literature rather than in
> mediaeval romantic literature that the Irish Heroic tales find
> their closest parallels.[2]

Murphy's conclusions are hardly original for the medieval Irish themselves likened the heroes of the Ulster cycle with those from the Trojan War, curiously enough as Trojans rather than the victorious Greeks. A 12th-century Irish poem compared the

Ulster King Conchobar with Priam of Troy, Cú Chulainn with Troilus, Fergus with Aeneas and Conall Cernach with Hektor.[3] So let's see how the Ulster cycle stacks up against the Homeric epics.

Homer and the earliest Irish tradition

The *Iliad* and the *Odyssey* are two extensive poems relating events during and following the siege of Troy by the Greeks, an event traditionally set to *c.* 1200 BC, during the Late Bronze Age in Greece in the later phases of Mycenaean culture. This coincides with the ancient Greeks' perception of an 'Age of Heroes' that was loosely set to 1400–1200 BC.[4] These two works are commonly assigned to a Greek poet by the name of Homer who lived in about the 8th century BC, a half-millennium after the supposed dates of the events that he describes. The actual text of the two Homeric epics was only standardized in the 2nd century BC.[5] In short, there is a gap of about 1,000 years between the supposed 'historical present', the period to which tradition assigned the Trojan War, and the earliest written evidence with which scholars must engage.

For the sake of comparison, we will focus on the earliest version we have of the *Táin Bó Cuailnge* in the rest of our discussion. The *Táin* depicts a major cattle-raid involving the southern half of Ireland against Ulster that Irish annalists set to 19 BC. The name of the author is unknown but there are elements of the story that suggest that it – or at least some elements of it – had some form of existence by the 7th century and many have argued that there was probably a primitive version by the 9th century. But the earliest full text was in the *Lebor na hUidre*, where it was written in *c.* AD 1100 by three different scribes. Like the Homeric poems, the gap between the supposed 'event' and the written account available to scholars is in the order of a millennium.

The text of the two Homeric epics runs to *c.* 30,000 lines of verse. The earliest recension of the *Táin* is a mere 4,160 lines.[6]

Authorship

The *Iliad* is clearly not the product of a single inspired author in the way that the *Aeneid* is the single work of the Roman poet Vergil. Rather, through its various inconsistencies, shifts in dialect, and other hints, there is little doubt that the Greek epic has been assembled over time. In fact, the noted classicist Ulrich von Wilamowitz-Moellendorff (1848–1931) dismissed the *Iliad* as 'a miserable piece of patchwork'.[7] The achievement of Homer in its creation is often seen as that of the poet who did his best to iron out the discrepancies and provide a somewhat imperfect artistic whole.

The *Táin* is clearly an assemblage of different elements and some of these are even listed as separate *scéla* (tales) in a 10th-century index of Irish tales.[8] Like the *Iliad*, it is also replete with inconsistencies and doublets of incidences. In fact, in the first recension in the *Lebor na hUidre*, we are clearly seeing a scribe who is trying to determine the 'real' story from the different versions before him.[9]

Hildegard Tristram has argued that the different incidents were not assembled together until the late 10th or early 11th century.[10] She notes that all of the genuinely Old Irish tales mentioned in the lists tend to be short and it was only in the middle or late 10th century that we begin to find longer texts, initially Irish translations of longer Latin narratives. Gearóid Mac Eoin viewed the compositional process as beginning with earlier anecdotes, originally oral, that were written down while newer anecdotes may have been created in imitation; but for him it was in the 9th century that these were coupled together to make longer narratives.[11] More recently Máire Herbert argued that the *Táin* was essentially a 9th-century product that was revived several centuries later when classical influences were having a major impact on Irish literature.[12]

If we wish to project a Homer into the Irish situation, it is the author of the later 2nd recension that is found in the *Book of Leinster* who did his best to produce a coherent account, including the addition of an opening to the tale that actually explained the motivation for the cattle-raid in the first place.

Verse versus prose

The Homeric epics are recited in verse – to be precise hexameter – where every line consists of six feet, each foot comprising either two long syllables or one long and two short syllables. The importance of verse composition is that poetry is more likely to be transmitted word for word both because it is easier to recall and also because any changes must be made according to the same metrical rules as the line's original formation. For this reason we can find instances where sacred verse such as the Rig Veda of India was successfully transmitted orally for many centuries before being committed to writing and, even today, the oral version takes precedence over any written version. In short, the integrity of the work is more likely to be sustained over a long period of time if it has been transmitted in verse.

The *Táin* is essentially a prose tale with verse scattered through it and some of the earliest evidence we have for a *Táin* story occurs in several early poems. So were the *Táin* and other early Irish tales originally composed in verse? To argue this would be an extremely hard sell among Celticists.[13] While we have clear instances such as the *Lebor Gabála* where prose narratives appear to be expanded versions of the verse sections, we also have many examples from the tales where the verse sections appear to be merely poetic paraphrases, often very abbreviated, of narrative prose.[14] And, on occasion, we even have what would appear to be verse passages that are older than the prose matrix in which we find them but that appear to have been designed to enhance a still earlier context in prose,[15] or verse passages that are so integrated with the text that an episode requires both formats for a clear understanding.[16] The situation is essentially that the earliest writing in Irish contains works combining prose *and* poetry and there is no case for assuming that the earliest tales were entirely composed in verse. Anything that was originally composed in verse might carry relics of a deeper past than the prose narrative in which they have become embedded. In addition, we also find what has been called 'formulaic prose' (i.e., passages of alliterating prose arranged in clearly determined accent units) that may be the detritus of earlier, more extended, verse passages. It has even been suggested that some of the verse passages may be deliberately marked in the text to signal that they were to have been performed from memory, or in other words that they had a specifically oral origin,[17] and that the more descriptive passages relating to the appearance of warriors, their weapons, chariots and horses, were originally memorized in verse.[18]

The storyteller

From whatever date one wants to initiate the *Iliad*, the vehicle of its transmission was the professional poet who performed his craft orally. How these extremely long Homeric epics were subsequently recorded is problematic although Michael Haslam sees no alternative to a poet dictating to a scribe.[19] It should be noted that as the historical present of the tales is set to the Mycenaean civilization, it coincides with the beginning of writing in Greece, the Linear B inscriptions. This would open the possibility that there could have been contemporaneous written accounts of the Trojan War (assuming that it actually occurred). However, classical scholars have emphasized the fact that the Linear B inscriptions are purely economic and there is no evidence that they were employed in the writing of literature (or history if one wishes to accept the Trojan War as real).[20] So it is generally presumed that the medium of transmission must have been oral, which requires generations of storytellers at least to the 5th century BC if not later.

The source of the earliest Irish tales is complicated. The keepers of traditional lore – origins, law, genealogies and history – were the *filid* (*fili* in the singular). They were not simply poets but multitaskers (their name might be best translated as 'seers') who, for our purpose, were acting the role of the *senchaid*, the authority in all things ancient. The irony is that although they were the vehicles by which ancient traditions were passed on orally, we obviously do not have a single example of their oral transmissions (unless one assumes that Fergus was really raised from the dead and his recitation of the *Táin* was dutifully recorded verbatim by Irish stenographers). All of our sources for the earliest Irish tradition derive from monasteries and the monks who have left us with our only written evidence. So while we may plausibly conjecture that there existed an oral tradition of ancient Ireland propagated by the *filid* before writing came to Ireland, we have no direct evidence for this. And the question of how the presumably oral tradition of the *filid* managed to make the leap from a professional class of poets to the monks has generated a variety of theories including the *filid* reciting to monks who took dictation; monks, having heard the oral recitations of a *fili*, returning to their monasteries to write them out in their own words; to *filid* acquiring the ability to write in the monasteries and there producing their own tales. In a recent review of the whole problem of orality and literacy, Elva Johnston[21] reminds us that the *filid* and the monks did not inhabit totally different worlds and there are even cases of individuals being both clerics and *filid*. That both would be present at formal recitations for the political elites where traditional narratives would be read out or recited would ensure that the people who wrote or copied out the tales should have been familiar with them. Indeed, the traditional tales played a major part in underwriting the legitimacy of the ruling elites. As Tomás Ó Cathasaigh has it, the *filid* and clerics (and jurists) were all part of a 'single literary and scholarly establishment'.[22]

Oral tradition

One of the great accomplishments of Homeric scholarship has been establishing the oral nature of the poems in the context of oral performances among traditional societies in the Balkans and Africa. The repetition of set phrases or whole lines is a common feature of oral composition, especially where the poet must work within the format of a fixed verse. Sometimes we find precisely the same line repeated as here, where Aeneas lies wounded but his mother, Aphrodite, protects him lest a Greek:

5.317 *khalkòn enì stéthessi balòn ek thumòn héloito*
5.346 *khalkòn enì stéthessi balòn ek thumòn héloito*
   'strike the bronze spear through his chest and strip the life from him'

Moreover, there are many epithets that are frequently repeated, especially when they not only serve the needs of sense but also the metre of the line, for example where the Greek leader Agamemnon arms himself:

3.334   *amphi d' ar ómoisin báleto zíphos arguróelon*
         'across the shoulders he slung the sword with the silver nails'

and then enters into combat:

3.61   *Atreídes de erussámenos zíphos arguróelon*
        'the son of Atreus, drawing the sword with the silver nails'

It is estimated that about 20 per cent of the Homeric poems consists of lines that are partly or wholly repeated elsewhere.[23]

It has been argued that in Greek epic, the formulaic nature of the phrases in the poems would have helped to preserve accurate descriptions of the material culture of ancient Greece over periods of centuries. For example, of 84 descriptions of shields in the *Iliad*, all but 18 consist of standard epithets that permit one to distinguish two basic shield types, one of which, it has frequently been argued, must be based on a Mycenaean archetype.[24]

When we examine the Irish evidence, we encounter a literary landscape that does include at least repeated stock descriptions.[25] In the first recension of the *Táin* we find, for example, eight references to warriors wielding a *claideb órdurin* 'gold-hilted sword', which we might compare to the use of the Homeric *zíphos arguróelon* 'sword with silver nails', a weapon that has been employed as evidence that the Greek sword described dated to Mycenaean times.[26] But there is a particular characteristic of early Irish literature that distinguishes its descriptive passages from those of Homer. This concerns the most descriptively rich sections of the tales where the Watchman Device is employed. This involves an observer who combines a keen ability to describe the appearance of people with a total ignorance as to their identity relating his descriptions to someone who can name the characters. The problem here is that the early Irish had an abhorrence of repetition. For example, in a series of descriptions of the chief Ulster warriors just before the climatic battle of the *Táin*, each warrior is depicted in terms of appearance, apparel and arms. Taking only the descriptions of shields (Table 3.1), one can easily see that while the term for shield was almost universally the same (*scíath*) the shields might differ in colour (for

Table 3.1: Shield descriptions from TBC[1] 3589–3827.

Name	Shield	Shield description
Conchobar	*gelscíath*	*co túagmílaib óir*
Cúscraid	*scíath*	*béimnech co fáebar condúala*
Sencha	*scíath*	*erradach co túagmílib*
Eógan	*cromscíath*	*co faebar condúala*
Lóegaire	*scíath*	*bémnech co fóebar condúalach*
Munremur	*dubscíath*	*co mbúailid humae*
Connad	*dercscíath*	*co mbúaili chaladargait*
Rochaid	*cúarscíath*	*co túagmílib ildathacha*
Celtchair	*cromscíath*	*co fáebur conndúala*
Feradach	*scíath*	*co mbúailid óir*
Eirrge	*bocóit*	*líath*
Menn	*scíath*	*glas*
Fergna	*scíath*	*derg*
Furbaide	*scíath*	*bémnech co n-imlib óir*
Erc	*scíath*	*taulgel...co cobrud óir*

example 'white' (*gel*), 'dark' (*dub*), 'red' (*derc*)), or shape (for example 'curved' (*crom* and *cúar*)). After that we have further descriptions employing repeated phrases, such as *co fáebar condúala* 'with scalloped rims', *co túagmílaib* 'with animal decorations', and *co mbúailid* 'with bosses (of X)', and there is a compulsion[27] to differentiate each of these such that of the 15 shields described below, only those belonging to the pairs Cúscraid-Lóegaire and Eógan-Celtchair are actually described with the same words.

Foreign influences

While the Homeric poems may appear to be archetypically Greek, during both their historical present in the Mycenaean era and all the subsequent periods of their possible composition the Greeks were in contact with their Near Eastern neighbours. These Near Eastern societies had their own myths, legends and literatures that the Greeks certainly encountered and absorbed and these no doubt influenced Greek mythology and provided both contexts and incidents that fed the imaginations of the

Greek poets whose poems were ultimately transformed by Homer. As Sarah Morris put it, 'it may be a greater challenge to isolate and appreciate what is Greek in Homeric poetry than to enumerate its foreign sources'.[28]

Central to understanding the foreign influences on native Irish tradition is naturally the fact that the tradition was recorded within a Christian environment by monks who were thoroughly conversant with both the Old Latin Bible and St Jerome's Latin translation. The opening line of the *Lebor Gabála* begins not in Irish but Latin, *In principio fecit Deus celum 7 terram*, and only then provides an Irish translation ('In the beginning God created heaven and earth'). When searching for possible foreign influences, our first port of call will generally be the Bible.

The subject of classical literary influences on the *Táin* has been argued for nearly a century. When the Latin Fury, Allecto, makes a guest appearance in the *Táin*, where she is identified as the Irish war-goddess, the Mórrígan, one could hardly claim that the writer was totally unaware of Latin literature. Indeed, it has often been argued that the *Táin* represents an Irish attempt to manufacture an epic in imitation of Vergil's *Aeneid*, with Cú Chulainn serving as the Irish equivalent of either Aeneas or, for those who look even further backwards to the *Iliad*, Troilus or Achilles. The debate concerning the degree to which the *Táin* may have been influenced by Greek or Latin epic will no doubt continue, but there are some issues on which there is some consensus.

Although there are some striking parallels between the Homeric poems and the *Táin*,[29] there does not seem to be much of a case for Irish monks encountering Homer in the original Greek, although they did know some of the Greek language.[30] But it is doubtful that the monk who copied out the Greek alphabet in one manuscript and then complained 'there's an end to that…and my seven curses go with it!'[31] was a great fan of the Greek language much less the more archaic language of Homer. It is more likely that their knowledge of the Greek epic was gained through Latin sources, such as the *Ilias Latina*, a super-condensed text produced in *c.* AD 60 that provided the standard schoolbook version of the *Iliad* in the Middle Ages.[32] Moreover, Homer had miraculously been discredited in the Middle Ages. As he had lived long after the Trojan War, it was argued that he was not a reliable witness to its events. Instead, Europeans turned to some early examples of 'found footage', tedious works that purported to come from eyewitness accounts of the Trojan War. The *De excidio Troiae historia* ('The history of the destruction of Troy') was a Latin translation of a supposedly first-hand account of the Trojan War by Dares Phrygius, who Homer claimed was a Trojan priest (it was actually a Latin fake composed in about the 5th century

AD). The Irish had early access to it and it was even translated into Irish as the *Togail Troi* by the 10th century, when it had a major impact on Irish literature. In addition, there was the diary of Dictys Cretensis,[33] a companion of the Cretan leader Idomeneus, who also provided an eyewitness account of the Trojan War, written in Phoenician no less, and then buried for over a thousand years in a lead box (we are now talking of a fraud of Hollywood proportions!) before being translated into Greek and then Latin and served to a gullible public.

If direct Greek influence on the *Táin* is unlikely, the influence of Latin learning evidenced in the works of Vergil, Latin translations of earlier Greek material, and the various commentaries, now seems to be far more pervasive than previously imagined. This has been painstaking argued by Brent Miles in a recent book[34] that makes it clear that those quilling the *Táin* were fully conversant and frequently guided, at least in their language and imagination, by the works on the Latin shelves of their monastic libraries. In Table 3.2 are listed some of the most prominent Latin texts from which an Irish monk, designing the descriptions or actions of his Irish heroes and heroines, might have been influenced. Most of these were translated into Irish and they are generally the earliest translations of Latin literature into a European

Table 3.2: Some major Latin works known to the medieval Irish.

Author	Work	Date	Irish translation	Date
Publius **Vergil**ius Maro	*Aeneid*	BC 1st century	*Imtheachta Aeniasa*	*c.* 12th century
Publius **Ovid**ius Naso	*Metamorphoses*	AD 1st century	No translation	
Dares Phrygius (attributed)	*De excido Troiae historia*	AD 5th century	*Togail Troí*	*c.* 10th century
Dictys Cretensis (attributed)	*Ephemeridos belli Trojani*	AD 4th century?	No translation	
Publius Papinius **Statius**	*Thebaid*	AD 1st century	*Togail na Tebe*	*c.* 12th century
Publius Papinius **Statius**	*Achilleid*	AD 1st century	*Achilleid*	*c.* 12th to 13th centuries
Marcus Annaeus **Lucanus**	*Pharsalia*	AD 1st century	*In Cath Catharda*	*c.* 12th century
Orosius and others	*Alexander chronicle*	AD 5th century	*Scéla Alexandair*	*c.* 10th century

vernacular (no French, Spanish or Italian translations of these classics are as early as the Irish).[35] The Irish translations are generally only partial and very free, frequently 'improving' descriptions by importing elements from the native literature. For example, while Polydorus gets a standard Homeric burial in the *Aeneid*,[36] the Irish translator gives him a good Irish burial instead.[37] In addition to these were several other tales from classical literature such as an account of the wanderings of Ulysses,[38] which the Irish apparently cobbled together from a variety of sources to create their own distinctive classical 'romance'.[39] Along with the Bible, these classical texts will need to be kept in mind as we examine the earliest tradition of the Irish.

Language

The language of the Homeric poems is obviously Greek and although predominantly composed in the Ionic dialect there is also evidence for the use of both the Arcadian and Aeolic dialects as well.[40] It is argued that the Homeric works do not appear in the language of a single time but are a composite of the various poetic dialects that contributed to the two great poems over a period of centuries.[41] The one thing that the language is not is the actual language of the Mycenaeans as we have it in the Linear B inscriptions, nor is it written in a language that was directly descended from Linear B.[42] In other words, one cannot use a purely linguistic argument to prove that the poems were originally composed in the palaces at Mycenae, Tiryns or Pylos by Mycenaean poets.

Linguistically, the language of the *Táin* is generally Middle Irish (*c.* AD 900–1200) although there are passages that are very easily convertible into Old Irish (*c.* AD 700–900), the language employed in the composition of some of the poetic evidence for a *Táin* story. For still earlier evidence of writing we have the ogam inscriptions (*c.* AD 400–700) that provide us with our knowledge of the most primitive state of the Irish language, a state that is similar to that of the still earlier inscriptions left by the Gauls. From this we have a very rough idea of what the Irish language should have looked like during the 'historical present' of the Ulster tales set to the first centuries BC/AD. As with the case for Homer, the differences between the language at the time the *Táin* is set and the language in which we find it written down are so great that we cannot regard the language of the *Táin* as an Iron Age document (see below).

Literary archaeology

The material culture of the Homeric epics, such as the weapons, has been studied for at least 150 years.[43] While much of 19th-century Homeric scholarship was content to treat Greek epic purely in literary terms, the excavations of Mycenae and Troy by Heinrich Schliemann in the 1870s had an enormous impact on the perception of the ancient poems. As the noted classicist Sir Walter Leaf put it:

> It must not be forgotten that the world of Homer is a real world, not a world of fancy. This is evident in every line…It is not as if we were transported into a mere realm of fairyland, where the poet could imagine and impose upon us such scenery as he thought fit. Whenever we can test the actualities of the poem we find that they are all events possible, and in many points they coincide in a surprising way with the results which recent discoveries have shown us[44]

This attitude, that Homer provides a guide to a real world, has been a major element of Homeric research for well over a century. The archaeological issues are far from resolved as scholars have long argued over the precise chronology of this 'real world'. Generally, the areas of dispute concern to what extent elements of the poems may be assigned to the deep antiquity of the Late (Mycenaean) Bronze Age (c. 1600–1100 BC) rather than the succeeding Dark Ages (c. 1100–800 BC) or the approximate period of Homer (late 8th century).[45] A good indication of the seriousness of such pursuits are the 25 volumes of *Archaeologia Homerica*, in which both the material culture and society of the Homeric poems are examined in detail from both textual and archaeological perspectives.

If one reviews the disputed territory of the antiquity of the world depicted in the *Iliad* and *Odyssey*, then modern approaches tend to set it much closer to the 8th century, the time of Homer himself, than the Late Bronze Age world that he purports to describe.[46] This is argued in general terms (Homer's world is incompatible with the palace system of the ancient Mycenaeans[47] and its economic complexity,[48] and fails in its portrayal of Mycenaean warfare[49] and burials).

On the other hand, elements of material culture, especially those 'fossilized' in fixed phrases or epithets, and sometimes attached to specific characters in the tales, have been traced back to the Mycenaean period or at least several centuries before Homer. Classic examples of putative relics of the Mycenaean age are the descriptions of boar-tusk helmets and the tower shield of Ajax.[50] The fact that the swords are routinely described as bronze and some are fitted with silver pegs is also adduced to support a Late Bronze Age date,[51] while a passage treating a mere lump of iron as a highly precious metal accords far better with a date of around the 16th to 12th centuries BC, before the widespread use of iron (c. 1000 BC).[52]

We have seen in Chapter One that the earliest extensive examination of the antiquities of early Irish literature occurred in 1873 with Eugene O'Curry's *Manners and Customs of the Early Irish*. O'Curry treated the overwhelming body of early Irish literature as essentially true. In reviewing the weapons described in the tales he attempted to distinguish between the spears of the Fir Bolg and those of the Tuatha Dé Danann by recourse to the specimens of weapons from the collections of the Royal Irish Academy.[53] His discussions were then reviewed and improved as well as illustrated by Sullivan.[54] Naturally, with Irish archaeology in its comparative infancy, the material presented involved artifacts dating anywhere from the Neolithic to the Middle Ages as well as misidentifications of halberds for spearheads or swords. Nevertheless, Sullivan's approach was analytical whereas the next major compendia of ancient Irish culture (viewed from its literature) by P. W. Joyce[55] tends to present the material culture more as background illustrations to what is otherwise a study of the descriptions from the early Irish texts.

Joyce was apparently unaware of J. v. Pflug-Harttung's[56] earlier attempt to date the *Táin* by comparing the descriptive evidence against that of archaeology. Although his conclusions are seriously flawed due to the then very incomplete understanding of the chronology of Irish prehistory, his was the first fully analytical approach. Believing that the use of iron in Ireland did not begin until c. AD 500 and that iron was not plentiful until AD 1000, he cited references to the metal in the *Táin* as evidence that its material culture was only as old as the 10th century, while the depiction of inhumation burials in the *Táin* was discordant with the prehistoric practice of cremation.

If Pflug-Harttung was a sceptic, William Ridgeway was a believer who cited an array of reasons for accepting the *Táin* as a reflection of Irish Iron Age society.[57] He specifically identified it with the same La Tène art style that dominated the Celtic-speaking regions of Western Europe during the Iron Age. The use of chariot warfare in the *Táin*, which had been associated with the Celts but had been abandoned both on the continent and in Britain, suggested that Irish literature preserved this Iron Age cultural legacy. So also did a description of a leaf-shaped brooch matched against an Irish La Tène-style brooch, and the swords depicted in the tales were compared with continental La Tène swords.

Throughout much of the 20th century the association between the descriptions in the Ulster tales and the Irish Iron Age were generally supported in the few studies undertaken. Sometimes even earlier dates were suggested. For example, Margaret Dobbs[58] argued that Medb's campaign route in the *Táin* that led her forces in a south-easterly direction was motivated by a desire to avoid the major series of linear earthworks (which were not mentioned in the *Táin*) that she believed had been constructed prior to the Iron Age. And waterbird ornament on metal bowls described in both the Ulster cycle and in some of the Mythological cycle tales could best be paralleled with the earlier Hallstatt culture of continental Europe. Helmut Bauersfeld examined all the evidence for weaponry in the *Lebor na hUidre* and tried to match it against the archaeological record, although his material ranged from the Middle Bronze Age to the Iron Age.[59] His study was outstanding for its time (1933) and had its database been expanded beyond a single (albeit critical) manuscript and, perhaps, been written in English, it might have had far greater impact than it has had.

In an attempt to resolve the problem of the arrival of Celtic-speakers in Ireland, T. G. E. Powell employed the evidence of the Ulster cycle to portray what he labelled the Overlord culture, centred on the Ulster and Connacht capitals, and argued that 'it would not be unreasonable to place the state of affairs reflected in the *Táin* stories within the century 50 BC–AD 50, or somewhat later'.[60]

The most influential supporter of a roughly Iron Age date was the distinguished Celticist Kenneth Jackson, who suggested that the tales were probably created around AD 400.[61] Although he cited some archaeological evidence, such as the use of chariots, his arguments were primarily based on the similarity of social conventions found in the Ulster cycle and those attributed to the continental Celts by classical writers, including headhunting, contesting the champion's portion at feasts and clientship. Also, historical evidence was adduced: the fall of the Ulster capital Emain Macha in the 4th or 5th centuries and the reapplication of 'Ulster' to only the eastern counties in the north suggested that the tales must predate these events. Jackson's thesis ultimately supported the notion that the Ulster cycle provided what he called a 'window on the Iron Age'.

The Iron Age foundations of the Ulster tales were also accepted by John Hamilton who compared passages concerning architecture in various tales from the Ulster cycle with his recent excavations of the Iron Age fort at Clickhimin in the Shetlands.[62] Various details such as storeyed buildings constructed around the inner perimeter of the fort, along with depictions of shields and chariotry, led Hamilton to conclude that:

> Though the characters in the stories may be fictional, the background and setting for their legendary exploits appear to be based on fact.

When the stories were first composed they must have incorporated
a great deal of authentic detail essential for their acceptance and
appreciation by the audiences to whom they were addressed.[63]

A more sceptical approach to the antiquity of the descriptions in the Ulster tales
began to appear in 1981 when the author initiated a series of articles comparing
various aspects of material culture such as the swords,[64] the forts,[65] and the general
material culture of the *Táin*.[66] In these and several other articles I argued that in those
cases where the description was sufficiently detailed to test against the archaeological
record, it suggested that they were not drawn from the Iron Age but rather the early
medieval period. Similar conclusions were drawn by Niamh Whitfield, who examined some of the major items of ornament described in early Irish literature.[67]

While not totally disregarding the archaeological evidence, another critical
approach to the antiquity of the Ulster cycle has emphasized that our only evidence
for the tales suggests that they were literary compositions created in a monastic environment by men who were well versed in Latin literature.[68] If 'Irish epic literature is
unlikely to have been orally composed and transmitted',[69] then claims that it should
reflect an Iron Age past become hardly credible. Much of the pagan mythology found
in the *Lebor Gabála*, for example, had passed through a biblical filter that did everything it could to link the ancient Irish with the Hebrews short of turning them into a
lost tribe.[70] And the elevation of Emain Macha in the Ulster tales could be dismissed
as fabrication designed to enhance the political capital of the neighbouring monastic
centre of Armagh.[71]

Mythology

The Homeric poems contain a good deal of mythological figures, not only bickering
on Mount Olympus and taking sides during the Trojan War but also actually inter-
acting directly with the mortals in the story. The goddess Athena, for example, once
drives the hero Diomedes' chariot, and Diomedes injures the goddess Aphrodite. The
ancients were not always impressed by this mixture of gods and mortals and in the
6th century Xenophanes of Colophon described Homer's views of the gods as inac-
curate and implausible.[72] In his dismissal of Homer as a reliable witness to the war,
Dares Phrygius claimed that the Athenians thought Homer was mad to have gods
and mortals together on the battlefield.[73]

The god Lug appears in the *Táin* and elsewhere in the Ulster cycle (after all he
was Cú Chulainn's 'real' father). In a broad critique of Kenneth Jackson's attempt to

view the Ulster cycle as a legitimate document from which one might infer something about an Iron Age past, Nicholas Aitchison argued that a major distinction between the Mythological cycle and a document like the *Táin* was unwarranted and that the *Táin* was replete with so much mythology that we should 'question the very idea that the contents of any of this literature has a "basis in reality".[74]

Aitchison's objections return us to the critical question of the context of our written sources and whether they can bear the weight of archaeological scrutiny. While I think few would argue against Aitchison's position that there is a mythological back-story to many of the Ulster tales, that alone should not be grounds to dismiss the imagined world depicted in the tales as too fantastic to bear serious examination as a cultural historical document. We have already seen that the mythological aspects of the *Iliad* have hardly deterred archaeologists from examining it in terms of Greek archaeology. And, adopting the perspective of a Martian archaeologist (who would dismiss all of Earth's religious scriptures as myth), we have long had a rewarding scholarly industry of biblical archaeology or archaeological assessments of the material culture depicted in the Rig Veda of the Hindus[75] and the Avesta of the Zoroastrians.

Excavation techniques

How does one excavate a line or a word from a literary document? Just as in field archaeology, our techniques must be adjusted to our research goals. In examining the earliest Irish tradition we have several main targets. Paramount is that we want to know the age of the material culture and behaviour depicted in the tales. Have any descriptions of life attributed to the Neolithic, Bronze or Iron ages managed to survive all the eroding factors of time, cultural influence and language change, to emerge in the medieval literature of Ireland? Can we identify the world or at least elements of the Dreamtime with a real world of archaeology or is it purely an imagined world concocted in the mind of a medieval monk from a variety of sources ranging from his own world, Latin literary works, and the spark of his own inspiration? So our null hypothesis will be: the earliest Irish tradition provides an archaeologically accurate picture of the world it purports to describe. This is what we hope to test and this goal must be emphasized because, occasionally, some have confused the aims of such an approach. For example, Nicholas Aitchison dismissed the results of reearch that concentrates

> on minor aspects of content (for example, the description of
> swords). This is just the type of incidental detail which could

easily have been altered or 'updated' during the process of manuscript copying.[76]

There would be justice in this criticism if the purpose of the analysis were to determine the date of the entire text or original composition (whatever that means?). But, as we have seen with regards to Homer, it is only the incidental details, the frozen descriptions, that provide the evidence for a deeper Mycenaean past. Obviously there may be frequent revisions of descriptions in tales recorded over centuries. What we are interested in is discovering if there are aspects of culture that have not been 'updated'. We seek the Irish equivalents of Ajax's tower shield or the boar-tusk helmet of the ancient Greeks. And although we can broadly arrange our tales in chronological periods of early and later, there is no reason to concentrate solely on the earliest tales since a 'relict' of the Iron Age past might survive only in a later tale.

Here are some of our 'excavation' techniques.

Etymology

In assessing the antiquity of a word or line from an archaeological perspective we have three factors to take into consideration. The first is the word itself and its own antiquity within the Irish language. Take, for example, the Old Irish *coire* 'cauldron'. This is a word of great antiquity in Irish and goes back beyond even Celtic to Proto-Indo-European, where we find a related word in Sanskrit *carú-* 'cauldron' and Old English *hver* 'pot, bowl, kettle, cauldron'. This etymology at least indicates that the word employed should have been thoroughly native to the earliest Irish. On the other hand, the early Irish words *cailech* and *cailice* 'chalice, cup, goblet' both derive from Latin *calyx* and here we may suspect no great antiquity for the object beyond the medieval period in which Latin loanwords were flooding into Irish.

Admittedly, we can also find loanwords that are more problematic. In the tales the word for 'tent' is *pupall*, which is not a native word in Irish but a Latin loanword from *papilio* 'tent' (see Chapter Six). The fact that the Irish had recourse to a loanword *may* be indicative that they only acquired the object when they acquired its name but this need not be so. After all, the tent is probably one of the oldest forms of habitation known to humans and it is hard to imagine that the Irish were ignorant of employing some animal skins as a shelter until they came into contact with the Romans in Britain. There are many other loanwords that also do not require a late importation of a concept. For example, the Old Irish word for 'gold', *ór*, is a loan from Latin *aurum*, yet we know of gold-working in Ireland from the Early Bronze Age (*c.* 2300 BC onwards). So the mere fact that an item or concept was served up with a loanword does not guarantee that the item was foreign or new to the Irish; they may have simply replaced their native term with a new one that they felt was more prestigious.[77]

On the other hand, when we find an entire semantic field reliant on loanwords, then we may begin to suspect that we are dealing with a cultural and not just a linguistic loan. The Old Irish word for 'arrow' was *saiget*, a loan from Latin *sagitta* 'arrow', the word for 'bow' was *boga*, a loanword from Old Norse, and the word for 'bowstring', *sreng*, was also borrowed from Old Norse *strengr* 'bowstring'. If there does not seem to be anything Irish about the vocabulary relating to archery, which occurs very occasionally in the Ulster tales, we should not be too surprised. While the Irish did employ the bow for millennia, the evidence of (flint) arrows disappears by about 1500 BC and archery is not really attested in Ireland again until the Viking raids from the 8th century onwards. Obviously, we still must be careful how we interpret such linguistic evidence. The observant reader, for example, might well ask why the word for arrow should come from Latin (and therefore date to around the 5th–6th centuries AD) while the words for the rest of the bow only appeared several centuries later, summoning up incongruous images of clueless Irishmen running around in the intervening centuries *throwing* arrows at one another until the kind-hearted Norse taught them how to shoot the arrows from a bow. Nevertheless, here we do seem to have evidence that any reference to archery in the earliest Irish tradition is not an accurate image of the past but either a classical motif or reference to a medieval type of warfare.

Description

The second aspect of assessing the antiquity of the cultural motifs in the tales is the description of the object. Let us take, for example, the sword. Archaeologically, true swords began to appear in Ireland *c.* 1200 BC and several centuries earlier we find rapiers with very long and narrow pointed blades. Naturally, swords were also employed throughout the Iron Age and the later period when the tales were written and manuscripts compiled until the present. A sword (*claideb*) described as 'beautiful' (*cain*)[78] does not really get us very far. On the other hand, when we find Cormac's men armed with 'swords inlaid with gold wire',[79] we have enough to go on to exclude all of the various classes of Irish prehistoric swords (see Chapter Seven), as such ornament does not appear in Ireland until the time of the Vikings.

Context

Another useful clue regarding a particular object is the context of its appearance or use. To return to the sword, we will also be interested in its precise use. Employed routinely for hacking off heads at a single blow or when Cú Chulainn cuts down a forked branch with one strike of his sword, all suggestions are that the business edge here was the blade and not the point.[80] Such contextual descriptions provide us evidence that we are dealing primarily with a slashing sword and not a rapier or thrusting sword.

From these three perspectives – etymology, description and context – we can attempt to build up a mental model of what the object looked like or how it might have been manipulated. Only then can we apply our model to the archaeological record and attempt to determine where it fits best.

Archaeological problems

While a comparison of our reconstructed literary image with the archaeological record may provide us evidence for accepting or rejecting our null hypothesis, quite often it leads to an ambiguous result. There are several reasons for this.

Insufficient literary description will be quite frequent because there is often so little linguistic or literary evidence that we cannot form an image to compare against the archaeological record. If, for example, we simply have a word that translates as 'cup' or 'spear' and we have no idea of its size, use, appearance or even material of manufacture, it could be assigned to any period of Irish prehistory or later. In many cases we may also have some basic level of description but still insufficient to determine when it might fit into the material culture of Ireland. 'Woollen cloak', for example, could be applied to objects known from the Late Bronze Age to the Middle Ages. This denies us the chance to test our null hypothesis.

We also must be aware that we need both a start and an end date to fix an object or behaviour in time. For example, the discovery of beheaded victims in burials dating from the Iron Age may at first seem to be a striking confirmation of one of the major motifs of the Ulster cycle and classical descriptions of Iron Age Celts. But head-taking did not cease with the end of the Iron Age and the Irish continued this ancient pastime right through the medieval period.[81] The issue then is not just when did the Irish begin to decapitate their victims but when did they stop?

In addition, often enough we find objects described that lack any clear archaeological correlate. In some instances the problem is merely local: the object, such as a silver sword scabbard, might be unattested in the Irish archaeological record but we might find a possible match elsewhere in Europe. This is a problematic area since we do not want to spend too much time trying to anchor the Irish imagination in foreign parts, but we must also be aware that the medieval Irish had established monasteries and connections with royal families throughout Western Europe and were incredibly well networked. We also find objects that seem to lack any plausible referent in Western European archaeology, prehistoric or medieval, where we may well suspect that the inspiration derives not from ancient Ireland but the Bible or classical literature. References to a four-horse chariot would be such an example. And, finally, we will find objects mentioned that defy plausible description, such as Cú Chulainn's ultimate weapon, the *gae bolga* (see Chapter Seven).

A thought experiment

Before initiating our excavation of Irish medieval documents it may be useful to engage in a thought experiment of what might have happened over the course of centuries between the prehistoric accounts that our null hypothesis suggests we can recover and the documents that a literary archaeologist must deal with. In order to be as fair as possible I will try to design a probable past as favourable as I can that would benefit the null hypothesis. For this exercise I have selected the account that has been most frequently assigned to the Iron Age.

The first thousand years of the Táin

The annals suggest that the centrepiece of the Ulster cycle, the *Táin Bó Cuailnge*, occurred *c.* 19 BC,[82] a date that falls well within the Irish Iron Age (*c.* 750/600 BC – AD 400). Let us imagine for a moment that shortly after the great cattle-raid an Irish Iron Age *fili*, Katu-butos, serving as a war-correspondent embedded in the army of Queen Medb, began to compose various oral accounts of events during the cattle-raid to be recited at the *óenaigi* ('public fairs') throughout Ireland. He would have composed and delivered his recitation in the earliest state of the Irish language. This form of Irish would have been more comparable to the language of the ancient Gauls and looked a lot more like Latin both in respect to its sounds and inflected word endings than any of the later stages of Irish. To enhance memorability, let's adopt Cecile O'Rahilly's suggestion that the major descriptive passages in his *Táin* accounts were composed in verse. This could theoretically improve the chances that the poetic versions might be recited more or less verbatim over generations. This is certainly the case with liturgical texts such as the Vedas in ancient India, which were recited orally for centuries before they were ever committed to writing.

And we might note that at the end of the second version of the *Táin* there is 'a blessing on everyone who shall faithfully memorise the *Táin* as it is written here and shall not add any other form to it'.[83] Of course, it is a bit optimistic comparing the *Táin* to a sacred text such as the Rig Veda, where the precise recitation of the hymns was of critical religious importance but, as I said, let's give the null hypothesis as much help as possible. Still, we must acknowledge that as Jan Vansina in his classic study of oral tradition remarked, the reliability of the oral text is far more dependent on the method of transmission than time.[84] The audiences at Katu-butos' public performances no doubt would have included other poets. For medieval Ireland James Carney performed his own thought experiment and estimated about 500 poets;[85] for the Iron Age, where the evidence of settlement and population is extremely sparse, we might make a guestimate of 50–100 jobbing poets who would tell their own versions of the *Táin* stories. Without some cultural pressure to protect the oral integrity of the text (as practiced by the ancient Indians) within a century we might then already expect a number of different *Táin* stories in circulation.

How early could accounts of the *Táin* be committed to writing? The earliest evidence for writing in Ireland is to be found in the ogam inscriptions that are found along the edges of stone pillars presumably erected as memorials and containing little more than personal names and occasionally kinship affiliation (FIG. 3.1). The earliest of these date from about the early 5th century AD, so we must envisaged for our *Táin* tales at least a period of four centuries of purely oral transmission. Incidentally, some of the ogam inscriptions reveal personal names similar to some of those we also encounter in the *Táin*, the most intriguing being an inscription from Rathcroghan (Cruachain), the Connacht capital, which reads *Vraicci maqi Medvvi* 'of Fráech, son of Medb'.[86] Alas, this is not likely to be the Fráech of the *Táin Bó Fraích* (see Chapter Two), whose adventures began at Cruachain, since he was not the son of Medb and, moreover, the form on the ogam clearly indicates that this Medb was a male and not the famous Queen Medb. Another name from the Ulster cycle, Feidlimid, Conchobar's storyteller and the father of Deirdre, appears in ogam in the genitive case ('of Feidlimid') as Veddellemetto; similarly 'of Eógan' (the Ulster Eógan was the killer of Deirdre's lover) is Ivageni and the

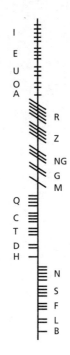

3.1. The ogam alphabet.

Ulster champion Conall is Cunovali. And these are the forms of the names in about the 5th century that would already represent some change from earlier Iron Age Irish. For example, 'of Fergus' is found in ogam as Vergoso but his Proto-Irish name would have been something like *Wiragusōs. And by the early medieval period our *fili* would now no longer be Katu-butos but, as indicated in the ogam inscriptions, something like Cattubuttas.[87]

Could Cattubuttas have written out the earlier oral tales in ogam? There is certainly evidence from early Irish literature that ogam could be applied to wood and there is even mention of wooden tablets, and anyone familiar with early Chinese books consisting of thin strips of bamboo or wood assembled together to form pages might regard ogam as a clumsy but still just possible means of recording early events. In early Irish literature the use of ogam on perishable objects such as wood, pegs or rods is generally for divination or employed by Cú Chulainn and his opponents to indicate a

3.2. Ogam inscribed stone from Ardmore, Co. Waterford, with two inscriptions that read: LUGUDECCASMAQI [MU] COINETASEGAMONAS DOLATI 'Of Dolativix the smith Lugud's son, tribesman of Nia Segamain' and BIGAISGOB 'assistant bishop'.

challenge; there is reference in one of the accounts of Bran's adventures written in quatrains on wood and a poet, worried about forgetting an incantation, committing it to four very long rods of yew.[88] But ogam is generally regarded so cumbersome that it is unlikely that it could have served for any extended piece of writing (FIG. 3.2). R. A. S. Macalister calculated that a 23-word Old Irish verse of 78 letters (which took up a little more than 5.5 inches in his text) would require 250 ogam strokes amounting to about 31 or 32 inches long.[89]

Unsurprisingly, we have no evidence of an ogam inscription written on any perishable material,[90] so its use in writing extended narratives is undemonstrated and unlikely.

By the 6th century the Roman script and the Latin language were flourishing in Ireland, providing a far more serviceable way of recording what would now be 500-year-old oral accounts of the *Táin*. The very earliest Latin writing, however, was largely devoted to ecclesiastical purposes and there is no evidence for a Latin version of the *Táin*. But from *c.* AD 600 we have our earliest evidence of poetry in Old Irish[91] and from the same century we recover three Old Irish poems that provide hints of some of the events and characters depicted in the *Táin*.[92] It is also in the 7th century that Irish tradition records the attempt of Senchán Torpéist (*c.* 580–650) to assemble the various elements of the *Táin* to produce a complete version.[93]

For reasons that we will soon discover, by about AD 700 Cattubuttas will have had to pass his poetic staff onto a *fili* called Cathbad, who will be our resident poet from 700 to 1000. As hinted at by our comparison of personal names, the early medieval Cattubuttas may have been able to recite his Iron Age predecessor's works in a language not too different from his own but what would Cathbad have made of them some 700 years after their creation? Here we find that despite its initial composition in verse, Cathbad would have run into very serious problems transmitting the original Iron Age text. By the 7th century the Irish language had endured an incredibly brusque change in pronunciation. The earliest Old Irish poetry was apparently based on alliteration and stress but by the 7th century this had been replaced by counting syllables. This was very bad news for one trying to preserve the integrity of a centuries-old prehistoric poem because by the time that we recover texts written in Old Irish, the language has suffered what we might crudely refer to as the 'great syllable slaughter.'[94] Where the earlier language had once looked more akin to Latin or Greek it had now shed many of its endings and internal syllables so that it looked much more like Irish. For example, the names of our former poets, Iron Age Katu-butos and early medieval Cattubuttas, would now be rendered Cathbad (the second and fourth syllables had been lost) and it would be unlikely that he could make a living spouting the original Iron Age version that would have been gibberish to most if not all of his audiences. Only the ogam stones reveal the primitive pronunciation; no Old Irish document retains it. While some have thought that this change reflected a very rapid 'mangling' of the Irish language in about the 7th century, John Koch[95] has suggested that, like classical Latin and vulgar Latin (or Proto-Romance), the two may have existed side by side for some centuries, with ogam essentially retained as an archaic language associated with the earlier religion. Once Christianity and Latin had filled this functional slot, Old Irish, the 'language of the people', was then free to become the standard written language.

An unbroken word-for-word transmission simply could not make it past the early medieval barrier and so we might expect that the original tales would have to be linguistically updated as the Irish language changed. Moreover, both Primitive Irish and Old Irish had been open to a current of loanwords, both from Latin and the British (Welsh) language of the earliest missionaries. These could be very broadly dated to the 4th and 6th centuries.[96] The world in which the *Táin* stories were performed or recorded was also changing or, at least, expanding. In terms of their being written down, the tales would have come in from the outside to the monasteries which, as we have seen, were intellectual powerhouses of early medieval Europe, enjoying not only access to the writings of the church but also a fair amount of access to classical literature, at least as it might be served up through Latin. The men who put quill to vellum to record the events of the *Táin* were also excellent Latin scholars and were familiar with the works of Vergil and the so-called authors of epic potboilers such as Dares Phrygius. They also had access to and frequently employed the *Etymologiae* of Isidore of Seville, the early Middle Ages equivalent of Wikipedia.

The monks never operated in a world of sublime academic isolation and by the 9th century they were in fact on the receiving end of Viking raids and settlements that gave them first-hand knowledge of Norse warfare. Alternatively, fleeing Ireland, they found themselves working in continental monasteries where they were exposed to a wider European world. In any event, the world of the 'keepers of the *Táin*' had changed again and the Irish language was open to further foreign imports, both culturally and linguistically, from the Anglo-Saxons and Franks. Around the 9th century or later several different versions of the *Táin* had been crudely joined in a cut-and-paste job and that is what we find in our earliest version copied into the *Lebor na hUidre c.* AD 1100. This version contains both doublets where we relive the same incident although with the victim's name changed or logical inconsistencies. For example, unless Cú Chulainn was into necrophilia, there was no reason for him to go off into the sunset with Findabair, the daughter of Medb, 809 lines after she had committed suicide. A far more literary and logical composition is to be found in the *Book of Leinster*, where many of the problems of the earlier recension were ironed out to make a more polished version of the *Táin*.

This brief summary of the possible factors that might erode or disturb the Iron Age package originally witnessed by Katu-butos is intended to provide an idea of what a literary archaeologist may be up against dealing with a 1,000-year-old story. And it hardly need be emphasized that we have confined our thought experiment to the most recent layer of the Dreamtime and not tried to explore the difficulties of tracing, say, Fintan and the other earlier colonists of Ireland back nearly 3,000 years earlier.

But it is now time to set aside the speculations of archaeological theory and grab our spades and trowels and begin excavating the Irish Dreamtime.

CHAPTER FOUR

The Archaeology of the Irish National Origin Legend

...the art of *consciously inventing* fiction is a late phenomenon in literature: and, on the whole, we may take it for granted that when an ancient author sets down an account of events, he is writing what he honestly believes to have actually happened.[1]

R. A. S. Macalister, 1928

The earliest events in Irish history comprise what John Carey has called the Irish National Origin Legend (INOL),[2] recorded primarily in the *Lebor Gabála Érenn* (LG) and summarized and synchronized with the Christian calendar in the *Annals of the Four Masters* (AFM). Although the overwhelming majority of the narrative of these sources consists of the succession of kings, the list of their battles, and natural occurrences, there is also a series of precisely dated innovations in technology, economy and culture. While these 'events' (other than the initial colonization of Ireland by Cesair) were accepted by many as truly historical up until the late 19th century, they are now presumed to be the least credible elements of Ireland's deep past. Nevertheless, it must also be admitted that there are also near 'hits' between the Irish texts and the archaeological record that do arouse our curiosity and at least some archaeologists have sought archaeological corroboration of these otherwise mythical events.[3]

What follows is an attempt to compare the written record of the *Lebor Gabála* and its attendant summaries in the *Annals of the Four Masters* with the archaeological record. I am well aware that some might wish to invoke Pinkerton's principle: to refute absolute nonsense is just as great as propounding it in the first place. But this 'nonsense' was taken to be historically accurate for nearly a thousand years and was on the curriculum of some schools in Ireland as late as the 1960s.[4] For this reason I think it does have some right to merit our consideration, even if we remain highly critical of its veracity. In his study of the history of hurling, Art Ó Maolfabhail remarked regarding the *Lebor Gabála* that it 'is considered by most scholars to-day to be pure fiction. Perhaps it is just that, but perhaps also the scholars of the twelfth century were in possession of historical traditions with at least some basis in fact'.[5] Let's see how big a 'perhaps' we are dealing with. This chapter is also intended to clear the way to analyze in greater detail the testimony of the much larger early Irish narrative tradition that encompasses some of the Mythological cycle and all of the Ulster cycle. We will deal with the literary references in the framework of an archaeological periodization of Ireland's prehistory.

Mesolithic (c. 8000–4000 BC)

Irish traditional chronology, tied as it was to a biblical chronology that could not entertain any settlement in Europe until after the Deluge, set the initial settlement of Ireland to 2958 BC, about 5,000 years after our earliest evidence for human occupation. Also, the earliest settlers in Ireland according to the INOL clearly derived from an agricultural population that did not exist there for the first four millennia of its settled existence.

Neolithic (c. 4000–2500 BC)

The earliest settlement of Ireland was associated with Cesair, who should have arrived during the Late Neolithic, c. 3000 BC,[6] at a time when the great passage tombs were being constructed. As the synchronization with the Deluge falls over a thousand years after the first farmers arrived in Ireland, many of the earlier actual events in Irish prehistory cannot help but be chronologically too recent in the written texts. For example, Cesair reputedly introduced sheep to Ireland[7] about 800 years after our earliest archaeological attestation of sheep. She and her father were buried under cairns, which would certainly have been possible for c. 3000 BC, but as cairns were actually introduced c. 3800 BC and continued to be used long after Cesair's 'landing', they do not provide a useful chronological anchor.

The second colonization under Partholón is set to 2680 BC.[8] Before he died in 2650 he had undertaken land clearances, which is the first record of forest clearings in the LG. While there is some slight evidence for Late Mesolithic clearances in Ireland, the real 'land-taking' began at the beginning of the Neolithic in c. 3800 BC, some 1,100 years earlier than the Irish traditional dates. Partholón's son, Slainge, died in 2667 and was buried in the cairn of Sliab Slangha,[9] an old name for Slieve Donard

4.1. Cairn on top of Slieve Donard, Mourne mountains, Co. Down. The cairn is traditionally associated with Slainge, son of Partholón.

in the Mourne mountains of Co. Down. There are two cairns on Slieve Donard although one, the larger and the probable cairn in question (FIG. 4.1), has been seriously damaged. There is enough evidence, however, to suggest that it may have been a passage tomb,[10] probably constructed sometime around *c*. 3000 BC.

Before any credence be given to the probable date of the tomb and the annalistic date it should be emphasized that most heroes and heroines of the past find themselves retro-filling megalithic tombs and barrows, their names attached to a monument of the distant past irrespective of its date (which, of course, was unknown to the compilers of the annals). In 1851 the great editor and translator of the AFM, John O'Donovan, noted the fact that the burial place of Bith, who accompanied Cesair, could both be located and was still in place. He optimistically remarked that 'If this carn be ever explored, it may furnish evidence of the true period of the arrival of Bith'.[11] This is a fascinating comment since it implies a certain amount of acceptance of the Cesair story but also a certain amount of scepticism as to the actual date of Bith. Anyway, while Partholón's son may have found himself buried in a roughly contemporary grave, tombs of the same period have also been filled with characters thousands of years more recent as well. Medb's cairn (PL. VI), for instance, a probable passage tomb on Knocknarea, Co. Sligo, commemorates a queen who died from a piece of cheese flung from a sling in the 1st century AD;[12] Ossian's (Oisín's) tomb, an Early Neolithic court tomb in Co. Antrim, was also erected thousands of years before its eponymous occupant, the son of Finn Mac Cumhail.

Partholón's colonization of 2680 BC was eventful, especially in terms of cultural innovations. During his time came the first guesting house, the use of the cauldron and the first brewing.[13] As for the guesting house, the period of substantial rectangular timber structures in Ireland was limited to the early Neolithic around 3800–3600 BC, after which houses tended to be less substantial circular and subcircular structures, until the Bronze Age when substantial roundhouses were constructed. Unassociated with guesting houses is the claim that during Partholón's time 'a short hollow surrounded every steading' (*cúas gar um gach liss re lind*).[14] The word *les* was normally employed to designate the interior space of a medieval ringfort that was surrounded by a bank and ditch and this is most likely the image actually held in the head of the author. There are, on the other hand, examples of small trenches around house foundations from the Neolithic onwards.

The cauldron (*coire*), be it wooden or bronze, is an artifact that emerges in the Late Bronze Age in around 1200 BC, over a millennium after Partholón; it continued in use through the Iron Age and the Middle Ages. The inception of brewing alcoholic beverages in Western Europe is generally set to the Beaker period, which in Ireland begins *c.* 2500–2300 BC. Brewing, of course, has continued from the Early Bronze Age until the present day and while the date of its arrival in Ireland may well have been of urgent concern to the thirsty scribe who penned this reference, it might seem ungenerous not to admit that here archaeology does provide a near 'hit' for the AFM. On the other hand, the scribe would also have known that one of the first things Noah did when he exited the Ark in *c.* 2958 BC was to plant the first vineyard, sample its produce and get drunk,[15] which would have pitched the invention of alcoholic beverages to just after the Flood and fortuitously kept it within the same temporal ballpark as the archaeological date.

It was also at this time that Partholón introduced plough[16] teams of four oxen.[17] As plough-marks have been recovered from 4th-millennium BC contexts in Britain it is likely that Ireland also possessed ploughs well in advance of the time attributed to Partholón. Querns, another Partholónian innovation,[18] are also recovered from the beginning of the Neolithic and the discovery of milk fats in Irish Neolithic ceramics suggests that the introduction of churning could also date to the early Neolithic. The initial importation of gold,[19] dated to Partholón's time by the LG, on the other hand, should be set to the Early Bronze Age where gold is found in Beaker contexts from 2300 BC onwards, so again we have a near 'hit'.

Partholón's colonization collapsed in 2380 BC,[20] during a really bad week when he and all 9,000 of his followers died of plague (leaving us with the classic mystery as to how we know anything about Partholón in the first place). The place where they died is identified as modern Tallaght (Tamlacht meaning 'plague-grave'), just south of Dublin.

Early Bronze Age

Nemed led the third colonization, arriving in 2350 BC,[21] a date that would fall within the early period of the Beaker horizon in Ireland. It is with Nemed that we find two forts erected in Ireland. While one might have hoped that the traditional sources would refer to familiar or at least impressive sites such as ancient royal capitals, instead we find ourselves puzzling over the location of these earliest forts that tradition assigns, appropriately enough perhaps, to the warlike province of Ulster.[22] Because we cannot identify the specific forts first mentioned, we are unsure of what the authors had in mind, leaving the definition of a fort somewhat fluid. While there are a few causewayed enclosures that date to the early Neolithic (*c.* 3800 BC), the first horizon of hillforts does not occur until *c.* 1000 BC. This would still leave the reference to forts on the order of a millennium too early.

The Fir Bolg also arrived during the Early Bronze Age, in 1934 BC,[23] and while they had a major impact on the political or tribal composition of Ireland they did not build any forts (nor clear any plains nor see any lakes burst forth).[24] The main item of material culture that changes at this time is the spear. Tradition reports that until then there were no pointed weapons in Ireland (or at least javelins or spears). But their last king, Eochaid, died in 1897 BC by the pointed spear of the subsequent invaders, the Tuatha Dé Danann.[25] While the earliest bronze spearheads date to *c.* 1700–1600 BC and continue on into historical times, flint javelin heads were known far earlier during the Neolithic and there was certainly no period in Irish prehistory with round or flat-tipped spears, as the texts describe for the Fir Bolg. Attempts by both O'Curry and Sullivan to match the 'pointless' spear of the Fir Bolg in archaeological collections are entertaining but, unfortunately, do not contribute to useful discussion (FIG. 4.2).

In 1896 BC the Tuatha Dé Danann assumed the kingship of Ireland, having defeated the Fir Bolg in the First Battle of Mag Tuired. Although this battle is described in detail in one of the tales (CMT1), we

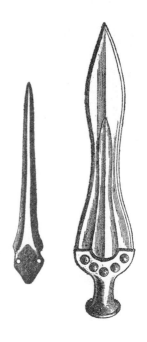

4.2. Two of W. K. Sullivan's candidates for the Fir Bolg *cruisech* '(blunt) spear'.

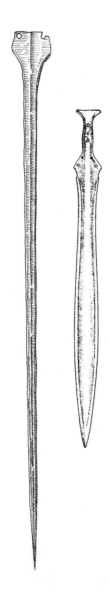

will restrict our examination right now to accounts in the LG. During the battle the Tuatha Dé Danann king, Nuadu, lost his hand and this was replaced ten years later by an artificial hand of silver,[26] which is the first mention of silver in Ireland. While we have (or rather had) a silver hand shrine of St Patrick from the early Middle Ages, there is nothing that comes remotely close to Nuadu's silver hand of an earlier date and, more importantly, the earliest major horizon of silver artifacts in Ireland is coincidental with Ireland's contacts with Roman Britain, over 1,500 years after the date ascribed to Nuadu.

The Tuatha Dé brought four talismans to Ireland that included the spear of Lug, the sword of Nuadu, the cauldron of the Dagda and the Lia Fáil, the stone of destiny.[27] We have already placed the spear and cauldron within their periods so it remains to locate the sword. The earliest sword-like weapons were rapiers, with their narrow elongated blades, that appeared a few centuries after the Tuatha Dé (FIG. 4.3). Actual swords that might be used for slashing (such as the one that hacked off Nuadu's hand) would not appear until around the 12th century BC (FIG. 4.4), leaving the traditional date about 600 years too early.

Board games were another innovation of the Tuatha Dé.[28] These are attested in the early medieval period and are comparable to some of the games introduced into Britain by the Romans but not found earlier in Western Europe (see Chapter Nine). Dice, on the other hand, are known from the Iron Age. The LG also makes reference to chariotry and horse racing at this time.[29] We will take up these topics in depth in Chapter Seven but we can note here that the earliest direct physical evidence of a wagon in Ireland dates no earlier than the 5th century BC and all of the material that is generally associated with either chariot parts or with horse-riding tends to date no earlier than the 3rd century BC.[30] As for the horse in Ireland, there is really no incontestable evidence much earlier than c. 1000 BC.

4.3. (*above left*) Middle Bronze Age rapier (length 80 cm) from Lissan, Co. Derry.

4.4. (*above right*) Late Bronze Age sword (length 61.5 cm) from Tempo, Co. Fermanagh.

Still within the Early Bronze Age we have the arrival of the Sons of Míl in 1700 BC. In 1544 Tigernmas assumed the kingship and introduced a number of technological improvements. It was during his reign that gold was first smelted, goblets and brooches were first covered with gold and silver and clothes were dyed different colours to mark social status.[31] In 1383 silver shields were introduced.[32] In 1328 we find the kings and chiefs now wearing chains of gold[33] and ten years later gold rings are worn. In 1209 wells were first dug.[34] And the most recent of the cultural innovations is set to 1024 BC when four-horse chariot teams are introduced.[35]

In an admittedly speculative article, Richard Warner has argued that some of the technological innovations indicated in the *Annals of the Four Masters* are such a good fit with the archaeological dates (as known in 1990) that they provide some support for the 'historicity' of native tradition reaching back into Irish prehistory.[36] Before we review Warner's arguments we should dismiss the Bible as a source for the Irish gold sequence as it already assumes its existence in the Garden of Eden[37] and does not concern itself with the evolution of gold-working technology. Warner remarked on the fact that the annals recognized two 'major revolutions in the use of gold in prehistoric Ireland', the first in the 16th century BC (gold casting) and the second in the 14th century BC (gold chains). He paralleled these with the archaeological evidence that assigned an initial date for the cold-working of gold to the 17th century BC and a second revolution involving the casting of gold to the 14th to 13th centuries BC. I summarize all the references to gold-working mentioned in the texts in Table 4.1.

The LG lists five gold-working events (not counting a later importation of a gold chariot in AD 9) although the Four Masters omitted the first despite the fact that it was included in their own version of the LG. In some ways it provides a better fit than

Table 4.1: Gold technology in ancient Ireland

Gold event	Annalistic chronology	Archaeological date
Importation of gold/ gold-working?	2650 BC	*c.* 2300–2100 BC[38]
Gold smelted	*c.* 1540 BC	*c.* 2000 BC *c.* 1400–1100 BC[39]
Goblets and brooches covered with gold	*c.* 1540 BC	*c.* 1000–800 BC?
Gold chains worn	1328 BC	1300–1100 BC
Gold rings	1318 BC	1300–1100 BC

4.5. Dress-fastener from Lattoon, Co. Cavan (maximum width *c.* 10 cm).

the others as it reckons the earliest importation of gold only a few centuries before we begin finding gold in Ireland.

The second event, the smelting of gold, is a bit problematic in terms of what is being celebrated. The Four Masters indicate that Uchadan, a smith, was the first person to smelt gold. They employ the verb *berbaid*, which basically means 'boils, cooks, melts' but can mean 'smelts' when applied to metals. Among the Early Bronze Age gold objects in Ireland are large discs and even larger lunulae (collars) that were hardly the product of a single gold nugget but would have required the melting of many nuggets or flakes together, so that melting gold should go back to at least 2000 BC if not earlier. We can also speak of melting gold around 1400–1100 BC in the context of alloying the metal with other elements such as copper or silver. These are pretty technical terms and one wonders whether we were meant to understand this achievement as simply allowing for the casting of gold objects. In this period smiths cast gold ingots that might be then stretched and turned into necklets and bracelets. By 900 BC we could interpret the smelting/melting to imply the casting of such objects as large gold dress-fasteners (FIG. 4.5).[40] Perhaps we gain a better grasp of what the annalists had in mind when we also read that this same Uchadan was also the first person to cover goblets and brooches with gold and silver. If we fudge the evidence in favour of the clever Uchadan, we might cite the occasional use of gold foil to decorate ornaments from around 800–700 BC[41] and such a technique could be pushed back even earlier to *c.* 1000 BC.[42] But reference to goblets covered with gold makes no archaeological sense, although we could cite some evidence for gold vessels from the Iron Age, *c.* 300 BC. The inclusion of silver here, however, pitches the most likely conceptual targets to early medieval Ireland or, more probably, the time of the Viking incursions when silver objects became more common.[43]

Reference to the introduction of gold chains in the 14th century is difficult to parallel unless we assume that what are described as 'chains' are really flange-twisted torcs (FIG. 4.6) that could date to the 13th century BC; gold rings might possibly be set to the same period if we use the word 'ring' in its most general sense. These are the

4.6. Flange-twisted gold torc from Tipper, Co. Kildare (diameter c. 38 cm).

earliest dates and we could continue with such ornaments from the Late Bronze Age into the historical period.

Finally, in AD 9 there was a raid overseas by Crimthann who returns with jewels, a gold chariot, a golden *fidchell* game board inlaid with gems, a sword inlaid with golden serpents, and a shield with bosses of silver.

Disasters

In addition to some items of material culture, Warner also proposed that there were good correlations between proxy evidence for environmental downturns and annalistic accounts of plagues and other disasters in the annals.[44] The proxy evidence derives from dendrochronology, where there is a record of oak ring-widths from the present back to 5450 BC. The pattern of ring-widths can be read broadly in terms of how well or badly the oaks responded to their environment and across the millennia there are a number of major narrow-ring events that signal serious climatic downturns (FIG. 4.7). Some of these find correlations with evidence for volcanic eruptions in Iceland or further abroad that are believed to have produced dust-veils which instigated disastrous weather conditions and, presumably, collapses in population. Warner's proposed correlations are summarized in Table 4.2.[45]

The first event explains how the colonization of Ireland by Partholón failed when the entire population of Ireland died of plague over the course of a week. Warner suggested that the dates applied by the Four Masters to these events may have been based

Table 4.2: Warner's correlation of annalistic and climatic disasters

Event	Annal date	Event	Dendro date	Correlated event
1	2380–2350 BC	9,000 people die within one week	2345 BC	Eruption of Hekla 4
2	1620–1544 BC	Three-quarters of the men of Ireland die	1628 BC	Eruption of Santorini
3	1180–1031 BC	Countless numbers die in plague	1159 BC	Eruption of Hekla 3
4	209–199 BC	Great mortality of cattle	207 BC	

4.7. The band of narrow rings seen in the lower part of this slice of oak indicates severe environmental stress between 1159 and 1141 BC.

on early Irish king lists that started from the historical period and worked their way back in time. He did not insist that the names of the kings be accurate nor the length of reigns be precise and that they may have been merely operating from a regnal generation of 15 years (the average length of the reign of the prehistoric king list).[46] But even if one accepted all this it would still be very difficult to see how Partholón's date could be reckoned by employing the Four Masters' list of kings as these only begin with the Fir Bolg, whose reign began 400 years *after* the Partholónian flu. Dates

94

of events before this should be governed by those of the preceding colonization of Cesair, which themselves must be synchronized against the biblical date of the Deluge rather than any Irish king list. And as the burial place was allegedly at Tamlacht, modern Tallaght, whose name means 'plague-grave', it is just as likely that the story was invented to explain the place name.

Event 2 mentions the death of Tigernmas and three-quarters of the men of Ireland. But the annals do not suggest that the people died because of plague but rather while worshipping the pagan god Crom Cruach on the feast of *Samain*.

Event 3 occurred specifically in the year 1031 BC at the end of the reign of Sirna Saeghlach. There are two features that should trouble any case for a correlation with a dust-veil event. First, the occasion of the plague in the AFM was a battle and, indeed, in the *Annals of Clonmacnoise* everyone died in the course of the battle and there is no mention of a plague.[47] The second problem is that an event that is suppos- edly tied into a regnal list is pegged to the end date of a king who, according to the Four Masters, ruled from 1180 until 1031 BC, or 149 years (at least the *Annals of Clonmacnoise* have him rule for a more realistic 21 years).

Event 4, involving the death of cattle around 207 BC, may, of course, only be a fiction created to explain the name of the reigning king, Breasal Boidhiobhadh ('destruction of cattle'), unless you believe the name was applied as a nickname to help recall the event.

To what extent may the annalistic disasters be randomly correlated against the narrow ring events? This is obviously difficult to determine but we should note that Warner only cited the four entries that he believed 'are described in the annals in terms that make them major disasters'. I would suggest the annals mention some other disasters as well for which there are no tree-ring correlations but that are every much as strong as those cited above. We have seen that a comparison between plagues or population collapse in the AFM and the tree-ring dates has targeted four narrowest- ring dates (2345, 1628, 1159 and 207 BC). But the AFM also lists a major plague for 1927 BC (death of the reigning king and 2,000 people) and another in 1258 BC where the king died and 'snow fell with the taste of wine which blackened the grass',[48] and in 892 the king also died of plague along 'with a great number about him'.[49] We also have another king dying of the plague in 1328 BC. One might wonder whether the annalists have been so generous in providing us with plagues (averaging one about every 300 years) that it would be difficult not to find a near hit with the tree-ring evidence.

As for the king lists providing a reliable chronology, perhaps over-idealized 15-year regnal cycles, the evidence is not very supportive. Of the 121 kings who reigned from the first Fir Bolg king to AD 1, only four of them actually reigned 15 years and their kingly lives ranged fairly widely, with the three longest and improbable reigns of 77, 80 and 149 years. Of the 121, 86 (or 72 per cent) were killed, usually in combat, and the only reason the figure is not considerably higher is that nine of the reigns were during a period of primitive power-sharing where each reigned for seven years before recycling the kingship. It is a bit difficult to imagine an average reign expectancy based on battle-death or assassination. It is also very difficult to accept a list of kings preserved since the Early Bronze Age, *c.* 1700 BC, for the descendants of Míl. As the high kingship of Ireland was itself a political ideology rather than a reality, extending it back for several thousand years seems implausible. If there ever were king lists, there should have been one for each of the more than 100 tribes of Ireland, so why we should recover a single list remains unexplained. And we cannot really dismiss the actual names of the kings, many of which are easily explainable through the Irish language. For example, there were at least 14 Eochaids that extended as far back as 1750 BC. The name means 'horse-rider' and the first four kings bearing that name lived before there is any evidence for the horse in Ireland.

While I am highly critical of any concept of ancient Irish king lists, I am also at least slightly sympathetic to those who find it difficult to understand how so many pages of medieval Irish text could relate a totally fabricated history. How much effort must have gone into generating the names of 120 kings who purportedly lived before the Christian era, as well as the years and events of their reigns? I can only suggest that anyone mesmerized by such detailed historical fantasy take a look at Roger O'Connor's (1762–1834) monumental antidote to insomnia, the *Chronicles of Eri*, which covers much the same ground as the *Lebor Gabála* but is purportedly a translation from the Phoenician (!) dialect of Scythia (a nice trick as the Scythians spoke an Iranian language in no way whatsoever related to Phoenician)[50] of an account of the wanderings of the Irish from Scythia to Ireland, originally written by Eolus, who lived some 50 years after Moses.[51] If you prefer more scholarly historical back-stories, Tolkien's *Silmarillion* and related works should suffice. Such extended fantasy histories are not only possible but only require the work of a single individual for their original fabrication.

Monuments

Although we can be wholly sceptical about the dates ascribed to the tombs of the various personalities in the literature, the foundation dates for the royal sites are worth testing against the evidence of excavation. One of the most important of the traditional dates is 668 BC, which marks the foundations of the Ulster capital of Emain Macha.[52] It should be emphasized that this is not the only date as the *Annals of Clonmacnoise* set the foundation to 450 BC and both the *Annals of Tigernach* and *Inisfallen* date it to 307 BC.[53] While the site experienced intermittent occupation from the Neolithic and Bronze Age, the main surviving landscape elements such as the mound and, especially, the surrounding ditch, which was reputedly marked out by its founder, Macha, actually date to *c.* 100 BC.[54] The foundation of Tara is still farther off the mark if we presume that the monument known as Ráth na Ríogh was the site. The annals would place the building of Tara (Tea's walls) to *c.* 1698 BC,[55] while excavations indicate that the bank and ditch were dug out at about the same time as those of Navan, i.e. about the 1st century BC–AD.[56] Although there are accounts of the foundation of Dún Ailinne (Knockaulin) in the *Dindshenchas* (the main collection of place name lore) it is difficult to put an absolute date on its foundation. The earliest mention of Dún Ailinne in the AFM is in AM 4169 = 1031 BC, but its actual construction has been set over 800 years later to the reigns of Setna Sithbacc[57] or his son, Art Mes Delmann (and several others), which would date to *c.* 100 BC, a good correlation with the archaeological evidence. Cruachain (Rathcroghan) offers the greatest difficulties because the site was known not only as the residential capital of the Connachta but also as one of the three great cemeteries of Ireland. The main site, Rathcroghan Mound, has been surveyed and reveals architectural features similar to Navan and Knockaulin so a best guess for it would also be *c.* 100 BC, but Rathcroghan is also covered with monuments and mounds of various ages,[58] prehistoric through to the early medieval periods, which renders any comparison between the monuments and the 'historical' dates hopelessly ambiguous. From the perspective of the Four Masters, its earliest mention is 1681 BC and there are four other references before about 30 BC,[59] when we come to the time of the Ulster tales.

Conclusions

A rough indication of how well or not the traditional chronology found in the *Lebor Gabála* and the *Annals of the Four Masters* corresponds to the archaeological record is given in Table 4.3.

Any attempt to evaluate the degree of correspondence should begin with the fact that most of the historical narrative of the *Lebor Gabála* purports to take place between *c.* 3000 (Cesair) and 1700 (Sons of Míl) BC. This period comprises the Late

Table 4.3. Summary of the correspondence of Irish tradition and archaeology. All dates are approximate and, dependent on the specific referent, many of the archaeological identifications should be preceded by a question mark.

Event	Traditional	Archaeology	Discrepancy (years)
Initial settlement	3000 BC	8000 BC	+5000
First livestock	3000 BC	3800 BC	+800
First land clearance	2700 BC	3800 BC	+1100
First cairns	3000 BC	3800 BC	+800
Guesting house	2700 BC	3800–3600 BC	+1000
Cauldrons	2700 BC	1200 BC	-1500
Brewing	2700 BC	2500 BC	-200
Ploughing	2700 BC	3800 BC	+1100
Querns	2700 BC	3800 BC	+1100
Dairy products	2700 BC	3600 BC	+900
Gold	2700 BC	2300 BC	-400
Forts	2400 BC	3800 BC/1000 BC	+1400/-1400
Pointed (metal) spears	1900 BC	1700 BC	-200
Silver	1700 BC	100 BC	-1600
Swords	1700 BC	1200 BC	-500
Board games	1700 BC	100 BC	-1600
Chariots	1700 BC	300 BC	-1400
Horse (racing)	1700 BC	1000 BC	-700
Tara's walls	1700 BC	100 BC	-1600
Gold smelted (cast)	1500 BC	2000/ 1400–1100 BC	+500 or -100
Gold vessels	1500 BC	300 BC/AD 700	-1200 or -2200
Silver vessels	1500 BC	AD 700	-2200
Gold brooches	1500 BC	1000 BC/AD 700	-500 or -2200
Silver brooches	1500 BC	AD 700	-2200
Silver shields	1400 BC	(silver) 100 BC	-1300
Gold chains	1300 BC	1300 BC	0
Gold rings	1300 BC	1300 BC	0
Ditch of Emain Macha	700–300 BC	100 BC	-600–200
Dún Ailinne	1000 BC?, 100 BC?	100 BC	-900 or 0

Neolithic and the Early Bronze Age in Ireland. In cultural terms, the innovations of this period in the archaeological record will be largely concerned with the new technologies of bronze and gold metallurgy. As nearly half of the traditional events are in some ways associated with developments in metallurgy, one should expect at least some fortuitous correlations with the archaeological record. If a 21st-century supporter of the traditional chronology reviewed the evidence in the table he or she might note several things in its favour.

First, while only one of the first ten events or innovations (the introduction of brewing) provides anything like a close fit with the archaeological record, nine of the ten are, like the archaeological dates, set earlier than all other events and so at least assume their correct relative position. As many of these derive from the beginning of the Neolithic, a date anterior to what could be admitted in the medieval world dependent on a Noachian chronology, their lack of precise correlation might be excused. The only exception is the cauldron, which is about 1,700 years too early (assuming one had in mind a metal cauldron).

Second, several innovations do come quite close to the archaeological dates: bronze spears, gold chains, gold rings and possibly the introduction of gold itself. The foundation dates of both Emain Macha and Dún Ailinne might also be regarded as near 'hits', although this is only because the traditional dates offer such a latitude of choice.

But the more sceptical would note that all of the objects mentioned also derive from the world of medieval Ireland. The most archaic 'innovation' was probably the chariot and even that is mentioned in the Irish annals as late as the 11th century. In other words, the list depicts the start date for items well known to the medieval Irish which may simply have been back-projected into a traditional chronology that had to constrain almost all of them to the Bronze Age, a period to which almost anything in the medieval period might find some form of ancestral presence. Also, I have been over-generous in linking the literary items to the archaeological record. For example, in the case of the medieval monk copying out a description of a brooch, he was probably imagining an instrument with a long metal pin for fastening one's cloak or tunic and not a Late Bronze Age dress-fastener (Chapter Nine). Hence, he probably had in mind a gold (gilded) or silver brooch from the 7th century AD or later rather than a prehistoric device that I have let slip in. Certainly, the objects made of silver are clear examples of discordances between the traditional chronology and the archaeological record.

Finally, the mechanism by which these events might have been retained, associations made with the reigns of Irish kings passed down over many centuries, is internally weakened by the fact that the first 13 'events' or 'discoveries' (45 per cent) were accomplished before 1700 BC, when the king lists of the Sons of Míl, the putative ancestors of the medieval Irish, began. This means that they date beyond a period where there would have been any reason to even maintain a king list in the first place, and the Four Masters hint at this themselves when they wrote the date for the beginning of the Milesian chronology in larger letters than all previous dates.

In general then, I think the case for the medieval Irish retaining a chronologically accurate recollection of the evolution of some events is extremely weak. Yet I have not examined every instance cited by Richard Warner and we will have cause to examine one of his best cases, derived from the literature other than the *Lebor Gabála* or *Annals of the Four Masters*, later in Chapter Eight.

CHAPTER FIVE

The Natural Environment

Landscapes are never described in our tales. In so far as the texts
tell us, the action of these tales could be taking place on Mars.

Ranko Matasović, 2009[1]

Although the early Irish have left us with a body of exceptional nature poetry, the earliest Irish heroic *scéla* rarely provide a context in which one can embrace the landscape in the way possible with some of the later historical tales. There are only occasional glimpses into past landscapes. In one 9th-century tale, for example, the author tells us that at the time of the story the future ecclesiastical capital of Ireland at Armagh was only a forest where the smiths of the Ulster king, Conchobar, worked.[2] In any event, as a prelude to our survey we may briefly consider the different landscapes in which our three avatars of the Irish *filid* lived.

Katu-butos, our Irish Iron Age seer, lived during what has been termed the Developed (300 BC–1 BC) and Late (AD 1–400) Iron Age.[3] In the centuries just before and at the start of this period we find evidence of an opening up of the landscape after several centuries of reduced agriculture and expanding forests.[4] From an environmental perspective Katu-butos was enduring what might be described as 'interesting times' for it was during this period that we encounter the 'Late Iron Age Lull.'[5] There are two lines of evidence for this lull – palynology, where the study of ancient sediments containing pollen permits the reconstruction of past environments, and dendrochronology, the use of the evidence of tree-ring dates to indicate fluctuations in building activities, at least those involved with the use of oak. Roughly between 200 BC and AD 200, across the entire island there is evidence that forests were reclaiming land that had previously been open to either cultivation or grazing. The causes of this are unclear and have included general climatic change, an environmental catastrophe induced by volcanic activity elsewhere in Europe, or social factors that may have led to a more mobile population. The evidence of the use of oak, which was a major building material throughout Ireland's later prehistory and historic period, also appears to have collapsed in the period between 40 BC and AD 300 (FIG. 5.1). Coupled with the evidence from palynology, this has led to the hypothesis that during the Iron Age there was a significant fall in population in Ireland and a major change in social behaviour. Indeed, some have even suggested that the death of Conaire Mór in 40 BC, which saw the end of his golden age, may be a legendary reminiscence of this major environmental collapse.[6] But it is also clear that the environmental studies may be over-doing the 'catastrophe', as there is also increasing archaeological evidence for cereals (wheat, barley, oats) and corn-drying kilns across this period as well.[7]

In the period in which Cattubuttas lived, c. AD 400–700, the landscape was experiencing major changes as we begin to see a marked rise in agricultural and building activity. Forests were being cleared once again, primarily to provide fields for pasture, and faunal remains from archaeological sites indicate that cattle were by far the most prominent livestock. Often, after the initial phase of pastoral use, there are signs of increased arable agriculture and by the 6th century there seems to be an intensification of almost all activities that we would associate with stable mixed-farming settlements – farmsteads, corn-drying kilns, trackways, timber buildings and by the 7th century we find watermills for grinding grain. Cattubuttas' world was not entirely a picture of progress as the annals also record occasional famines and plagues, most noteworthy being the Justinian plague (c. AD 540) that ensured that Ireland would also experience widespread mortality along with the rest of Europe.[8] Moreover, there is some palaeo-environmental evidence for a reduction in farming around AD 500 and a rise in pastoralism.

During the period in which the tales were being set down on vellum (AD 700–1000), their author Cathbad witnessed an acceleration of the changes experienced by his predecessor. Cereal cultivation became still more important and there was an intense period of mill construction to process the grains in the 8th and 9th centuries. Settlement types associated with pastoralism were replaced by those where arable agriculture predominated and by the 9th century, although cattle were still predominant, pigs and sheep were on the rise. Again, the annals suggest that alongside this evidence for agricultural progress there were also frequent enough bouts of bad weather, famine and plague, especially in the 8th century.[9]

It is now time to see how this landscape was portrayed in the earliest Irish tradition. We will begin with the trees, then other plants, both wild and domesticated, and conclude with the evidence for fauna. Unlike material culture and ritual behaviour, to be examined in the following chapters, the natural landscape is far less sensitive to revealing marked changes through time and so much of our discussion will be focused on description and determining whether any elements might possibly have been imported from outside of Ireland.

Trees

From the perspective of the Ulster tales, the arboreal landscape was primarily utilitarian: trees were generally mentioned in the context of how they might have been manipulated by people, or they served as metaphors for human behaviour. A number of trees, in particular, were generally described in relation to their use in warfare.

The alder (*fern*) was principally seen in terms of its use in the manufacture of shields and may itself stand in the place of 'shield';[10] we also find the troops of Ulstermen marching toward Caherconree described as a 'grove of alderwood', again a wall of shields.[11] In one very late tale emphasizing the different characteristics of trees, the alder is described as the 'battle witch of all woods' as it is 'hottest in the fight'.[12] And although not shaped as a shield, the Ulster hero Celtchair utilizes a hollowed-out alder log to protect his arm as he reaches through it to rip out the guts of a ferocious hound.[13]

Shafts of holly (*cuillen*) made convenient weapons, as we find in the *Táin* when Nad Crantaill travels with an arsenal of holly spears,[14] while Cú Chulainn makes chance use of a holly shoot to kill one of his opponents.[15] A spit of holly thrown at Midir puts out one of his eyes.[16] In addition to serving as a weapon, holly is also employed in making chariot poles.[17] It could also be burnt in a fire, preferably when green.[18]

Another tree suitable for turning into a spit was the rowan (*caerthann*): Cú Chulainn is trapped into violating his *geis* (taboo) of eating the flesh of a dog, roasting on a rowan spit.[19] It also has magical properties and is known as the 'wizard's tree'; for example, Étaín is magically transformed into a pool of water when she is struck by a rod of scarlet rowan.[20] The berries of a rowan tree are also high-lighted in a number of tales.[21]

Poles of hazel (*coll*) might be employed as weapons as when, during the *Táin*, charioteers cut rods of white hazel to serve as clubs.[22] Also, once sharpened, a hazel rod might be used as a convenient support for displaying the head of a victim[23] or to provide bent hoops to protect the severely wounded Cú Chulainn's mangled body.[24] Hazel was a preferred wood for the ceremonial staff, such as the one borne by MacRoth, the messenger of Queen Medb,[25] and perhaps served as such in the hands of Elcmar in the Mythological cycle.[26] Hazel was also intimately associated with both a drink made from hazelnuts[27] and the art of poetry[28] and was regarded as a wood that should not be burnt.[29] On the other hand, as a bush it seemed to be singularly inefficient for hiding from view one's extramarital dalliances.[30] Finally, a hazel grew through the grave of Buana, the wife of Mesgegra.[31]

The ash (*uinnius*) only appears in terms of its use in transport. In one instance there is reference to a yoke of ash attached to a chariot,[32] while elsewhere it is the dark wood that 'makes the wheels go'.[33]

Some trees that present branches with sharp thorns are primarily represented as fences or hurdles. Prominent among these was the hawthorn (*scé*), which could form a barricade,[34] or the idea of a thorny fence might be used to describe Cú Chulainn's hairstyle[35] while the sharpness of its thorns provided a comparison for the spikiness of his hair when he became distorted with rage.[36] The hawthorn was another tree that one was more than welcome to burn.[37] In TBC[3] the Mórrígan in the form of a scald crow perches on a whitethorn above the bogs that went around Cú Chulainn's district.[38] The blackthorn (*draigen*) was similarly employed as a barricade[39] although, on one occasion, it may also have been used as a club.[40] In TBC[3] it is also employed to make a false beard for Cú Chulainn where one would normally have expected the juice of a berry.[41]

The oak (usually *dair*) occupied a special place in the Ulster tales. Obviously, it was employed in the construction of buildings and defences[42] and also roadways across bogs.[43] Oak branches might be stripped to be used as clubs[44] or, in one instance, an entire oak tree was uprooted by Fergus to be used as a club.[45] The strength of the oak was also often emphasized and employed as a metaphor for warriors.[46] The same metaphor exists in classical literature, for example in the Latin *Iliad* two warriors are described as 'two oaks of savage war'[47] and in the *Aeneid* a slew of angry Cyclopes are likened to tall oaks,[48] but its metaphorical use need not be derived from elsewhere. In TBC[2] Cú Chulainn cuts an oak sapling, twists it and writes an ogam on it,[49] while TBC[1] uses the word *omna* 'oak' to describe the object on which he writes his warning ogam.[50] The same word for oak is employed several times in the expression of being pierced as 'an axe pierces an oak'[51] and also to indicate a tree of immense height, although the warrior giant Goll was even taller.[52] Finally, the oak provides mast (*mes(s)*) for pigs and its presence generally indicated the good rulership of a king.[53]

Another architecturally important tree is the yew (*ibar*), whose primary function in building was to provide a carved wainscot in the interiors of status buildings[54] or the door.[55] Yew also served for making a suitable surface for an ogam inscription[56] and for the making of drinking vats[57] and a yew tree provided a convenient resting place for the woman-warrior Scáthach.[58]

The one problematic tree is the pine (giús), which only occurs once in describing the construction of a house (see Chapter Six) that one would otherwise have presumed to have been built of oak.[59] Although many of Ireland's modern forests are now pine, these represent a modern reintroduction of a species in the 17th century that suffered a major collapse in c. 2000 BC. After this time pine pollen is generally absent from the pollen record of much of Ireland. And when the Iron Age (c. 400–200 BC) man found preserved in a bog at Clonycavan, Co. Meath, required a pine-based hair gel, the species of pine employed had been imported from southwest France or Spain (PL. XII).[60] What little evidence we have for actual pine trees suggests that whatever remnants of pine forests survived in Ireland they were not likely to have been employed in the construction of status buildings.[61] With few exceptions, the Irish word giús 'pine' occurs in non-native contexts, either with reference to the Bible and other exotic trees or in translations of Latin literature.[62] The exceptions, however, are troublesome since an area of Munster was called Giusach 'piney' and in an early 12th-century historical tale, the king of Leinster sets out to gather up three tall masts of pine.[63] There are also other words for 'pine' such as ochtgach, which may usually be rendered 'bedpost' or 'ridge post' but sometimes retains its original meaning of 'pine'; for example, in a 9th-century poem a hermit sleeps either in a pine forest or on a bed of pine branches.[64] Clearly there is a mismatch here, with the palynologists telling us that any industrial use of native Irish pine during the 1st millennium is highly unlikely, but sufficient literary evidence to suggest that there should have been a period in Ireland's imagined landscape when the pine was relatively abundant or that references to pine were created and perhaps maintained within a non-Irish context, perhaps in Scotland where much of the population was Gaelic-speaking and where some of the events of the tales occur.

There is, however, one other option that would render the references to pine as local. Although pine had largely disappeared after 2000 BC, the pine forests that covered Ireland before that time could have survived buried under peat. Iron Age or medieval Irishmen engaged in turf-cutting could have encountered rich remains of well-preserved and perfectly usable pine trees buried in bogs and collected them for building. This is a plausible theory that, unfortunately, lacks empirical evidence for the period in question, although bog pine was extensively employed in structural timbers for house roofs, thatching, tieing roof beams and wainscotting in the 18th and 19th centuries.[65]

The Irish did encounter the pine in classical contexts, the stem of a pine tree providing a handy eye-gouge for Odysseus to employ on the Cyclops,[66] for example, and there are also references to pine spears or stakes,[67] but it does not seem to have been associated with descriptions of buildings. The Bible offers only one reference to 'rafters of pine' but plucking the Irish architectural references from the *Song of Solomon*[68] would seem to be a long-shot. On the other hand, if the Irish were content to include 'cedar' under the meaning of pine, then there was very wide scope for regarding *giús* as a suitable material for building a royal hall, as cedar is commonly used in the Bible.

The nut (*cnú*) was obviously a food source, one of which was larger than a man's head, which led to a major dispute between King Mesgegra and his servant.[69] It could also be fed to swine.[70] It might also be used to indicate a very small thing[71] or compared to a heart.[72]

The apple (*aball* 'apple tree' and *uball* 'apple') occupied a curious role in the Ulster tales. As for its use as a food, we find Medb's daughter, Findabair, plying Fer Diad with 'fragrant apples over the bosom of her tunic' to entice him to fight his foster-brother, Cú Chulainn,[73] and there are references to an orchard of apples.[74] But more often we find the apple employed for its shape as a ball, either in an apparent juggling feat[75] or in a description of how apples would stick to the hairs on Cú Chulainn's head when he went into his battle frenzy.[76] It also might serve as a ball to trace one's passage on the ground.[77] We also find apples of gold,[78] including one that functioned like a horcrux in the Harry Potter books, that could only be split with the sword of Cú Roí.[79] The precious apple tree was not one for burning.[80]

Among the other trees with minor mentions we find the aspen or poplar (from *crithach* 'trembling'), which, with its 'palsied branch' is burnable,[81] but in one of the earliest poems that relate the story of the *Táin*, it may refer to a club (*fidot*).[82] The birch (*beithe*), which is also burnable,[83] may be laid down on the floor of a building as a cover along with rushes.[84] Otherwise, Cú Chulainn's multilayered hair is likened to the bright yellow of the top of a birch tree.[85] Elder (*trom*), with its tough bark, can be burned.[86] And there is a sanction against the burning of willow (*sail*) because of its association with poetry and bees.[87]

Plants

We can divide the mentions of plants in the Ulster tales into a number of functional categories.

Colouring

Among the plants mentioned we have those known primarily for their use as either a colouring agent or, at least, their own colour. Hyacinth (*buga*), for example, is always applied with reference to the blue colour of one's eyes,[88] while the standard for cheeks was foxglove (*siail*) for both beautiful women like Deirdre[89] and Étaín[90] and rough warriors such as Conall Cernach.[91] Of course, one might also have the complexion of a rose (*rós*)[92] or one could be as white as a white flower (*bánscoth*).[93] Hair might be as white as cotton grass (*canach*)[94] or the colour of primrose (*sobaire*).[95] The hair might also, presumably, be bristling, as in the case of Mugain of the furzy hair (the sister of Queen Medb and adulterous wife of King Conchobar, who flaunted her breasts in front of the young Cú Chulainn); furze (*aittenn*) was generally used to describe a rough landscape.[96] Hair could also be compared to heather (*fráech*)[97] or sedge (*seisc*).[98]

Clothing

May cotton grass (*canach*) was plucked and apparently woven into some material for warriors.[99] The only references to flax (*forcor* or *coipp* 'foam' = 'flax-heads'?) occurs in the insult: 'he belabours you as flax-heads (?) are beaten in a pond.'[100]

Domestic uses

Bedding generally consisted of fresh rushes (*lúachair*)[101] and reeds. The rushes would be cut by women.[102]

Edible plants

There is abundant evidence from early Irish texts that the fruitfulness of the land was very much dependent on the proper behaviour of the king and this idea is also reflected in the early stories. Conchobar, for example, could not give a false judgment lest the crops (*torad* 'fruit') fail,[103] while acts of inhospitality would destroy[104] mast and fruit. Very often we find a frozen expression 'corn and milk' (*ith ocus bainne*) used to describe the basics of sustenance,[105] sometimes extended to include also 'flowers' (*bláth*)[106] and 'mast and fruits'.[107] Among the Tuatha Dé Danann, the Dagda controlled both weather and crops.[108]

Among the edible but uncultivated plants was seaweed (*femm*), which was offered to Lugaid and Fergus by Cú Chulainn on several occasions,[109] along with watercress (*birar*)[110] and water parsnip (*fochlocht*). Watercress might also be used to cover a cup.[111] Deirdre sings the praises of the wild garlic (*crem*) of Scotland.[112] Leeks are also mentioned,[113] as well as puffballs.[114]

Cereals are seldom referenced in the tales and when they are, it is often in the context of what one is feeding to a prize animal rather than on the table. In *Fled Bricrenn* Cú Chulainn chooses barley (*eórna*) for his horse while Conall and Lóegaire feed theirs *airthend*, possibly translated as 'timothy grass' (*Pheum pretense*).[115] Briccriu fattens his prize boar for his contentious feast on corn (*arbar*) and wheaten cakes.[116] On the other hand, in a very late tale the Leprechauns promise to provide fields of wheat (*cruithnecht*) to the Ulstermen, although this is only after their king has been captured, as earlier they had threatened to snip off the ears of all the corn (*días*).[117]

The most obvious edible plant (if you were a cow) is grass (*fér*), which receives occasional mentions but other than being consumed by magical flocks of birds at Emain[118] it is used to manufacture a false beard for Cú Chulainn[119] and provides a special (and quite unnatural given the digestive system of a pig) feed for Briccriu's boar,[120] one which specifically excludes the consumption of heather (*fráech*).[121]

Medicinal and magical

Herbs (*luib*) and plants (*lus*) are applied medicinally, for example, to heal Cú Chulainn's wounds and cuts,[122] or when Fergus mac Léti stuffs herbs in his ears so that he can travel under water.[123]

Miscellaneous

Nera is told to take the summer fruits – wild garlic (*crem*), primrose (*sobairce*) and golden fern (*buiderad*) – with him to prove that he has come from a *síd* that is experiencing a different season.[124] Buttercups (*buide*) are to be found on Mag Breg.[125] Honeysuckle or woodbine (*féithlenn*) is noted for its taste[126] and its burning is forbidden.[127] And irritating plants such as the thorn (*dealg*),[128] thistle (*fothannán* and *omthand*)[129] and nettle (*nentog*),[130] all get a mention.

Insects

A few insects or worms are mentioned in the tales. The most prominent by far is the beetle or chafer (*dega* or *doel*), which is frequently employed to describe something that is very black,[131] such as eybrows[132] or eyes;[133] also, a dark blue cloak can be described as such.[134] In addition, it could also be used to describe someone with a poisonous tongue, most prominently Dubthach Dóeltenga (chafer-tongue).[135]

Bees (*bech*) are not usually mentioned in the context of honey except, presumably, in the list of ten swarms in the gifts of Cú Roí.[136] Elsewhere bees are usually mentioned only in terms of comparison, such as the yellow colour of Cú Chulainn's hair.[137] It should be noted that Pompelius Mela (*c.* AD 43) claimed that there were not only no bees in Ireland but scattering Irish soil about a hive would drive the bees out.[138] But if there were no bees in prehistoric Ireland we would have a really difficult time explaining the use of the lost-wax technique in bronze casting.[139] The ant (*sengán*) only occurs in the context of indicating Mac Cecht's dismissive perception of a wolf-bite, which he likens to that of an ant, fly (*cuil*) or gnat/midge (*corrmíl*).[140] The fly (*cuil*) is also mentioned in the *Táin*, with Cú Chulainn making chariot poles so smooth that a fly couldn't stand on them[141] and a disguised Cú Roí abusively calls Cú Chulainn a 'wretched fly' in *Fled Bricrenn*.[142] There is also the purple fly that evolves from a worm (*cruim*) in the story of Étaín.[143] The flea (*dergnat*) occurs as a destroyer of ale.[144]

Fish

Given Ireland's location, it is natural that fish and fishing are mentioned in the earliest Irish tradition and one would expect that during the reign of a just king there would be fruits of the sea.[145] Cú Chulainn routinely offers fish as a sign of hospitality[146] and one tale even reports that there is a *geis* that fish should not be in the bays at the mouths of rivers unless they are caught by him.[147] Fish is one of Cú Chulainn's basic sources of food while he defends Ulster in the *Táin*.[148] A certain Roncu is named as the fisherman of Conchobar who catches fish on his line.[149]

The preferred fish was the salmon (*éicne* or *eó*), which is offered in hospitality.[150] The leap of a salmon is a frequent expression in the tales with reference to one of the feats preformed by warriors[151] and we even hear of the 'salmon of valour' (*eó gaile*).[152] It is a salmon that leaps and catches Findabair's ring in the story of Fráech.[153] Salmon roe was also kneaded in wheat flour.[154] A characteristic of the salmon was its speckled skin.[155] The other favoured fish, the trout (*íasc mbrecc* 'speckled fish'), is mentioned on occasion, for example when Cú Chulainn managed to spear one from the Boyne,[156] and Medb fears that Conall will cut up her people as one cuts up a trout with iron flails on red sandstone.[157]

The slippery eel (*escong*)[158] occupies a particular place in the Ulster tales since this is the form that the war-goddess, the Mórrígan, takes when she wishes to harm Cú Chulainn.[159]

Finally, there is the odd reference to a *corrcenn* 'crane-head', which may refer to the swordfish.[160]

Reptiles

The one animal that Ireland is most famously devoid of is mentioned in at least nine different tales. In most of them, the snake (*nathair*), an inherited word no less and related to English *adder*, is closely associated with either venom or at least a venomous serpent.[161] This suggests that we are most likely dealing with a literary, possibly biblical motif that has been inserted into the Ulster tales. When Fráech and Conall go up against an Alpine fort guarded by a serpent, this is more likely to be a borrowed folkloric motif. Probably of greatest interest is the description of a sword ornamented with a snake.[162]

Perhaps we may number the dragon (*draic* and *drauc*, from Latin *dracō*), usually employed as a metaphor for the fierceness of a warrior, among the exotic reptiles.[163] It is interesting that when the two pig-keepers are transformed into dragons, they do not breathe fire but rather 'pour down snow on each other's land'.[164] Giraldus claimed that there were no dragons in Ireland,[165] but this was just another example of his sloppy scholarship since the *Annals of Ulster* (AU) reported a huge dragon (*draco ingens*) at the end of autumn in AD 734. Another clearly exotic motif is the leviathan (*lebedán*), who appears to act as the Norse Midgardserpent who encircles the world.[166]

Finally, we have a native water-monster that inhabits Dundrum Bay in Co. Down and was slain by the Ulster king, Fergus mac Léti. In the earliest version[167] it is known as a *muirdris*, while in the later version it is a *sinech*.[168]

Amphibians

Ireland is no better known for its amphibians than its snakes and the toad (*loscann*) only occurs once as some form of aggressive 'sharp, beaked monster'.[169]

Birds

Birds occupy a significant role in the mythological landscape of the tales as various deities or Otherworld figures may adopt the form of a bird. The war-goddess, the Bodb, may appear as a scald crow (*fennóc*)[170] or a raven (*bron* and *fiach*),[171] while the Mórrígan may also appear as a scald crow[172] or a black bird (*én dub*).[173] The two pig-keepers, among their many transformations, squabbled as hawks (*senén* 'old bird' = 'hawk' or 'crow').[174] Midir and Étaín appear as two swans (*ela*) around Tara.[175] Dispensing with her local low-cost Norwegian Air Shuttle, Derbforgaill journeys to

Ireland along with her servant in the form of swans.[176] Birds may also serve as messengers as when a gerfalcon (*gríb*) relates an attack on Emain by warriors from the Isle of Man,[177] while two ravens (*fiach*) spoke druidic secrets in the Otherword.[178] In addition they provide obvious items of comparison, such as that the colour of eyes may be like the eggs of a blackbird,[179] or that Fráech may be as white as the bird of Loch Ló,[180] or that the colour of Iubdán, the king of the Leprechauns, was that of a swan (*ela*) or the foam of a river.[181] Perhaps more interesting, we find them hunted and kept as pets.

The general term for 'bird' (*én*) occurs on many occasions. Cú Chulainn is often depicted as being especially proficient at hunting birds; for example, he brings down eight birds with a sling to impress the Ulstermen after his first raid[182] and he also kills (actually beheads with stones) pet birds perched on Ailill's and Medb's shoulders.[183] Challenging Medb's son Maine, he threatens to cut off his head in the same way as he would a blackbird (*lon*).[184] A king might also be prohibited from hunting birds as one of his *gessa*.[185] There are some passages which indicate that the hunting of birds was to obtain a meal.[186]

The most obvious consumable bird is the chicken (*cerc*) and there is a single mention of a hen's egg providing food,[187] while the cock (*cailech*) is only described as crowing.[188] The goose (*cadan*, *ged*)[189] and the 'barnacle goose' (*cauth* and *gigrann*)[190] were also consumed. In two different tales geese are linked with cranes.[191] Both the domestic fowl and geese are present in early medieval sites in Ireland,[192] so they would certainly have been known to Cathbad, and possibly Cattubuttas, but we lack any evidence for bird fauna from sites contemporary with the Iron Age (although we do know that domestic fowl were present in the British Late Iron Age).

The crane (*corr*) occurs either in association with the mention of wild geese[193] or in the frequently repeated description of Cú Chulainn's warp-spasm where he sucks one eye so far into his head that a crane could not reach it.[194] Although the crane is now absent from Ireland it has been recovered from a number of medieval sites so there is no reason to suspect that its mention derives from a foreign source.[195]

The swan (*ela* or *géis*) was noted for its ability to skim over the surface of the water[196] and its loud voice.[197] On his first raid, Cú Chulainn goes after a flock of swans as part of his returning party trick.[198] Cáer finds herself in a flock of 150 swans[199] and the upcast of Cú Chulainn's chariot wheels is likened to a flock of swans.[200]

Other than being singled out for its melodious voice,[201] the cuckoo (*cúach*) is described as a pet.[202] The corncrake (*tragna*) is portrayed as 'heavy' or loud,[203] the swallow (*ainnel* or *fannal*) is known for its swiftness[204] and its ability to lightly skim over water,[205] and the lark (*uiseóg*), naturally, ascends.[206]

Many references to birds either emphasize the valour of birds of prey or see them as harbingers of death and slaughter, such as when a falcon (*gríb*) brings news to the Ulstermen of a Manx attack.[207] Donnell the Red is likened to a falcon of dangerous valour[208] and among the gifts to his poet, Cú Roí leaves ten claws of the gerfalcon.[209]

The hawk (*sebac*) was a suitable metaphor for a warrior such as Cú Chulainn,[210] whose grasp is likened to that of a hawk's claws.[211] The Sons of Uisnech are called the 'three hawks of Slieve Gullion'.[212] Senb, the daughter of a druid, appears in the form of a hawk (*séig*).[213] And from three different tales we encounter the simile of a warrior attacking his opponents as a hawk would attack small birds.[214]

But the main bird of the tales is the raven or scald crow. Under the name of *badb*, which underlies the name of the war-goddess Bodb, we are dealing with a fierce bird[215] that is usually seen feeding on corpses.[216] It is no different with the more frequent names of *bron* or *fiach*, where ravens routinely feast on the dead.[217] It was a scald crow (*ennach*) that perched on Cú Chulainn's shoulder at his death.[218]

Mammals

The largest category of animals is the mammals, which can be divided into three groups. The first comprises references to non-native animals that generally provide metaphors for heroic behaviour. The second are the native wild animals that are usually incidental to the tales. Finally, there are the domestic animals upon which the economy was largely based.

Non-native mammals

Although the bear is known in Ireland from before its human colonization, the most recent finds tend to date to the Bronze Age[219] and it is suspected that the bear was extinct by the early medieval period.[220] The nature of the contexts in which it appears is entirely relegated to metaphors of warlike behaviour. The Ulster warrior Eirrge Echbél, for example, is described as a bear (*art*), violent and terrible.[221] Conall is described as a bear (*beithir*, a Germanic loanword)[222] as also the three Sons of Uisnech,[223] the two swineherds[224] and Ailill and Fergus.[225] In the *Fled Bricrenn* Cú Chulainn is a majestic bear (*math*)[226] and there are several references to fights likened to lions attacking bears (*mathgamain*).[227] Although the bear may have survived in Britain up to AD 1000, the regular metaphoric use of the animal does suggest a literary origin.

(above) The Rathiddy standing stone in Co. Louth near Knockbridge is traditionally regarded as the pillar to which the dying Cú Chulainn tied himself.

(right) The Lia Toll or Hurlstone near Ardee, Co. Louth. The hole was reputedly made by the near-sighted Ulster warrior Cethern, who mistook the 1.7-m-tall standing stone for the Connacht king, Ailill, and plunged both his sword and his fist through it.

III. (*above*) Dunseverick on the north Antrim coast was often represented as the farthest point in Ulster. The visible monuments date to long after the Ulster tales.

IV. (*left*) The impressive Staigue Fort, Co. Kerry, measures 27 m across and its walls stand nearly 6 m high.

V. (*below left*) Rathcroghan Mound, Co. Roscommon, is traditionally seen as the capital of Queen Medb, and encases circular timber structures comparable to those found at Navan Fort and Knockaulin.

VI. (*below*) Medb's tomb or *Miosgán Meadhbha* ('Medb's heap'), is an enormous stone cairn 60 m in diameter and 10 m high, presumably covering a Neolithic passage tomb.

VII. The 'Mound of Down' in Downpatrick, Co. Down, is traditionally identified as the seat of Celtchair mac Uthechar, one of the leading heroes of the Ulster cycle.

VIII. The earthen banks and mound that crown the summit of Navan Fort, Co. Armagh, the Ulster capital of Emain Macha.

IX. The beginning of the *Táin Bó Cuailnge* on page 55 of the *Lebor na hUidre*. Although faded, three different hands can be recognized on this 11th-century manuscript, which is housed in the Royal Irish Academy.

X. The beginning of the *Annals of the Four Masters* recounting the invasions of Cesair and Partholón.

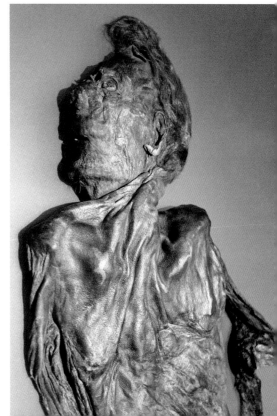

XII. (*below*) Clonycavan Man, Co. Meath, lived and died c. 400–200 BC. The man's hair was held upright by a hair gel, made from a species of pine that grew in southern France or Iberia.

XI. (*below*) An Irish warrior depicted in the *Book of Kells*. Note both the wearing of short trousers and the small round shield.

XIII. (*above left*) Oliver Sheppard's bronze statue of Cú Chulainn, originally made in 1911, was later placed in the General Post Office in Dublin, the headquarters of the Easter Rising.

XIV. (*above*) Statue of Cú Chulainn holding his foster-brother, Fer Diad, whom he has just slain in the *Táin Bó Cuailnge*. The statue stands in Ardee, Co. Louth, which derives its name from the encounter (*Baile Átha Fhirdhia*, 'the place of the ford of Fer Diad').

XV. (*left*) Oisin Kelly's evocative statue of the Children of Lir was made in 1964 and placed on display in the Garden of Remembrance in Dublin in 1966.

XVI. Queen Medb of Connacht was depicted on an Irish one-punt (pound) note (replaced by a pound coin in 1990). The other notes in the series featured genuine historical figures: Johannes Scotus Eriugena, Jonathan Swift, William Butler Yeats and Turlough O'Carolan.

XVII. Loyalist Cú Chulainn. Oliver Sheppard's statue of Cú Chulainn has here been re-employed to represent the Ulster Defence Association's resistance to Irish Unity.

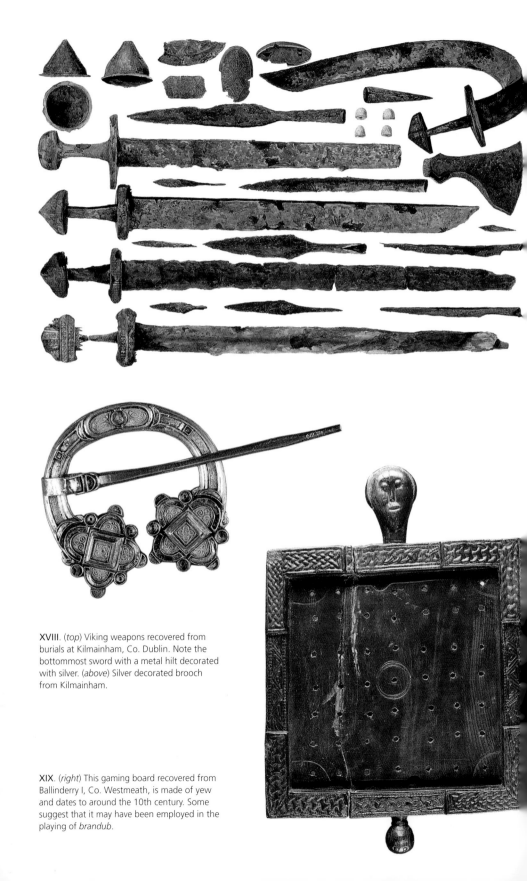

XVIII. (*top*) Viking weapons recovered from burials at Kilmainham, Co. Dublin. Note the bottommost sword with a metal hilt decorated with silver. (*above*) Silver decorated brooch from Kilmainham.

XIX. (*right*) This gaming board recovered from Ballinderry I, Co. Westmeath, is made of yew and dates to around the 10th century. Some suggest that it may have been employed in the playing of *brandub*.

The lynx (*lince*), another native species that fails to appear in Irish sites after about 6,000 years ago, also gets a mention.[228] The lynx appeared to survive in Scotland into the Iron Age but as its only occurrence in the Ulster cycle is a very late medieval tale and the Irish word is a clear borrowing from Latin *lynx*, it is most likely a borrowed literary motif, although quite from where remains uncertain.[229]

The lion (*léo*) is obviously a literary motif and a loanword that is also widely found in a number of tales as a description of Cú Chulainn,[230] Fergus,[231] Celtchair,[232] Eirrge Echbél,[233] Fer Diad,[234] and the three Sons of Uisnech.[235] The tiger (*tiger*), another obvious loan, seems to get a mention from a single tale.[236]

Native wild animals

In terms of citations, the major native wild animal in the *scéla* is the wild deer, which may appear under a variety of names. As expected, the stag (*dam*) may serve as a metaphor for a warrior[237] and it is just another form in which the two swine-keepers inflict mayhem on each other.[238] It may also be portrayed as prey, as when Cú Chulainn describes himself as a hound for the taking of deer (*oss*).[239] And when Fergus and Medb take a naked swim (shortly before Fergus is murdered) they are likened to a hart (*dam*) and a doe (*elit*).[240] Cú Chulainn is particularly proficient at both catching alive and hunting deer (although Giraldus would not have been impressed as he regarded Irish deer too fat to escape),[241] beginning with his first foray where he captures a wild deer (*os*,[242] *dam*,[243] *ag allaid*[244]) in the Fews mountains of Armagh, and later, during the *Táin*, he lives off venison (*osfeoil*).[245] In a late tale, we find that the herd of deer in the Fews that Cú Chulainn was driving belonged to Conchobar.[246] Perhaps this suggests the use of deer-forests, known from the Middle Ages,[247] where an area such as the Fews was seen as suitably remote from the cultivated fields on the Plain of Macha. The red deer was present in Ireland since the Neolithic and has been recovered from Navan Fort, the site of Emain Macha,[248] and regularly on early medieval sites.[249]

The hare (*fiamuin*) is noted for its swiftness,[250] as is the *íaru*, which has been translated 'weasel' (*Mustela nivalis*), although the only native Irish member of the *Mustela* genus is actually the stoat[251] (*Mustela erminea*);[252] it may be hunted.[253]

The otter (*doburchú*) occurs twice in the relatively early *Táin Bó Fraích*, once when it is simply hunted[254] but more interestingly with reference to harps (or better, lyres) that are protected in bags of otter skin.[255] The famous lyre recovered from the Anglo-Saxon burial at Sutton Hoo was held in a bag of beaver skin. Ireland lacks beavers (as Giraldus rightly tells us) and so a harp-bag of otter skin would be an obvious alternative. The only other certain reference to the otter is its role in drinking Cú Chulainn's blood in a late version of his death tale.[256] There is, however, a questionable reference to an *onchú* which has been possibly identified with the otter or leopard (but see below), perched on the shoulders of the Ulster troublemaker Dubthach.[257] The otter is among Ireland's native fauna and has been found on a number of early medieval sites.

The pine marten occurs in a single context: Medb has a pet marten (*togmall*) running around her shoulders that Cú Chulainn killed with his sling.[258] The marten is native to Ireland and has occasionally turned up on early medieval sites.[259]

There are little more than passing references to sea mammals such as the walrus (*rosualt*) and seal (*rón*),[260] and even a reference to a whale (*bledmall*),[261] and the whole skeleton of a whale (*míl mór* 'big beast) is also mentioned.[262] The seal is found on early medieval sites.

The fox (*sinnach*) receives sparse attention. On Fráech's hunting expeditions, foxes are hunted along with deer, hare and boar.[263] There is also reference to the track of a fox in grassland.[264] Finally, Fergus' exile is described as his being forced to live among wolves and foxes.[265] Although the fox may have been reintroduced (it was native but seems to have become extinct about 13,000 years ago), it has certainly been in Ireland since the Bronze Age.[266]

The wolf receives more mentions, appearing under a number of different names including *cú*, which otherwise designates the domestic dog.[267] Far more common is the use of *fáel* (often with *cú*) where we have the similes of a wolf among sheep[268] or attacking pigs.[269] The wolf is predictably employed as a metaphor for warlike behaviour as, for example, with Cú Chulainn[270] or with reference to raiding, a topic Kim McCone has dealt with in depth in his discussion of the wolf-like behaviour of Irish and other European warrior bands.[271] The same tales that employ *fáel* may also employ *mac tíre* (literally 'son of the land'),[272] as when Conaire Mór takes wolves as hostages to insure the good behaviour of their kind. Finally, as would be appropriate to a war-goddess, the Mórrígan takes the form of a she-wolf (*sod*).[273]

Some of the 'native' fauna are problematic. That a warrior might travel on water like a squirrel (?) or stoat (?) (*íaru*)[274] is hardly a typical expression today although both can swim, and the stoat is regarded as a particularly strong swimmer. It is noteworthy that the squirrel is not listed among the native fauna of Ireland (i.e., those that arrived either before or immediately after the last Ice Age),[275] nor is it recorded among the wild fauna recovered from Irish early medieval sites that do reveal the remains of otters, badgers and hares.[276] This is curious because the animal is mentioned in other

Irish texts such as the Irish Augustine's 7th-century study of miracles of the Bible, which pondered how wolves, deer, wild boar, badgers, hares and squirrels got to Ireland.[277] The earliest archaeological recovery of squirrel remains is from the 10th- and 11th-century Viking levels in Dublin.[278]

If the Irish *griun* really means 'hedgehog' (*gráineóg*), then it is known for its grip as Cú Chulainn's fingers and toes are likened to the curled claws of a hedgehog.[279] The identification of *griun* with hedgehog in the *Táin* is problematic, however, in that the hedgehog does not appear to be native to Ireland, was specifically excluded from the native fauna by Giraldus,[280] and its earliest occurrence on an Irish archaeological site is from 13th-century Waterford,[281] suggesting that it may have been introduced by the Normans or, possibly, somewhat earlier by the Welsh if one accepts Mac Coitir's attractive theory that Irish *gráineóg* was formed under the influence of Welsh *draenog* 'thorny little one, i.e. hedgehog'.[282]

Domestic mammals

Dog

The dog is generally cited in contexts that emphasize its function as a watchdog, either of a settlement or flocks, a hunter and a fighter, for which reason it is generally translated as a 'hound' rather than just 'dog'. The basic word for the hound is *cú*, which is most famously embedded in the warrior name of Sétanta, Cú Chulainn 'the hound of Culann', who is also frequently described as the 'hound of Ulster'.[283] The element *cú* is often found in compounds as *árchú* 'battle-hound', *mílchú* 'hunting dog'[284] and in some late tales as our troublesome *onchú*, perhaps some ferocious type of dog if not an otter or leopard.[285] Measurements of dog skeletal remains from the Late Bronze Age site of Haughey's Fort,[286] which lies near to Emain Macha, and those recovered from the high-status early medieval occupation at Knowth, Co. Meath, indicate that the largest dogs would be roughly comparable in size to an Alsatian.[287]

Like Cú Chulainn other heroes can also be likened to hounds, such as the three Sons of Uisnech,[288] Cú Roí (whose name also contains the word for hound),[289] and the Three Red-Hounds of Cualu.[290] The names of the greatest watchdogs are known, including Ailbe, the guard-dog of Leinster,[291] and Conbel, who guarded a half of a province.[292] For this reason the hound was a suitable royal gift, as when Conaire Mór presented the hosteller Da Derga with 27 hounds on silver chains.[293] That the dogs might be kept on leads is indicated in other tales as well.[294] The hound appears to have been an integral part of any retinue and if placement is indicative of social status, they were reckoned above the accompanying servants. When driven into exile, the Sons of Uisnech leave with their warriors, women, 150 hounds and servants.[295] Cormac sets out with his own warriors, women, boys, hounds and servants.[296] And Senchán maintains a retinue of 150 professors, second professors, hounds, male servants, women and craftsmen.[297] That the hounds were highly prized is also clear from the account of Ailbe, the Leinster hound that was sought by the rulers of both Connacht and Ulster.[298]

The hounds were obviously employed for hunting,[299] both adults and also pups (*cuilén*).[300] The *Dindshenchas* relate the use of a hundred hunting dogs on a wild boar hunt.[301] Cú Chulainn describes himself as a hound strong for combat[302] and when Cethern, the bane of the Ulster ambulance service, enters the fray in the *Táin* his *mílchú* runs before him.[303] Some hounds are such effective killers[304] that they have Otherworldly origins. The most famous are the three most ferocious hounds, all from a single litter: the hound of Culann whom Cú Chulainn slew,[305] the hound Ailbe owned by Mac Dathó, and the hound of Celtchair, Dóelchú, whose master had to put him down but died himself from a drop of the hound's poisonous blood.[306]

On occasion we find references to pet dogs such as Baiscne, the young hound of Medb,[307] or the lap dog (*messán*) of Boand.[308] Osteological evidence for lap dogs is known from the early medieval period: the smallest at Lagore had a shoulder height of only 26 cm. According to Irish tradition the lap dog was introduced into Ireland from Britain in the years around AD 186 by Cairbre Músc, who obtained one by a devious ploy to circumvent the British prohibition against an Irishmen acquiring a lap dog.[309] Unfortunately we lack sufficient dog remains to know precisely how early a specially bred smaller dog appeared in Ireland.

The female (*sod*) is rarely mentioned although they were clearly used as hunters.[310] In a late tale Fergus kills a ferocious she-hound,[311] while from the Mythological cycle we find that as an infant, the future mother of Conaire Mór was chucked in a kennel with a bitch and her offspring to die.[312]

Finally, we have the prohibition against eating the flesh of a dog set on Cú Chulainn, the violation of which leads to and foreshadows his death.[313] Dogs were clearly eaten during the Late Bronze Age and this practice continued into the Iron Age, where there is evidence for the consumption of dog at Tara;[314] too few dog remains were recovered from Knockaulin and Navan Fort to make such an assessment. Evidence for the consumption of dog flesh is generally absent from early medieval sites although around the 10th century some of the residents of medieval Dublin had been reduced to eating dog.[315]

Cat

The cat (*catt*) occupies a peculiar place in comparisons. When Cú Chulainn's charioteer wishes to employ reverse psychology and encourage the champion to try harder,
he reminds him that his opponent has gone over him as a tail goes over a cat.[316] A
swift action is likened to a cat making for cream.[317] And one of the feats of a warrior
is known as the cat-feat.[318] On one occasion magical cats from Cruachain are
unleashed on three Ulster heroes vying for the championship of Ulster.[319] Also, the
cauldron that prevents the deadly spear of Celtchair going into complete meltdown is
filled with the blood of cats and dogs.[320] In their mice-killing capacity, they are satirized for not doing enough in one tale.[321]

The domestic cat, which appears on early medieval sites in Ireland, was probably
introduced via contacts with Roman Britain.[322] It is absent from the faunas recovered
from the few Iron Age ceremonial sites at Tara, Knockaulin and Navan Fort.

Cow

The primary unit of wealth in early medieval Ireland was the cow and this is abundantly attested in the tales where there is a large vocabulary devoted to describing
cattle (*ag, búar, cethrae, crod, éit, indile, slabrae*) including with respect to age, e.g.
calf (*gamnach, lóeg*), bull-calf (*tairbíne*), sex, e.g., cow (*bó, ferb*), heifer (*samaisc,
sesc*), reproductive capacity, e.g. bull (*damrad, tarb*) vs ox (*dam*) and dairy use, e.g.
'milch cow' (*blichtach*), dry cow (*lulgach*). As might be predicted, the bull (*tarb*)
might be employed as the appropriate metaphor for a warrior.[323] On the other hand,
one of the insults directed at a flagging warrior (see 'cat' above) was to say that his
opponent had gone over him as a cow goes over a calf.[324]

The association of cattle with dairy products is substantial. One of the major
fears of Cú Chulainn in the *Táin* is that the Ulstermen will be either deprived of their
milch cows[325] or that they will be forced to slaughter them for meat during the
winter.[326] Elsewhere in the *Táin* the Mórrígan milks a cow with three teats.[327] As an
act of mourning for the death of Cú Chulainn's son, the Ulstermen prevented the
calves of the province from going to their cows.[328] In another tale we read of a wonder
cow that yields milk for 29 nuns.[329] At one time it was suggested that dairying
appeared in Ireland quite late, in the early medieval period,[330] and if so, this would
have provided a useful chronological index for this motif in the tales. But more recent
analysis of the residue of fats in Irish Neolithic pottery has indicated that the Irish
have been milking cattle since the 4th millennium BC,[331] so milking per se cannot be
used to indicate a late date for this element of the economy.

Cattle are also associated with beef, frequently in an expression that combines beef with pork, for example, in the *Táin* Fergus directs that Cú Chulainn receive an ox (*dam*), a flitch of bacon and a barrel of wine,[332] an expression found in other tales as well.[333] Elsewhere we find that cattle were broiled,[334] and in one tale seven oxen are consumed at a feast.[335] Cattle were also associated with ploughing in a very few of the tales;[336] the hospitaller Blaí maintained a plough-team with each herd and, as the name *seisrech* indicates (*sé* 'six'), the plough-team consisted of six beasts.[337] And for ultimate traction is the log or stock in the hand of a giant that would require 20 yoke of oxen to drag.[338]

The size of the herds varies. The only mention of the number of heifers accompanying a bull (*tarb*) occurs in the *Táin*, where the Donn Cuailgne is with 15 heifers.[339] The mother of Fráech gives her son 12 cows from the Otherworld[340] and each of these 12 yielded a measure of milk for 50.[341] These figures are roughly in accord with the (idealized?) herd size expected of a *bóaire of excellence*, a relatively affluent landowner in early medieval Ireland.[342] The law tracts dictate herd sizes for individuals up to the 20 cows, 2 bulls and 6 oxen required of a *bóaire of adjudication*,[343] while landowners of higher status distribute their livestock across a variety of vassals or clients. So the larger herds that we have in the literature might be regarded as still realistic. Eochu, for example, maintained 40 milch cows (*lulgach*) for feeding children,[344] the hospitaller Blaí had 140 cows in each of his seven herds,[345] Conaire made a gift to Da Derga of 100 cows,[346] Ailill and his wife Medb attempted to acquire Mac Dathó's famous hound for 160 milch cows,[347] and the greedy Athairne's fort held 700 head of cattle.[348] Also, large numbers of driven cattle may not be exaggerations as 140 cows were required for provisioning a raid on Cuailgne[349] and Ailill loses 100 milch cows and 140 oxen in a raid,[350] while Ailill Find loses 540 cattle in the same way.[351] In fact, the number of cattle recovered in these raids is actually rather unimpressive compared with the number of cattle reportedly seized in the annals from 985 to 1059, where the average for each of ten raids listed was 1,100.[352]

In the initial contest of wealth between Medb and Ailill, each has their herds brought from various areas of Connacht,[353] while in one tale a girl drives cattle, pigs and sheep together.[354] This raises the issue of the balance of the basic livestock of cattle, pigs and sheep. In late prehistoric sites there is no evidence of parity of numbers, with cattle or pig proving the majority in all cases except for Dún Aonghusa, where the island situation favoured the predominance of sheep. Otherwise, sheep run an exceptionally poor third to cattle and pigs. In the list of Cú Roí's gifts, however, we find him bequeathing 10 oxen and 10 sheep/goats but 100 pigs.[355] Also, in the law text *Críth Gabhlach* the 'standard' requirements in terms of livestock numbers for an *ocaire* is 7 cows, 1 bull, 7 pigs, 7 sheep and 1 horse[356] while a higher-ranking *bóaire of adjudication* should have 20 cows, 2 bulls, 6 oxen, 20 pigs, 20 sheep, 400 hogs, 2 brood sows and 1 saddle horse.[357] These figures are at variance with the recovery of animal bones from our few Iron Age sites that indicate cattle or pigs as the most numerous livestock, with sheep hardly represented.[358] So when we find a raid that returns with 100 milch cows, 140 oxen and also 300 'small livestock' (sheep, goats?), we may suspect that the tale is more likely to derive from the economy of the time of Cathbad rather than the Iron Age or the earliest medieval period.

Although the great importance of dairying is widely in evidence, the heroes of the Ulster cycle are very rarely depicted actually drinking milk but rather an alcoholic beverage. Only in one instance, where the Ulstermen are holed up in a fort dying of thirst, do they seem to crave milk, which the ultimate greedy poet Athairne dumps over a cliff rather than sharing it with his defenders.[359] Milk is also intended for children.[360]

Cattle also appear in ritual, the most prominent being the *tarbfeis*, the bull-feast from which a king would be chosen.[361]

Despite the importance of the cows, there is little full description. There is a classic reference to red-eared white cows,[362] a description that just might be referring to a breed also identified in early Britain.[363] There are also references to a moiled (hornless) cow,[364] and a calf three hands high,[365] and the etymology of *erc*, with reference to Iuchra's cattle, indicates that they were spotted or red.[366]

Finally, we find cattle employed in an 8th-century chat-up line that, outside of medieval Ireland, might just work in the state of Texas but get a slap anywhere else. When the Ulster hero Noíse, standing on the banks of the Ulster capital of Emain Macha, first sees Deirdre, the most beautiful woman in Ireland, he remarks within her hearing: 'mighty fine heifer walking by'.[367]

Pig

After cattle the pig is the most widely attested domestic livestock and in addition to the general term for pig (*muc*) the *scéla* provide a variety of different words indicating sex, e.g., sow (*crain*[368]), boar (*torc*,[369] *tríath*[370]), litter (*crithail*[371]), and its use as meat, e.g., salted pork (*tinne*[372]). References to the pig do not always indicate whether the animal described is domestic or wild, although various adjectives for 'wild' are sometimes added. That a hero might be likened to a boar is hardly unexpected; Cú Chulainn, for example, is described as a 'brave boar'.[373] While the Irish encountered classical references to warriors likened to boars,[374] I doubt that we need look outside of Ireland for this motif in Irish literature.

When Ailill and Medb match their possessions, the herds (muccrad) of pigs are driven in from 'woods and sloping glens and solitary places'.[375] Herds of pig belonging to Conchobar were driven to the Fews mountains.[376] There is a curious incident where seven maidens, inviting their own abduction, drive their herds of cattle, pigs and sheep together.[377] Conaire Mór gives Da Derga 100 fattened pigs,[378] and the same number was left by Cú Roí to his poet.[379]

That the consumption of pork was of high status is most clearly seen in the story of Mac Dathó's pig, which was the object of contention between the men of Ulster and Connacht as to whom would go the champion's portion and the right to divide the pig.[380] Another association of royalty with pork consumption is the strange exchange between Cú Chulainn, who was off performing one of his boyhood deeds, and his king, Conchobar, who peckishly informs him 'if I had a roast pig, I should be alive'.[381] But this hardly competes with Fergus, who could only be sated by seven pigs,[382] which, coincidentally, was the number of women he required unless he enjoyed the services of his own wife. Just as the Otherworld might produce cows yielding limitless milk, it could also provide resurrectable pigs that might be slain, consumed and then brought to life again.[383] There are few useful descriptions of pigs other than the mention of a black boar with bristles in the story about Dá Derga's hostel.[384]

As mentioned above, a recurring motif is the combination of beef and pork (tinne) at meals.[385] Another accompaniment to pork was boiled cakes.[386]

Horse

In the Ulster cycle horses occur most frequently in the context of the chariot, which was pulled by a team of two horses. Although the AFM indicates that four-horse chariots were introduced in 1024 BC, this motif never occurs again in the Mythological tales, although we find it often enough in the Ulster cycle where it is likely borrowed from classical literature (see Chapter Eight). There are two primary words for horse, the older being ech, which would generally indicate an elite horse, a noble steed, and a gabor, which at times could indicate the same status of animal as an ech[387] but might also refer to a far less prized animal such as the mangy old horse yoked to the comical Iliach's chariot in the Táin.[388] Another word, grafand, occurs in the Táin where it describes the horses of Ulstermen racing to assemble against Medb's army.[389] The mare (láir) is occasionally mentioned, most notably in the dismissive verdict of the failure of Medb's army in the Táin that is likened to a herd of horses led by a mare.[390] And mares provide another victim for the (tedious) simile of a lion attacking a herd of (take your pick).[391] The herd of horses was a *graig* (probably a loanword from Latin *grex*).

In terms of description there is an enormous disparity between the sparse descriptions of cattle and pigs and the adjectival overkill with respect to the horse. Will Sayers has isolated around 150 discrete adjectives that are used to describe the horse in the Ulster cycle, noting one description alone that ran to 22 adjectives.[392] He cites as a major inspiration for these descriptions the *Etymologiae* of Isidore of Seville, the book that was so valued by the early Irish that they exchanged the *Táin* for it. Isidore provides an extensive list of all the features that one would employ to describe a horse as well as its behaviour, almost all of which we can recover from the Ulster tales.

The horse is depicted not only as a draft animal but also occasionally as a combatant in its own right. As part of a test to determine the champion of Ulster, the three contestants confront not only a very formidable opponent in the form of Ercol but also his nasty gelding (*gerrán*), who manages to kill the horses of Lóegaire and Conall.[393] More famous is the defence of the dying Cú Chulainn by his own horse, the Liath Macha.[394]

In addition to the role of the horse in warfare, chariots were also raced. In one of the *Dindshenchas*, Ireland is called 'the land of swift horses'[395] and there are a number of references to horse races, most prominently the one between Macha and the Ulster king's chariot team in the origin tale of Emain Macha.[396] Fast horses were prized and Conaire Mór gave Da Derga 100 such horses,[397] while Medb attempted to bribe Fer Diad to fight his foster-brother Cú Chulainn with a gift of five horses.[398] Cú Roí's legacy ran to an extravagant 10,000 horses.[399]

The consumption of horse flesh is obliquely attested in the literature, for instance when there is an injunction against entering a chariot for a period of 27 days after one has eaten horse meat as well as in the case of a number of saint's lives that inveigh against the consumption of horse.[400] Remains of clearly butchered horses are reasonably well attested at both Tara and Navan Fort during the Iron Age.[401]

Sheep/goat

Although there are not a great many mentions of sheep they do suggest that these animals had some economic importance. The oldest word for sheep (*oí*), described in one tale as the poetic word for the animal more usually designated the *caera*,[402] is among the animals in Cú Roí's legacy, where they number 'ten-hundred'.[403] During the contest to see who had the greatest number of possessions between Medb and her husband, great flocks of sheep were driven in to be counted.[404] Among them is a ram (*reithe*) worth a cumal, the usual unit of value for a cow.[405] On the two occasions where the drivers are mentioned, they are women. Girls drive cattle, sheep and pigs together in one tale,[406] while Fráech and Conall come across an old woman herding sheep in the Alps.[407] The sparks in Cú Chulainn's mouth when he undergoes his spasms are said to be as large as the skin of a ram (*molt*).[408] The familiar image of a wolf among the sheep occurs in at least two of the tales.[409] Finally, there is the famous description of the suicidal Deirdre trapped between the murderer of her lover and the man who ordered the hit, likened to an ewe between two rams.[410]

The goat hardly gets a mention in the Ulster tales. The white skin of a she-goat (*erp*) was used to cover the harps at Cruachain.[411] In a late version of the death of Cú Chulainn we find the hero confronting the monstrous Children of Cailitin who bore heads resembling those of goats (*boc*) and rams,[412] while among the legacy of Cú Roí are small domesticated livestock, which is glossed either sheep, goats (*gabor*) or heifers.[413] The goat is not regarded as particularly important either in law texts or in faunas of any period, although definite evidence for the animal does occasionally turn up in later prehistoric excavations.[414]

Conclusion

Unlike architecture and, especially, material culture, the natural environment and economy of the ancient tales is not particularly time sensitive: changes in the flora and fauna were so slow that a simple checklist from the Iron Age is just as likely to be repeated in the medieval period. Of the various arboreal species, for example, we have seen that only one tree, the pine, poses a problem as to whether it derived from a purely native environment or indicated that the imagined world and its architecture was Scotland instead of Ireland. There are two reasons to suspect that we may be dealing with a transferred literary motif. The first concerns the use of pine in building a high-status hall, where elsewhere the building material is described as oak. In general, this makes poor sense in that pine is naturally neither insect nor weather resistant, so the construction of an entire house of pine hardly trumps one built in the more desirable oak (although, it must be admitted, the ancient pine (Scots pine) of Ireland was probably more durable than its modern replacements). The use of bog pine is, of course, possible but so far unattested for the period in question. Second, although the pine is hardly mentioned in the Bible, the cedar, a tree at least within the same general family, is used in the construction of high-status buildings, for columns, interior walling and roof planks.[415] If Solomon could build in cedar then, perhaps, it was also possible that the capital of Connacht might be constructed in a similar wood. But is should be noted that there is no evidence that the early Irish confused these woods as they employed the loanword *ced(a)ir* or *cedrus* to translate 'cedar'. Of less import is the prohibition against burning willow that was certainly not observed in the Iron Age[416] or early medieval period,[417] where it has been recovered from ring ditches associated with cremation burials.

Among the animals there are few to concern us. Obviously, the *nathair* 'snake' does not make a good fit with the Irish environment and its appearance in no less than nine of the tales does require some consideration. Regarding its etymology, we are dealing with an inherited word; there is no reason to see the name of the snake as a loanword. It is likely then that the Celts, who were the linguistic ancestors of the Irish, brought both the name (*natrak-*) and the concept of a snake with them to Ireland. Of the ten references to serpents, six of them are specifically associated with venom, suggesting that we are dealing with the motif of a poisonous snake. There are at least two sources for this motif in serpent-less Ireland. One is the Bible, where occurrences of the snake are frequently associated with their venom.[418] The other is neighbouring Scotland, which was well within the purview of the world of the Ulster cycle. It has only one species of serpent, the adder, the only poisonous snake that is found throughout Britain, but this may have been sufficient for the earliest Irish to both retain their linguistic ancestor's name for the snake and the memory of its danger.

Among the wild animals, we are most likely dealing with literary motifs in some instances, for instance bear, lynx, lion and tiger. We have seen that there are two slightly problematic animals of minimal citation: the squirrel, which so far refuses to yield up identifiable bones on early medieval sites, and the hedgehog, which gives all the appearance of being introduced in the Norman period, after the date that it is possibly mentioned in our manuscripts.

Other than the cat and horse, all the domesticated animals described in the texts have been in Ireland since the Neolithic (and there is even evidence for the wild cat from the Mesolithic,[419] although the tales no doubt have the domestic cat in mind). The domestic horse appears in Ireland by *c.* 1000 BC, so it was well known to the Iron Age Irish and in all subsequent periods. It might be noted though that while the horse was consumed during the Iron Age, at least at the major ceremonial centres, there does not seem to be any reflex of this in the tales. The extended descriptions of the horses appear to have been generated by a reading of Isidore of Seville rather than any local equine-praise poetry. It is also doubtful that our Iron Age *fili*, Katu-butos, would have engaged in poetic references to the domestic cat, which probably entered Ireland only as contact with Roman Britain intensified towards the end of the Iron Age.

As for the main domestic livestock, the primacy of cattle followed by pig does not seem to have undergone any major change from at least the Iron Age, probably the Bronze Age, onwards, into the beginning of the medieval period. On the other hand, the parity of sheep among lists of animals does seem to be a product of the world of Cathbad rather than his predecessors.

In short, the Ulster tales provide us with a general picture of the Irish landscape (mixed on occasion with exotic animals from the Bible or classical literature) that could date from at least the Bronze Age until the Middle Ages.

CHAPTER SIX

The Built Environment

Tara – every high, every conspicuous place
On which are dwellings, strong forts;
Tara – every peaked, pointed place
Except for *Emain*, the far-seen.[1]

I n the last chapter we saw how there was very little evidence of recollection of
Ireland's past landscape, other than that Armagh stood where once there was only
forest. The built environment was similarly taken for granted although we do find
a reference which claims that about the time of Conchobar 'there was at that time in
Ireland neither ditches, fences nor walls'.[2] In actual fact, the Iron Age was a very good
time to stumble into ditches, or climb fences and walls, as we will see below.

The archaeological evidence for the built environment of our Iron Age poet,
Katu-butos, is a matter of extremes. On the one hand, he could have frequented the
major ceremonial sites of Tara,[3] Navan Fort (Emain Macha),[4] Knockaulin (Dún
Ailinne)[5] and Rathcroghan (Cruachain),[6] the first three of which have seen extensive
excavations while the fourth, the Connacht capital, has been the subject of a major
geophysical survey. In all these sites we find traces of a large enclosure marked out by
a bank and ditch and within three of them enormous circular timber structures consisting of concentric rings of posts. But outside these elite sites there are only a few
somewhat less extravagant sites before we plummet to odd traces of huts and hearths
and other slight indications of Iron Age settlement. One feature that is increasingly
being uncovered is the ring ditch, a small enclosure surrounded by a ditch which may
be variously interpreted as a small settlement site, a ritual site (when there is absolutely no trace whatsoever for occupation in the interior), or a ploughed-out barrow
(especially when there are traces of mortuary remains). There are at least 28 such sites
now dated to the Iron Age.[7] As for the homes of the ordinary farmer, there is some
very meagre evidence for circular houses, built of either upright posts or wall-slots,

measuring about 6 m in diameter.[8] In addition to the incredibly sparse evidence for domestic structures, there are also a number of linear earthworks, large barriers running across the Irish landscape consisting of one or more banks and ditches and, in some cases, timber palisades. As we have already seen in the last chapter, building activity involving oak only flourished up until about 50 BC, after which there is no more evidence for structures built of oak until *c.* AD 250 or later.

Cattubuttas, who recited his poems in AD 400–700, occupied a world the architectural evidence of which was only marginally better than that of his Iron Age predecessor. By now the large Iron Age ritual sites had fallen into disuse. The ditch surrounding the Ulster capital at Navan Fort, for example, had originally been dug to over 4.5 m in depth, but by the time of Cattubuttas the bottom 3 m had already silted up (FIG. 6.1). The earlier ceremonial places were now being replaced by the churches of a new religion. These ecclesiastical sites, along with monasteries, obviously are not part of the imagined world of the earliest Irish tradition. By the 6th and 7th centuries a series of new settlement types emerged. These comprised the earliest ringforts, bank and ditched enclosures usually measuring *c.* 28–35 m across, surrounding a house and possibly other structures. Most ringforts provided settlement for the well-to-do farmer and were usually surrounded by a single ditch but on occasion we find two or even three ditches that are often presumed to indicate the higher status of the site. In addition we also find the earliest cashels – equivalent structures

6.1. The Navan ditch, initially dug in c. 95 BC, and the relative dates of our three *filid* and the *Táin* according to the Irish annals.

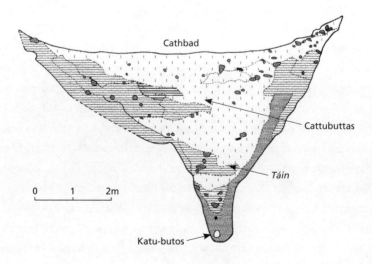

built of stone – and crannogs, artificial islands, presumably defensive sites, constructed offshore in Ireland's countless lakes; the impressive architectural remains of these latter sites consist of timber platforms and walls.

Cathbad composed or recited his stories during one of the most architecturally visible periods in Irish history (AD 700–1000). By the end of his time the Irish landscape was covered with over 60,000 settlement enclosures, comprising primarily ringforts and cashels (c. 45,000 in number), and crannogs (1,200 are known). As time went on there is some evidence that there was a progressive alteration in the architecture of the ringfort. The earlier flat ringforts were gradually replaced, at least in some areas, by raised platforms, and it has also been suggested that sites tended to be relocated towards good arable soils rather than the earlier primarily pastoral lands.[9] The interiors of the sites were occupied by either a circular or rectangular house averaging on the order of 6 m diameter (or 6 or 7 m long if rectangular) that constituted a single-room dwelling although, frequently enough, there might be a small attached adjunct building. Around 550 houses are known. From this period there are also found souterrains, underground passages and chambers, normally walled with stone, that may have been initially built in the 6th or 7th centuries but usually date to the 8th to 12th centuries. They number in the region of 3,500. Naturally, this is also a period from which we recover many of the monuments of the early Christian church in Ireland.

We will begin our survey of the built environment with the least substantial sites and work our way up to the major provincial capitals.

Field camps

There are several words that describe the military encampment in the field. The commonest is *dúnad* 'encampment', a word derived from the Old Irish word for 'fort' (*dún*). The context of its use is often so vague that it is difficult to determine whether it is referring to an architectural entity, the type of fortified field camp that the Romans erected on campaign, or whether it is being used socially, merely to describe an assemblage of people camping together. Certainly there is almost no description of the appearance of such an encampment nor any certain evidence that they were protected. There is a slight possibility that they might have had a rampart or ditch but this is uncertain. In the *Táin*, when Conchobar rallies the Ulstermen for the final battle he urges them to sharpen their swords, fight the battle, dig a ditch (*búrach*) and strike their shields.[10] While the Ulster Division may certainly have dug ditches in the First World War, it is difficult to imagine what purpose would be served by ditch-digging as one was preparing to attack an enemy position. Furthermore, we are reminded in another tale that at that time there were no 'ditches (*clad*), fences nor walls; the plain on every side was unbroken.'[11] As the Irish were familiar with the descriptions of military camps in their account of the siege of Troy[12] and other 'classical' battles where the erection of a palisade or digging of a ditch (and even the building of towers) seems to have been absolutely standard, there is really very little if any evidence that these descriptions 'contaminated' the native view of a field camp.

Before setting up a camp (*gabáil dúnaid*),[13] the area might be cleared. Who precisely did the hard work is not indicated except for the instance when an unfortunate work-team of ten cupbearers (*deogbaire*) and ten warriors were slaughtered by Cú Chulainn while they were establishing a camp.[14]

Another common term for a 'camp' was *longphort* whose, the context of which in the Ulster tales is identical to that of the *dúnad*. The word *longphort* (as well as Welsh *llongborth*) is a compound of two Latin loanwords (*longus* and *portus*, i.e. *long* 'ship' plus *port* 'place, shore') but had clearly come to mean something more general than simply a place to tie up and protect boats. It was glossed *castrum*, the Latin word for an army camp. Annalistic references to the *longphort* for the 9th and 10th centuries designate exclusively Viking encampments, a specific type of defensive site situated adjacent to a river and which could be secured by a ditch, bank or palisade, and after much searching Ireland appears to have begun revealing some of its Viking camps.[15] They are first recorded in the annals for the year 841, and the annals indicate the existence of at least 20 such sites that provided staging areas for Viking raids. However, by the early 10th century *longphort* was also applied to native fortified sites as well.

Often the *dúnad* is paired with *longphort* and since they mean pretty well the same thing this provides a real headache for translators who render this as 'camp and stronghold'[16] or 'fort and camp'[17] or throw in the towel and just use one word, 'encampment'.[18] To compound the redundancy there is a third word for 'camp', *sosad*,[19] the use of which is indistinguishable from the other two and which may even be paired with *longphort*.[20] In one instance we also find *costud* 'camp, a halting', probably from Latin *custōdia*.[21]

Those living in the camps lived in a tent (*pupall*), a word that the Irish borrowed from Latin *papilio*,[22] which basically means 'butterfly, moth' but was adopted as Roman military slang to indicate a 'tent'. It occurs numerous times in the course of the *Táin*, from which we can assemble a functional rather than a descriptive image. Throughout most of the tales there is no description of the tents themselves other than about three instances where we find reference to multicoloured tents in the legacy of Cú Roí[23] or Emer's erection of a multicoloured tent over the body of Cú Chulainn in a very late tale.[24] The only other mention of a specific colour for a tent is the 'bright scarlet' tents that were erected on boats.[25]

The tents obviously possessed a door but during the *Táin* the Ulstermen become so excited that they burst through the back wall of their tent, naked.[26]

Tents are associated with the major leaders (Ailill, Fergus, Medb) and their forces and it is within them that the leaders received both other royalty such as Cú Roí or each other. The tents housed sleeping equipment (beds *(coilcthech)* and blankets *(brothracha)*) as well as more general items.[27] Little else is mentioned of their interior function other than the deliberately scatological reference to Medb urinating on the floor of her tent during the *Táin*.[28]

In addition to the tent we also find a reference to an 'open tent' *(bélscálan)*, which, like the tents, was built during troop movements.[29] A more common alternative is Irish *both* 'bothy, hut' which, again like the tents, was erected by Medb's army in the *Táin*[30] or, when harassed by Cú Chulainn, could not be set up.[31]

The bothy is, of course, not limited to military campaigns and we also find some evidence for 'hunting booths' *(fian botha)*. Deirdre in her *ménage à quatre* had three such booths that served three separate functions: cooking, eating and sleeping.[32] The *both* could also serve for sheltering livestock[33] and in at least one instance it was explicitly a shed for cattle *(bóboth = 'cowshed')*.[34]

In addition to shelters for the troops, the Irish raiding parties also constructed pens and sheds for their cattle. On its way through the Cooley peninsula, Medb's army constructed cowsheds or byres (Irish *lías*) for their attendant herds of cattle,[35] which explains the place name Lías Líac. Such sheds could also be erected as more permanent structures, as suggested by reference to a *gamlías* 'winter-shed'.[36]

Ever since the initial settlement of Ireland in the Mesolithic, *c.* 8000 BC, the occupants probably built temporary shelters, although it is unlikely that they employed skins until the Neolithic when both domestic animals (cattle, sheep, goat) and red deer appear to have been introduced. In a practical sense, then, the concept of a tent could be of native origin although we have no certain evidence of them other that two Iron Age pegs excavated beside the Corlea trackway that certainly look like tent pegs (FIG. 6.2).[37] Nevertheless, throughout the prehistoric period many if not most sites offering evidence for occupation yield palimpsests of stakeholes whose posts probably supported temporary structures.

On the other hand, as the word for 'tent' is clearly a loanword from Latin, we can ask whether the tented Irishman is primarily a foreign import or literary motif? On

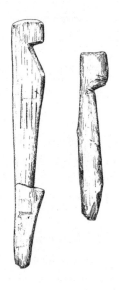

6.2. 'Tent' pegs from Corlea, Co. Longford (lengths 19.2 and 13 cm).

the neighbouring island, for example, Roman soldiers traditionally slept eight to a tent made of cattle or goat hide and there was enough raiding in Britain by Irish warriors that they could not have avoided encountering tents. The curious thing is that the Irish, like the Welsh,[38] borrowed a word from the jargon of the Roman soldier and not from the classical texts where heroes might sleep, once protected by a ditch and rampart, in their tent (*tentoria*).[39]

Some slight literary parallels may exist. The Bible is not an obvious source although there is mention of a multicoloured door of a tent.[40] But when Emer places Cú Chulainn's body under a tent, this is reminiscent of the excavation of Queen Ethelthryth whose body, preserved from decomposition, had a tent spread above it for the benefit of those who wished to venerate her.[41]

The fort

With few exceptions, the population of the early tales occupied fortified sites. From the perspective of the *Lebor Gabála* and the annals, the earliest forts were established in the time of Nemed, c. 2340 BC, and these are identified as Ráth Cinnech in Oneilland, the northern part of Co. Armagh, and Ráth Cimbaeth in Seimhne, Island Magee in Co. Antrim.[42] Unfortunately, neither place name has survived to indicate the monument intended.[43] Later, when the Sons of Míl established themselves, they also began building forts (1671 BC) and six are listed,[44] although again none of their names has survived to be identified in the modern landscape.[45]

There are a series of words that can be translated as 'fort' in the Ulster tales and although some of them may tend to a more specific shade of meaning in certain contexts, most are infuriatingly interchangeable. The primary term in the literature is *dún*, a word of impeccable Celtic origins that also survives in Welsh and Breton as *din* and was known in ancient Gaul as *dūnon*. The word thrives in abundance across the Irish landscape in both medieval and modern place names. It was often interchangeable with *dunaid, daingen* and *din* (a word that basically indicated a point or spike and was extended to mean 'height' and then 'fortified height').[46] Some other terms for fort occur either rarely or are obviously coordinate with primary words such as *dún*. These would include the ubiquitous Irish place name term, *baile*, and a Latin (and ultimately Germanic) loanword *borg*.[47] Another term for 'fort' is *cathair*, the meaning of which is not confined to a fort but also may include a castle or even a monastery. There are several intriguing hints as to its appearance. Cú Chulainn, for example, is able to chant a spell so that Cú Roí's *cathair* 'revolved as swiftly as a millstone'.[48] This not only suggests a circular structure but also hints at one of the specific meanings of *cathair*, 'a stone enclosure'. This is further supported by an albeit 12th-century tale[49] that describes how Cú Roí's *cathair* was built from every pillar-stone in Ireland. Finally, there are two other words that are not only very frequently encountered in the tales but also very common elements of Irish place names, the *ráth* and the *les* (see below).

In the Ulster cycle we find instances of forts being named after people, such as Dún Sobairche (modern Dunseverick, Co. Antrim), reputedly named after a great-great-grandson of Míl and counted as one of the three main forts of Ireland;[50] today's visitor would certainly understand the mystique of the site given its spectacular location but probably be underwhelmed by the meagre architectural remains, likely all stemming from the historical period (PL. III). Situated on the north Antrim coast, Dún Sobairche serves as sort of a Timbuktu in the Ulster tales, a place about as far away north as one can hope to go. Medb, for example, is reported to have raided as far north in Ulster as Dún Sobairche.[51] Another example of the name of a fort drawn from a person's name is that of Dún Forgaill, named after Cú Chulainn's reluctant father-in-law.[52] Elsewhere we find a hero specifically associated with his own *dún*, 'Celtchair in his *dún*'.[53] This has been identified as a major fortified site in Downpatrick, Co. Down (The 'Mound of Down'). Possession of more than a single fort is suggested in the Mythological cycle tale *Tochmarc Étaíne* in which the Dagda had two main forts (*primdún*).[54] The word *dún* could be applied to the greatest pro-vincial royal sites, such as Emain Macha[55] or Cruachain,[56] and to the residence of Culann, the smith of King Conchobar. Just as the Ordnance Survey of the early 19th century recorded the great houses of the gentry, the budding Ulster hero Cú Chulainn was instructed by his charioteer on his first crossborder raid as to the names of every chief fort and other fort between Kells and Tara, on his way to slay the three sons of Nechtan Scéne in her fort.[57]

If we put ourselves in the position of a visitor to a *dún* we can list its various named components. The first thing of notice would be the 'green' (usually *faithche* but sometimes *airlann*[58]) that surrounded or was set before the entrance of the fort.

This is a standard motif and it was the staging area for a meeting between people at a fort but also served other purposes. Fráech, for example, hunted animals right up to the green of the Connacht capital of Cruachain.[59] The green at Cruachain could also serve as a playing field[60] and at least part of the green at Emain Macha served as the designated *cluichemag* 'playing field' for the boy-troop in Ulster.[61] On the green we might occasionally expect to find one or more pillar-stones,[62] tall trees,[63] or, in the *Dindshenchas*, a well.[64] The green also occurs in Irish translations of classical literature.[65]

The enclosure itself was surrounded by one or more ramparts. How these ramparts were constructed is only occasionally hinted at. In one episode of the *Táin* Cú Chulainn drove his chariot so frantically that its iron wheels dug deep into the ground and cast up enough earth and stone, ranging from gravel to boulders, to make a *dún* and a *daingen* (another word for 'fort'); this suggests either a stone-faced fort or one in which the rampart at least included a large quantity of stones.[66] A stone-faced fort is also suggested by a reference to the 'bright-faced fort of Delgae'.[67] An element in the death tale of Cú Roí involves his people attempting to build a magnificent fort (*daingen*) out of every pillar-stone (*coirthe*) in Ireland. His treacherous wife attempts to pass off his approaching enemies as builders carrying 'stones and oak' for constructing the fort.[68] A possible reference to a timber palisade is suggested in a tale where the Ulstermen break into a fort by ripping out the stockade to make a breach.[69] The height of the fort is not given and the hints are not entirely clear. In the *Táin*[70] Cú Chulainn attacked and fired a fort so that its buildings were the same height as the outer walls which, if this refers to the walls of the ramparts, suggests that the buildings within the fort were much higher than the ramparts surrounding the site. A similar expression occurs in the rematch, when Cathbad laments that the forts were burnt so that they were no higher than the rooms and outhouses.[71]

The main words for 'rampart' are *múr* (a loanword from Latin *murus* 'wall') and *doé*. In addition to a rampart's obvious functions of defence and to provide a platform for watchmen,[72] it is also where Deirdre's lover Noíse was wont to sing when he first met her.[73] The height of the rampart is unknown and little can be gained from the fact that Cú Chulainn was able to jump over a rampart into a fort, mistakenly believing that his opponents in the contest for the Ulster championship had managed to jump it themselves (in fact they had been tossed over the walls by a giant).[74] We might also add to these rampart words *táible* 'rampart', another clear Latin loanword (*tabulae*), and one which does occur in the earliest recension of the *Táin*.[75]

The number of ramparts surrounding a *dún* is only occasionally specified and there is clearly some evidence that there might have been as many as three or more about a fort. For example, Cú Chulainn returns from his weapons training (to which his potential father-in-law, Forgall Manach, sent him to die) by leaping across the three ramparts of Forgall's *dún* and then hopping back, carrying his future wife and her servant.[76] A figurative reference can be seen when Cú Chulainn 'cast up three ramparts of (dead) men around the battle'.[77] Less clear, perhaps, are a series of references to 'three ridges' about a house or hall. The Irish word *fuithirbe* can mean anything from 'a unit of land' to 'ridge' or 'furrow' and it is used to mark off anything from the approach of the three quarrelling wives visiting Briccriu's hall[78] to the distance which defenders drove attackers away from Da Derga's[79] and Da Choca's[80] hall; and Fedelm leapt over three ridges (ramparts?) from the hall of Briccriu.[81] The word seems to have evolved from 'ridge' to the 'piece of land surrounded by a ridge'[82] and it may well be linked to the concept of a fort with a triple enclosure.

A few tales also suggest the existence of a palisade (*sonn*). For example, in the second version of the *Táin*, the house of Culann the smith is surrounded by a palisade rather than a rampart.[83] That the palisade was of timber posts is indicated where Conchobar and his men 'with their right hands they tore down the stockade'.[84] In some instances we are met with clearly fictitious defences such as a rampart of iron[85] or an island with a silver wall around it crowned with a copper palisade.[86] Here we can well suspect the influence of classical literature (Statius' *Thebaid*, for example, makes reference to ramparts or walls of iron[87]). It might also be noted that in the same passage in Statius describing an iron wall we also find a reference to a 'triple wall', which according to Vergil surrounds a castle in Hades.[88]

Human heads might also be displayed hanging from the palisade.[89] The height of the palisade is not recorded although the *Táin* does mention that when Sétanta was attacked by the hound of Culann, the Ulstermen running (unnecessarily) to his rescue climbed over the palisade in their haste rather than using the gateway that was wide open.[90]

Both *ráth* and *les* may indicate a fortified enclosure but the *ráth* is more properly assigned to the ramparts or walls of the enclosure while the *les* comprises the open space or courtyard that has been enclosed. This distinction, however, is not always maintained and, for example, we even find the word *ráth* glossed as a *les*.[91] One of the clearest examples of its use occurs in the Mythological cycle where the Fomorians oppress the Tuatha Dé Danann and reduce the Dagda to serving as a rampart-builder (*ráthbhuide*), forced to construct the *ráth* of the evil king Bres.[92]

Although the fort is the major residence of the elite there are hints in a few tales that there were also unenclosed houses surrounding or in the suburbs of a fort. From the Mythological cycle we find Étaín and Ailbe on a romantic engagement 'in a house which lies outside and beyond the *dún*',[93] while from the Ulster cycle we learn that Emer is with the daughters of landowners who 'lived around the *dún*' of her father, Forgall.[94]

The word *ráth*, like *dún*, is applied to the names of the royal sites, such as Ráth Cruachain,[95] and to the forts of the various heroes, such as Ráth Cathbaid,[96] or Eógan mac Durthacht's residence at Ráth Airthir.[97]

Once the visitor has crossed the green, he or she goes through a door or gate (*dorus*), which usually lacks any useful description unless we include a reference to Scáthach, the woman-warrior who instructed Cú Chulainn in the arts of warfare, who had the gate to her *dún* decorated with severed heads.[98] There is also occasional reference to a doorkeeper.[99]

Once past the gateway, what would one expect to find in a fort? In a few instances we find livestock enclosed within the *les*: 700 head of cattle in Athairne's *dún*,[100] 540 livestock recovered during a raid on Ailill Find's fort,[101] and, in a foreign fort, cattle and a captive woman are kept in a serpent-guarded *les*.[102] There is evidence from the early medieval period that livestock, particularly cattle, might be kept within the enclosures, presumably at night, to prevent theft.[103] This is also suggested in the account of Cú Chulainn's naming, where the smith has the gate to his *les* shut and his hound is released to guard his cattle.[104] In one tale it is presumably livestock that are being routinely attacked by a ferocious hound on a nightly basis.[105] In addition to livestock one might also expect to find a dung heap in the courtyard, such as the one that the obnoxious Briccriu and his wife toppled into[106] or where Lóegaire was tossed by a giant.[107] For the medieval period, this certainly receives some support from the ringfort at Deer Park Farms, Co. Antrim, where dung beetles and lice indicative of livestock were recovered.[108]

From the perspective of an attacker, a prime goal would be gaining access to the *les*,[109] either through the gate or, alternatively, by climbing over a rampart.[110] In terms of human population there are very few hints as to how many might occupy a fort. On one occasion Fergus kills 27 of the warriors stationed in Dún Dá Benn.[111] In another tale, there are 50 warriors in a *les*,[112] while Cú Chulainn manages to kill 400 men in the fort of Garmán.[113] For the ultimate estimate we have Conaill mac Gleo Glais, who brags that within his fort of Dún Colptha he could provision all the Ulstermen, both living and dead, for a year.[114]

But in general, once through the gate and in the *les*, we would expect to find the main house or hall and other domestic structures, of the sort that we will examine below. The *les* is where you might be invited into the fort by a king[115] or wounded men might be carried in for treatment.[116] While a tree might be found in front of the *les*, presumably outside on the green, you could also find a tree within the *les* as when Fergus uproots a massive oak in Mac Dathó's *les* that he uses to bash in the men of Connacht.[117]

Despite the ostensibly defensive nature of the fort, there is very little in the tales regarding actual attacks. The fort of Ailill Find was under attack for a week.[118] The Ulstermen killed everyone in the fort of Temair Luachra, which accounted for its abandonment.[119] Some late tales describe the slighting of forts where the walls are broken down and all the buildings are levelled.[120]

In addition to the fortified site, we also occasionally find references to the tower (*túr*), a Franco-Norman loanword (*tour*) with a good biblical pedigree (e.g., the tower of Nimrod), that also serves for Ulster heroes or enemies; Cú Chulainn, for example, kills Bodb 'in his tower'[121] and, in its metaphorical sense as 'hero' there is reference to a fair tower (hero) in the death tale of Cú Chulainn.[122]

Translating the literary evidence concerning fortified sites into archaeologically testable descriptions is difficult and generalizations must be built on the flimsiest of references. Here we are only concerned with the forts in general and not the major royal sites.

The AFM maintains that fort-building in Ireland was initially established between 2400 and 1600 BC, i.e. the Early Bronze Age. But as we have already seen, the chronology of the earliest forts makes a poor match with the archaeological evidence. The first period of serious fort building is *c*. 1200–1000 BC, when we find the erection of Late Bronze Age hillforts across Ireland. Although these sites show some evidence of occupation during the Iron Age, this would appear to have been undertaken on already abandoned monuments. The next major period of enclosure with banks and ditches corresponds to the erection of the major provincial capitals *c*. 100–1 BC which we will examine below. After another half-millennium or more we find the erection of the early medieval ringforts, which continued through to the period in which the tales were initially written down.

The Ulster tales relate that forts were enclosed by a bank of stones and earth, and a ditch. These features are generic and found across all periods in which forts were erected in Ireland. Of greater interest is the literary evidence that forts may have had ramparts either built of or faced with stone.

Stone-walled forts are known from the Late Bronze Age (*c.* 1000 BC) at Dún Aonghusa, Co. Galway, and Mooghaun, Co. Clare, and even if abandoned long before the composition period of the earliest Irish tradition, there would still be enough visible that they could easily have been worked into any prehistoric narrative. The next major period of stone-walled fortification coincides with the cashels of the early medieval period that should date from *c.* AD 700 or later. Unless the stone forts reflect reimaginings of much earlier monuments of the Late Bronze Age, it is most likely that the tales depicting stone forts are describing early medieval cashels (FIG. 6.3).

Another interesting element of the fort descriptions is that some seem to have been surrounded by up to three ramparts. Trivallate hillforts are known from the Late Bronze Age hillfort horizon, dating to around 1000 BC. The next major phase of their existence is the early medieval period, during which about 20 per cent of ringforts are surrounded by two or more banks and ditches, an arrangement interpreted as indicating high-status sites.[123] But here we should probably distinguish between the irregularly spaced banks and ditches that might surround a Bronze Age hillfort and the regular and closely spaced banks that surround some of the early medieval ringforts. When Cú Chulainn is portrayed leaping across three ramparts, it is far more likely that the author is imagining a series of closely ranked ramparts

6.3. The stone walls of
Drumena Cashel, Co. Down.

of the historical period rather than a trivallate hillfort such as Haughey's Fort. Here Cú Chulainn would have a 55-m gap between the first bank and ditch and the second, and then another 25 m to go before the outer ditch. This is a steeple chase, not a heroic leap. Indeed, this same triple-jump motif can be found in literature representing the historical period. In one of the many stories concerning Mongán, a 7th-century figure, a warrior jumps across three ramparts of a fort and lands in the *les*.[124] In addition, the instances in the tales where there is evidence for three banks are associated with characters who are presumed to be high status, such as Forgall Manach and Briccriu. In any event, it is most likely that the tales reflect Irish native trivallate ringforts of the early medieval period (FIGS 6.4, 6.5) rather than any earlier monument.

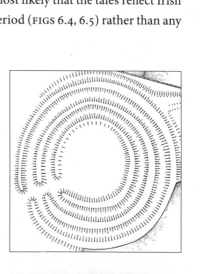

6.4. (*right*) Plan of the trivallate ringfort (120 m across) at Lisnagade, Co. Down.

6.5. (*below*) Trivallate fort at Lisleitrim/Kiltybane, Co. Armagh.

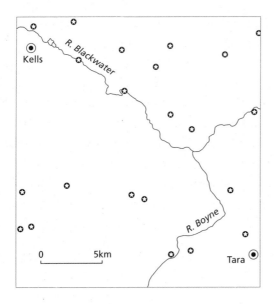

6.6. The early medieval ringforts that Cú Chulainn might have encountered between Tara and Kells.

A third aspect of the fort descriptions is their number. As we have seen, almost any hero in the Ulster tales may be associated with his own fortified site and when Cú Chulainn makes his initial journey between Tara and Kells he asks his charioteer to point out and name all the forts along the road.[125] But other than the major provincial capitals and several other ceremonial sites, we really cannot fill the Iron Age landscape with forts. On the other hand, a chariot driven between Tara and Kells, keeping to the east of the Boyne and Blackwater, could encounter at least a half dozen early medieval ringforts (FIG. 6.6).[126] There is a tale concerning historical characters of the 7th century, involving the chief Ulster poet Eochaid Rígéices, who is tested by a group of youths who wish to expose his ignorance. They bring him to a large fort and ask him to identify who lived in it. Eochaid, ignorant of the answer, replies in his defence: 'Too many build forts to keep them all in mind.'[127] In sum, the motif of the fortified settlement occupied by each major warrior is far more compatible with the early medieval period than the Late Bronze Age, not to mention the even less likely Iron Age.

The house

House

In the tales, the commonest word for a house was *tech*[128] and it was used generically for the dwellings of everyone from kings,[129] nobles and hostellers[130] to smiths,[131] stewards[132] and even barbers.[133] The element *tech* also appears in compounds to indi-cate a dormitory, literally 'sleeping-house' (*cotalthech*),[134] a cook-house (*cuchtarthech*),[135] a guest-house (*tech n-óiged*)[136] and various named 'warrior-houses'.[137] Naturally, there were also various words to describe the 'drinking-house'.[138]

The largest house was the *bruiden*, the hostel[139] or feasting hall, which is fre-quently mentioned in the tales. There were reputedly six hostels in Ireland main-tained by Mac Dathó, Da Derga, Forgall Manach, Da Reo, Da Choca and Blaí,[140] yet the term is employed beyond these, for example, Dún Dá Benn.[141]

Wall

The various walls and partitions within a house have a variety of names. The main term is *fraig*, which is defined as the interior wall of a house viewed from within.[142] This is certainly the presumption when the word *clíath* is used to describe the wall that the enraged Celtchair pierces with his lance after having run through Blaí the hospitaller.[143] We generally presume we are dealing with wattled or plank walls except for some of the more extravagant late tales where the wall may be of metal.[144] We also find the *slis* 'wall', which describes the wall in Briccriu's hall[145] and also Mac Dathó's hall where the bodies inside the hall are piled as high as the walls.[146] All of these suggest a wattled wall consisting of intertwined rods of some pliable tree such as birch.

A major exception to the wattled wall is the triple-walled structure at Temair Luachra, where the Ulstermen are lured into a building consisting of two outer walls of oak but an iron interior wall which would be heated to burn the Ulstermen alive.[147] The inner and outer walls are generally taken to indicate oak planks around an iron core. Richard Warner has compared the triple-wall arrangement in the tales to the smaller figure-of-eight structures at Navan Fort (with somewhat comparable structures from Knockaulin; FIG. 6.7).[148] The parallel is possible but we also have multi-walled structures from the early medieval period such as Deer Park Farms, Co. Antrim, although here there are only two walls with an insulating core[149] (FIG. 6.7), a bit more practical than iron. Warner argues that the insertion of 'iron' in the tale stems from a possible scribal error. A source for such a motif is not readily apparent. Of course, we do have Nebuchadnezzar's attempt to burn Shadrach, Meshach and Abednego all together in what must obviously be a sizeable furnace with a doorway.[150] Also, Orosius has Perillus of Athens fashion a large hollow bronze bull into which victims are shoved before it is heated from below.[151] But neither of these could be described as iron houses.

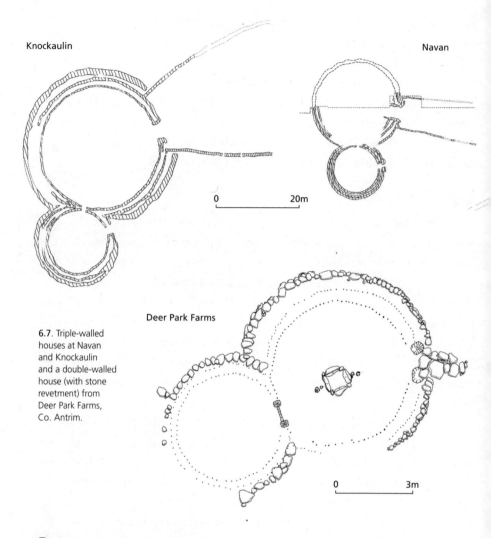

Knockaulin

Navan

0   20m

Deer Park Farms

6.7. Triple-walled houses at Navan and Knockaulin and a double-walled house (with stone revetment) from Deer Park Farms, Co. Antrim.

0   3m

Door

The door to a house or hall receives much attention in the *scéla* with a variety of terms employed that do not necessarily differentiate between the door of a house and the gate of a fort. The door or gate itself may be the *addorus*,[152] more often the *dorus*. Although one might presume a single door for most houses, we find a considerable variety in the number of doors. Étaín finds herself confined to a house without a door but lit by a window and skylight.[153] In the larger halls or *bruiden* we find many more doors. Mac Dathó's hostel had seven doors to accommodate the seven roads that led into it and 50 beds between each two doors.[154] Scáthach also has a house with seven doors,[155] while there were 12 doors into the hall of the Leprechauns who would confront Fergus mac Léti.[156] Da Derga's hostel had seven doors (or else-where nine doorways[157]).[158] On the other hand, Da Choca's hall was set at the junction of four roads as was reputedly the case for all the hostels,[159] and Dún Dá Benn also had four doors.[160] The *bruiden* of Da Choca was located on top of a hill and there were several other structures associated with it, housing the womenfolk and nobles.[161] The material from which the door was made is only cited in the exceptional examples of iron doors[162] concealed within a door of yew three feet thick[163] and the doors of gold of the Leprechauns.[164]

The door valve (*comla*) itself is mentioned by name in a number of tales where we would normally just employ the word 'door'.[165] One exception to this is the strange arrangement of Da Derga's hostel, which possesses seven doorways but only one door valve 'that is turned to every doorway to which the wind blows'.[166] The word can also be used figuratively as when Celtchair is termed 'the Ulstermen's doorway of battle'.[167] One alerted the occupants or doorkeeper to one's presence by striking a wooden door-knocker (*baschrann*) on the door valve.[168] The door valve itself was fastened to a door-post (*airsa*).[169]

The lintel (*fordorus* or *imdorus*) is occasionally mentioned and we might expect that in high-status sites, such as the feasting hall of Briccriu, it would be ornamented with carvings.[170]

As for the size of the door, one of the shortest of the tales provides some, admittedly strange, evidence so please permit me a 'Giraldus moment' to repeat the death tale of Lóegaire Búadach. Mugain of the furzy hair, the wife of King Conchobar, had an affair with the king's poet, Aed mac Ainninne.[171] Their liaison was discovered and the randy poet was seized and condemned to death, Conchobar granting him his choice of execution – death by drowning. But the wily poet had selected this manner of death with good reason: every time Aed was dragged to the shore of a lake he cast a spell on the water that dried the lake up. So the band of executioners hauled the poet all around Ireland until they at last came to a lake, Lough Lai, which did not respond to Aed's charm. A servant saw the henchmen drowning the poet and he ran to his master, Lóegaire, to alert him of the humiliation that a poet might be drowned in his own lake. Lóegaire grabbed his sword and leapt to the poet's defence, but bounding out through the door of his house he had an unfortunate domestic accident, striking the top of his head on the lintel and spattering half his brains on his cloak. Lack of brains being little impediment to a true Ulsterman, Lóegaire still managed to kill 30 of the executioners before he collapsed and died. In the confusion the poet made good his escape.

6.8. Door jambs and collapsed lintel from Deer Park Farms, Co. Antrim.

The obvious question is whether Lóegaire was extraordinarily tall or the door extremely low? We do have some archaeological evidence from the time of Cattubuttas that might suggest a possible answer. At Deer Park Farms, Co. Antrim, a site with remarkably well preserved remains, a house was found with its door preserved all the way from the oak threshold and two timber door jambs to its lintel.[172] The evidence of the tree-rings indicates that the jambs were made from timbers dating to AD 648. And what is of most interest to us here is that the height of the door, between the threshold and the bottom of the lintel, was only a little over 1 m in height (FIG. 6.8). So an angry warrior, impatient to get outside his house and begin slaughtering people, could easily neglect to duck sufficiently and smash his head against the lintel.

Floor

The floor (*lár*) is almost never described. That there might be some stone is indicated in *Fled Bricrenn*, where Cú Chulainn leaves his two footprints 'in the flag on the floor of the hold.'[173] There is also reference to a fantasy floor of copper in a very late tale.[174]

Window

The glass window is clearly a borrowed concept (though not from the Bible), as can be seen from its name in Irish, *seinistir*, a loanword from Latin *fenestra*. Briccriu's solarium had windows of glass[175] as did the bower prepared for Étaín.[176] Later tales even use a more recent loan with *fuindeóc*, borrowed from Old Norse *vindauga* 'wind-eye', as in the case of the woman-warrior Scáthach, whose bower had seven windows.[177]

Pillar

Internal pillars for the grander buildings are described, frequently made out of some precious (and fantastic) material. The commonest word for structural pillars is *úaithne* (*tuir* is also used) which may be of gold in some very late tales,[178] silver,[179] *findruine* (some time of white metal),[180] copper, as in the pillar that Conchobar would rap to call attention,[181] or even glass or crystal.[182] The use of metals in the description of pillars could easily have been lifted from the Bible, where we have pillars overlayed with gold, or made of silver or brass.[183]

Roof

The construction of the roof is only hinted at in the tales. A number of the stories refer to the *cleth*, the rooftree or ridge-pole. An axe may be raised high to the roof-tree[184] or, when it has been used to cut off a giant's head, the head may be tossed so high[185] while a spy spots three naked Bodbs on top the rooftree of Da Derga's hostel.[186] The ridge-pole may also be expressed with *ochtach* (which also indicates the elusive pine tree), as when the three competitors for the championship of Ulster toss a wheel as high as they can (Conall's wheel reaches the ridge-pole, Cú Chulainn's carries the ridge-pole off the top of the hall).[187] There are also fantasy references to a ridge-pole of *findruine*.[188]

Below the ridge-pole we find rafters (*sparr*, a loanword from either Old Norse or Middle English), to which both Conall and Lóegaire make for when trying to escape giant demonic cats.[189]

There is only one reference to thatching (*tugae*).[190]

Solarium

Despite Ireland's weather, a number of the tales posit the existence of a solarium (*grianán*) or sun-house.[191] Solariums are attributed to Emain Macha,[192] and Dún Dá Benn.[193] Actual descriptions of the structure itself within the tales are sparse but there appear to be some common elements. To begin with, there are mentions of windows in the *grianán* of the Mac Oc,[194] with the woman-warrior Scáthach possessing a solarium with seven windows between every two of its seven huge doors.[195] The most detailed account concerns Briccriu's building of a solarium on the same level as the couch of King Conchobar and fitted with glass windows, one of which was above his own couch so he could watch the inside of the hall.[196] Although sometimes simply translated as a balcony, here that will not quite do as the compartment requires a window to see into the building.

Architecturally, a solarium would require a raised timber floor, which is generally regarded as absent from the domestic remains known from the Iron Age through to the early medieval period. An Irish writer would encounter a brief description of a solarium in Isidore[197] that focuses on the fact that it is open to the sun and cites the instance where David spies Bethsheba for the first time from what he takes to be a solarium (most translations simply indicate 'roof'). As for classical literature, this provides a far more likely source but from where? The Irish were so solarium obsessed that they inserted one into their translation of Statius' *Thebaid*.[198]

Bed

For a genre that focuses so much on military mayhem, it is amazing to see how much vocabulary and description is given over to beds.

The bed was associated with the *imdae*, which denotes either the area in which one slept, as a separate bedroom or merely a space that might be partitioned off from the rest of the house, or the bed, couch or bench itself.[199] There are a number of issues regarding the *imdae*, such as their precise locations and their number. The law texts, for example, prescribe eight *imdae* for the house of a noble but we find 12 *imdae* for the warriors of Ulster in Briccriu's house along with an elevated one for Conchobar;[200] Da Derga's hostel had seven *imdae* between each of the seven doorways (=49 *imdae*); Mac Datho's hall had 50 *imdae* between each two doors;[201] and there were 150 *imdae* in the house of three women who greet Cú Chulainn on one of his quests,[202] as well as Ailill's hall,[203] Scáthach's solarium,[204] and the Otherworldly house of Labraid.[205] We may suspect that the excessive numbers of beds may have been driven by classical examples. Homer, for instance, describes the palace of Priam as containing 50 stone sleeping chambers for the sons of the king and an additional 12 chambers for his daughters and their husbands.[206]

There were two general names for bed: *lige*,[207] which is also found in the word for a sickbed (*serg-lige* or *othar-lige*),[208] and, more commonly, *lepaid*.[209] Both words might also be used in an expression indicating that one was in a bad way, i.e. in an evil bed (*drochlepaid* or *drochlige*).[210] Some late tales also use *tolg* 'bed, bedchamber'.[211]

There were two basic types of bed. The first consisted only of strewn rushes (*cossar* indicates strewing rushes out for a bed). These might be prepared on campaign in the field[212] as well as in a hall. The second was a feather-stuffed mattress (*coilcthech*) and a recurrent image in the tales is the exploding mattress that sends feathers flying everywhere.[213] Such mattresses could be set up in the field – Ailill sleeps on one in his tent[214] – or in Briccriu's newly built hall.[215] A house might contain both beds of rushes and stuffed mattresses.[216]

The bed might have a post or bench (*colba*) that is once described as being of either red enamel or copper.[217] Otherwise, the bedpost provides a handy anchor for the treacherous wife of Cú Roí to tie her husband's hair to as she plans to have him assassinated.[218] The *séol* may indicate the bedstead, at least in some instances.[219]

There are several words for pillow in the tales. At the beginning of the second recension of the *Táin* where Medb and Ailill begin their 'pillow talk', their heads rest on a *cerchaill*, a loanword from Latin *cervical* 'pillow, bolster'.[220] The *adart* 'pillow, cushion' of the tales is repeatedly described as filled with feathers.[221]

The bed could be covered by a quilt (*breccán*)[222] whose underlying etymology ('speckled thing') suggests that it was striped or chequered like a plaid, but more often the term for a bed covering was a *brothrach*,[223] which derives from *brothar* 'hair, fur'. There is even one tale where an ornamented white linen sheet (*lín-anart*) is employed.[224]

The organic preservation at Deer Park Farms allows us to imagine the appearance of an early medieval bed. Two beds were found up against the wall of one of the best-preserved structures, a house some 7 m in diameter. The best preserved consisted of a base of large branches covered with smaller branches and twigs, topped with straw and fibrous material. At one end was a bed-end, a wooden beam that had been perforated to hold at least 15 upright rods that probably supported a wattle screen.[225]

Furniture

Although there is a native word for 'seat' (*suide*) that refers to the royal throne,[226] the more frequently employed word for a chair or throne (*cathaír*) is an obvious loanword from Latin *cathedra*, and when described in any fashion it tends to be a fantastic description such as the silvery chair[227] at Da Derga's hostel or the reference to a chair of crystal.[228] And even the humble 'stool' is borrowed from Latin if we understand the single occurrence of *scamun* (< Latin *scamnum*) correctly.[229] The word for 'table' (*mías*) is also a Latin loanword from *mensa* and again we only find fantastic descriptions of their construction in silver, bronze and *findruine*.[230]

Weapon racks

Five tales mention the presence of spear-racks (*aidlenn*) where the warriors would store their weapons,[231] while the sword might be stored on the *alchaing*.[232] Shields were mounted on wooden pegs (*berraide*)[233] or hooks (*delg*).[234]

Souterrain

The standard word for souterrain (*úam* 'cave') is not employed in the tales but its existence appears to be alluded to in the *Táin* where opponents of Cú Chulainn will not escape even if they 'take refuge underground';[235] similarly, the reluctant doctors who wish to avoid being killed by the wounded Cethern will be slaughtered even if they hide underground or in a locked house.[236] To these references we might add that to Mann, who dug deep chambers underground and placed a large treasure in them to ward off a plague.[237]

From an Irish perspective the presence of souterrains in the tales may appear to be an anachronism as they do not emerge in Ireland until the 6th century at the earliest. But here we have a problem because Irish souterrains are centuries more recent than similar examples in Scotland that appear by the 3rd century BC[238] and so an Irish Iron Age Katu-butos could possibly have known of their existence although it is still far more likely that we are dealing with a medieval anachronism, as the motif would make little sense in the context of Iron Age Ireland.

Pillar-stones

In addition to pillars inside houses, the tales frequently refer to stone pillars (usually *coirthe* but there are some other words as well[239]) that appear to litter the landscape and provide convenient objects against which one might splatter both hounds[240] and men.[241] On several occasions pillars, dressed either with a mantle[242] or a crown,[243] fool a warrior into attacking them, which at least gives an impression of the height of the stones; one source speaks of a four-cornered pillar-stone.[244] Cú Chulainn places withies or rings on pillar-stones as a challenge[245] while his enemy, the Mórrígan, takes the form of a bird and perches upon one.[246] Most famously, it is against a pillar-stone that the mortally wounded Cú Chulainn ties himself so that he will die standing upright (PL. I).[247]

The location of pillar-stones is occasionally mentioned. They are said to stand before royal forts[248] and there is one (in an admittedly very late tale) on the green of Emain Macha,[249] an enormous one at the fort of Cú Roí,[250] and another at Cruachain.[251] One tale records that a third of a stone was buried in the ground with two-thirds above it – the stone was then pulled out by Cú Chulainn and thrown.[252] An apparently random pillar-stone turns up on the floor of Da Derga's hostel, and the mighty Mac Cecht chucks it at an attacker.[253] While they usually appear alone, there are occasions where two pillar-stones are found together[254] and seven are mentioned at Cú Roí's fort.[255] As to the occasion of raising a pillar-stone, the account of the destruction of Da Derga's hostel informs us that one would be raised to signal a 'rout' (while a destruction would require a cairn).[256] An 11th-century tale from a different cycle, concerning the 7th-century figure Mongán, informs us that it was the custom of the Ulstermen to raise a pillar-stone whenever they made their first kill,[257] while in the tale depicting the drunken detour of the Ulstermen, the charioteers raise pillar-stones (here using *columa*, a Latin loanword) for the shelter of their horses.[258] Finally, there is passing reference to the Lia Fáil, the stone penis (*ferp* from Latin *verpa*) that stood at Tara on the chariot course.[259]

Archaeologically, it is impossible to assign the references to any distinct period. Standing stones have been dated to the Early Bronze Age (at least Early Bronze Age burials have been found at their base), the Iron Age (where we find on occasion La Tène decoration) or the early medieval period (where they provided a surface for ogam inscriptions, the earliest form of writing in Ireland).

Bridge

The bridge (*drochet*) receives occasional mention. We learn, for example, that the bridge of Cairbre is over the Boyne.[260] Otherwise the references are to a magical bridge in Scotland which Cú Chulainn must cross on his way to and from his training, but that buckles up under anyone who tries to cross it.[261] There is also reference to a forebridge (*airdrochat*).[262]

Fence

There are several references to fences. As we have seen, one author specifically denied their existence in Ireland in the time of Conchobar when he claimed that there were no ditches, fences (*airbe*) nor walls.[263] While the story of Da Derga's hostel mentions the existence of 'silvery hurdles' (*clíath*),[264] the *Dindshenchas* more realistically mention hurdles composed of thorns and brambles.[265] Another word for fence (*cró*) is used figuratively when Cú Chulainn is called a 'marshalled fence of battle'.[266]

Linear earthworks

Linear earthworks are extensive lines of banks and ditches (and sometimes timber palisades) that form large barriers to movement or mark off major social territories. Archaeologically, there is evidence for massive linear earthworks constructed during the last centuries BC (FIG. 6.9). These include a section of the famous Black Pig's Dyke[267] (which draws its name from a folk tale where a magician-teacher transformed himself into a pig and was driven across the landscape, rooting up the land; FIG. 6.10)[268] and the Dorsey ('doors, gates'), which appears to be a double line of defences in south Armagh, the final phase of which is the same date as the main building phase at the Ulster capital of Emain Macha (*c.* 100 BC).[269] And further south we find the Dún of Drumsna,[270] what appears to be a major barrier against crossing the Shannon, that possibly dates to the first centuries BC.[271] There are also traces of other linear earthworks running north–south near the Down–Armagh border known popularly as the Dane's Cast, and which have been interpreted as an early medieval division between the truncated remnants of Ulster in County Down after the fall of the Ulster capital.

We have already seen that at least one of the authors of the Ulster tales denied the existence of such defences for the early centuries BC and AD. On the other hand, a century ago Margaret Dobbs argued that the course of the *Táin* from Rathcroghan to Cooley was dictated by a desire to avoid attempting to penetrate Ulster across its linear earthwork defences; in other words, the course of Medb's army did not turn north earlier because it was hindered by an unmentioned barrier that had been erected before the time of the *Táin*, *c.* 1500–500 BC.[272] The argument is subtle but unconvincing as there is both an expressed motive for the meandering course of the invading army (it was being deliberately stalled by its leader Fergus who was reluctant to lead it into his former home)[273] and there is still no sound reason why such an earthwork would have not been mentioned as it was surely a far more impressive ruin in the Iron Age or early medieval period than it is today. The *Táin* does reference one possible linear earthwork: the last act of the dying Brown Bull of Cuailnge was to dig up a ditch forming Gort mBúraig 'enclosure of the trench'. Kay Muhr has identified this with the Dane's Cast.[274] The Mythological cycle similarly offers little, except for a reference to the Dagda possessing a magic club that, when dragged behind him, 'left a track as deep as the boundary ditch between two provinces'.[275]

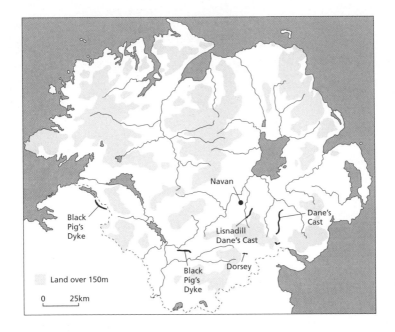

6.9. The linear earthworks of Ulster.

6.10. Aidan Walsh's excavation of the Black Pig's Dyke near Scotshouse, Co. Monaghan.

As mentioned above, it is notable that these monuments, which can stand as much as 6 m high today and can be up to 10 km long, tend to play no part in the lists of events recorded in the Irish annals and nowhere do we intercept them as artificial monuments created by the early Irish. To the custodians of the Dreamtime they are the product of magic clubs and irate wonder-bulls or a more recent shape-shifting schoolmaster pig.

Specific sites

The annals and the tales mention a large number of sites, usually fortified, that are associated with the personages of the Mythological and Ulster cycles. Among the most familiar is certainly Brug na Bóinne, now known as Newgrange. While the monument clearly dates to c. 3000 BC, the descriptions of this enormous passage tomb are of an Otherworld palace and not the interior of a burial chamber. In short, we are dealing here with a reconstruction where a tale has been back-projected into an existing monument that already had a well-established aura of antiquity.[276] In some cases it is modern writers who back-project identifications. For example, P. W. Joyce announced that Da Derga's hostel had been discovered in 1879 when what were taken as the remains of a mass slaughter were found under a large mound.[277] Although the initial account of the excavation[278] was in error in treating it as the site of a Viking slaughter, that should have been enough to indicate that the human remains there did not belong to a group of raiders who attacked King Conaire Mór in 40 BC (the site is actually an early medieval Irish cemetery into which a Viking burial was inserted).[279] These and other burial monuments thus offer very poor material on which to fix the dates of the earliest Irish tradition although we will return to this subject when we examine the evidence for mortuary practice.

Far more promising, one would think, might be the various sites mentioned in the Ulster tales. Unfortunately, these have either been excavated rarely or the excavations have been so small that we cannot draw secure conclusions. Here are a few examples of the more important and, perhaps, more securely identified sites.

Dún Sobhairce. Identified with the modern Dunseverick, Co. Antrim, and according to the AFM founded in 1699 BC. The site has not been excavated and all that remains are some remnants of a stone castle and some house foundations, all clearly of the historical period.[280] There are some ground features that may be earlier and the site was certainly known in the early medieval period as the annals indicate that it was sacked by the Norse between about 871 and 926. Tom McErlean has

6.11. The Giant's Sconce, Co. Derry,
the probable site of Dún Dá Benn.

recently argued that the discovery of 500 Roman silver coins, dating to the 2nd century AD, only 1 km west of Dunseverick, may suggest that the site itself was occupied as early as the Iron Age,[281] but there is really no hard evidence for this.

Dún Dá Benn. This is a prominent site serving as a northern capital in the *Mesca Ulaidh* and from which the drunken Ulstermen set out one night in their chariots for Dundalk and instead found themselves in Kerry. Its precise location has been disputed with the earlier identification of Mount Sandel more recently (and logically) replaced by the Giant's Sconce (FIG. 6.11).[282] The first monument appears to be a Norman motte that might have had antecedents if it had been built on an earlier ringfort, as was the case for several other mottes that have been excavated. The Giant's Sconce, also unexcavated, is more likely to be an early medieval cashel rather than any earlier monument.

Ráth Celtchair. This is the fortress of Celtchair, one of the most illustrious and fearsome of the Ulstermen. There is no description of his own fort but it is has been identified as the 'Mound of Down' (PL. VII), located in Downpatrick, Co. Down, on admittedly slender evidence (far more secure is the medieval name Dún Lethglaise, which is first mentioned in the annals in AD 496 or 498). Located on a drumlin, the site is enclosed by an outer ditch and internal bank measuring *c.* 215 × 165 m. Within the enclosure is a mound some 8 m high. A recent excavation of the site by Phil Macdonald suggests that while there was some earlier Late Bronze Age activity, the surrounding enclosure and mound were most likely constructed in the immediate pre-Norman and 12th-century Norman periods.[283] From this, we may well wonder what the medieval redactors of the Ulster tales were referring to.

Dundrum. The visible remains of this site are those of a Norman castle built during the decades around 1200, when it was known as Castrum de Rath, but there are references in the annals to a pre-Norman *Dún Droma* 'fort of the ridge', suggesting that the hill had been fortified before the Norman incursion. The site was identified with Briccriu's fort of Dún Rudhraighe as Dundrum Bay is known as Loch Rudhraighe. But this identification is not entirely secure as there is no other association between Briccriu and the bay, in which elsewhere in the Ulster tales we read of Fergus mac Léti's encounter with a sea monster. Whether one accepts the identification or not, the earliest evidence for occupation and defence on the site (a possible 70-m diameter enclosure) is of early medieval date.

Dún Rudhraighe. If one does not accept Dundrum as the seat of Briccriu, an alternative, suggested by Phil Macdonald,[284] is Water Hill Fort, which is located inland at Lough Brickland, originally Loch Bricrenn, and generally assumed to mean the 'lake of Briccriu'. Overlooking the lake is an elliptical henge-shaped enclosure, 52 × 45 m, which might make a possible candidate. This site is unexcavated.

In general, the forts that litter the *scéla* are either monuments such as Newgrange that long pre-date any of the events in the tales or they are sites which, at least so far, cannot be ascribed to the prehistoric period. What little evidence we have suggests that the Ulster cycle comes much closer to describing the built landscape of medieval Cattubuttas or Cathbad rather than that of the Iron Age Katu-butos. But there is one possible site-type that may be an exception: the tales also describe in some detail the provincial capitals, the so-called 'royal sites', and here we have the evidence not just of surveys but also excavations.

The royal sites

Cruachain

The Connacht capital is frequently mentioned and described in the tales in detail[285] and it is clear that there was at least some first-hand knowledge of the monumental ritual complex of Rathcroghan-Carnfree. A variety of sources[286] emphasize the identification of Cruachain as one of the great royal cemeteries of ancient Ireland, where there were 'barrows for every noble couple'. This is certainly consonant with both the probable etymology of the name Cruachain, if from *crúach* 'mound',[287] and the fact that there are over 35 monuments in the area that are identified as mounds or ring barrows.[288]

Cruachain is often termed a *ráth*[289] but sometimes a *dún*.[290] Seen from the perspective of a visitor, one must note that in addition to a royal hall or palace there were some other monuments, although not mentioned in any detail. These would include a 'cave'[291] which is generally identified with Oweynagat, 'the cave of the cats'.[292] This is a natural limestone feature that one enters by way of a souterrain. The problem here for the dating of this monument is establishing whether the souterrain was later inserted into the original natural entrance of the cave (which would push the date of the motif of an Otherworld cave back into geological time) or whether the cave was discovered when the souterrain was dug, which would indicate an early medieval date for the concept of the 'cave'.

There is also repeated reference to a *síd* 'mound' in the tales,[293] which is most likely associated with Rathcroghan Mound (PL. V).

The primary monument of the tales is the *rígthech* 'royal house' of Ailill and Medb.[294] This palace is presumably surrounded by a rampart as this is where the warrior-pensioner Conall sat fixing spears,[295] and the *Dindshenchas* recall the 'dun ramparts' of Cruachain.[296] Another tale indicates that heads were brought out to the palisades.[297] And, as usual with any fortified enclosure, there is also a green in front of the fort that can be viewed from Medb's *grianán*.[298] There is also reference to a number of other houses as well as the palace. Medb, for example, can put up the three contending heroes for the Ulster championship in separate buildings,[299] and Fráech was summoned to the 'house of council' at Cruachain.[300] There is also a bath.[301] As for the palace itself, we will examine this in the context of the Standard Irish Palace Description below.

Emain Macha

Some of the tales demonstrate that their authors had at least some field knowledge of the Ulster capital, which is situated only a few kilometres west of the ecclesiastical capital of Armagh. A number of references help anchor Emain Macha in its landscape. Cú Chulainn, for example, relates in the second recension of the *Táin* how he learned to swim in the Callan river,[302] which flows just to the east of Navan Fort. The first recension has Cú Chulainn swimming in the pool at Navan.[303] The pool goes unnamed but there is only one likely candidate: the body of water today known as Loughnashade which is immediately adjacent to the Navan enclosure and which was probably known as Lough Cirr in the Middle Ages (FIG. 6.12).[304] As is usual, one approaches the enclosure by crossing the 'green' (*faithche*).[305] There is mention of a gate of Emain (*dorus nEmna*)[306] and a watchman.[307] On a few occasions we have mention of the rampart (*dóe*)[308] or, employing a Latin loanword (*tabula*), we find Cú Chulainn's father shouting a warning to the Ulstermen from atop the rampart (*taibled*) (PL. VIII).[309] The father shouts his last warning from on top of the 'Mound of the Hostages in Emain' (FIG. 6.13),[310] a scene which when reprised in the second recension is changed to the 'stone of the hostages in Emain'.[311] There are several other references to a mound (*sídbrug*), actually 'Otherworld mound', at Emain Macha.[312]

As for actual descriptions of the building(s) within the enclosure, other than remnants of the Standard Irish Palace Description,[313] there is not much information. In a late (12th-century) tale we are told that there were three buildings at the site: the Croebruadh for the king's palace, the Croebderg for the spoils of war, including the heads of enemies, and the Téite Brecc, where the arms were stored.[314]

Archaeologically, the descriptions of the monument locate it at the site of Navan Fort and recall the major features one encounters today – earthen ramparts and mound. The mention of a 'stone of the hostages' is a problem as there is no stone visible today. There was, however, a 17th-century land-grant that mentioned 'the great stone called Crewroe' as a boundary marker; Creeveroe is the neighbouring townland to Navan and reflects the modern spelling of Croebruadh, the 'ruddy branch', the name of Conchobar's hall.[315]

Standard Irish Palace

Over a century ago it was recognized that there was a Standard Irish Palace Description that served Cruachain,[316] Emain Macha[317] and Briccriu's hall essentially in the form of variants on a common template.[318] The descriptions concern the general layout of the interior of the building, the composition of the structure and its roof. The version depicting Cruachain in the *Fled Bricrenn* in its simplicity seems to be closest to a basic formula involving both alliteration and repeated syllable counts. In short, parts of the passage resemble one of those nuggets of oral formulas that one so eagerly searches for in the works of Homer. Here is the description of Cruachain arranged to highlight what I suspect are the core elements and what I have taken to be later prose additions in italics.

6.12. Navan Fort (Emain Macha) with Loughnashade
in the foreground (and limestone quarry inbetween).

6.13. The mound (Site B) at Navan Fort,
which covers the '40-metre structure'.

secht	cúarda	*and ocus*
secht	n-imdada	*ó thein co fraig.*
airinich	créduma	*ocus*
aurscartud	dergibair.	
trí stéill	chréduma	*i*
taulaic in	taige.	
tech	ndaruch	*co*
tugi	slinned.	*Di senistir déc and co comlathaib glainidib friu. Imdai Ailella ocus Medba immedon in tige.*
airing	airgdidi	*impe ocus*
steill	chréduma.	
Seven	ranks	*there and*
Seven	compartments	*from fire to wall.*
Frontings	of bronze	*and*
Carved work	of red yew.	
Three posts	of bronze	*in the*
Socles?	of the house.	
House	of oak	*with*
Roof	of shingles.	*There were twelve windows with a covering of glass. The chamber of Ailill and Medb was in the middle of the house.*
Rails	of silver	*around it and*
Posts	of copper.	

The other examples generally follow the same format and order of presentation but insert further information outside the prosified verse. On occasion, the other sources make a substantive change; for instance while *Fled Bricrenn* appears to retain the formula *tech ndaruch* 'house of oak', the *Táin Bó Fraích* description of Cruachain has inserted in clear prose *De gíus dognith a tech* 'it was of pine that the house was made'.[319]

If we take a composite picture of these descriptions we can summarize the general appearance of a royal palace in the Ulster tales (with the more important deviations).

The building is arranged into seven (or nine) ranks with seven compartments from the fire to the wall. This sets up the image of a central fire with ranks of compartments, seven deep, extending to the wall of the building. The ranks (*cuarda*) can be taken as circles, so that we have a very large circular structure with concentric rings of posts.[320]

The three bronze posts are problematic in that their location in the *taulaic* (socles?) or *aulaic* (wall?) of the house is unclear, although this might be taken to be the ledge or border of the compartment.

Precisely how the seven radiating (presumably sleeping) compartments are to be imagined is a problem because this leads to inconsistencies with other descriptions. For example, at Emain Macha the king is supposedly surrounded by his 12 chiefs[321] and the most pertinent medieval Irish law tract to our subject, the *Crith Gabhlach*, specifies that a king's palace should have a statutory 12 compartments.

The house, here presumably the basic structure such as the many post uprights, was of oak. For some reason (discussed in the previous chapter) this was altered in the *Táin Bó Fraích* version to pine. The roof of the house was covered with shingles or tiles, presumably of wood. In terms of interior styling, the compartments were adorned with bronze, possibly silver, and certainly carvings of yew.

We can now make an attempt to assess these descriptions in terms of the archaeological or literary record. It is to the latter that we can turn for at least some of the exaggerated opulence of the descriptions, such as the pillars and decorations of bronze and silver. As we have already seen, a medieval monk would certainly have plenty of examples from the Bible of the use of metals in the building of structures and the descriptions of Solomon's palace, decorated in cedar, and with brass pillars.[322] As we have also seen in the previous chapter, the substitution of pine for oak in describing the hall of the elite is difficult to explain prompting my feeble attempts to link it to biblical descriptions of palaces built in cedar or the author having Scotland rather than Ireland in mind. In addition, there were always classical descriptions of opulent buildings such as Dido's temple from the *Aeneid*.[323] But what about the basic construction?

Our Iron Age poet, Katu-butos, could have regaled his audiences with the high deeds of his heroes at the major provincial courts of Emain Macha (Navan Fort), Cruachain (Rathcroghan), Tara and Dún Ailinne (Knockaulin, the capital of Leinster). Excavation has revealed large timber structures that date to about the 1st century BC at two of these sites (Navan Fort and Knockaulin) and remote sensing has uncovered evidence of a similar structure at Rathcroghan. The existence of a corresponding structure at Tara is not known although, like the other three, it possesses a surrounding bank and ditched enclosure. If there was a real Iron Age template for the Standard Irish Palace Description, one might presume that these provided the likeliest candidates. Moreover, as the structures were basically sealed by the 1st century BC and AD, if the tales accurately describe these monuments, then it would reveal the type of privileged information that would support a memory of the Iron Age. This is especially true of Navan, the structure of which was encased in a stone cairn and buried under an earthen mound; the corresponding site at Rathcroghan is also encased in an earthen mound.

Navan Fort offers the closest parallels to the Standard Irish Palace Description. There is a large circular structure, 40 m in diameter, consisting of a massive central post, dated to 95 BC, surrounded by 6 concentric rings of oak posts numbering about 280 altogether (FIG. 6.14). The comparable Knockaulin structure comprised an outer double post-ring 43 m in diameter within which was another post-ring 20 m diameter and within that a small 'tower', the base of which was indicated by a wall-slot about 6 m in diameter (FIG. 6.15). The focus at Rathcroghan is Rathcroghan Mound, c. 90 m in diameter and between 4 and 7 m above the surrounding plain. An ambitious programme of remote sensing has established that the mound incorporates a probable series of circular structures, the largest of which is a double-ringed enclosure of posts c. 32 m in diameter, within which there is evidence for other concentric circles though not necessarily contemporary (FIG. 6.16).[324]

The similarity with the Standard Irish Palace Description is the presence of an unusually large circular structure that consists of concentric rings of upright posts. Navan offers a circuit of six ranges around its central post, only one off the seven indicated in the description.[325] Moreover, the post uprights at Navan are all of oak. This, unfortunately, is the end of the matter, as there was no evidence whatsoever for occupation on the floor of the Navan structure. The building may have carried some form of roof because the outer ring of posts had been reinforced with additional posts, suggesting that they were load-bearing. But there is a strong suspicion that no sooner had the building been erected then it was filled with limestone cobbles up to a height of 2 m, its outer perimeter fired and then covered with sods to form a large mound. We have already seen that the tales record the presence of a mound at Emain Macha and so when Cú Chulainn's father, Sualtaim, shouts his warning to the Ulstermen atop the mound that their lands have been invaded, it renders it unlikely that the creators of the *Táin* were aware that their elaborate palace was actually buried under the mound on which Cú Chulainn's father stood. The only alternative to this would be placing Sualtaim's feet on the top of the centre of a slight ring ditch near the mound.

The corresponding building at Knockaulin (Mauve phase) resembles the Iron Age palace descriptions even less, since there is no question of it serving as a roofed

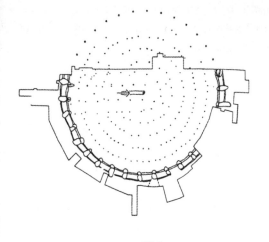

6.14. The '40-metre structure' at Navan. Note the ramp for erecting a massive central post, and the reinforcing posts around the perimeter.

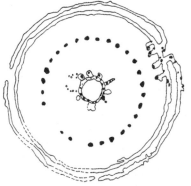

6.15. The central 43-m structure at Knockaulin. The excavator interpreted its central feature as a wooden tower.

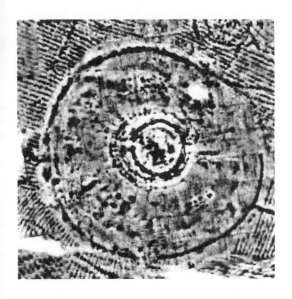

6.16. Magnetic gradiometry image of Rathcroghan Mound indicating an outer timber revetment (c. 80 m across) and inner multi-ringed structure.

structure, given the distance between the several concentric rings. The excavator reconstructed it as an open-air ceremonial precinct with possible seating in the outer ring, a sort of wood henge in the middle and a tower at the very centre.

As various scholars such as Nicholas Aitchison have frequently emphasized, there is a major disparity between the Standard Irish Palace Description, which depicts a large residential structure, and the evidence from the Irish 'royal' sites, which are interpreted as large ceremonial structures.[326] This is all the more plausible as these sites are surrounded by hengiform arrangements of an outer bank and inner ditch more appropriate to a ritual site than a residential one.[327] Smaller alternative structures would also appear to be ceremonial. For example, at Lismullin, Co. Meath, we have a double row of post-rings, 80 m in diameter, enclosing a central ring 16 m in diameter and a posted gateway between the two enclosures that all date to *c*. 450–220 BC (FIG. 6.17).[328] The site is oriented on the Pleiades and is also interpreted as a ceremonial site.

In short, while Katu-butos certainly may have found venues for his poetic talents during the Iron Age, these large ceremonial buildings do not make a very convincing match with the literary evidence.

During the period in which Cattubuttas plied his craft (AD 400–700), we have only the remains of domestic structures in ringforts, which would have measured

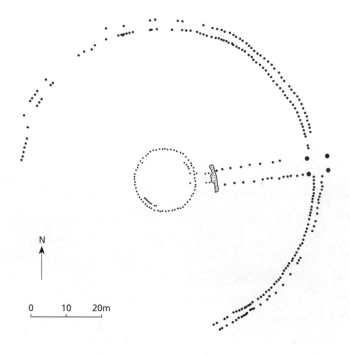

6.17. Large Iron Age ritual structure at Lismullin, Co. Meath.

N

0   10   20m

c. 6 m across and make very poor comparisons indeed with our literary descriptions of elaborate halls. At this time there were a few large structures across the sea that may have served as halls in Anglo-Saxon England, but these were rectangular in shape, as were the much larger halls that followed in the Late Anglo-Saxon period.[329] In short, as the most recent survey of Irish early medieval settlement argues:

> Despite the fantastical descriptions in some of the Irish narratives
> for massive, otherworldly houses with multiple doorways, there
> is no archaeological evidence in Ireland for buildings of the scale
> found elsewhere in north-west Europe in the early mediaeval
> period...or even in Anglo-Saxon England.[330]

Cathbad, who flourished AD 700–1000, would have generally encountered small timber structures in the secular world, although there would be a gradual shift to rectangular structures after *c.* AD 800. But there is also some evidence for larger buildings that might have provided a model for the Standard Irish Palace Description. That large communal or status buildings did exist is suggested by the annals that, at this time, are generally regarded as reliable, although we need not always accept the body counts. In any event, they record the destruction of feasting halls and the deaths of kings and a substantial number of their followers. For example, in 972 one such house was burnt along with a loss of 70 men.[331]

More importantly, the evidence of archaeology is not entirely quiet on the existence of such large buildings, although the prime example is extremely controversial. At Lissue, Co. Antrim, Gerhard Bersu excavated a ringfort, *c.* 40 m in diameter, which appeared to enclose a structure that extended almost to the inner bank, in other words almost 40 m across. The building appeared to consist of an outer palisade wall surrounding six concentric rings of posts with a central hearth (FIG. 6.18). As no other contemporary site has paralleled Lissue, the interpretation of the ground plan has been frequently disputed.[332] Nevertheless, Bersu's interpretation has been accepted by Richard Warner, who has been engaged in sorting out the Lissue excavation report, and Lissue could certainly provide an excellent model for the descriptions of the Standard Irish Palace. Moreover, there is literary evidence that suggests that Lissue was Lis Áeda, the house of one of the major claimants to the kingship of Ulster who reputed died in his 'roundhouse' in AD 886.[333]

The evidence for a large feasting hall has led us to an interesting predicament. If we dismiss these palace descriptions as a combination of native status buildings such

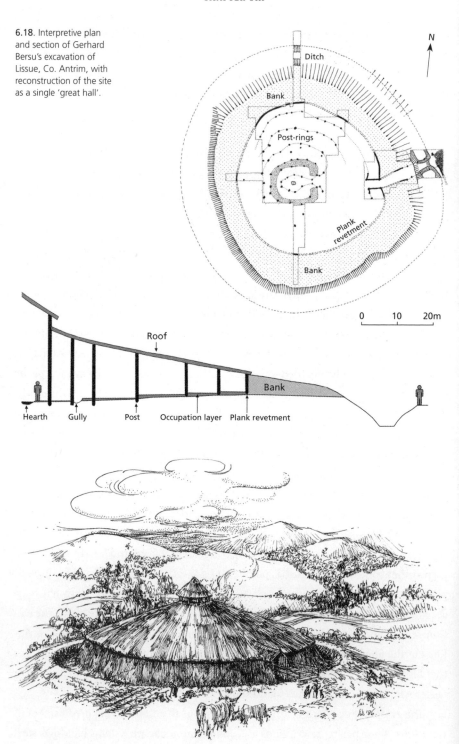

6.18. Interpretive plan and section of Gerhard Bersu's excavation of Lissue, Co. Antrim, with reconstruction of the site as a single 'great hall'.

N

Ditch

Bank

Post-rings

Plank revetment

Bank

0　10　20m

Roof

Bank

Hearth　Gully　Post　Occupation layer　Plank revetment

as Lissue tarted up with the use of metals that could have been borrowed from the Bible or classical sources, we are still left with explaining why these halls were imagined to stand on the few sites that we now know are of Iron Age date and that produced comparably monumental buildings? All other sites mentioned so far, in terms of the existing archaeological evidence, are anachronistic, probable medieval sites that have been back-projected to the Iron Age. Why are the ancient capitals different?

Reconsidering the capitals

In a major study of the ancient 'royal' sites of Ireland, Nicholas Aitchison emphasized the differences in interpretation between the actual Iron Age sites of Navan Fort and Knockaulin and the depictions of those as the royal capitals of Emain Macha and Dún Ailinne.[334] The literary evidence suggested that the provincial capitals were residential fortified sites that served as the main political centres of a politico-cosmological scheme that divided Ireland into five provinces. The archaeological evidence, on the other hand, revealed the sites to have been ceremonial enclosures whose banks and ditches were not specifically defensive nor was there much evidence for permanent residential occupation. He argued that these ancient sites were essentially appropriated during the early medieval period in order to support the political aspirations of the Uí Néill, the major political dynasty of the northern half of Ireland. Similar statements have been specifically applied to Navan Fort, in terms of the generation of a large body of literary lore in order to enhance the importance of neighbouring Armagh.[335]

While this approach is certainly defensible, it still leaves one wondering why early medieval Irish spin doctors, intent on creating a series of provincial capitals that were under an Uí Néill high king resident at Tara, latched on to four ancient monuments which appear to belong to the same (Iron Age) chronological horizon and possessed similar surface features and, in the cases of two, possibly three, subsurface circular buildings that had either collapsed or been buried under mounds for centuries. If the medieval Irish wanted to create a politically useful past, they did not randomly select anonymous monuments. Rather, I suspect that Navan, Tara, etc., all still retained a great cultural valence around which there were likely to be a whole series of tales. Certainly this was the case in ancient Greece where Homer depicted a Greek army, stemming from a series of similarly dated Mycenaean sites (Mycenae, Tiryns, Pylos, etc.), attacking Troy. As we have seen, archaeological assessments of the Homeric poems tend to agree that there is a major discordance between the palace systems that archaeologists have uncovered at Mycenaean sites and Troy and their depiction in Homer, which tends to be anchored around 800 BC, 400 years after the *floruit* of Mycenaean civilization.[336] But while the sites may have long been abandoned, Greeks of the 8th and 7th centuries BC were depositing ceramic and other offerings in the monuments that they attributed to the leading figures of the Trojan War as part of a hero-cult. So might we envisage the major Iron Age ritual sites of Ireland as ancient monuments about which there was a still sufficient oral tradition to ensure that their significance was still recalled centuries later. By that time their social context had evolved so much that they were reinterpreted as provincial capitals. There may even have been some recollection that they once housed enormous circular buildings, but when it came time to describe them in detail the early medieval monk reached for large contemporary structures such as Lissue enhanced with literary models to provide a suitable arena for royalty.

Conclusions

Many of the descriptions of the built environment are too generic or describe structures that have changed so little that we cannot really confine them to any of our three periods. Moreover, our knowledge of Iron Age buildings, other than the major ceremonial sites, is so poor that it is impossible to distinguish whether many of the literary descriptions should be assigned to the time of Katu-butos or later. Still, there are some very broad conclusions that we may try to make.

The earliest probable horizon depicted in the tales (where literary memory may be contemporary with archaeological remains) are the references to the major provincial centres of Tara, Emain Macha and Cruachain[337] (Dún Ailinne does not really play a significant part in the tales). The importance of these sites, however that might be understood, seems to have survived through the first millennium AD much in the same way that Homer's Mycenae, Pylos, Tiryns and Troy survived as places of major importance in the *Iliad* and *Odyssey*. On the other hand, the descriptions of these ancient sites, both Irish and Greek, need not and probably were not based on an inherited memory, conveyed by an oral literature, of their detailed appearance. Rather, the *filid* employed some of the surface or landscape details of what were already for them ancient monuments to flesh out the stories in their landscapes, for example by having Cú Chulainn swim in the Callan River or Loughnashade or Sualtaim shouting a warning off an Iron Age mound.

The next possible horizon might be that which yielded the Standard Irish Palace Description. The core of this description does suggest that there was once an oral formula for describing the construction of the ancient halls. How early this might be is very difficult to establish. While there are certainly some resemblances between the depiction of a (probably) large circular building of concentric rows of posts and the '40-metre structure' at Navan,[338] we could also make a similar claim for the medieval royal site of Lissue that would place the description much closer in time to our actual texts. It is difficult to weigh these two possibilities against one another. Lissue, so far, stands out as an admittedly controversial exception to all the other architectural evidence that we have for the early medieval period, where well over 500 houses are nowhere near its dimensions. Also, we do not have intermediary sites between the Iron Age horizon of the 1st century BC and Lissue, the date of which insecure but probably around the 9th to 10th centuries.

Whenever the basic template of the palace was created, it seems clear that it was expanded upon by monks who were very well acquainted with descriptions of buildings of comparable status in both the Bible and classical literature. So before we gain our first image of these buildings, they have been thoroughly renovated with pillars of precious metals, windows and rich furniture of a world that was certainly not that of Katu-butos.

As for the very general descriptions of the non-royal centres, these seem to be a product of the early medieval built environment rather than an earlier Iron Age landscape. It is not simply that we can easily envisage the literary descriptions in terms of our excavations of early medieval ringforts but also because the frequency of the forts in the tales is so high that it makes a far easier match with the fort-filled landscape of Ireland from the 8th century onwards than it does for any period of prehistory. The occasional reference to trivallate forts also makes a very good match against the medieval evidence. To search for trivallate forts from an earlier period, we would have to go back to the Late Bronze Age, c. 1000 BC, a time when the defensive architecture is not as comparable to the descriptions in the tales as the later medieval forts. As for the stone forts described in the literature, these too can be most easily compared with the cashels of the medieval period. Of course, one could argue that both the trivallate forts and the stone forts were inserted into the tales, not on the basis of their existence in the contemporary landscape but as ancient (and abandoned) prehistoric monuments, in the same way as we have seen ancient funeral monuments conscripted to serve as burial chambers for much later heroes. Nevertheless, I think the world of early medieval Ireland provided a much more convenient template for those who created the built environment of the Ulster tales.

CHAPTER SEVEN

Warfare and Weapons

Ogma unsheathed the sword and cleaned it. Then the sword told
what had been done by it, because it was the habit of swords at that
time to recount the deeds that had been done by them whenever
they were unsheathed.[1]

In 1897 BC the Fir Bolg, having just learned that the Tuatha Dé Danann had
invaded Ireland, dispatched their toughest warrior, Sreng, to spy on the enemy.
He set off with his sword, shield and two spears (typical of any warrior) but also
wearing a four-cornered helmet and carrying an iron club. Seeing him approach, the
Tuatha Dé sent out one of their own warriors, Bres. Encountering one another, they
were both astonished and fearful of the other's weapons and Sreng crouched down
and hid behind his shield as did Bres. They then discovered that they both spoke Irish
(as they had a shared ancestry from Nemed) and they compared their weapons in a
form of show and tell.[2] They were most impressed with the differences between their
spears. Sreng displayed his heavy javelin that he called a *cruísech* and Bres foresaw
that such a weapon would result in 'broken bones' and 'gushing gore'. For his part,
Sreng was in fear of Bres's sharp pointed *sleg*, as tradition had it that no one in Ireland
had encountered a sharp pointed weapon until the coming of the Tuatha Dé Danann.[3]

This scene was seized upon by Eugene O'Curry to distinguish between the
weapons of two of Ireland's past ethnic groups, and he scoured the archaeological
collections of the Royal Irish Academy to find the appropriate weapons described in
the *Cath Maige Tuired*.[4] His discussion was then augmented and illustrated by W. K.
Sullivan.[5] The *sleg* was identified with a range of Irish Bronze Age spearheads but the
compulsion to find a weapon that did not look like a typical sharp-pointed spear, a
Fir Bolg *cruísech*, lured O'Curry and Sullivan to compare the literary descriptions
with weapons ranging from continental swords to Irish halberds, daggers and
rapiers (FIG. 4.1).

Warfare

That the Ulster cycle is primarily concerned with warfare is obvious when we examine the cultural vocabulary (architecture, material culture, names of plants and animals, etc) and score the words according to the number of different tales in which they occur. The top ten most widely found in order of frequency are: *claideb* 'sword', *gae* 'spear', *scíath* 'shield', *carpat* 'chariot', *dún* 'fort', *slabrad* 'chain', *bratt* 'mantle', *sleg* 'spear', *cris* 'belt', and *cú* 'hound'. The Mythological cycle is quite similar and its top five items of material culture are the sword, chariot, shield and two different words for spear.[6] It is clear, then, that warfare is the primary semantic field of the Oldest Irish tradition.

In the Iron Age at the time of Katu-butos the evidence for weapons is hardly abundant. The sword was of iron (though there is also evidence for wooden (toy?) swords as well) but Katu-butos may not have wanted to show off his 'fun-sized' sword outside his homeland as the blades of Irish swords were embarrassingly short, the longest only reaching about 58 cm; most were severely reduced versions of continental and British swords.[7] The hilts were made of organic material such as bone, antler or wood, or, if we trust a slightly questionable description of Irish sword hilts by the 3rd century (AD) Gaius Julius Solinus, 'the tusks of great sea mammals'.[8] That longer swords may have existed is suggested by the remains of a (now lost) sword from Lambay Island. Also, Katu-butos may have encountered a sword with a metal hilt in the shape of a man had the Ballyshannon swordhilt, found off the coast of Donegal, ever found its way to shore in the first place; it was an import from Gaul and not native Irish. Katu-butos would have carried his sword in a scabbard, made of bronze, and highly decorated in the La Tène style. Naturally, the scabbards were as short as the swords they contained.

Katu-butos would also have carried a spear whose head ranged in size and could have been about as long as the sword he was carrying.[9] At the opposite end of the spear there may have been a bronze spear-butt whose form could range from a long tube to a flat doorknob. From the sparse evidence surviving we might also permit Katu-butos to defend himself with a wooden shield covered with leather.

The later Cattubuttas would have continued the tradition of fighting with a relatively short sword although now we find some types with a blade that expanded as it neared the point, which indicated its use as a slashing sword. Also, from the Germanic world, presumably via the Anglo-Saxons, there appeared single-edged swords like the scramasax. All the swords known so far have organic hilts and they would be regarded as small, certainly compared with the Viking swords that followed them. The longest Irish sword has a total length of 66.7 cm while the shortest Viking sword known in Ireland, dismissed as a toy sword by some, is still 10 cm longer.[10] The spear-heads would tend to be either leaf-shaped or with a shoulder as one finds among the Anglo-Saxons. By now if not earlier (our knowledge of Iron Age Irish shields being so poor) the Irish had adopted a small round shield with a metal boss in the centre.

The weapons of Cathbad's time see a continuation of those of the earlier period with the addition of new weapons borrowed or modelled on those from the Germanic world. The Vikings introduced truly massive slashing swords with metal hilts, some-times ornamented with precious metals. The blades may also have been decorated with damascening. The earlier spears, which were usually fastened with a single rivet, now might have several rivets as well as ferrules. The Norse reintroduced the bow and arrow to Ireland and the remains of a wooden bow, dating to about the 10th century, were recovered from Ballinderry 1.[11] Viking sites in Ireland have also yielded hun-dreds of iron arrowheads.[12] And to the previous weapons one should now add the axe which the Irish took to as a cheaper substitute for the sword.[13] For protection, the Irish maintained the shield with its small metal boss but otherwise lacked helmets and the only evidence for chain mail remains undated.

Sword

The sword was the primary weapon of the hero in the Ulster tales. In the contest for the championship of Ulster, the silver medallist, Conall, is defeated by a group of Geniti (ferocious female warriors) and in flight he leaves his spears, but the *Fled Bricrenn* notes that he does manage to hang on to his chief weapon, his sword.[14] Our archetypical warrior-poet, Cathbad, also carried a sword that he brandished over Nes, with whom he would eventually father the Ulster king, Conchobar.[15]

As a major weapon, the sword was an appropriate high-status gift. In a very late tale full of excruciating exaggeration, Fergus presents 3,000 swords.[16] Like King Arthur, several heroes wielded very special swords. The earliest of these was borne by Nuadu, who was armed with one of the great talismans of the Tuatha Dé Danann, a special sword that guaranteed victory when unsheathed.[17] A few swords bore names although the Irish were not in the same league as the Norse, who had over 175 named swords.[18] The Ulster king, Fergus mac Léti, had a special sword, the *Caladbolg*,[19] whose name is cognate with that of the Welsh *Caledvwlch*, borne by King Arthur and which is more widely known in some form of Latin corruption as *Caliburnus* or *Excalibur*.[20] Fergus employed this in his fight against a sea monster in Lough Rudraige.[21] After his death it was passed onto Fergus mac Róich (his possible doublet).

The later Fergus famously had this sword stolen while he was in dalliance with Medb but returned to him in the final battle of the *Táin* where, when he was confronted by Cú Chulainn and told to desist from slaying his fellow Ulstermen, he gripped it with both hands and lopped off the tops of three hills.[22] Cú Chulainn bore the *Cruaidin Catuchenn* 'hardhead steeling', which could cut through stone, tree and bone and was useful in depriving the giant Goll of his head.[23] The partner of Deirdre, Noíse, also carried a special sword gained from the sea god Manannán mac Lir which was later employed to behead himself and his two brothers with a single stroke.[24]

The sword was naturally worn on the left side[25] where it is often specifically located at the waist[26] or on a belt.[27] It might, however, also be worn over the shoulder.[28] Only once do we find someone with his sword on his right side and that is ascribed to the giant Goll who wields a sword 30 feet long.[29] And only in the case of Fergus mac Róich and his *Caladbolg* do we find someone requiring both hands to wield his sword.[30]

There are three main words for the sword in the tales: *claideb*, its diminutive *claidbíne* 'little sword' and *colg*.[31] By far the most frequent word for 'sword' is *claideb* (the diminutive is very rarely employed) but the *colg* is mentioned over 30 times. A similar word to *claideb* also occurs in the Brittonic languages, for example Middle Welsh *cleddyf* and Cornish *cledhe*, where it also indicates 'sword', and all these words appear to derive from a root meaning 'beat, strike', which makes good sense if the sword was basically for striking or slashing. More important, however, is the fact that the Irish word is not inherited from some earlier Celtic form; it is a loanword from British that entered Irish in about the 6th century,[32] or possibly a century earlier.[33] In fact, the Roman *gladius* 'sword' may be a loan from Celtic **kladyos* 'striker'. In short, *claideb* is a name that Cattubuttas or Cathbad might have applied to a weapon, but not the Iron Age Katu-butos.

When considering both the construction and provenience of a sword, it is useful to keep the blade and hilt separate, as the two might have very different origins. In the tales the blade attracts no less than 58 adjectives while the hilt is qualified by another 21 adjectives.[34] Many of these are not particularly informative: a sword might be *caín* 'beautiful'[35] or *cródae* 'bloody'[36] and blades are frequently described as red, in obvious anticipation of their gory use.[37] But some of them do give us a physical image of what the authors of the tales might have had in mind. The most frequent adjectives employed are, in order: *trom* 'heavy',[38] *mór* 'large',[39] *tortbullecha* 'heavy striking',[40] *cruaidghér* 'hard-sharp',[41] and *clas-lethan* 'grooved-wide'.[42] The blade, it seems, is living up to the etymology of the word and is often described as a large, heavy slashing blade. How large the sword was we cannot tell, as the few measurements provided involve a considerable dollop of hyperbole, such as in the case of Conaire Mór's giant bodyguard Mac Cecht, who has a sword 30 feet long,[43] or a problematic comparison with several warriors having swords as long as a weaver's beam.[44] The inspiration for comparing the length of a weapon to that of a weaver's beam is fairly certainly the Bible, in which Goliath's spear is likened to a weaver's beam.[45] Máire West has recently argued that the Irish words translated as 'weaver's beam' and employed to indicate what the prophetess Fedelm held in one hand when she foretold the destruction of Medb's army, the length of swords or the shins of a woman who seeks admission into Da Derga's hostel, actually indicated a 'weaving sword' or a 'fringe sword', weaving tools which tend to measure somewhere between about 20 and 50 cm.[46] The names of these tools (*claideb garmne* and *claideb corthaire*), she suggests, were mistaken glosses on the Latin *liciatorium* that was used to describe the length of Goliath's spear and did indeed mean 'weaver's beam'. Her arguments make good sense for Fedelm's weaving tool but raise problems when comparing the length of a hero's sword with a weaving instrument that only measured *c.* 20–50 cm, perhaps a bit larger. This is roughly the same size range of Iron Age (average *c.* 38 cm) and early medieval Irish swords (the longest measuring 66 cm). Consequently, why would the author of the passage tell us that men bore 'three black huge swords'[47] whose length was well within the range of an average (pitiful) Iron Age sword?

The image of a slashing sword is reinforced by an analysis of precisely how the *claideb* was used. On at least 21 occasions the verb associated with its use is *benaid* 'strike, beat, hew'. This verb is regularly employed in describing decapitations but also in basic combat, such as when Cú Chulainn becomes so irritated with one of his would-be opponents that he 'struck Etarcomol on the crown of his head and clove him down to the navel'.[48] In addition to these 'edge-centred' acts we also have the description of how the Ulstermen, when telling of their combats, would lay their swords over their thighs and if they lied, the blade would turn against them.[49] Swords are also used for some fine cutting as when Connla, Cú Chulainn's son, crops his father's hair with a single stroke,[50] just as his father had inflicted the same humiliation on the hapless Etarcomol.[51] A food dispenser for Fráech is described cutting up joints of meat in the palm of his hand with his sword.[52] One of the displays of marshal skills involved the edge-feat of the sword.[53] And on several occasions we find a sword being thrown, either against an opponent[54] or at a flock of birds.[55]

On the other hand, we also find that the business end of the sword could be its point, as when Cethern, falling for one of the oldest ploys in the world, runs his sword through a pillar-stone (PL. II) disguised as his adversary,[56] or when Cú Chulainn probes the trap the Ulstermen find themselves in when he runs his sword through the walls of the iron house into which they have been lured.[57] There is also the strange image of Cormac's nine followers who twirl the points of their swords on their fingers and the swords then extend themselves.[58] Fergus swears by the point of his admittedly very special sword[59] and Cú Chulainn threatens to bend every joint and limb beneath the point of his sword.[60] But these are rare exceptions to an overwhelming image of a slashing sword where the point could obviously also be employed.

To all of these descriptions we can add the mention of a single-edged sword carried by the Connacht ambassador[61] and the god Lug.[62] Such a sword clearly derives from after the Iron Age when the Irish adopted Germanic sword types that resembled the Anglo-Saxon scramasax (FIG. 7.1F).

The adjectives describing the hilt are generally more specific and the most frequent are *órduirn* 'gold-hilted',[63] followed by *intlaisse* 'inlaid',[64] *argat* 'silver',[65] and *dét*

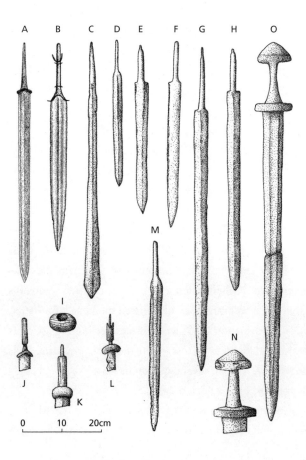

7.1. Irish swords of the Iron Age (A – Ballinderry; B – Lisnacrogher; I – Dungarvan; J – Lough Gur); of the early medieval period (C – unknown; D–F, H, M – Lagore; G – Newstead; and Viking (N, O, P – Kilmainham/Islandbridge).

0   10   20cm

'tooth'[66] or perhaps 'ivory' (there is also mention of a white hilt).[67] There are also at least a half dozen mentions of an *elta dét* 'hilt-guard ivory',[68] which utilizes a Germanic loanword (*elta*) to indicate the hilt-guard.

The image of the *claideb* is thus a large, heavy slashing sword with a hilt either of some organic material or, more often, of metal such as gold or silver, which can be inlaid. The sword is large and strong enough to cleave a man in two or behead a victim.

In the Ulster tales, the diminutive *claidbíne* 'little sword, dagger' is confined to Cú Chulainn in the *Táin*, where he wields either four or eight swords in one or both hands with a full sword (*claideb* or *colg*) in his other hand.[69]

The word for the second type of sword, *colg*, has cognates in other Celtic languages but these do not return the meaning 'sword' but rather some other pointed object, such as Old Welsh *colginn* 'awn (of barley)'. Even in Irish the word does not simply indicate a sword but 'anything pointed, piercing instrument, sting, stab, thrust'. The one possible exception to its general meaning is the name of the Caledonian king, Calgacus, whose name might mean 'possessing a sword' and into whose mouth Tacitus places his best-known quotation (the Romans 'have made the world a desert and called it peace').[70] This same Calcagus helps supply the original name of Northern Ireland's second city, Derry, which was originally (at least before the Christian association of St Columba) known as *Daire Calgaich* 'oak-grove of Calgacus'. Etymologically, then, the *colg* would appear to have been some type of stabbing or thrusting weapon the business end of which was its point rather than its blade.

Descriptions of the blade of the *colg* are not very informative: the blade is *crúaid* 'hard'[71] or *airnocht* 'bare'.[72] It may also be *díriuch* 'straight'.[73] And descriptions of the hilt are entirely limited to some form of organic hilt of tooth, tusk or ivory.[74]

Only twice do we find the *colg* in action and both instances also employ the verb *benaid* 'strike'. In the second recension of the *Táin*, Cú Chulainn's foster-brother Fer Diad struck Cú Chulainn with an 'ivory-hilted' *colg* that goes into Cú Chulainn's breast.[75] In one of the oldest references to the *Táin* we also hear how Cú Chulainn will strike a 'backstroke with his *colg*'.[76]

Although one can make a limited case for distinguishing between a *colg* and a *claideb*, they appear to be worn in the same way, i.e., either suspended from the left side[77] or over the shoulder.[78]

If we draw all this evidence together we find a weapon that both in terms of its etymology and the descriptions of its hilt indicates a thrusting sword with some form of organic (and never metal) hilt; the descriptions of its use, involving a slashing action, are, however, comparable to the *claideb*.

Where do we put these weapons in time? It is clear that the *claideb* makes a very poor fit with what we know about Iron Age weapons. The swords of Katu-butos' time were short, organic hilted, primarily used for thrusting and not called a *claideb* (FIG. 7.1A, B, J, K, L). The swords of the Ulster cycle are large, heavy, slashing swords that might have organic hilts but more often are described with decorated metal ones. By the time of Cattubuttas, Irish swords were somewhat larger and with their expanded blades certainly could have served for slashing. The introduction of a weapon similar to the Anglo-Saxon scramasax could also account for the few descriptions of single-edged swords. The references to grooved swords are, unfortunately, useless for dating purposes because wide shallow grooves on swords can be found from the Iron Age to the Viking period.[79] There would, of course, still have been the problem of the metal hilts decorated with gilt-copper alloy, silver strips or sheet silver, which would only appear in the time of Cathbad.[80] In short, it appears that the *claideb* was probably introduced in the time of Cattubuttas, but much of its description was updated after the Norse incursions into Ireland. One way out of tying the sword descriptions to earlier than the Viking raids on Ireland is to suggest that the Irish obtained the image of their main weapon from abroad. By the 5th century we occasionally find both silver and gold employed in covering the hilts of swords in southern Scandinavia and in the 6th and 7th centuries a new sword type was being taken up across the Germanic world, including Anglo-Saxon England, which included metal hilts, some of which were either gilded or of solid gold. By the 9th century there are pommels and guards decorated with silver,[81] which clearly matches some of the descriptions of the Ulster tales although there is no evidence for Anglo-Saxon hilt forms in Viking Dublin.[82]

An alternative to looking abroad for archaeological parallels is recourse to the literary evidence available to the Irish. Although the Bible might be our first stop, we can note that other than the odd case of a 'flashing' or 'two-edged' sword there are almost no actual descriptions of swords in the over 460 citations in the Bible. The only instance offering a not very convincing parallel with the Irish derives from the Apocrypha,[83] where Jeremiah gives to Judas a 'golden sword' (*gladius aureus*), but this seems to be slight reason for all the descriptions of gold (hilted) swords in the Ulster tales. As for classical parallels, there are a few possibilities but classical sword descriptions are seldom as detailed as the ones we find in the Ulster tales. Gilded swords appear in both the *Aeniad*[84] and the Latin *Iliad*,[85] while Vergil also provides us with an ivory sword[86] and a 'broad' sword (*ense...lato*),[87] one of the frequent descriptions in the Ulster tales. But these are not particularly forceful parallels and, in fact, it seems probable that when an Irish translator encountered descriptions of weapons in Latin, he shook his head despairingly and muttered 'boring' and then inserted typical descriptions of Irish swords.[88] This is particularly the case with the Irish account of the Roman Civil War where we not only have numerous references to Irish weapons but Julius Caesar even arms himself as if he were Cú Chulainn and performs an Irish weapons feat.[89]

The *colg* could linguistically go back to the Iron Age and the etymology of its name is congruent with the small Irish Iron Age swords. Its organic hilt could also be compatible with the time of Katu-butos or his successor Cattubuttas. In fact, recently a sword hilt made of whale bone has been recovered from Collierstown 1, Co. Meath, dating to the 5th or 6th centuries.[90] In this sense, it might be a genuine relict from an earlier time than when the tales were written down in the medieval period, comparable in a way to Homer's description of bronze swords with silver nails. But the few occasions depicting its use suggest that by the time the tales were recorded, the weapon was imagined to function the same way as a *claideb*, or in other words as a slashing rather than thrusting sword.[91]

The sword was carried in a scabbard for which the Irish employed three words. The first, *ferbolg*, literally 'man-bag', was usually the term for the sack in which one carried board-game pieces, but in the *Táin* it is also once used to describe a sword scabbard, here made of white silver and rings of gold.[92] More common is the *intech*, which is generally described simply as 'warlike' (*badb*).[93] Finally, there is *trúaill* 'scabbard' where we find one 'with interlaced design of bright silver'[94] or of *findruine*.[95]

Although metal scabbards are known from the Irish Iron Age (FIG. 7.2), these are of bronze and not silver or the white metal that is indicated by the word *findruine* as they are consistently described in the tales, at least where metal is involved. Silver scabbards are unknown in Ireland although

7.2. Iron Age scabbard of bronze from Lisnacrogher, Co. Antrim (length 55.4 cm).

they can be found on the continent at least as early as the 5th century, and by the 6th century there are silver mounts known from neighbouring Anglo-Saxon scabbards. Leather scabbards with interlace designs are also known from Ireland. As for external literary sources, scabbards are not described in the Bible nor our usual classical sources.

Judging by what little evidence we have, it is unlikely that the scabbard descriptions are residual images derived from the time of Katu-butos but rather, once again, they are more comparable to the later use of silver in scabbards on the continent.[96]

Headhunting

One behavioural act is intimately associated with the sword – the decapitation of one's fallen opponent, a practice abundantly in evidence among the continental Celts and frequently utilized to emphasize the archaic nature of the Ulster cycle. From the very beginning of the *Táin* the prophetess warns Medb that her invasion of Ulster will result in her leaving 'a thousand severed heads'[97] and Cú Chulainn does everything he can to fulfil this prediction until, at the end of his life, he himself is beheaded by Lugaid.[98] The taking of an opponent's head as a war trophy was so much a part of the ritual of warfare that, on occasion, defeated warriors actually requested that they be beheaded by their opponent, e.g. Lugaid to Conall.[99] Once a head had been detached it would serve as a trophy that might be brandished at your enemies,[100] impaled on either a spit,[101] a forked branch,[102] a stone,[103] or the ramparts of a fort.[104] The Ulster hero Conall claimed that he never passed the night without the head of a slain Connacht warrior as his pillow.[105] The most elaborate treatment involved removing the brains from the skull of an opponent and mixing them with lime in order to form a more solid ball-like trophy.[106] Such a brain-ball was stolen by the Connacht champion, Cet, who later slung it at Conchobar embedding it in the Ulster king's own skull until it leapt out because he over-exerted himself in his delusional attack on 'Jewish' trees.

There are two issues with employing head trophies as a chronological marker in early Ireland: how old is the practice and how was it accomplished? The great Neolithic passage tomb of Knowth also boasts evidence of Iron Age occupation and burial, including the interment of two males who had been decapitated[107] and so head-taking may well have been known to Katu-butos during the Iron Age (the burials are dated *c.* 40 BC–AD 100).[108] But this does not tell us that the occurrence of head-taking in the tales must necessarily be a direct legacy of such Iron Age behaviour. For a scan of the annals clearly indicates that while beheading was sporadically recorded from the 2nd century onwards, by the 9th century through to the 12th century, the Irish were routinely taking either each other's heads or exchanging decapitations with their Norse intruders (FIG. 7.3).[109] In short, it would have been difficult for an Irish writer, working in the time of Cathbad, to describe warfare without including some coverage of beheading. In fact, when the Irish set about translating classical works such as Dares Phrygius' anaemic account of the Trojan War, they couldn't resist inserting instances of head-taking that were never there in the Latin original.[110]

As for the method of beheading, if we recall that Iron Age swords are quite small, they would hardly be capable of hacking off a head with a single blow as is routinely described in the *scéla*. On the other hand, there is little doubt that a metre-long heavy Viking sword could do the job; possibly some of the wide-bladed swords

7.3. Headhunting in the Irish annals. Black heads = decapitations involving Vikings; grey heads = decapitations among the Irish.

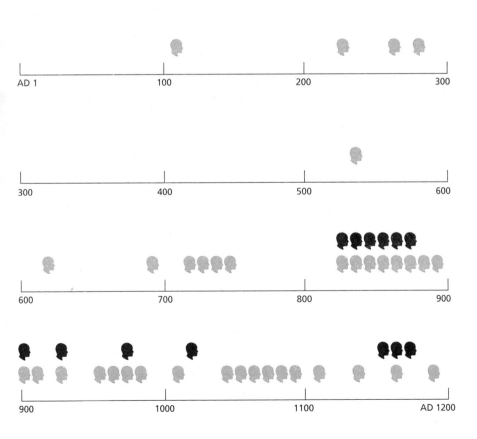

7.4. Decapitation with various swords: (upper left) typical Iron Age sword; (upper right) longest Iron Age sword; (lower left) early medieval sword; and (lower right) Viking sword.

of the early medieval period might also serve (FIG. 7.4). This is a fine call because I can hardly claim that one could not remove a head with an Irish Iron Age weapon (theoretically you could cut off a head with a penknife) but I doubt that it could be accomplished with anything remotely like the panache one finds described in the Ulster tales.[111]

Spear

While there were few names for swords in early Irish, there was a large vocabulary concerning spears that Eugene O'Curry believed were associated with the different population groups of Ireland.[112] Some of them are confined to a single individual such as Cú Chulainn who, as a boy, played with his *bun(n)sach*, literally a 'rod or staff' but here clearly a wooden javelin that Cú Chulainn would toss into the air and then catch before it landed (a motif possibly lifted from classical literature).[113] When older, Cú Chulainn possessed two differently named small javelins, a *cleittíne*[114] and a *certgae*.[115] Although small, these weapons could do considerable damage, as when Cú Chulainn casts his *certgae* at Buide which 'went into his armpit, and his liver on the other side broke in two at the impact of the spear.'[116] Another weapon, the *luinech*, is also confined in the Ulster tales to Cú Chulainn; its only distinguishing feature is that it is red.[117] In addition he possessed the *Duaibsech*.[118] Celtchair mac Uithechair was associated with the *lúin* 'lance' which he employed to kill a particularly savage hound.[119] It was also employed by Dubthach when he had it on loan from Celtchair, having been handed down to Celtchair from all the way back to the Battle of Mag Tuired.[120] This spear is so potent that when its 'spear-heat' seizes it, sparks fly from its head and it must be quenched in a cauldron,[121] an act that W. K. Sullivan argued was a poorly understood reference to the tempering of steel.[122] In the Ulster tales the spear of Cúscraid is likened to a *caindel* 'candle, light', evidently a metaphor for a spear. This weapon is described in detail, with a silver band running from the shaft to the grip or with the bands of silver alternating with rings of gold from the butt to the socket.[123] Another metaphor is *tuire*, a tower or pillar, invariably the pillar of a palace, which is used to describe very large spears.[124] Conall Cernach employed his Cúlglass in avenging Cú Chulainn's death.[125] The warrior with an aversion to doctors, Cethern, used a *bir*, which usually refers to a stake, spike or spit but here is a thrusting spear, which he plied on his enemies and of which he was also on the receiving end.[126]

The commonest terms are *gae* and *sleg*, which might suggest that they should be formally distinguished. Unfortunately, the distinction between a lance and a javelin is not always clear. In most cases where there is action described, the *gae* functions as a javelin. On occasions it is equated with both a *certgae*[127] and a *clettíne*,[128] both indicating a javelin. In other duels, Cú Chulainn throws his *gae* at his opponent, Nad Crantaill,[129] while elsewhere he is on the receiving end of 14 javelins hurled by Medb's followers.[130] The *gae bolga* (see below) that Cú Chulainn employs to kill his foster-brother Fer Diad is also simply referred to as a *gae*.[131] The descriptions of the *gae* vary considerably, so that it is clear that the name covers a variety of weapons. It is sometimes described as 'broad-bladed'[132] and 'long'.[133] The spearhead was also riveted on,[134] in one case with three rivets,[135] and in the case of the great warrior, Celtchair, 30 rivets were required.[136] In one instance the rivets were of gold.[137] A peculiar motif is the double-pointed *gae*, with a sharpened head on the butt as well as the head.[138]

The *sleg* is another word that can be used generically for 'spear' or for either a throwing weapon[139] or a thrusting weapon. While one might imagine that one weapon is a lance and the other is a javelin, we still find Cú Chulainn brandishing his two spears (*sleg*).[140] When his javelin (*clettíne*) smashes Buide's ribs and pierces his heart, it is also called a *sleg*.[141] On the other hand, Conall thrusts his *sleg* through the back of Illann, and there are many other examples of warriors dispatched by a thrust from a *sleg*.[142] When one has scraped away the less informative descriptions of the *sleg* (for example as 'sharp', 'strong', 'shining'), we are still left with a considerable variety of adjectives. They may be 'broad',[143] 'ridged'[144] and 'rivetted'.[145] In the

Táin, Illann carried a *sleg* with a 'bent point',[146] while the aged and naked Iliach had two 'gapped' spearheads.[147] The most elaborately described was one borne by Fergus that had three rings and bands of silver.[148] Fergna had a spear with a gold socket,[149] and the spears of Cú Chulainn and Fer Diad included 'thongs of hard flax'.[150] This reference to the use of an *amentum*, a leather strap attached to a javelin that increased both the distance that it could be thrown and its accuracy, unfortunately only occurs in this relatively late insertion into the *Táin*. The Irish were certainly aware of the use of the *amentum* as it was briefly described in Isidore and they employed it in their translations of classical literature.[151] For this reason we may be suspicious of any claim that this is a relict of earlier days, although that may be possible (the Gauls, for example, also employed the *amentum*).

Very frequently (in the sense that no warrior would be caught dead without one) we find the Ulster heroes carrying a *sleg cóicrind*, a five pronged or pointed spear[152] (Cú Chulainn carries two).[153] Several are described as having a ring of silver[154] or gold[155] with deluxe versions such as those carried by Bodb's group having ribs of gold, silver and bronze[156] or 50 rivets of *findruine* along with gold.[157] This weapon defies classification and has no obvious biblical or, as far as I can find among the texts obviously known to the medieval Irish, classical parallels.[158] Although not discussed by Sullivan, he did consider the appearance of the *faga fogablach*, which was described in the Book of Lismore, a 15th-century manuscript, as a weapon that had 'five prongs or barbs that were on each side of it, and each sickle or barb of them would cut a hair against a stream'.[159] Sullivan illustrated such a weapon with what he classified as a 'military fork' (FIG. 7.5), but precisely what the medieval Irish had in mind (a trident with two extra prongs?) remains a mystery.

7.5. 'Military forks' of iron that W. K. Sullivan used to illustrate the *faga fogablach*. The larger is c. 27 cm long.

The *sleg* also came in a fun-sized version, the *slegín*.[160] And in contrast to the *sleg* and *gae* we have the *foga*, evidently a smaller spear that served as a javelin. As with the *selg cóicrind*, a number of the descriptions indicate a forked weapon.[161] One is described as possessing rivets of burning gold[162] while another has thongs attached and rivets of *findruine*.[163]

The *láigen*, yet another weapon that the RIA dictionary treats as a 'broad-headed' spear, is clearly large as it covers the *lúin* of Celtchair and Dubthach.[164] While one might regard such a heavy spear as primarily being used for thrusting, in at least one tale we learn that it can also be cast and in so doing can kill nine men at a single go.[165]

The *manaís* is defined by the RIA dictionary as 'a large spear with broad head and sharp point' that, by now as the reader can see, is pretty well indistinguishable from most of the other spears. In some contexts it is clearly a thrusting weapon, as when Cú Chulainn suggests to Fer Diad that since they have not managed to kill each other with throwing spears they might as well have a shot at bringing their duel to an end with 'great long spears' for thrusting.[166] In another tale, after Maine has skewered Conchobar with his javelin (*sleg*), he then plies his *manaís* on him.[167] On other occasions, however, there is some evidence that the weapon could be thrown.[168] A recurring description tells us that it is mounted on a 'slender shaft'[169] or a shaft of ash.[170] We also read that the spear was 'perforated',[171] or bore 'neck-rings'.[172]

Finally, we have that problematic weapon of the Fir Bolg, the *cruísech*. In the *Táin*, the *cruísech* is used interchangeably with the *manaís* (here it is described as venomous).[173] Medb is also described as possessing a *cruísech* that is 'keen, sharp-edged and light'.[174] We will return to the *cruísech* below when we discuss the First Battle of Mag Tuired.

If we try to compare this abundance of spear terminology with the archaeological record we must face the depressing problem of a real paucity of archaeological evidence. For the Iron Age, for example, we only have about half a dozen spearheads that we can assign to this period.[175] Moreover, the appearance of the spearhead in Ireland, from its emergence in the Early Bronze Age until the historical period, has not changed so radically that it permits us to date most of the descriptions with any great confidence. There are both narrow and wide spearheads, leaf-shaped and shouldered. And that the shaft may be of ash tells us next to nothing as that was the main material for spear-shafts throughout both the prehistoric and historic periods.[176]

I once suggested a comparison between references to 'gapped' spears and types of perforated spears known from the Late Bronze Age[177] and, more interestingly, from the Iron Age, where small perforations are to be seen in spears from Roodstown,

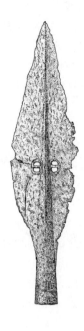

7.6. Gapped spear from Corrofin, Co. Clare (length 22.0 cm). The blade is iron while the eyelets are bronze inlays.

Co. Louth, and Corrofin, Co. Clare (FIG. 7.6).[178] But it is more likely that this is not intended as a design element but to suggest that they were simply rusted through, as they are associated with a comical attack of a naked old warrior riding in a dilapidated chariot. On the other hand, descriptions involving silver ornament mean that a large number of the spears simply have no place in the Irish Iron Age. In fact, Catherine Swift has compared the elaborate *caindel* of Cúscraid, with its rings of silver and gold, to a Viking-period spear from Woodstown, Co. Waterford, whose socket was ornamented with bands of silver.[179] As we have seen above, rivets, either functional or for decoration, are often mentioned in the tales, sometimes in large numbers on a single weapon. From the Iron Age, we have a spearhead from Lisnacrogher, Co. Antrim, that possessed two rivets. Generally, the number of rivets seems to have increased over time and multiple decorative rivets are well known from Viking Age sites in Ireland;[180] there is certainly no evidence for multiple decorative rivets from Iron Age Ireland.

Finally, there is a factor of negative evidence. Generally, we would not equate the lack of some item being described in the tales with its genuine absence but there are so many descriptions of warriors with their full kit, especially anything that might be taken as bling, that the absence of any mention of bronze spear-butts is a problem. These comprise the second largest category of metal objects dated to the Irish Iron Age (over 65 examples are known; FIG. 7.7). As we have seen above, the only

7.7. Example of doorknob spear-butt, from Coleraine, Co. Derry (length 8.6 cm).

references we have to a pointed spear-butt derives from Fintan's band in the *Táin*, which suggests a shaft with a spearhead on both ends (the Ulster cycle equivalent of a Sith's double-pointed light sabre?). The Iron Age spear-butts terminated in either knobs or, when tubular or conical, flattened ends, and were certainly not intended as weapons, although iron ferrules could be found on some Iron Age spears on the continent. And even from the later Viking period where two possible ferrules have been recovered, they do not appear to have been attached to a spear.[181] Had the tales routinely described the shiny metal butt of the spearhead, this would have displayed the type of privileged knowledge that should have been confined to the Iron Age and indicated a genuine retention of an ancient cultural motif. It would have been the Homeric version of a boar-tusk helmet or full-body shield. But the descriptions of the spears fail to do this.

Special spears

Cú Chulainn possessed two very special spears whose descriptions generally invite puzzlement. The first of these is the *deil cliss*. These words are employed in all three recensions of the *Táin* and are generally associated with some form of a heavy-duty javelin (*sleg*) or some other form of projectile. Cú Chulainn carries eight of his small javelins in one hand and the *deil cliss* in the other.[182] The puzzling part of its description is that it leaves the warrior on the receiving end riddled like a sieve (but see the discussion of the *gae bolga* below).[183] There is some attempt to explain how this might happen when Fóill mac Nechtain is killed by the *deil cliss* that consists of an iron ball that is capable of penetrating his shield and then passing entirely through his head, carrying out an equivalent portion of his brains.[184]

The *deil cliss* is nothing to Cú Chulainn's one weapon of absolute destruction, the *gae bolga*. It use was taught to the young Cú Chulainn by the woman-warrior, Aífe, with whom he trained and who bore his only son. Cú Chulainn reserved its employment for when he was pushed to his absolute limit, as was the case with Lóch,[185] Fer Diad,[186] Eochaid Glas,[187] the Fomorian Cet,[188] and his own son, whom he intended to train in its use.[189]

We will now see why this marvellous weapon has defied all attempts to render it archaeologically plausible and there are serious reasons to suspect that at least some of those who quilled descriptions of its use had little idea what they were trying to describe in the first place. Anyway, we can start with the one clear fact: the *gae bolga* was thrown as a javelin. After this things begin to get really strange. In the case of two of his victims, Lóch and Fer Diad (this is regarded as one of those doublets in the first recension of the *Táin*), the spear's point of entry is the victim's anus.[190] As there is not the slightest hint in these episodes that Cú Chulainn's opponents were stupid enough to moon the 'Hound of Ulster', we are dealing with a serious problem of how this might have happened.[191] In the second recension, Lóch and Fer Diad die from a wound directly into the heart.[192] And to round things off, the trajectory of the *gae bolga* that kills Eochaid Glas went straight down into the victim's head.[193] The hurling of the spear also poses problems in that the first two recensions of the *Táin* are agreed that Cú Chulainn launched the *gae bolga* with his toes.[194] If this were not difficult enough, in both cases in the *Táin* and also in the story of how Cú Chulainn slew his son, the spear was also launched in water. Finally, there is the peculiar way that it behaves after it has entered the body. The descriptions in the *Táin* are agreed that although the *gae bolga* has only a single barb on entrance, once embedded in its opponent the barbs increased to 24 or 30, tearing the internal organs apart. We are left, then, with the image of an aquatic, toe-launched, spring-loaded, anus-seeking javelin, an item we can't even find on eBay and which has pushed the imaginations of graphic artists illustrating Cú Chulainn magazines for years (FIG. 7.8).[195]

O'Curry described the *gae bolga*, the etymology of which he took to mean 'belly-spear', but understandably did not attempt to connect it with archaeological evidence.

7.8. *Gae bolgas* from graphic noveis: left – Will Sliney's *Celtic Warrior The Legend of Cú Chulainn*; middle – Patrick Brown's *The Cattle Raid of Cooley*; right – Gary Hamilton's *Cúchulainn: Champion of Ulster).*

He did introduce a poem that indicated that it originated in the East and was fashioned from the bones (skull) of a sea monster who died in the Red Sea, and was eventually handed on until it came to Cú Chulainn.[196] Many have presumed that the best indication of how the weapon may have appeared should derive from the etymology of *bolga*, which has been variously translated as 'bulging', 'broad-headed', 'death-dealing' and 'gapped'.[197] The latter, understood by O'Rahilly to indicate 'a weapon like a pitchfork' might, perhaps, be compared with a perforated spear but it is hard to imagine that the only other example of such a 'gapped' spear is the one referred to above in the description of the old warrior, Iliach. The linguist Julius Pokorny took the literal reading of *bolg* 'bag' and finessed this into 'bladder', concluding that the *gae bolga* was an Inuit harpoon with an attached bladder.[198] This neatly explains the association with a water launch but there is no evidence that Cú Chulainn had difficulty distinguishing between men and seals. O'Rahilly himself preferred to understand *bolg* as 'lightning' and interpreted the weapon as the lightning spear, or in other words a thunderbolt weapon, derived originally from the solar deity and the Otherworld (and the two Fergus's *Caladbolg* would be 'hard lighting').[199]

Classical literature does not offer an obvious solution to the description of the *gae bolga* except for one, admittedly rather remote, possibility (but see also Chapter Eleven). In the Irish translation of Statius' *Thebaid*, the hero Theseus threw his 'great Marathonian spear' at Creon, and it passed through a gap in his armour and 'drove a thousand points through his skin,'[200] which is not far off the description of how the *gae bolga* renders multiple wounds. The Irish translation makes it clear that we are to envisage a thousand spearpoints (*arrinde*) exploding through the skin. But this is not

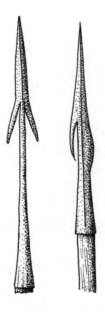

7.9. Barbed javelins
from Nydam 1 and
Vimose, Denmark.

actually what Statius' original poem conveys.[201] Here the spear penetrates what would appear to have been iron chain mail and it is through a thousand of its rings that the blood of Creon spurts most spectacularly. The Irish translator may have, of course, deliberately mistranslated the scene to accord with the behaviour he knew of Cú Chulainn's ultimate weapon. On the other hand, this may be a case of a misinterpretation or a reimagining of an earlier Latin work that resulted in the creation of the motif of an exploding spear.

An alternative approach is to ignore conjectures regarding the etymology of the name and ask whether there is anything in the archaeological record that might remotely do the job described in the *scéla*? The weapon we are looking for must obviously be a javelin and, because of the difficulties in removing it from its victim, a barbed javelin[202] might make a good prototype for this weapon. While such weapons are so far absent from Ireland, barbed javelins (FIG. 7.9) were current in Germanic Europe, certainly in the time of Cattubuttas.[203]

Sling

One of Cú Chulainn's favourite weapons was the sling. The basic word was *táball* or *cranntábal* ('wooden-sling'), which was a loanword from Latin *tabella*, leading to the suggestion that the weapon had a wooden handle. To all intents identical was the *tailm*, although this word is not clearly associated with a wooden handle. There is no description of the sling itself although, in the hands of Cú Chulainn, it was capable of taking out the shaft of a chariot,[204] Medb's troops,[205] pets perched on Medb's shoulder,[206] Medb's servant,[207] and even wounding the Irish war-goddess who supported Medb, the Mórrígan.[208] But it was not Cú Chulainn but Furbaide who launched a piece of killer cheese from his sling that dispatched Queen Medb.[209] Cú Chulainn's son was also adept with the sling.[210] The other notable use of the sling was by the Connacht champion Cet who fired from his sling the calcified brain-ball of the Leinster king, Mesgegra, which caused a slow but fatal wound to Conchobar.[211]

The motif of a hero with a sling may summon up images of David and Goliath,[212] but comparisons with the biblical accounts are neither many nor particularly close. There are also no close classical parallels with Cú Chulainn's use of the sling, although slings are frequently recorded.[213] The sling has of course existed probably since the Palaeolithic and the Iron Age hillfort of Maiden Castle in Dorset reputedly yielded some 40,000 sling stones. So far we lack any comparable evidence in Ireland for the use of massed sling-warfare,[214] but in the case of such a simple weapon, it may still be a local motif. Giraldus regarded the Irish as exceptionally skilful at throwing missiles.[215]

Bow and arrow

One of the more obvious ways that the Irish *scéla* distance themselves from any classical texts is their general avoidance of references to archery. Mentions of the bow and arrow, both of which are expressed in Ireland through Latin and Germanic loanwords, are limited to a few very late tales,[216] or to the *Táin* but in contexts where Cú Culainn's leather apron[217] or shield[218] is capable of repelling arrows along with spears and javelins. No warrior is actually depicted drawing a bow and it is likely that the few references in the *Táin* have simply been drawn from classical literature where archery is ubiquitous. In fact, it has been claimed that there is no certain evidence that the bow was employed in Ireland between 1500 BC and AD 800.[219] Giraldus tells us that the Irish were initially terrified by Norman archery but soon learned to adopt the bow.[220]

Club

There are a number of terms for club[221] in the tales, and these may be divided into two types: wooden and metal. In a very early text[222] we find the *fidot*, a word defined as both a 'cudgel' but also a word for 'aspen'. In the first recension of the *Táin*, charioteers arm themselves with such (aspen?) clubs,[223] while in the second the rods (*fidslat*) are of hazel.[224] The commonest word for a club is *lorg* and it too is applied to wooden clubs, made of oak[225] or blackthorn.[226] But the *lorg* could also be made out of iron[227] and, in the case of the three Manx giants housed in Da Derga's hostel, at the end of the iron club was a chain that had on its tip an iron pestle.[228] Built on the previous word, the *lorgfhertas* was capable of taking a man's head off.[229]

Although the club is certainly found in Irish translations of classical literature,[230] there is nothing in these descriptions to hint that this is not a motif that could be grounded in Ireland and it need not be imported.

Axe

Despite the fact that Giraldus depicted the Irish as a race of axe-murderers (FIG. 7.10),[231] until well into the Middle Ages the axe was not a typical weapon of the Irish and there is little or no evidence that this weapon, so at home among both the Anglo-Saxons and the Vikings, is to be found in early Irish literature. The only extensive references to an axe (*bíail*) are in relation to the decapitation contest in the *Fled Bricrenn*, where the disguised Cú Roí carries an axe that is specifically employed to cut off his own (reattachable) head.[232] Once we scrape away the hyperbole (it was so

7.10. According to Giraldus the quarrelsome Irish always carried an axe to inflict injury on one another.

heavy that a plough-team would have been required to shift it) all we are left with (perhaps) is that it possessed a blunt side and was not double-edged.[233]

Shield

There is probably no item of material culture in the tales that received more varied descriptions than the shield. Although there are a few rarely used terms, the basic word for shield was *scíath*. As was the case with the sword and spear, shields were named, the most famous being that of the Ulster king, Conchobar. His shield, the Ochoin, would scream whenever the king's life was in danger. It reputedly had four golden points and four coverings or rims of gold.[234] It protected Conchobar from the onslaught of Fergus in the climactic battle of the *Táin* but when his son employed it to defend himself against Illann, the son of Fergus, in a late version of the Deirdre story, it ultimately led to the death of both.[235] Conall Cernach also carried a named shield, the Bucrui or Lámthapach, that was speckled with rivets of *findruine*.[236] Many other warriors are identified with named shields but these are not described.[237]

The shield was worn or carried on the left side, as to be expected, and born with a shield strap (*scíathrach*).[238] There are a number of detailed descriptions of its use in combat with warriors seeking to attack from either over the rim or below it. This indicates that it was not a full-body shield as carried by the Greek hero, Ajax (and one of the most frequently cited examples of a Mycenaean relic in the *Iliad*).[239] There are particularly graphic accounts of the duels between Cú Chulainn and Fer Diad. Cú Chulainn, targetting Fer Diad's head, leapt onto his shield and sought to strike from above the rim but Fer Diad threw him off with a blow from his elbow[240] against the shield and then, on a second attempt, with his knee.[241] In their final encounter, as soon as Fer Diad heard that Cú Chulainn was about to launch his *gae bolga*, he lowered his shield to protect the lower part of his torso. Cú Chulainn then launched a spear over the rim into Fer Diad's breast. When our hapless victim then tried (a bit late, mind you) to raise his shield to protect the upper part, Cú Chulainn launched his *gae bolga* into Fer Diad's bowels.[242] These descriptions suggest the modest size of the shield and this is only countered, possibly, in a scene where Cúscraid's men drop down on one knee with the rim of their shields reaching their chin.[243] If the shields were resting on the ground, this would indicate a shield of about 1 m in height, more than enough to protect just about anyone's chest and groin at the same time. But we cannot be certain that Cúscraid's men actually rested the bottom of their shields on the ground.

In terms of the group use of shields, we find that Medb had to travel with a screen of shields over her head[244] and the Sons of Uisnech formed a 'fence' around Deirdre with their shields.[245] The closest thing to an actual shield-wall in the sense employed by the Norse or Anglo-Saxons occurs in the story of the death of Cú Chulainn, when the Ulstermen 'build a wall of shields',[246] and also in a very late tale where the Ulstermen locked shields.[247]

The shield might also be used aggressively, as can be seen by references to a *scíath bémnech* 'smiting shield'.[248] The rim might be razor sharp too, as when Cethern performed his Captain America feat by throwing his shield, taking out Maine, his charioteer and even his horses.[249] The most famous shield accident occurred when Cú Chulainn's father, Sualtaim, attempted to rouse the Ulstermen to aid his son, but while exiting Emain Macha in his chariot accidentally decapitated himself on the scalloped rim of his shield (this still did not shut him up).[250] Moreover, the shield could be employed in the 'edge-feat', one of the tests of warrior ability.[251] Finally, the shields might form a platform, as when the women in Medb's army, acting like frenzied groupies, begged their men to raise them up on their shields so that they could catch a look at the glamorous Cú Chulainn.[252]

We have about a hundred descriptions of individual shields in the Ulster cycle where we find both recurring elements and almost wilful variation in description. In terms of colour, for example, the shields may be black,[253] red[254] (and dark red, dark purple), yellow, blue, white, silver,[255] and variegated. Of greatest interest are the white shields, such a those described in the *Fled Bricrenn*,[256] that employ the Irish *cailc*, a loan from Latin *calix* 'limestone, lime', which was employed in whitening shields. One of the other words for shield was *finnén*, literally, 'little white one', where it is presumed that it has been applied because of the practice of whitening shields.[257]

The shape of the shield is critical for determining its chronology but also problematic as the *scéla* suggest the existence of several different shapes. One of them, indicated by adjectives such as *fotal* and presumed to indicate a 'long or oblong shield (?)' in the *DIL*, could indicate some form of rectangular or sub-rectangular shield.[258] Perhaps the best case for a rectangular shield can be found in the descriptions of Conchobar's Ochoin, which has four golden points or edges.[259] Otherwise, shields tend to be described with various adjectives suggesting that they were 'curved'.[260] While this has been taken to indicate that the shields were convex[261] rather than round, references to at least two of the curved shields occur in contrast to descriptions of 'long' shields and so a contrast between long [rectangular] and curved [round] makes better sense. Moreover, even a rectangular shield is likely to be concave. There are some additional hints at round shields to be seen in the occasional reference to a shield with 'five circles of gold', which Cecile O'Rahilly translated as 'a shield made of five concentric circles of gold'.[262] Such descriptions suggest that we are dealing with a circular shield. And while an asymmetrical shield might be thrown as a weapon, it is easier to imagine a large deadly frisbee being hurled by Cethern, taking out a warrior, his charioteer and horses.[263]

Evidence for Iron Age shields in Ireland is limited to two examples, one of which consists only of the bronze boss. The other, from Clonoura, Co. Tipperary, was rectangular and made of alder with an oak grip, and covered with leather (FIG. 7.11).[264] The critical aspect for us is that it was rectangular, and that is also the type of shield we encounter in Iron Age Britain among the native populations as well as with the Romans. Early medieval shields in Ireland, however, at least those portrayed in manuscripts, are round, as were those of the contemporary Anglo-Saxons and later Vikings, although the author of *Beowulf* does mention that his hero carried a 'towering' shield when he went up against the dragon.[265] We are working with precious little hard evidence to sustain a contrast between rectangular shields of the Iron Age and round shields both before (in the Late Bronze Age) and then after in the early medieval period. If we can read the few instances of 'long' shields and the four-cornered *Ochoin* as rectangular shields, then there is at least a possibility that there was some

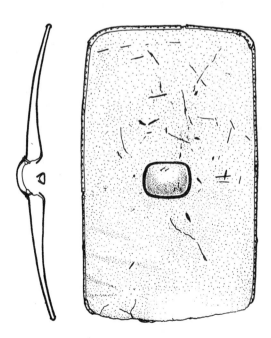

7.11. A wooden (alder) shield covered with leather from Clonoura, Co. Tipperary (length 55.4 cm). The wooden grip is made of oak and the marks on the shield were probably made by spears or swords.

recollection of Iron Age shields in Ireland. In fact, the Ochoin assumes an importance somewhat similar to that of Ajax's large body shield in the *Iliad* in that the supposed 'relic' is tied with a specific individual. The idea of a large protective shield also arises with reference to Cú Chulainn when he plants his shield 'in the ground to form a protective barrier which warded off javelins',[266] although this occurs in one of the transparently late passages associated with the scythed chariot. And this reminds us that our 'long shields' just might possibly be inspired by classical literature; the Gauls in the *Aeneid*, for example, carry 'long shields' (*scutis...longis*).[267]

The rims are frequently enough described as 'scalloped',[268] a motif for which I have failed to find a source. The rim itself may be made of gold,[269] silver,[270] *findruine*[271] or bronze.[272] In the centre of the shield was the boss that could also be of gold,[273] silver,[274] *findruine*[275] or bronze.[276] The shield itself would have been usually of wood (or leather)[277] although there are references that suggest that either the shields were made of metal or at least gilded,[278] silvered[279] or of copper.[280] And when the aged warrior Iliach enters the battle in his dilapidated chariot, he bears an iron shield.[281] Finally, the shields themselves may be decorated with concentric circles of gold,[282] animal designs in silver or gold,[283] emblems[284] and, going completely and uselessly over the top, carbuncles and precious stones.[285]

In general we probably have a mix of some native descriptions and literary borrowings. All the curved shields are more likely to be assigned to the medieval period rather than the Iron Age. But the idea of a long (rather than round) shield might also owe something to classical literature as we have seen from the *Aeneid*, which also gives us good examples of shields employing precious metals such as gold[286] and Aeneas himself carries a bronze shield.[287] Iliach's iron shield also finds a parallel in the *Aeneid*.[288] The Bible also supplied plenty of references to gold shields[289] and one bronze shield,[290] but none of silver.

Armour

The fact that references to helmets occur in all recensions of the *Táin* and in at least 13 other tales in the Ulster cycle indicates that their presence is more than sporadic, although it must be admitted that many of these tales are among the most recent. The basic word for helmet was *cathbarr*. Although some of the helmets are adorned with long descriptions, the commonest adjective is *círach* 'crested',[291] and here the evidence is quite strong that we are dealing with a motif lifted directly from classical literature such as the *Aeneid*.[292] Also, as was the case with the Fir Bolg Sreng, we have references to the helmet being rectangular.[293] Other features include describing the helmet as gold,[294] ornamented with gems and crystal and stones from the East,[295] and specifically Arabia.[296] In the late version of Cú Chulainn's death, his avenger, Conall, strips the helmets off those he has slain.[297] In another tale we find that the helmet is of little use in deflecting Cú Chulainn's deadliest weapon, the *gae bolga*.[298] There are several other words for helmets or headgear but they are not described.[299]

Body armour is also a frequent motif associated with a rather large vocabulary although seldom involving any useful description. In some cases the Irish have clearly borrowed this vocabulary from either Latin, e.g., *arm* 'armour' (Latin *arma*), or Germanic (*bróc* 'greave'), when Fráech's men, like good classical warriors, wore greaves of bronze.[300] Two terms are of greatest interest. One is the general word for a breast-plate or corslet, *lúirech*, a loanword from Latin *lorica*. It is generally restricted to late tales[301] but it does occur in the *Táin* where we find iron breastplates protecting horses.[302] The armour (on humans) was apparently put on by pulling it over one's head.[303]

Another important piece of armour is the *conganchnes* 'horn-skin' that was worn by Lóch,[304] Conganchnes mac Dedad[305] and, most famously, by Fer Diad.[306] Curiously, this horned-skin, which supposedly defended one against any weapon, did not protect the chest as Cú Chulainn's deadly cast of his *gae bolga* went over the top of it and penetrated Fer Diad's heart.[307]

Mythological cycle

The Mythological cycle boasts two extensive descriptions of warfare where the future of Ireland was allegedly decided in battles fought in different locations that, however, shared the same name (Mag Tuired: the first near Cong, Co. Mayo, and the second near Lough Arrow, Co. Sligo).

The First Battle of Mag Tuired (1897 BC)

This battle between the Fir Bolg and the Tuatha Dé Danann is described in some detail although we lack any thorough description of most of the weapons. The *claideb* 'sword' appears here but not the *colg*. That the sword is intended for slashing is indicated not only by its description in combat but also by the fact that Sreng hacks off the arm of Nuadu, the king of the Tuatha Dé.[308] Here we also get a curious reference to swords with curved blades.[309] There is also a reference to what might be taken for grooves on the swords[310] and decoration on the blades,[311] at least the latter of which is more suggestive of Frankish or Viking weapons.[312]

The warriors carry two spears that are standard throughout the literature and the range of spear terms, as we have seen above, has suggested a distinction between the spears of the Fir Bolg and those of the Tuatha Dé Danann. While the latter carry a *sleg*, a typical weapon throughout the Ulster cycle, the Fir Bolg wield the *cruísech*, a weapon whose thick shaft and general heaviness are emphasized along with the broad point (O'Curry translated *mael* as 'pointless')[313] and keen edge.[314] The distinction later becomes immaterial because, in the spirit of fair play, each side manufactures their own weapons for their opponents so that both sides are armed with a *sleg* and a *cruísech*.[315]

The shields are coloured or emblazoned[316] or covered with lime.[317] In battle their bosses may be broken and, interestingly, 'the glued seams of their shields were torn'.[318] There is also a reference to 'hooked shields'.[319] The warriors wear both helmets (*cathbarr*) and armour (*lúirech*) that require repairing over the course of the battle. [320] Finally, it might be noted that the battle is fought entirely on foot and there is no mention of the use of horses or chariots.

The Second Battle of Mag Tuired (1870 BC)

The Second Battle of Mag Tuired, between the Tuatha Dé Danann and the Fomorians, was fought with much the same type of weapons as we encounter in the later Ulster cycle. Elatha, the Fomorian king, carries two silver spears (*gae*) with riveted shafts of bronze and a gold-hilted sword (*claideb*) inlayed with silver and gold studs.[321] Here too we find the motif of throwing a sword at someone, when Dian Cécht disapproves of his son's ability to restore Nuadu's severed hand.[322] Both the common word for sword (*claideb*) and the more native word (*colg*)[323] are employed in this tale, which is linguistically earlier than the account of the First Battle. Moreover, the author conveys an account of the importance of the sword in ancient times, especially in times of battle, when swords would recount deeds done by them, and demons would speak from them because weapons had once been worshipped and utilized in swearing oaths.[324]

We do gain an insight into the production of weapons where the smith guarantees to repair any spear that separates from its shaft.[325] A brazier guarantees that he will produce rivets for spears, hilts for swords and bosses and rims for shields.[326] And the carpenter agrees to produce shields and spearshafts, at least indicating that the main body of the shield was wood.[327] In describing the actual production process when the smith Goibniu produces swords (*colg*), spears (*gae*) and javelins (*sleg*), he does so in three strokes (as also do the carpenter and brazier in their tasks). Although the material of manufacture is nowhere indicated, this suggests forging iron and not casting the bronze weapons that would have been expected if this battle had really been set before the Iron Age. As for the Fomorians, they are depicted wearing helmets (*cathbarr*) and armour (*lúirech*) and employing the spear (*manaís*) in their right hand while their sword hung from their belt.[328] Just as Cú Chulainn often employed a sling, so also does his divine father Lug, who uses this weapon to kill the major champion of the Fomorians, Balor of the Evil Eye.[329]

There is some evidence for archery,[330] and charioteers are mentioned in passing[331] – their chariots, goads and horses are even named,[332] yet they play absolutely no part in the battle.

Assessment

It hardly need be said that the weaponry and armour described in these two tales bear little resemblance to their imagined dates, which would set both battles in the Early Bronze Age, a time in which we would not find swords, helmets or armour in Ireland. Had the battles been fought *c.* 1900–1700 BC, we might expect the opposing sides to be slashing at each other with halberds or, perhaps, some very rare daggers; in fact, bronze axes were far more plentiful at this time than any other potential weapon, although we are on the eve of the introduction of the bronze socketed spearhead. Moreover, the bow and arrow was still in use at this time, but we can hardly make much out of references to the bow and arrow in the Second Battle as they employ Latin and Norse or other Germanic loanwords to describe the weapons. One aspect of interest is that both battles are fought on foot and the chariot is not even mentioned with respect to CMT1 and only as a sort of appendage in CMT2. A True Believer, I suppose, could argue that this proves the antiquity of the tales as it sets them well before the advent of chariotry in the Iron Age. But given all the other anachronisms (including the Dagda's use of coins employing an Old English loanword[333]), this 'negative evidence' is hardly compelling and the description of weapons here is little different from the Viking or earlier Germanic elements found in the Ulster cycle.

Conclusions

The earliest material horizon we seem to be able to recover in the Ulster tales *might* date back to the Iron Age, when the ancestor of the *colg* '(thrusting) sword' would be at home both lexically and archaeologically. But by the time the Ulster tales were

7.12. Iron Age warrior (left) from the time of Katu-butos (with rectangular shield, short sword and spear with bronze spear-butt), and mediaeval warrior from time of Cathbad (with round shield and large slashing sword).

committed to writing, the fact that this sword was primarily for thrusting had been forgotten and it was treated similarly to the later *claideb* '(slashing) sword' (FIG. 7.12). Lexically, the *claideb* was borrowed into Irish in about the 5th or 6th centuries and this may well have been in accompaniment with new Roman/British type weapons imported about that time. So Cattubuttas could have composed tales mentioning both the *colg* and the *claideb* but our descriptions of the latter weapon often seem to have derived from a still later period when the Irish became acquainted with the large and highly decorated swords from the Germanic world, especially those of the Norse who raided and settled in Ireland. The descriptions of the scabbards in which the swords were carried are most probably of the medieval period, although exact matches are hard to come by. The routine references to silver and *findruine* suggest a medieval date (rather than Iron Age) prompted by objects physically known to the Irish rather than a product of literary inspiration from the Bible or classical literature.

Most of the spears mentioned in the tales could be of almost any period from the Early Bronze Age onwards (the tales are generally silent on whether we are dealing with bronze or iron spears) except for those whose description includes gold, silver or *findruine*, which would suggest a date during the medieval period. Multiple rivets may also be a later medieval marker.[334] We have also seen that one series of items, the bronze spear-butts, although they would certainly have been known to the world of Katu-butos, are nowhere mentioned in the Ulster tales.

If the descriptions of the shields are taken to indicate that they were round, then most of the shields in the Ulster tales are of medieval origin. And while there may be exceptions to round shields, the few descriptions of rectangular shields may have been influenced by Latin literature.

The other accessories of war such as bow and arrow, armour and helmets do not find comparable archaeological *realia* in Ireland across the time investigated and in almost every case we can probably make a stronger case for a foreign literary source for these motifs.

CHAPTER EIGHT

Transport

Their mode of fighting with their chariots is this: firstly,
they drive about in all directions and throw their weapons
and generally break the ranks of the enemy with the very
dread of their horses and the noise of their wheels; and when
they have worked themselves in between the troops of horse,
leap from their chariots and engage on foot. Thus they
display in battle the speed of horse, [together with] the
firmness of infantry.

Julius Caesar on the Britons[1]

While names like Ferrari, Lamborghini and Maserati might predispose us to assume that Italy had completely cornered the fast vehicle market, the ancient Romans also held the chariots of the Gauls in high esteem. The Gaulish name for a vehicle, *karros*, was borrowed by the Romans as *carrus* (our 'car'), while the Gaulish *carbanton* 'chariot' provided the origin for the Latin *carbentum* 'coach, carriage, chariot'. But when Julius Caesar invaded Britain in 54 BC he was surprised to find himself confronting British warriors attacking in chariots, as the chariot had already disappeared from the arsenals of the Gauls.[2] Its last mention in Britain in the context of combat was in AD 84.[3] So here we have a cultural item, closely associated with the Celtic-speaking peoples of the continent and Britain, and well anchored in the Iron Age. As we have seen in the preceding chapter, the *carbad* 'chariot' ranks fourth in terms of the number of Ulster cycle tales in which it occurs (over a hundred times alone in TBC[1]), and already by the time of W. K. Sullivan one could argue that war chariots belong 'not to a later period than the second or third century of the Christian era'.[4] This argument, in various guises,[5] has evolved over succeeding generations to support the proposition that the chariots described in the Ulster cycle may be genuine relics of Iron Age Ireland.

Archaeology

Surveying the equestrian landscape of the Iron Age, one could hardly miss the fact that horse-bits comprise the largest class of La Tène metalwork in Ireland. Numbering around 140 examples, they are almost exclusively made of bronze, with the exception of two bits of iron.[6] As to whether the bits indicate horse-riding or paired draft, the evidence is equivocal. There are only a few instances of two bits being found together, which might suggest paired draft. There is also some evidence for asymmetrical wear or decoration on only one side of a bit, which again might suggest it was for a horse pulling on one side of a team.[7] But the only reason why one might not regard most of these bits as evidence for riding horses is the allure of the literary evidence that so forcefully emphasizes chariots and charioteering rather than horse-riding.[8]

The existence of wheeled vehicles in Iron Age Ireland is undoubted and includes disc wheels that date to the 5th or 4th centuries BC and which would have supported a farm cart or wagon. As for the actual remains of chariots, the evidence is extremely meagre. Unlike Britain, where there are at least 20 known chariot burials, there is no evidence of a chariot burial (so far) in Ireland, so any argument that chariots existed in Ireland must be built on stray finds of metal or well-preserved wooden artifacts that may have adorned or served a function on a chariot. What we do have are some bronze horn-like fittings that may have served as decoration on a yoke (FIG. 8.1). To this could be added a bronze terret (FIG. 8.2), a device fixed to the yoke through

8.1. Possible horn-like chariot mount for the end of a yoke, from Lough Gur, Co. Limerick (height 16.4 cm).

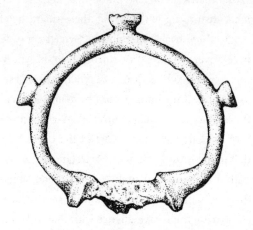

8.2. Bronze terret from Co. Antrim (height 4.7 cm). The reins would pass through the terret, which was mounted on the yoke.

which the reins would be passed, and some possible examples of lynch pins (FIG. 8.3). There is also evidence for a wooden yoke (FIG. 8.4) that was presumably associated with paired-horse draught rather than oxen,[9] and other pieces of worked wood, found along an Iron Age timber road, may have been parts of wheeled vehicles.[10] This is the only concrete evidence for chariots in Iron Age Ireland. If Katu-butos had travelled to Britain he would have discerned some major differences between the Irish chariots and those of Britain. While one terret is known from Co. Antrim in the far north of Ireland, it is clearly an import. As British terrets number nearly 600, we must presume that the reins of Irish vehicles passed directly through the yoke

8.3. Lynch pin from Dunmore East, Co. Galway (length 11 cm).

8.4. Wooden horse yoke from near Dungannon, Co. Tyrone (length 1.24 m).

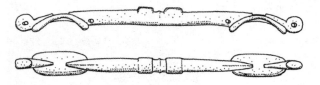

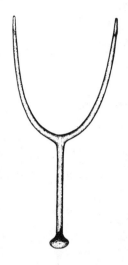

8.5. Y-piece harness component of bronze from Coleraine, Co. Derry (length 31 cm).

rather than a metal terret mounted on it. Also somewhat disturbing is that while there might be about one to three Irish lynch pins known (there is debate here), over 130 are known from Britain. And while there seems to be a dearth of lynch pins and terrets in Ireland, Katu-butos would have also known that there was a (usually bronze) Y-shaped object (FIG. 8.5) that formed a part of the horse harness, that number over a hundred in Ireland but are essentially unknown in Britain.[11] It has been suggested that we cannot apply a quantitative approach to comparing the Irish evidence with that of Britain or the continent because Ireland lacks the burials and settlement evidence found elsewhere,[12] but I would think that when the quantitative evidence consists primarily of chance finds, then it is indicative that in terms of chariots, there are still some striking differences between Ireland and Britain.

The evidence for wheeled vehicles during the times of Cattubuttas and Cathbad is equally poor. The hub of a spoked wheel of presumably early medieval date was recovered from Lough Faughan crannog, Co. Down,[13] and vehicle trackways continue through to the medieval period. Of considerable interest are the depictions of chariots on six of the 235 high-crosses (FIG. 8.6), some of which have been argued reflect actual scenes from the Ulster cycle.[14] To this may be added references to

8.6. Chariot depicted on a high-cross at Monasterboice, Co. Louth.

chariots in the law texts, one of which, dating to *c.* AD 700, defines a 'highway' as a road wide enough that the chariots of a king and a bishop can pass each other.[15] One of the last references to a chariot occurred in 811 when, according to the *Annals of Ulster*, neither horse nor chariot was allowed to attend the fair of Tailtiu. Even later in 1020 we find reference to 'the abbot's chariot' going up in flames during the burning of Armagh, although this may have referred to an old relic.[16]

It should be noted that there is evidence for horsemanship, especially after the Viking incursions, where we find iron horseshoes, saddles and stirrups as well as highly decorated bridles.[17]

Chariots in the Ulster cycle

There are an enormous number of references to chariots in the Ulster tales, exceeding a thousand mentions. In the first recension of the *Táin* alone there are 157.[18] The chariot (*carpat*)[19] was a two-wheeled vehicle pulled by a team of two horses that, as we have seen earlier, appears to have been described under the influence of the descriptions of horses set out by Isidore of Seville. Under extraordinary circumstances we might find a magical chariot pulled by a single horse.[20] The horses were driven by a charioteer (*ara*) whose name is occasionally recorded, especially that of Láeg, the charioteer of Cú Chulainn, who possessed all three charioteering skills guaranteeing the swiftest arrival at the intended destination irrespective of terrain.[21] There was also Ibor, the charioteer of Conchobar who drove Cú Chulainn on his first raid. The Second Battle of Mag Tuired from the Mythological cycle also includes lists of the names of not only charioteers and horses but even the chariots themselves and the goads employed by the charioteers, although the use of the chariot in the battle itself is not actually described.[22] According to one brief text, charioteers were seated with the musicians (horn-blowers and flute-players) in the king's hall.[23]

The warrior sat immediately behind the charioteer. These positions were unimaginatively rendered in Old Irish as *ara* 'charioteer' (from **are-sed-s* 'he who sits in front') and *eirr* 'chariot-warrior' (from **er-sed-s* 'he who sits behind'). The primary function of the chariot appears to have been to convey the warrior to the battle, offer him a platform for intimidating or impressing his opponents and provide him with a convenient vehicle for carting away or displaying the heads of his victims if he was successful or a swift escape if he was not. Nevertheless, there are also occasions when the warriors might engage each other from chariots, although the term *cairptech* 'chariot-warrior' was rarely applied.[24] One of the great slaughters of the *Táin* occurs when Cú Chulainn mounts his scythed chariot from which he dispatches innumerable warriors, horses and hounds in Medb's army.[25] That the text actually refers to a 'scythed' chariot is problematic as the key word in question, *serda*, can also mean 'Chinese' or at least 'oriental'.[26] But this particular vehicle certainly appears to be a borrowed literary device onto which has been heaped a mountain of fantastic description.[27]

Although chariots were normally depicted as being driven by males, there are also references where women were behind the reins. For example, Cethern's wife resupplies her husband's weapons, which she brought in her own chariot,[28] and we also find Conchobar's daughter serving as *ara* for her father.[29] Most other female drivers tend to be alone and from the Otherworld.[30] Chariots were highly valued commodities. Medb had nine[31] that travelled in a formation around her (but not so close as to soil her clothes),[32] while Conchobar had at least 13 (12 of which failed Cú Chulainn's stress test in TBC[1] and 17 in TBC[2]).[33] Whenever Medb was looking for a bribe (other than her daughter or her own enticing thighs) she would offer a chariot. Various members of Medb's army were offered bribes of chariots valued at seven cumals (worth a cow or female slave) if they would take on Cú Chulainn,[34] although the one offered to Fer Diad in TBC[1] was worth thrice that[35] and, by the second recension, inflation had taken it to four-times seven cumals,[36] which was quite generous as that was worth a cumal more than the chariots that Ailill and Medb themselves were carried in.

The chariot was associated with a number of rituals. For example, a chariot moving clockwise was indicative of a good omen,[37] while a chariot on a withershins course was taken as an insult, challenge or evil omen.[38] At Tara there stood a standing stone (a 'stone penis') at the end of a race-course for chariots against which the axle of a successful candidate for the kingship would scream.[39] Also, the chariot of the prospective king would tilt up before anyone regarded as unqualified tried to mount it.[40]

The classic descriptions

Although there are many references to different parts of the chariot, there are also nine instances of formulaic descriptions that are clearly interrelated and contain the remnants of an original core.[41] As with the Standard Irish Palace Description, we are again in the realm of ancient Irish verse,[42] as can be seen from these alliterating lines of 4/3 or 3/3 syllables describing the chariot of Conall Cernach in *Fled Bricrenn*:[43]

Carpat fidgrind	*féthaidi*
da droch finna	*umaide*
sithfe find	*forargit*
cret aurard	*drésachtach*
cuing druimnech	*dronuallach*
dá n-all dúalcha	*dronbudi*

chariot of fine wood	smooth-finished
two wheels fair	of bronze
pole of white	silver
frame high	creaking
yoke ridged	with solid coils(?)
two reins coiled	solid yellow

Conall, as the second-place finisher in the contest for the championship of Ulster, is depicted in a more modest chariot than Cú Chulainn but a classier one than the bronze medallist, Lóegaire. While the descriptions are basically the same, Conall's wheels are made of bronze while those of Cú Chulainn are of iron; Conall's chariot has a *síthbe* 'pole' that has a silver mounting while the pole of Cú Chulainn's chariot is of white silver with a mounting of *findruine*. Elsewhere in the earliest recension of the *Táin* we find Cú Chulainn approaching Fer Diad in a 'beautiful roomy chariot (*carpat*) of white crystal, with solid gold yoke (*cuing*), with great sides (*tarbclár*) of copper, with shafts (*fertas*) of bronze, with a harness(?) (*lungeta*) of white gold, with framework (*crett*) of narrow compact opening…and so on.[44]

There has been a series of articles discussing the probable material referents to the Irish vocabulary employed in describing chariots that are technical but, as they generally concern perishable parts of the chariot, are not critical to our discussion.[45] Moreover, textual analysis suggests that over time, the meaning of some of the terms probably became lost to those who composed the tales. David Stifter, for example, has demonstrated how passages describing chariots in the first recension of the *Táin* were simplified by the author of the second recension, who appeared to be less conversant with the objects he was describing.[46] The starting point for most recent discussion of the Old Irish chariot is a paper by David Greene which examined 14 key terms found in the earliest chariot descriptions in the Ulster cycle. The results of Greene's discussion were summarized in a much reproduced drawing by Liam de Paor (FIG. 8.7).[47] Greene's portrayal of the Irish chariot as 'a

8.7. Reconstruction of an Old Irish chariot
by David Greene and Liam De Paor.

simple two-wheeled cart' has often been regarded as a rustication of the type of light chariots excavated on the continent. Raimund Karl has reviewed the evolution of our reconstructions of Iron Age chariots and has published his own image of a Celtic chariot whose parts have been labelled with their Irish terms (FIG. 8.8).[48] He emphasizes that the literary descriptions are not exact descriptions of Iron Age vehicles but that chariots continued in use during the early medieval period and these were little altered from their Iron Age predecessors; in other words the literary descriptions are not actually of Iron Age vehicles but of quite similar medieval chariots that survived in Ireland.

We are at a point where we would do well to list some of the possible interpretations of our literary evidence:

1. The *scéla* preserve descriptions of Iron Age chariots as they existed in Ireland or folk memories of British or Gaulish chariots if the Irish had only recently arrived in Ireland.
2. The *scéla* provide descriptions of contemporary early medieval vehicles that generically resemble earlier Iron Age vehicles.
3. The *scéla* provide descriptions of chariots drawn from other literary traditions such as the Bible and classical literature.

As the reader may be trying to get his or her head around the practicality of driving a chariot made out of white crystal,[49] let us tackle the third option, a classical source, first and then try to sort out the more intractable options afterwards.

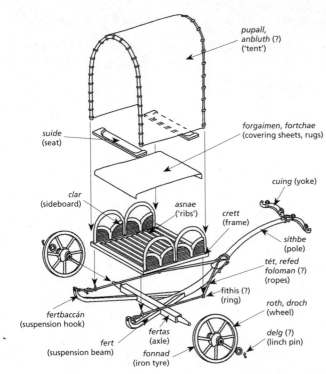

8.8. Reconstruction of an Old Irish chariot by Raimund Karl.

pupall, anbluth (?) ('tent')

forgaimen, fortchae (covering sheets, rugs)

suide (seat)

cuing (yoke)

clar (sideboard)

asnae ('ribs')

crett (frame)

síthbe (pole)

tét, refed foloman (?) (ropes)

fithis (?) (ring)

roth, droch (wheel)

fertbaccán (suspension hook)

fertas (axle)

delg (?) (linch pin)

fert (suspension beam)

fonnad (iron tyre)

In order to discuss the source of the chariot descriptions, the reader should take a look at Table 8.1 where the names of the parts of the chariot are taken from the formulaic descriptions but the material of composition derives both from the formulaic descriptions and any other tale[50] where the composition is provided. Also included are two chariots from classical literature.

The great reliance on describing various parts of the chariot as composed of precious metals or stones rather suggests that the descriptions have been larded with quite a lot of hyperbole. While the medieval Irish could always have generated these fantastic descriptions on their own, classical composition (and less likely the Bible)[77] certainly offered suitable models that they could embellish. Fanciful chariot descriptions go back at least to Homer's portrayal of Hera's chariot in the *Iliad* that has gold bridles, harness and yoke, bronze wheels, and a nave and pole of silver.[78] More accessible sources for such descriptions would have been Latin works such as Ovid's *Metamorphoses*, where we find a golden axle, pole and wheels, silver spokes and a yoke of chrysolites and jewels,[79] or a much later 5th-century AD source such as Sidonius, where again a crystal yoke, ivory spokes and a pole of yellow metal are engaged in pulling a chariot.[80] Among the striking parallels are the use of crystal in

Table 8.1: Parts of the chariot and the material of composition in the Ulster cycle and some classical sources.

Part	Name	Material	*Iliad* 5.721–732	*Metamorphoses* 2.107–109
chariot	*carpat*	wood,[51] crystal,[52] *findruine*[53]		
wheel	*droch*	gold,[54] bronze,[55] iron[56]	bronze	gold (silver spokes)
wheel	*roth*	*findruine*,[57] bronze, iron[58]	golden (felly)	
pole	*síthbe*	wood,[59] silver,[60] *findruine*,[61] bronze[62]	silver	gold
shafts	*fertas*	*findruine*,[63] bronze,[64] copper[65]		
frame	*crett*	wood, tin[66]		
yoke	*cuing*	gold,[67] silver[68]	gold	chrysolites, jewels
bridle	*all*	gold[69]	gold	
harness?	*lungeta*	gold,[70] *findruine*[71]		
bridle-bits	*pellec/bellec*	gold,[72] silver[73]		
side-piece	*tarbchlár*	copper[74]		
goad	*brot*	silver[75]		
goad	*flesc*	silver[76]		
axle			iron	gold
nave			silver	

both one of the *Táin*'s descriptions[81] and in classical literature and the use of silver to describe both the pole and yoke, which is also found in classical descriptions. Finally, there is some similarity between the ordering of the elements described in the three formulaic passages where the chariots of the three contestants for the championship of Ulster are contrasted (wheels, pole, yoke and bridle) and Homer's description of Hera's chariot. In some cases, and these are unaccounted for as we have no reason to believe that the early Irish had access to Homer,[82] we can find near translations of the Greek text into Irish: for example, we can highlight *éx argúreos rhumòs* 'of silver (the) pole' and *sítfe find forargit* 'pole white and silvered' or *khrúseion kalòn zugón* 'gold (and) good yoke' and *cuing druimnech dronordae* 'yoke ridged firm-golden'.

David Greene's reconstruction of the Old Irish chariot was based on the earliest texts (7th to 8th centuries) that generally portrayed a vehicle which was at least reasonably plausible, unencumbered by embellishments of crystal and gold. Linguistically, almost all of the terms associated with the chariot could be explained from Celtic antecedents and there was no clear evidence of foreign loanwords, which served to convince Greene that the Irish chariot was 'a largely indigenous development'.[83] The question then arises as to whether the chariot descriptions reflect inherited descriptions of an indigenous vehicle that has been 'pimped' by Irish monks well acquainted with the image of chariots in classical literature or whether the classical passages themselves served as a source for the Irish descriptions? Let's return to this after we have compared the archaeological evidence with our literary descriptions.

The different reconstructions of the chariot highlight one of the great problems of comparing the literature with the archaeological evidence. Most of the terms are entirely generic. The words for wheel, yoke, pole, harness and frame could all be equally applied to a wagon or farm cart as a chariot. It is only in the detail of description that we exclude a wagon (the Irish *carpat* has two wheels instead of four), an Irish jaunting car (there is only one front pole on a *carpat*), or a farm cart (the *carpat* appears to be very light and easily dismantled). And, most obviously, it is occupied by a charioteer and a warrior in the tales (though we also have saints driving chariots in medieval literature).[84]

Lacking well-preserved remains of vehicles from the Iron Age and subsequent periods, we are dependent on the metallic finds that, as they were increasingly replaced by iron, diminish rather than increase through time. The most numerous horse-associated find of the Irish Iron Age are the 140 odd horse-bits that, as we have seen, may have been as much for horse-riding as for draught. For the purposes of argument, however, we will assume that they were for paired draught.

The word for horse-bit or bridle found in the earliest texts is *all*, later replaced by the loanword *srían* (< Latin *frenum* 'bridle').[85] These earliest examples are described as curly, firm, yellow and inlaid.[86] If we presume we are dealing with horse-bits, then the Iron Age objects make a reasonable fit as the loops might be referencing the different curved links and as all but two are of bronze, the yellow colour would be appropriate (bronze is yellow or gold before it develops a green patina). Elsewhere in the *Táin* we have reference to bridles of gold that we might take to be hyperbole. There is also evidence for enamelling the end studs of some of the rings: red enamel

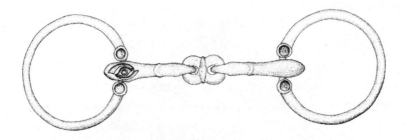

8.9. Bronze horse-bit still retaining its original gold-coloured patina and with studs showing traces of red enamel. From Lough Beg, Co. Antrim (length 32.5 cm).

was recovered from a stop stud from a horse-bit from Lough Beg, Co. Antrim (FIG. 8.9).[87] But while the descriptions may fit with the Iron Age, it is not the only period to which the horse-bits might be assigned as iron horse-bits of the medieval period might also be plated with bronze.[88]

Another group of items potentially associated with chariots are bronze fittings that Barry Raftery suggested were probably employed to ornament the ends of a yoke[89] or some other part of the chariot. The most archaic descriptions of the yoke have it *druimnech* 'ridged', which is graphically depicted in a riddle exchange between Cú Chulainn and his intended wife, Emer, where we learn that a woman's cleavage seen at the top of her tunic is like the lovely plain beyond a yoke.[90] Generally, the material descriptions of the yoke suggest that they were entirely of solid gold/gilded,[91] or silver/silvered.[92] That the yoke was specifically ornamented with a horn-like attachment at its ends, as one might expect from the meagre archaeological evidence, does not seem to be part of the literary description.

In a recent study of fantastic technology in early Irish literature, Will Sayers has translated the description of the yoke of Cú Chulainn's phantom chariot as: 'the yoke with gilded terrets (pointed and gilded)'.[93] If the text is correctly translated (there is always room for doubt with respect to some words), we would have a very problematical reference to an Iron Age yoke. On the one hand, it would provide evidence that the reins of Irish chariots passed through metal terrets that are commonplace among Iron Age chariots in Britain. But it would also be problematic in that, as we have already seen, only one terret has been found in Ireland, of presumed British manufacture, while 600 are known from Britain. The archaeological evidence suggests that Irish vehicles did not employ terrets but that the reins passed through perforations in the yoke itself. If an Irish text is describing a yoke with terrets, it is more likely describing a British chariot!

Finally, we have the problem of the Y-pieces, the large bronze objects that are shaped ostensibly like a spur but are at least twice as large as a medieval spur. They appear to have served as an important part of the bridle of a horse and would have been well known to Katu-butos (whom archaeologists would love to ask how precisely they were employed!). There is nothing about the descriptions of the horse-bits that would seem to indicate with any certainty that they were referring to this enigmatic large bronze object. While negative evidence is always going to pose problems of interpretation, we are discussing an item of the first centuries AD that numbers over a hundred and constitutes the second largest category of Irish Iron Age artifacts. As they were an element of Iron Age 'equine bling' associated with the transportation of elites, their absence from the Ulster tales is noteworthy. Or, to reverse the argument, had we solid evidence for their existence from our literary sources, this would provide the type of privileged information that would confirm an Iron Age date for the motif, i.e. a reference to an ancient object that was unknown to subsequent periods. On the basis of this argument, coupled with our failure to match the literary descriptions of Iron Age yoke (?) ornaments and the reference to a post-Iron Age element such as silver, even in reputedly early texts, the case for regarding the descriptions as reflecting exclusively Iron Age vehicles is found wanting.

The physical evidence for chariots in the following period, until the last mention of a chariot in the 11th century, is extremely poor outside of depictions of chariots on high-crosses. These often heavily eroded images (FIG. 8.6) generally represent religious processions and offer precious little actual detail other than the spoked wheels, pole and harness (although the dog, apparently standing on the pole of a chariot from a high-cross at Ahenny, is certainly a novel touch). There is, of course, also written evidence, including the law texts and saints' lives, that demonstrates the importance of the chariot centuries past the supposed *floruit* of the Ulster tales, but these do not offer graphic descriptions of the vehicle. Here we recall Raimund Karl's conclusion that the texts were describing chariots from early medieval Ireland that were similar to those of the Iron Age and performed the same functions in society.[94] So we now return to the question: were the formulaic descriptions of chariots based on the appearance of chariots in the time of Cattubuttas or were they still the products of Irish monks whose minds had been dazzled by the images of chariots in classical literature?

There are a number of objections to deriving the formulaic descriptions of the Old Irish chariot from a classical model. Firstly, much if not all of the vocabulary relating to the earliest descriptions of the chariot is native Irish and, in some cases, shares cognate terms known in Gaul so that we can well suspect that they were employed during the Iron Age. Secondly, the earliest Irish descriptions are not loaded down with precious metals and gems, so if we propose that Ovid or Sidonius or some unknown translation of Homer stimulated the Irish to create their own descriptions, we must also explain why they stripped away most of the references to silver poles, golden yokes, etc., and then reintroduced them several centuries later. When it came to describing things, the medieval Irish could hardly be labelled as 'minimalists'. Thirdly, the earliest Irish descriptions often emphasize physical attributes such as 'hard', 'polished', 'strong', straight', 'ridged', etc., that are not found in the more extended classical chariot descriptions, at least as far as I can determine. Fourthly, the classical descriptions are not presented in the type of terse formulas seen in the Irish but rather in a far more expansive style: the yoke of crystal depicted by Sidonius, for example, was acquired 'in early winter, when the ice of the young world began to increase the bulk of the Caucasus, was compacted of a piece of the Tanais by dint of the northern frosts...',[95] requiring an Irish monk to run a red quill though most of the description. And finally, although the axle and spokes are mentioned in the *scéla*, they are not described as in classical literature; nor is the nave really mentioned in the Ulster tales.

Nevertheless, it is also enormously unlikely that the Irish would construct formulaic descriptions of chariots that do resemble those of the classical world unless they had been influenced by similar passages in Latin literature. We have already seen that they employed Isidore of Seville in constructing their descriptions of the horses pulling the vehicles and it seems (to me at least) that the resemblance of the earliest Irish vehicle descriptions to those found in classical literature are too close to be put down to independent invention.

Squaring this circle is a real headache but here is the best model I can come up with. During the Iron Age the Irish possessed an inherited Celtic vocabulary pertaining to chariots, elements of which were shared with both the Britons and Gauls. Whether they had formulaic descriptions of Iron Age chariots embedded in their oral literature is a moot question. The Irish came into contact with Latin literature during the later time of Cattubuttas, c. AD 400–700. That the descriptions require certain linguistic developments that appear to be no earlier than the 5th century helps confirm the earlier threshold date and, perhaps, the fact that the syllable count varies from the earliest archaic metre might suggest a somewhat later date.[96] The descriptions then were made in a loose imitation of classical descriptions. In some cases the verse depictions adhered more closely to the actual vehicles of the early medieval period while others were composed that employed the metallic hyperbole seen in the classical descriptions. There need not have been an earlier 'purely Irish' phase and a later 'classical' phase of imitations; rather, the Irish learned classes responded to classical stimuli in different ways. And it should be emphasized that this argument does not impinge in any way on the existence or otherwise of chariots in Iron Age Ireland (that is purely an archaeological matter); it only pertains to the date of the earliest *image* we retrieve of such vehicles in the *scéla*.

Wagon

Much less frequent than the chariot was the wagon, which was known under several names, *carr* 'cart, wagon' and *fén* (or *fénae*) 'cart, wagon', with no clear distinction between them. For example, Nad Crantaill's formidable arsenal of weapons initially arrives in a *carr* in TBC[1] but then we learn that they are in a *fénae*.[97] Either vehicle was clearly for heavy traction such as hauling wine to keep the men of Connacht lubricated during the *Táin*,[98] or carting in the tail of a fattened mega-pig to a feast,[99] or hauling a cartload of anachronistic arrows.[100] There are also references to Cú Chulainn possessing a 'four-wheeler'[101] and to nobles from Norway being conveyed to Dún Dealgan in both chariots and 'four-wheelers' (*cethairríad*).[102] The 'four-wheelers' are very likely lifted from classical literature, such as the *Aeneid*.[103]

Horse-riding

The traditional position is that the Ulster cycle depicts a world where the chariot was known but where horse-riding had not yet been introduced. David Greene further supported this hypothesis in arguing that there is no native word for 'trousers' in Irish, an item of apparel that horse-riding would seem to call for.[104] This proposal is part of a widespread model found in the epic traditions of other peoples that there was a period of chariotry that preceded horse-mounted warriors. The rejoinder to this is that epic traditions such as those from Greece and Ireland were essentially concerned with elite warriors who could afford chariots as prestigious weapons, while horse-riding, which was regarded as less prestigious, was excluded from the arsenal of the epic heroes.

In reality, horse-riding is not entirely absent from the tales of both the Mythological and Ulster cycles although it is often found in ambiguous contexts or in the later texts. The main word indicating a horseman is *marcach*, which David Greene suggested might have been borrowed from the Welsh who had adopted horse-riding from the Romans.[105] But Ranko Matasović treats *marcach* as a native Irish derivative (along with its British cognates) from a Proto-Celtic word (*markāko-* 'having a horse').[106] It does occur in the first recension of the *Táin* where Maine's 30 horsemen are drowned and where Lugaid rides to Cú Chulainn with his 30 horsemen to arrange a non-hostility pact.[107] In addition, in the second recension we learn that Fer Diad rode horses.[108] In other tales we find clear evidence of horse-riding when Eochu's long blond hair straddles the horse upon which he is riding,[109] and 50 horsemen are attributed to Eochu Bec.[110] Given the fact that both these examples involve men whose very name means 'horseman', we should hardly be surprised by their association with riding. In the death-tale of Conchobar, the king is ordered by his physicians not to mount a horse lest the calcified brain-ball lodged in his skull should leap out.[111] Horsemen also occur in the story of the 'Destruction of Da Derga's hostel'[112] but here we are dealing with a tale rooted in the Mythological cycle where riding is more often encountered.[113] For this reason, even when dealing with an early tale from the Ulster cycle that finds Fráech and his men mounted on horses and riding to Cruachain, we can explain this by the fact that Fráech's mother was from the Otherworld.[114] Most other instances of horse-riding occur in contexts where the word for 'horseman' seems to alternate with chariot-warrior or involves a chariot which has lost a horse,[115] or the tale itself is very late.[116] A single reference[117] to saddles (*sadall*), employing what is presumably an Old Norse loanword, hardly supports the antiquity of horse-riding in the tales. So, were Greene and others right? Do the tales accurately reflect a period (the Iron Age) when the Irish utilized chariots but did not yet know horse-riding?

The chariotry-first model does seem to be unlikely for a variety of reasons. To begin with there is historical evidence such as Tacitus' description of the Battle of Mons Graupius (AD 83), where the Roman general Agricola confronted the Caledonian army of Calgacus who employed both chariotry and cavalry.[118] This makes it difficult to imagine that across the Irish Sea the Irish did not also engage in riding horses. Certainly the other Celtic-speaking peoples engaged in horse-riding, as Barry Raftery reminded us, pointing to the testimony of classical authors and images on Celtic coins indicating that horse-riding was widespread; in Ireland it should hardly have been exceptional.[119] Given the number of Irish horse-bits and our uncertainty regarding whether they were intended for ridden horses or draught horses, it seems that horse-riding should not be regarded as a criterion for dating the tales.

Roads

Roads are mentioned under a variety of names in the Ulster cycle although these rarely provide the type of additional description that we must gain from outside the *scéla*. We know that roads were important in early medieval Ireland and they are well discussed in the law texts where the building of roads near a royal seat or in a strategic place increased the price of the surrounding land.[120] We also learn from such texts that five types of roads were distinguished: the *slige* 'highway', *rót* 'road', *lámraite* 'byroad', *tógraite* 'curved road' and *bóthar* 'cow-track'. Some of these names and a number of others are employed in the Ulster tales.[121]

The *slige* 'highway', defined in the law texts as a road wide enough for two chariots, is the commonest term employed in the Ulster tales. Initially indicating the act of felling trees to clear a way, its etymological origins are occasionally reflected in the tales. For example, Medb digs up a road through the Cooley mountains so that it might serve as a monument to her raid.[122] The highways are occasionally associated with names, including 'the road of Cualu'[123] or Mid-Luachra,[124] and on one occasion we find a road (Slige Ercail) named after Ercail, who was killed in the siege of Da Choca's hostel.[125] Major sites such as Tara[126] and, reputedly, every hostel[127] would be approached by four roads. The condition of the roads varied seasonally (in winter the roads were dirty while in summer 'smooth and safe' and this dictated when one might plan a raid).[128] Another word for a primary road was *rámat*.[129]

Although the descriptions of the roads are rather meagre, the *tóchar* 'causeway' provides one of the most intriguing problems in evaluating the chronology of the Dreamtime. In the Mythological cycle, during the reign of Eochaid Airem (142–116 BC), the king placed on Midir four Herculean tasks, one of which was to build a causeway over Móin Lámraige. Summoning up an enormous work crew, Midir directed them to first lay down a foundation of tree trunks and then cover it with clay, gravel and stones to form a causeway across the bog, the best causeway in the world.[130] Richard Warner and others have identified the bog with the modern townland of Laragh, Co. Longford, wherein lies Corlea Bog, which was crossed by the largest timber trackway (FIGS 8.10, 8.11) found in Ireland, constructed in 148 BC.[131] As the bog swallowed up the trackway soon after it was constructed one could dismiss any notion that a thousand years later one could generate a contemporary account of its construction. Warner argued that this indicated that 'some of the material in the Ulster cycle was remembered from pre-Christian times and reflected actual prehistoric events and monuments.'[132]

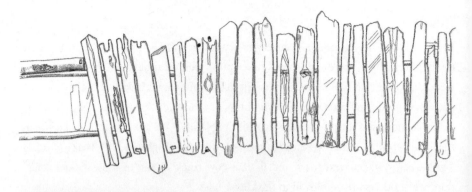

8.10, 8.11. Trackway found at Corlea, Co. Longford. The oak plank sleepers, measuring about 3 to 4 m across, rested on long runners of birch logs. The oak timbers consistently dated to 148 BC.

The association of the building of the Corlea 1 trackway with the events recorded in the 8th- or 9th-century rendition of the *Tochmarc Étaíne* is one of the most striking correlations between archaeology and the Dreamtime. There are two aspects of this correlation that need to be considered: the precise location of the trackway according to the tales and the closeness of the archaeological fit to the literary description. After a review of the place name and other evidence, Dáithi Ó hÓgain concluded that while it was impossible to make a 'definite identification' of Móin Lámraige with Corlea, there was at least some reasonable circumstantial evidence that the two may have been the same.[133] The literary description envisages one of the most monumental work projects in early Ireland and the Corlea 1 trackway, consisting of roundwood runners on which were lain split-oak sleepers measuring 3.5 to 4 m across, required something on the order of 25 hectares of oak trees (300 to 500 oaks) that had to be processed and hauled onto site in about a thousand cartloads.[134] For this reason, the event of the trackway's construction, it is argued, may have entered folklore and been recalled still many centuries later, long after it had disappeared from view.

When we compare the physical description of Corlea 1 with the account in the *Tochmarc Étaíne* we find some similarities but also some differences. In the tale, Eochaid sends a steward to observe the progress on the trackway and his presence so irritates Midir that the work was not finished properly; the archaeological evidence also suggests that the Corlea trackway was not completed properly.[135] On the other hand, according to the tale, no one had ever set foot on the bog before, but the evidence of Barry Raftery's excavations indicates that there were at least eight earlier trackways across the bog, beginning in the Neolithic (4th millennium BC). While most of these were architecturally much simpler brushwood trackways, Corlea 6, which dated 2268–2250 BC, was also constructed of large oak sleepers. Corlea 7, which dated to the 5th to 6th centuries AD and much closer to the date of the *scél*, only consisted of some traces of a hurdle, so was most unlikely to have engendered such a story. Of course, it should be recalled that most bog sites have already had their upper layers removed, so it is always possible that there may have been a spectacular trackway more recent than Corlea 1 that has long gone up in flames but it is safer to work with what we have. Where the literary and archaeological evidence deviates most is in the actual construction methods employed. Corlea 1 required pairs of birch trees to be set down as runners, atop which were set massive oak planks, frequently fixed in position with wooden pegs. But the trackway built by Midir only employed tree trunks as a foundation over which was laid clay, gravel and stones to form a road surface very different from the fine timber-surfaced road at Corlea 1.

Here I think it would be churlish not to accept Warner's argument that the tale does retain remembrance that once a magnificent road had been built to cross a specific bog, but this ancient memory was not sufficiently well preserved to perpetuate a precise description of the Iron Age trackway.

Ships and boats

Although references to boats occur with some frequency in the *scéla*, they are very rarely described in much detail. Moreover, although there are a number of terms for different types of vessels, with few exceptions most of these are loanwords. The one exception, the archetypal Irish boat, the currach or curragh (*curach*)[136] was glossed with *phaselus* 'a bean-shaped vessel'. These may have been small hide boats as one traditionally might expect, for example where Bláthnait is carried off in a hide coracle,[137] or the presumably small boat that carried Cú Chulainn's son from Scotland to Ulster.[138] On the other hand, the same word is used to describe the boats that Cesair and her fleet of soon-to-be-drowned colonists arrived in,[139] as well as the fleet of 150 vessels employed by the reavers to attack Da Derga's hostel, each currach carrying an average of 33 raiders, perhaps arranged on five benches (*cúcsescurach* 'five-benched boat', able to seat 30 men).[140] A late tale has a giant (Goll) arriving in Ireland in a suitably enormous currach with a prow as big as a mountain and the poop still higher. Here the boat was fitted with three ranks of oars.[141] These vessels were used both on rivers[142] and on the open sea.[143]

The stories also mention the *bárc* 'ship', here to be compared with Latin *barca* 'ship', and which on one occasion is described as being built of wood.[144] Rarely used, and only in the later tales, is also the *laídeng*, sometimes translated 'galley', which was borrowed from Old Norse *leiðangr* 'a levy, often involving a ship'.[145] Fergus sailed to Scotland in his *ibrach*, presumably a boat made of yew (*ibar*) or at least named 'yew'.[146]

Even the main word for a ship, *long*, derives from Latin *longa* or was at least influenced by it. It occurs in the *Táin* where a stream of blood rising from Cú Chulainn's head is compared to the high mast of a ship.[147] Although we generally seem to be dealing with a large vessel, propelled by the wind,[148] and arranged in fleets,[149] the *long* could also refer to smaller vessels. One recurring motif is the concept of the bronze ship that was employed by Cú Chulainn's son,[150] as well as Senbec, who magically propels his boat on the Boyne,[151] and in the Otherworld.[152] That bronze ships are known from classical literature suggests a probable source for this particular motif.[153]

Another possible loan, *nó*, was used to describe what was generally a small oar-driven boat, although by the time of one of the later tales such a boat could hold 30 people.[154] Here again we find references to metal boats, but copper rather than bronze.[155] Finally there is the infrequently used *ether* 'boat, ferry'.[156]

As for the various parts of the vessel we have the oars (*ráma*),[157] whose few descriptions are a bit impractical unless one finds gilt oars[158] or, presumably to

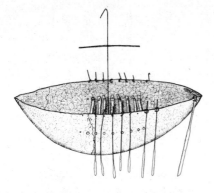

8.12. Gold boat (length 19.6 cm) found as part of the Broighter hoard, Co. Derry. The boat displays a mast, sail and benches for 18 oarsmen.

accommodate the giant rowing the ship, iron oars,[159] plausible descriptions. The rudder (*lúi*) only occurs as a metaphor for Fergus' missing sword.[160] Finally, the sail (*séol*) may be a Germanic loanword and usually occurs in contexts referencing the height of the sail-mast (*séolchrann*).[161] Sails help drive the pirates across the sea to attack Ireland,[162] but they are also employed a few times in presumably native Irish vessels.[163]

Our archaeological evidence for ships from the Iron Age until the Viking period is naturally minimal, given the fact that boats were built of highly perishable hide and wood. We do have a wooden dugout from Gortgill, Co. Antrim, and the partial remains of a flat-bottomed wooden boat from Lough Lene, Co. Westmeath, that dates to the Iron Age and reflects Mediterranean (here Roman) building techniques. There is also some iconographic evidence as well, most noteworthy being the famous Iron Age gold boat from the Broighter hoard, Co. Derry, which depicts a boat with 18 oars, eight benches, a steering oar and a mast for a sail (FIG. 8.12). Later we have an 8th-century pillar-stone from Bantry, Co. Cork, and some of the later high-crosses. And, finally, we have parts of Viking ships (never a whole). And then there is a very sizeable body of literature that includes descriptions of medieval boats.[164] There is no obvious diagnostic evidence from the Ulster cycle that would permit us to assess the date of the boats depicted in it on the basis of the available archaeological evidence.

Conclusions

The chariot has been one of the primary pieces of evidence employed to support the thesis that the Ulster cycle preserves authentic images of Iron Age Ireland. A review of the evidence, both archaeological and literary, leads to a conclusion that falls somewhere between those who advocate that the Ulster tales provide a 'window on the Iron Age' and those who believe that descriptions of chariots may have been borrowed from the classical texts that were available to the medieval Irish monks who copied and created the tales. The hard archaeological evidence of Iron Age paired draught is both poor and equivocal regarding the existence of chariots before the iconographic evidence of high-crosses and contemporary references to the chariot in the Irish laws and other early medieval documents. Given the fact that chariots were well known in Iron Age Gaul and Britain, as well as in early medieval Ireland, it would seem pretty absurd to deny their existence in Iron Age Ireland at the time of Katu-butos. The question is not whether the Iron Age Irish possessed or lacked chariots but rather do the Ulster tales accurately depict the chariots of the Iron Age?

Given the paucity of chariot-associated material in the archaeological record, it is obviously difficult to compare the literary descriptions with the handful of existing objects and any argument is going to be based on evidence that would hardly stand up in court. If one is sceptical of Will Sayer's translation, the descriptions seem to lack reference to terrets, so one might claim that this does provide some negative evidence for their portrayal of Irish Iron Age chariots. On the other hand, the absence of any clear reference to the large Y-pendants that are characteristic of Irish horsemanship and not found in Britain is a somewhat more serious omission and does damage the case for an Iron Age provenience. Moreover, we might have hoped for some reference to the gleam of metal on the tips of the yokes if the tales were referring to Iron Age chariots. In short, I suspect that if Katu-butos had composed poems detailing the appearance of Iron Age chariots, like the Standard Irish Palace Description they did not manage to make it intact into Old Irish. Rather, it is a bit easier to accept that what we have are descriptions of early medieval Irish vehicles that were stimulated, in various degrees, by those known to the early Irish from classical literature.

The one element that is most difficult to brush aside is the possible memory of a truly magnificent trackway built in the 2nd century BC that was incorporated into the story of Midir.

CHAPTER NINE

Material Culture

He was called Eochaid Eadghadhach because it was by him the
variety of colour was first put on clothes in Ireland, to distinguish
the honour of each by his raiment, from the lowest to the highest.
Thus was the distinction made between them: one colour in the
clothes of slaves; two in the clothes of soldiers; three in the clothes
of goodly heroes, or young lords of territories; six in the clothes
of ollavs; seven in the clothes of kings and queens.

Annals of the Four Masters, AM 3664 (1536 BC)

Although there is a wide variety of references to material culture in the Ulster
tales, most can be divided into a handful of well-defined categories such as
weaponry and transport, which we have already covered. Here it remains to
examine some of the other major categories – dress, ornament, containers, musical
instruments, games and some miscellaneous technology – to determine where they
might belong in place and time.

Dress

Unlike their Anglo-Saxon neighbours, who confined their sartorial enthusiasm
largely to describing war-gear,[1] the early Irish were also fascinated with depicting
the flashier apparel of their heroes and heroines and they frequently did so in considerable detail. In the opening of the earliest version of the *Táin* we immediately
confront the early Irish penchant for insuring that no two people invited to a party
will arrive dressed the same. Cormac's first troop rides by wearing multicoloured
cloaks and tunics that fall to their knees; the second troop wears dark-grey cloaks
and tunics that fall to their calves; and the third troop are decked out in purple
cloaks and tunics that run all the way to their feet.[2] And so when we later encounter

Table 9.1: Cloaks of the Ulster warriors in the *Táin*.

Name	Description of cloak (*bratt*)	Colour
Cúscraid	*húainide*	green
Sencha	*dubglas*	dark grey
Eógan	*corcra*	purple
Lóegaire	*buide*	yellow
Munremur	*odarda*	dun-coloured
Connad	*glas*	grey
Reochaid	*corcra*	purple
Amorgene	*húaine*	green
Celtchair	*riabain*	striped
Eirrge	*dublúascach*	black swinging
Menn	*brec*	multicoloured
Fergna	*derg*	red
Furbaide	*drgscoigthi*	beautiful
Erc	*corcra*	purple

the line-up of Ulster heroes in the *Táin*, we are not surprised to find them all colour coded (see Table 9.1.)

It is evident from the table that there are some overlaps: Cúscraid and Amorgene both wear a green cloak, although Cúscraid wears a bordered tunic while Amorgene wears a hooded white one. And while Eógan, Reochaid and Erc all wear purple cloaks, only the latter two wear the same type and colour of tunics (white-hooded with red insertion). It might be noted that while the Old Irish laws make it explicitly clear that a purple cloak is an exclusive marker of a king or his son,[3] such sumptuary laws are not strictly applicable to the Ulster tales where, for example, we might have expected Cúscraid, son of King Conchobar, to be wearing a purple cloak rather than some of the other warriors mentioned. Niamh Whitfield has suggested that the adoption of purple as a royal insignia was borrowed from Roman practice, possibly as early as the 5th century when Old Irish *corcair* 'purple' was borrowed from Latin *purpura*.[4]

The basic apparel of a character in the Ulster cycle consisted of a tunic (*léine* or the shorter *inar*),[5] which was a long garment worn under all other clothes[6] and which, as we have seen, extended to anywhere from the knees to the ankles. In fact, the fringe could be a bit higher than the knee but no more than a hand-breadth if one trusts the *Triads of Ireland*, summoning up images of an overzealous headmistress measuring the hems of her students' dresses.[7] The tunic, often described as white in colour, could be embroidered in a variety of other colours, especially red,[8] occasionally gold,[9] and even with animal designs.[10] At the top of the garment there was frequently a *culpait*, generally translated collar or hood, and those tunics with red insertions were frequently part of a fixed expression 'a tunic with a white hood and a red insertion' (*léne gelchulpatach co ndergindled*).[11] But the top of the tunic should not have been too high otherwise Cú Chulainn would not have been able to ponder the pleasant view of Emer's cleavage when he first courted her.[12] The material of the *léine* is presumably wool or linen but on occasion, involving both men[13] and women,[14] we find references to silk (*síta*).[15] The general rule, at least among the Anglo-Saxons, was that the only person who would willingly wear wool (as opposed to linen) directly against the skin was likely to be a monk in training for sainthood.[16] The *inar*, glossed as *tunica* 'tunic', could also be of silk,[17] or satin,[18] and in one instance we find Cú Chulainn's charioteer, Láeg, dressed in a filmy *inar* of deerskin.[19]

The tunic was tied at the waist with a belt (*cris*), which not only served to bind in the tunic but could also be a place to hang one's purse,[20] one's sword,[21] the decapitated head of one's enemy,[22] a calcified brain-ball,[23] or even birds that have been collected.[24] On some occasions the word for belt is employed to describe a piece of leather defensive clothing (*cathchris* 'battle-belt'), which extended all the way up to Cú Chulainn's arm-pits.[25] It is interesting that, like Ajax's shield in the *Iliad*, it was fashioned from seven oxhides.[26] Its presence in the Ulster tales is most likely a borrowing from the classical world, where we find Paris wearing a 'seven-fold leather cuirass' in the Latin *Iliad*.[27]

Over the tunic was worn or, actually wrapped, the mantle (usually *bratt*[28] but occasionally *fúan* or *lenn*) which, as we have seen, could be of a wide variety of colours and, in the few places it is mentioned, was composed of wool.[29] The mantle was a prized possession and a suitable prestigious gift: Conaire Mór, for example, gave Da Derga 100 mantles.[30] It was wound around its wearer (up to five times) and fixed with a brooch. Being essentially a rectangular blanket, it might also serve as such and when the Ulstermen look for shelter and find but a small hovel, Briccriu reports that it lacks both food and mantles.[31] By the time of Charlemagne, the cloaks had become much smaller on the continent but the emperor hung onto his native Frankish dress complaining that the smaller cloaks, which he dismissed as napkins, were incapable of covering one in bed, keeping the elements off while riding a horse, or preventing arse-freeze when he had to relieve himself.[32]

The hood or cape (*cochall*, borrowed from Latin *cucullus*) might then be worn over the *bratt*.[33] In late tales, Cú Chulainn's charioteer, Láeg, was kitted out with a hood of satin.[34]

Other garments included the shirt (*caimmse*, a loanword from Latin *camisia*, itself a possible loanword from Gaulish, and glossed *léine*).[35] The *fúathróc*, translated as apron or girdle, was worn both by Cú Chulainn and Fer Diad as well as some of the characters involved in the destruction of Da Derga's hostel.[36] A warrior might wear several layers of 'aprons' ranging from silk or silky satin close to his body to a leather one that was clearly designed for defensive purposes and, even iron,[37] which nevertheless still failed Fer Diad when he wore it to protect himself against Cú Chulainn's *gae bolga*.

Organic remains of clothes are a rarity, even in Ireland where bogs and water-logging have assisted in preservation, so there is much that we do not know. Moreover, unlike their Anglo-Saxon neighbours, the early medieval Irish did not bury their dead dressed but rather in shrouds, although we do occasionally find personal ornaments. As for clothes of linen and wool, all of these had already appeared in Ireland by the Late Bronze Age and there is even an instance of a belt woven from horsehair.[38] During the Iron Age, in the time of Katu-butos, we have some evidence for woollen clothing but the best evidence derives from bog bodies such as the one from Gallagh, Co. Galway, where a (presumably sacrificed or executed) male was clothed in a leather cape. Later in the Iron Age we find at Baronstown West, Co. Kildare, the burial of an adult male, reputedly with a woollen textile and pieces of a leather garment. Although undated there is some suspicion that an otter-skin cape recovered from Derrykeighan, Co. Antrim, may also date to the Iron Age.[39] In short, our hard evidence for Iron Age dress in Ireland is meagre indeed and the literary descriptions of the composition of the clothes, be it wool or linen, could date to anywhere from the Late Bronze Age to the medieval period. This is confirmed by the recovery of woollen and linen material from six sites dating to the early medieval period.[40] 'Dressed in a tunic with a belt and with a mantle thrown over' would be a fair description of most male populations in late prehistoric north-west Europe.[41] Because of this, it is difficult to evaluate the suggestion that the tunic with a heavy cloak fastened on the right shoulder with a brooch was borrowed from the Romans, whose officials were similarly attired.[42] As we have evidence for native Iron Age textiles, belts and, most importantly, brooches that may have served to fasten a cloak, it is hard to exclude the possibility that the basic dress depicted in the Ulster tales does reflect Iron Age dress.

With the introduction of Christianity, we find representative art – such as high-crosses and manuscript illuminations – that provides us with good evidence for early medieval dress which by and large can be paralleled with contemporary liter-ary descriptions found in the Kings cycle.[43] Niamh Whitfield, for example, has shown how the garments and ornaments worn by Becfhola, a fictional character whose deeds are anchored to real personalities of the 7th century and whose story was first composed in the 9th or 10th century, can be matched against the archaeo-logical record from the 7th to 10th centuries.[44] Becfhola wears a purple *bratt* and a *léine* with red-gold embroidery. That essentially this same description can also be applied to Fergus in the *Táin*[45] and others in the Ulster cycle suggests that it is far more likely that the descriptions of clothes in the *scéla* have been anchored in the sartorial world of early medieval Ireland rather than recall the specific dress of Iron Age Ireland.

Those descriptions of clothes made from silk or satin certainly suggest a medi-eval rather than earlier date. The earliest appearance of silk in Britain is during the Roman period where it has been recovered from several sites,[46] but it seems unlikely that this rare fabric was then woven into the descriptions of Iron Age tales in Ireland at such an early date. The presence of silk in Anglo-Saxon graves, from which we have fairly abundant evidence of textiles, is limited to a single silk thread and it is absent from the royal Anglo-Saxon burials where one might have expected to see it, although it was (probably) present among the Merovingians on the continent.[47] But we have literary evidence from Anglo-Saxon England, such as Adhelm's *De Virginitate*, that speaks of sleeves with silk borders in the 8th century. By the 9th century Byzantine silks had certainly become available in the West and silk is recorded frequently enough on Viking-age urban sites, including Dublin, where over a hundred fragments were recovered,[48] and Waterford.[49] There is also some circumstantial evidence that silk may have appeared in Ireland as early as the 8th century if some of the see-through garments illustrated in the Book of Kells indicate silk clothing.[50] As the manufacture of satin initially employed silk threads, it too should be regarded as a medieval motif, at least in Ireland, and it is generally pre-sumed to be one of the innovations occasioned by the Viking intrusions.[51] In addi-tion to silks, Mairead Dunlevy has suggested that some of the other possible later innovations in dress would have been light-coloured tunics, cloaks with borders, hoods and the shorter tunic, the *inar*. All of these are regularly attested in the Ulster tales and, as we have seen, a fair number employ loanwords from Latin.[52]

There is one item of dress not depicted in the Ulster tales but encountered in Irish iconography (both carvings on high-crosses and illustrated manuscripts; PL. XI). Although classical authors mention the wearing of trousers (the Irish *triubus* 'trousers' is a loan from French), especially on soldiers and horse-riders, they are not part of the standard warrior descriptions that we find in the Ulster tales. Moreover, on the basis of the customs of Celtic-speaking peoples in neighbouring lands, the practice of wearing trousers has at least been suspected for Iron Age Ireland.[53] Christopher Hawkes believed that trousers were introduced to Ireland at the same time as La Tène fibulae, and that they were part of a major innovation in dress.[54] If one presumes that an Iron Age Irishman looked like the captive Iron Age Briton (FIG. 9.1) depicted on a bronze fragment, we would have a fair idea of the possible dress of Katu-butos. Maria Fitzgerald has suggested that the wearing of trousers may have been confined to (presumably low-ranking) soldiers and people who had to work outdoors, but may have been rejected by the elite who are not portrayed wearing trousers.[55] Another, more remote possibility, perhaps, is that as the Vikings tended to wear trousers,[56] the Irish found such garments unsuitable for depicting their own ancestors.

9.1. Image of captive Briton wearing checkered trousers from a bronze statue.

Ornaments

The ornaments depicted in the Ulster tales are primarily the brooches or pins that fastened the *bratt* 'cloak', and these were an integral part in depicting the appearance of any of the characters (Table 9.2).

Table 9.2: Brooches in the Ulster tales.

Name	Origin	Meaning	Shape	Material	Other
bretnas	? < *Bretain* 'Brittany' or 'Britain, Wales'	brooch	round, heavy headed[57]	gold,[58] silver[59]	inlaid with gold,[60] with headpieces of gold[61]
delg	Proto-Celtic *delgo-*	pin, brooch	lead-shaped,[62] circular[63]	gold,[64] silver,[65] *findruine*,[66] tin,[67] iron[68]	golden inset[69]
eó	'point, sharp, pin'	brooch		gold,[70] silver,[71] bronze[72]	
brotga	? cloak/spike + *gáe* 'spear'			silver,[73] bronze[74]	
casán	*cas* 'twisted'	brooch		silver[75]	
cúaille	*cúal* 'bundle of stakes'	stake, brooch		iron[76]	
dúalldai	*dúal* 'lock of hair, fold'	brooch		gold[77]	
duillend	*duille* 'leaf'	brooch		gold[78]	
frithchuman	'bent clasp'	hook		bronze[79]	
mílech	*míl* 'animal'	brooch		gold,[80] silver,[81] *findruine*[82]	inlaid[83]
muirnech	? *muirenn* 'spear'	pin		copper[84]	
roth	*roth* 'wheel-shaped, circular'	brooch		gold,[85] silver,[86] bronze[87]	
síbal	< Lat *fibula*	pin		gold,[88] silver[89]	With head animals[90]
tanaslaide	thin-beaten?	thin pins		gold[91]	
túagmíl	*túag* 'arch' + *míl* 'animal brooch'	clasp		gold,[92] silver[93]	

The brooches are distinguished by a series of different names (generally built from native Irish vocabulary), their composition and whether there was additional ornament, although most still cannot be matched against specific objects in the archaeological record. From the Irish Iron Age we have about 30 fibulae (or safety-pin brooches), and about 40 pins with ornamented heads. All the Iron Age brooches and pins are made of bronze with the exception of two iron brooches. If we read the descriptions literally, then we can see that in terms of composition, these make a poor fit for the Iron Age dress-fasteners. Very few of the Ulster cycle brooches are described as being of copper or bronze and although there are two mentions of iron pins, these are problematic examples. The iron *delg* 'pin' is actually worn by three Britons,[94] while the iron *cúaille* worn by the macho Celtchair[95] is probably meant to indicate an exceedingly crude stake-like device for a rough warrior rather than one of the safety-pin brooches that have been found in iron. In any event, there is evidence for iron brooches in the medieval period, such as the penannular brooch found in a woman's grave from Betaghstown, Co. Meath, dated between the 4th and 7th centuries.[96]

If we employ material of composition as a filter for dating the descriptions then the overwhelming majority should belong to the medieval period. While it might be argued that terms like gold and silver were only intended as indications of colour (hence a shiny bronze object might be described as 'golden') this is contradicted by the several instances where the various metals have been ranked against each other, indicating that the differences were not regarded as superficial references to bling but to the actual composition of the object.[97] And if it is argued that the descriptions of Iron Age objects have merely been exaggerated with precious metals, then they are no longer Iron Age objects. The one caveat that can be admitted is that the ornaments, at least the gold ones, need not be of solid gold, since such objects were exceedingly rare (and possibly imports). Usually, gold brooches are actually made of silver or bronze that has been gilded.[98] The shift to gilding in brooch manufacture probably occurred around the 7th century but by the late 9th or early 10th century brooches tended not to be gilded.[99] The shift from bronze to silver brooches itself was also in about the 7th century, although bronze continued to be employed for lower-status objects.

The etymology of the various terms for brooches is not particularly helpful as many of them are exceedingly vague, such as *delg* 'thorn' and *eó* 'point'. On the other hand, a few of the names go beyond the obvious. The *bretnas* 'brooch' may indicate that the style of brooch has been borrowed from the Britons and, hence, is not native.

It occurs at least 16 times in the Ulster tales and is worn invariably by natives (and in the TBDD where foreigners abound it is worn by the sons of King Conaire and the *filid* 'poets'). The *mílech* 'with an animal' and *túagmíl*[100] brooches signal some form of zoomorphic image, and while some of the Iron Age brooches in Ireland feature stylized bird heads[101] these only ornament the foot section of the brooch so that they would be nearly invisible to a viewer and, thereby, make a poor match for someone describing warriors from afar. Far better is the abundant evidence for animal designs on the faces of a brooch that could actually be easily viewed.[102] Zoomorphic penannular brooches tend to be dated from the 5th to 7th centuries.[103] And the *roth* 'wheel' certainly suggests some form of circular brooch, which has no parallels among Irish Iron Age brooches but could serve to describe any number of medieval penannular brooches, which themselves may have been introduced as early as the 4th or 5th centuries although fully circular brooches date later.[104] But the earliest of these were of bronze: in the tales two of such brooches are described as of gold,[105] although the *Táin* does depict one warrior with a *roth* of bronze.[106]

One of the brooch types has been especially singled out for discussion. On four occasions in the tales we find reference to a *delg nduillend* 'leaf-shaped brooch' that is worn by Medb, Sencha, the two Cormacs, and Cú Chulainn.[107] Medb and Cú Chulainn wore a gold brooch while the others wore one of *findruine*. Early in the 20th century Ridgeway compared the 'leaf-like' description with some of the Iron Age brooches known in Ireland (FIG. 9.2) to try to support an Iron Age date for the *Táin*.[108] This was dismissed by Kenneth Jackson, who believed that the description might not have been confined to the Iron Age brooch and who also regarded the context of its citation to be relatively late.[109] There are eight leaf-bow brooches known from Ireland and these probably date anywhere from the 3rd century BC onwards and there is no certainty as to when they were abandoned, although Hawkes

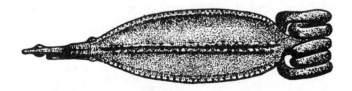

9.2. Leaf-shaped brooch of bronze (length 8.1 cm). No provenance.
Identified by some as the *delg nduillend* 'leaf-shaped brooch' of the Ulster tales.

9.3. A kyte brooch from Co. Kilkenny. Among the Irish medieval brooches, this is perhaps the closest to resembling a leaf, although palmettes might be found decorating some penannular brooches.

believed that the fibula in general died out in Ireland in the 1st century AD.[110] If one wishes to compare the concept of a leaf-shaped brooch with the archaeological record, then it must be admitted that Ridgeway's old identification is still the most convincing, as the Iron Age leaf-shaped brooch is an archaeological category for a select set of brooches in both Britain and Ireland. There are always alternatives, such as the medieval kyte brooch (FIG. 9.3), but they are not as compelling as the Iron Age brooch.[111] On the other hand, when we review the variety of ways the leaf-shaped brooch is articulated in the texts (*duileand-dealc, delg nduillech, delgi duillech, duilend*) it is difficult to treat these as examples of a frozen expression that has survived in oral poetry since the Iron Age.

Headgear

There are a number of terms associated with headgear in the Ulster tales that appear to vary in function from royal crowns down to headbands which served to keep hair out of one's eyes (Table 9.3). As can be seen from the table, the great majority of descriptions involve an object of gold, though here we also sometimes find evidence for the use of precious stones. At the top of the social scale are the crowns worn by Ailill, which are variously described as a *benn*,[112] *imscing*[113] or *mind*,[114] a word that basically means 'treasure' but is often employed contextually to indicate a 'crown'. Queen Medb also has a golden *mind*[115] but so do many of the other warriors and other categories of people such as druids[116] and jesters.[117] Also kitted out with special headgear is Cú Chulainn's charioteer, Láeg, who wears a headband, variously described as a *clár*,[118] *gibne*[119] or *lann*,[120] the latter of which is also attributed to other

Table 9.3: Headgear in the Ulster tales.

Name	Meaning	Composition	Additional
barr	crown	gold[130]	
benn	diadem	gold[131]	
cáelbar	kerchief?		ornamented[132]
cenn	headpiece		gem-flashing[133]
cennbarr	head covering		ornaments of glass and *findruine*[134]
clár	headband		studded with precious stones[135]
gibne	headband	precious stones,[136] gold,[137] *findruine*[138]	
imscing	crown	gold[139]	
lann	plate	gold[140]	
mind	crown	gold,[141] silver[142]	
sníthe	circlet	gold[143]	

charioteers[121] and even poets.[122] Finally, we have some very flashy headpieces such as the *cennbarr* worn by Bodb's troops.[123]

Understandably, Irish museum shelves of any period do not tend to be stuffed with crowns. Nevertheless, from the Iron Age we do have two objects, the Cork Horns (FIG. 9.4) and the Petrie Crown, that, while lacking a certain function, are generally interpreted as elaborate headgear.[124] They are of bronze and while generally dated to the Iron Age it has also been suggested that they may date as late as the 5th or 6th century. The descriptions of crowns in the tales make a poor match for these, not just because the literary evidence indicates gold crowns but also because there is no trace in the descriptions that these crowns looked like horns. The only potential evidence, suggested long ago by Margaret Dobbs,[125] were the nicknames Ferbend 'man with horns' and Ferbenduma 'man with bronze horns', applied to several warriors in the Ulster cycle. Ferbend was explained in the *Cóir Anman*[126] as he who had two silver horns and one gold horn in his helmet. But on the occasion in the Ulster cycle[127] where *bend* is employed on its own, it refers to a golden crown or diadem and not a horned helmet, while there is no hint that any of the helmets described in the Ulster tales is horned. This is unfortunate because one of the most striking – and

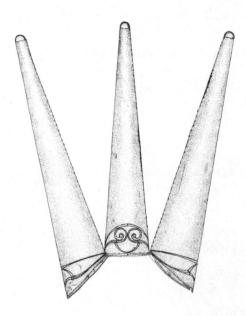

9.4. The three bronze Cork horns (length of central horn 26.2 cm). When originally discovered there were supposedly traces of leather attached to the bronze.

9.5. The so-called Tandragee idol (its original find spot is uncertain) is conjectured to date to the Iron Age. There are at least two competing interpretations concerning its identity. As it appears to hold a severed arm, it has been compared to Nuadu, the king of the Tuatha Dé, who lost his arm at Mag Tuired. Others interpret the nickname of Conall Cernach, not as 'victorious' but rather as 'having an excrescence' and see the figure as a 'horned' god. Moreover, Conall fought two duels with one arm tied to his side in order to grant 'fair play' to a one-armed opponent.

elusive – stone sculptures suspected of being of Iron Age (at least 'pagan') date (an early medieval date, however, cannot be excluded) is the so-called Tandragee idol (FIG. 9.5), which depicts a figure who seems to wear a horned helmet (other interpretations could be advanced as well). The fact that the figure appears to be holding an arm (at least to me) suggests that we may be dealing with an image of Nuadu, the Tuatha Dé Danann king who lost his arm in the First Battle of Mag Tuired.[128]

As for the *cennbarr* worn by Bodb's troops that are covered with ornament of glass and *findruine*, this is reminiscent of a *cennbarr* worn by Flann, the paramour of Becfhola whom we saw above is to be found in the Kings cycle. He too wears an item of headgear 'of gold and silver and crystal'. Niamh Whitfield has discussed this item in the context of Irish and European archaeology, where its most consistent parallels lie in the early medieval period.[129]

Rings

Under the category of rings is anything that might be worn around the neck, arm or finger (Table 9.4), and it will be with the latter that we begin our brief discussion.

The rings worn on the hand are assigned to both the finger and the thumb and are made of gold or silver. From the Iron Age we have some evidence for bronze finger-rings, one found on the middle finger of a burial from Lambay Island.[144] Rings, of course, continued through to the early medieval period and are also known from the 5th or 6th centuries onwards in Anglo-Saxon burials. And, here, like the Irish descriptions, some rings appear to be so large that they were probably worn on the thumb.[145] Gold rings are known from the 9th century. The ascription of gold and, certainly, silver to the Irish rings certainly suggests that these were derived from medieval rather than prehistoric images.

The description of arm-rings or bracelets is surprisingly rare in the tales. Among the blandishments that Medb employs to entice Fer Diad to fight Cú Chulainn are many bracelets,[146] and each warrior in Bodb's troop is described as wearing a bracelet.[147] As for the composition of the bracelets we read once that they may be of gold,[148] and in another instance, harpers are described with rings of crystal about their arms.[149]

The Irish Iron Age yields a small number of bronze bracelets, including a superbly decorated one possibly from Newry, Co. Down. Also from this period, although ranging as late as the 4th century AD, are a number of bracelets made of glass.[150] The motif of gold (and silver) bracelets is also known in the Kings cycle and attributed to the Hiberno-Viking period when gold arm-rings are well known in Ireland.[151]

Table 9.4: Rings in the Ulster Tales.

Name	Meaning	Material
*buinne*157	arm-ring	
fail	arm-ring	gold,[158] crystal[159]
mílech	arm-ring	silver[160]
muntorc	neck chain	silver[161]
muince	neck-ring[162]	
dornasc	finger-ring, arm-ring[163]	gold[164]
fornasc	thumb-ring[165]	
ordnasc	ring, thumb-ring	gold,[166] silver[167]

Perhaps most interesting of the various rings is the neck-ring, the presence of which in the Ulster tales is meagre in the extreme. Ten neck-rings (*muince*) are part of the legacy of Cú Roí but then glossed in such a way as to suggest that they were actually arm-rings.[152] And in the *Táin* there is a single reference to torcs (*muntorc*), here made of silver, around the necks of the 'warriors of Irúath'.[153] The archaeological evidence for torcs in Iron Age Ireland is also not plentiful and involves at least some indication of importation from abroad, including in the case of the original components of the Broighter torc, a necklet from Lambay.[154] The fact that the only reference in the tales that describes the composition of a torc identifies it as silver certainly pitches the probable date of this motif to the Hiberno-Viking period after AD 800, when silver neck-rings are well known in Ireland.[155] The only way to move it earlier is to presume that the motif was transferred from Britain, where two silver torcs were recovered from the 7th- or 8th-century Norrie's Law hoard in Fife.[156]

Containers

There are at least 20 different names for containers in the Ulster cycle (see Table 9.5) and this represents only a fraction of the over 150 terms for containers known from early Irish sources.[168] The description sometimes indicates their composition, their size and their association with particular beverages, such as mead, wine or ale.

To these descriptions we can add the occasional addition of metal ornament on the vessels. The most famous are the three cups presented to the three contestants in

Table 9.5: Vessels in the Ulster cycle.

Name	Origin	Translation	Contained	Made of
airdech	Latin	beaker	mead[169]	gold[170]
án	Irish	cup		bronze[171]
baíglenn	unknown	goblet		
ballán	Irish	mug		
bleide	English	goblet	mead[172]	silver[173]
clíab		basket		
cochmae	Latin	vessel	gold[174]	
coire	Irish	cauldron	oxen and pigs,[175] calf,[176] heifer,[177] ox,[178] porridge[179]	bronze[180]
coppán	Latin	cup, beaker		silver,[181] bronze[182]
corn	Irish	drinking horn	mead[183]	silver,[184] buffalo[185]
cuäch	Latin	cup	wine,[186] water,[187] ox and bacon,[188] mead[189]	wood,[190] bronze,[191] *findruine*,[192] gold,[193] jet[194]
cuad	Latin	cup		
dabach	uncertain	tub, vat	water,[195] wine,[196] mead,[197] ale[198]	bronze,[199] wood[200]
escra		drinking or dispensing bowl		silver[201]
ían		cup		
lann	Latin	trencher(?)		copper[202]
lestar	Brittonic	vessel	mead[203]	iron,[204] bronze,[205] silver[206]
long	Latin	basin	water[207]	silver[208]
ulmías	½ Latin	dish, table	salmon[209]	
ommar		pail		
tulchube	½ Latin	cup		

the Ulster championship: Lóegaire's bronze cup has the figure of a bird chased in *findruine* on its base;[210] Conall has a vessel of *findruine* with a bird chased in gold; and Cú Chulainn receives first prize with his golden cup formed from precious stones.[211] Finally, there is the gold and silver ornament on a drinking horn made from buffalo,[212] where the Irish word *búaball* is clearly borrowed from Latin *būbalus*.

In assessing the antiquity of the various words for vessels, the first hurdle on which most of the words fail to be plausibly Iron Age is their derivation, generally from Latin words (we should not be too alarmed about the English loanword *bleide*, from Anglo-Saxon *bledu*, as it occurs in an extremely late tale). From the time of Katu-butos, the only vessels that we are somewhat confident of him knowing would be *án* 'cup' (if it is indeed derived from an Indo-European root),[213] the *ballán*, a native Irish word from *ball* 'member' that also yielded *baillén* 'small drinking vessel' and *ballóc* 'vessel', *corn* 'horn' and *coire* 'cauldron'.[214] The cauldron word is very old and has cognates in other Indo-European languages. Archaeologically, the cauldron has been known since the Late Bronze Age and continued in use through the Iron Age and into the early medieval period. Unfortunately, there is insufficient description and archaeological evidence to distinguish to which period the *coire* of the Ulster tales should be assigned.

The second obstruction to declaring a vessel of Iron Age date is the fact that so many of them are described as silver which, other than the occasional Roman find, should be dated to the early medieval period of Cattubuttas or later. It might be noted that silver cups are also found frequently in the Bible.[215] Bronze bowls are known well enough from the Iron Age although, other than a gold bowl from the famous Broighter hoard that also yielded a gold boat, gold vessels are also quite rare in the Irish Iron Age. There is a clear case for associating bird head ornamentation with Irish (and British) Iron Age bowls but these are not found chased on the base but rather are part of the handles, which are not so described in the Ulster tales.[216]

As for parallels from classical literature, there are to be sure examples of vessels made of precious metals that could have stimulated Irish descriptions, but here we find that the Irish tended to go one better. For example, Statius was content to describe a 'goblet (*paterem*) fair-wrought with figures (*signis*) and shining with gold.'[217] You can almost see the Irish translator shaking his head that this won't really do before he translated it: 'ornamented goblet, fashioned of gold and silver with a great variety of forms and monsters of the earth.'[218]

It is difficult, then, to recover from the descriptions in the tales any object that must be regarded as exclusively Iron Age, and most of the vessels should probably be assigned to the early medieval period. Yet there are two aspects of these descriptions that call for some further comment.

Firstly, if one peruses the composition of the different vessels, they are of wood or metal; there are no descriptions of a ceramic vessel. In the time of Katu-butos, ceramic vessels, apparent in the archaeological record for nearly 4,000 years, had disappeared around the transition from the Late Bronze Age to the Iron Age (c. 8th to 6th centuries BC).[219] The Irish would have occasionally encountered imported ceramics from Britain and the continent over the period c. AD 500–800.[220] By the 8th century AD the Irish also began manufacturing their own clay pottery (souterrain ware) but this was confined to the northeast part of the island and full-scale ceramic manufacture does not appear until the Normans. The Ulster tales are silent regarding ceramics and even if we expanded our survey to include all of the vocabulary associated with vessels in Irish well into the Middle Ages, we would still be hard pressed to identify a specific word for clay-made pottery.[221] So in the time of Cathbad, an Ulster monk either copying or composing stories set supposedly many centuries earlier was, on the one hand, aware that food was prepared, cooked and served in clay vessels (as well as wood) but, on the other hand, avoided describing this practice. Why?

One obvious explanation is that we have here some negative evidence that the vessels described in the tales were drawn from the Iron Age. The total absence of ceramic descriptions could be used to argue that the accounts of feasts were even earlier than the 5th century, as one might have expected the authors of the tales to have incorporated descriptions of imported wine serving vessels from the continent. We generally presume that these imported wares were largely confined to aristocratic use. In a recent study, Cormac McSparron has speculated on the social differences between the use of souterrain ware, which was too small to have been very effective in preparing large quantities of food for feasts, and the rest of Ireland which avoided making or using souterrain ware and, according to McSparron, presumably enjoyed much larger communal feasts where the food was prepared on spits or in large cauldrons.[222] If this is so then we are faced with the irony that the area of Ireland that appeared to have moved to a more egalitarian form of dispensing food was also that area that most revelled in descriptions of sumptuous feasts. The explanation may be somewhat simpler if we accept that souterrain ware was basically used in domestic contexts but was not regarded as appropriate for depiction in a feast.

A second observation regarding the vessels concerns their contents. While both water and alcoholic beverages (mead, wine, ale) were depicted as being consumed, there are but few mentions in the tales of the Ulster cycle of someone actually drinking milk, despite the fact that milk and cattle were the bases of the Irish economy. The most plausible explanation is again that the past imagined in the tales was one almost entirely confined to elites and so there was no reason for the diets of most of the population to be described. So our evidence for milk consumption is confined to such incidents as thirsty warriors craving milk that the poet Athairne will not share.[223] Another tale is associated with the Mythological cycle but also borders on Christian hagiography: in the *Altram Tige Dá Medar* 'The fostering of the house of two vessels', we encounter the lacto-philiac Eithne who sustains herself for decades on milk from a special cow, served to her in a goblet of gold.[224]

Musical instruments

Royalty in the Ulster tales was regularly entertained by a variety of musicians. These included harpers,[225] pipers,[226] horn-blowers[227] and lute players.[228] Except for a very late reference to a gold timpan,[229] there is hardly any further description of the instruments and we cannot always be certain that our modern translations are accurately identifying the instrument intended. As most of these instruments consist largely or entirely of organic material, the dating of the introduction of any of them into Ireland is hazardous in the extreme. For example, we find evidence for pipers in the Ulster tales that should date from the first centuries BC. This would not be temporally impossible as there is evidence that the Romans possessed bagpipes, and so the instrument could have come with the Romans to Britain and passed on to Ireland anytime later, but we only have the literary descriptions as evidence. A similar comment could be made on what might presumably have been a medieval lute that occurs in a number of the tales. The one instrument that we have the best chance of comparing with the archaeological record is the lyre. In the *Táin Bó Fraích* we read that in the halls of Queen Medb are:

> Harp-bags of skins of otters about them (the harps) with
> ornamentation of Parthian leather on top of which was ornament
> of gold and silver...harps of gold and silver and *findruine* with
> figures of snakes and birds and hounds of gold and silver.[230]

That the harp-bags were ornamented with leather from Asia might alert us that this is a late and probably borrowed motif, but the description of both the lyres and the

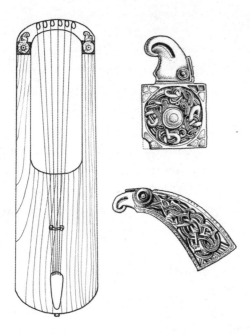

9.6. A reconstruction of the Sutton Hoo lyre (left and above right) with its gilt bronze bird decoration and a further example from Taplow.

bags in which they were carried does offer some opportunity for discussion. We have remains of lyres from two royal Anglo-Saxon burials at Taplow and Sutton Hoo. The Sutton Hoo lyre was contained in a bag made of beaver skin, which we can treat as a rough parallel to that described for Cruachain, where the bag was in otter skin (once again: there are no beavers in Ireland). While the Cruachain lyre featured decoration of gold, silver and *findruine*, that from Sutton Hoo was of gilt bronze. The Irish lyre was decorated with snakes, birds and hounds while those of both Sutton Hoo and Taplow had bird ornament (FIG. 9.6). The similarity between the lyres in these 7th century Anglo-Saxon burials and the description found in a presumably 8th century Irish tale seem close enough to reconstruct the imaginative horizon to which the Irish author of *Táin Bó Fraích* might be assigned although, of course, we are dealing with a musical instrument that has a pedigree stretching back to the 3rd millennium BC. And, just to complicate matters further, a Scottish cave site has yielded wooden remains of what has been identified as the bridge of a lyre that dates back to the Iron Age.[231] But the decoration described in the Ulster tale places this instrument a bit more comfortably in the early medieval period. Although they are mentioned, neither harps nor lyres are described in the Bible in the type of detail we need to compare with those in Irish literature, so we need not look there for their inspiration.

Games

We encounter several types of games in the Ulster tales: field games, lots and board games. The field game is generally identified as a form of hurling, a sport in which Cú Chulainn was particularly adept. The game required a stick (*lorg ána*[232] or *cammán*[233]) and a ball (*líathróit*) and involved driving the ball past one's opponents into a hole (*poll*) which, if translated literally, conjures up images of tactical team golf. Presuming here that *poll* actually indicates some form of goal (and we have no idea how large), we find one account in the boyhood stories of Cú Chulainn that when confronted with 150 opponents, he could drive all of his balls into their goal while they could not get a single one of theirs into his.[234] The stick was presumably of wood (we can dismiss the mention of a bronze hurley and silver ball as exaggeration[235]) and we are not informed what the ball was made of but it was obviously something sufficiently strong for Cú Chulainn to whack it through the guts of a ferocious hound.[236] Good comparanda have recently been uncovered in Iron Age graves in the far west of China dating back to *c.* 400 BC that comprise three leather balls and eight polo sticks,[237] so the technology of hurling should have been well within the technology of Iron Age Ireland. The game was played in a special playing field at both Emain Macha[238] and Cruachain.[239] It is hardly surprising that there is no archaeological evidence to indicate the date of such a field sport in Ireland but as ball and stick games are found all over the world there is absolutely no reason that it might not have been an Iron Age pastime. There is, in any event, some iconographic evidence from Britain of a ball and stick game going back to the 3rd century.[240]

There is better evidence, both literary and archaeological, for board games and these have generated considerable discussion.[241] The main games played in the Ulster tales are *fidchell* 'wood-sense', *brandub* 'raven-black' and *búanbach* 'lasting blow?', and the tendency to translate the first two as 'chess' or 'draughts' should really be resisted as chess was not introduced into Ireland until the Anglo-Normans and so it is fairly clear that these games are something very different. There is no full description of a gaming board, the pieces played on it nor any indication of precisely how the game was played, but there are occasionally useful although sometimes contradictory hints as to how we should understand the games. There are certainly far more references to *fidchell*, which was played on a board with an unknown number of squares (or lines) and that could be regarded as a valuable object. The *fidchill* board in *Táin Bó Fraích* was supposedly made of *findruine* and the pieces of gold and silver,[242] while another tale depicts a silver board ornamented with precious stones, gaming pieces of gold, and a bag for the pieces (usually referred to as 'men') made from woven chains of bronze.[243] A key area of distinction in board games is whether we have a special piece such as a king and an uneven number of pieces for each side (typical of a tablut-type game where the object is for a superior force of attackers to capture a king before he manages to make it to safety on the side or corners of the board), or no distinctive piece and an equal number of pieces on each side. The tablut-type games have fairly easily understood rules while one text emphasizes the difficulty of learning to play *fidchell*.[244] It might also be noted that Irish tradition reckoned that *fidchell* should have been introduced by the Second Battle of Mag Tuired, *c.* 1870 BC, although the scribe who copied this tradition had his doubts as he believed that the game had been invented at the time of the Trojan War, which he synchronized with the battle, and so there was no time lag allowed for its diffusion to Ireland.[245]

Although there is some conflicting evidence, the comparison of *fidchell* with the Roman game of *ludus latrunculorum* seems to be favoured by most scholars.[246] Partial remains of a Roman gaming board were recovered from a burial at Colchester dating to the 1st century AD and while we cannot assume that this was for *ludus latrunculorum* the game was widely played over the Roman world and could have served as a predecessor to *fidchell* as it is described in early Irish sources. In short, it is always possible that *fidchell* could have been originally borrowed from the Roman world during the later Iron Age and there is some linguistic support for such an early date. The name of the Irish game is cognate with the Welsh board game *gwyddbwyll* and Old Breton *guidpoill*, which suggests that they all shared this game at a time when either their common ancestral language was the same or, at least, before we can detect loans between the different dialects. An ancestry harkening back to the time of Katubutos is linguistically very plausible.

The second major game is *brandub* and while references to it in the Ulster tales are far less frequent, there is sufficient evidence from other Irish sources to indicate that this was a tablut-type game with unequal sides. In terms of size and layout, it probably best matches one of the more extraordinary discoveries of Hugh Hencken's excavation of Ballinderry Crannog 1:[247] a wooden playing board that is dated to the 10th century (PL. XIX). But all this does is fix the date of this game contemporary with the sources describing it and it is impossible to determine how much earlier in north-west Europe such games were played or when they may have entered Ireland. All we can say is that in Britain, Ireland and throughout Scandinavia this tablut- or tafl-type game was extremely popular until it was eventually pushed out by the spread of chess, first to England around the 11th century, and then Scandinavia and Ireland in the 12th century.

Miscellaneous items

There are a number of other categories of material culture that offer some evidence of their date that we treat below.

Chains

Chains occur relatively frequently and with a variety of functions. In some instances the chains are employed for securing either an animal[248] or a man.[249] In others they are intended to serve as a yoke between two or more individuals (people or animals), such as two birds yoked together with a chain of gold[250] or silver.[251] So far no chains of any type have been recovered from the Irish Iron Age although suspension chains, employed for hanging metal vessels, are known from neighbouring countries[252] and a pre-Roman slave chain was recovered from Llyn Cerrig Bach. There are at least two potential sources for the motif of silver chains. The single reference to a silver chain in the Bible[253] hardly seems to be sufficient to explain the motif nor can I find any obvious sources in the classical literature known to the Irish.

The extraordinary range in sizes of chains might all find parallels in the real world. While birds linked by chains may be regarded as implausible, there was a very small silver chain suspended from the Tara brooch[254] (although bird yokes were as likely to be gold as silver)[255] and ornamental chains, again of silver, are known from the Viking period.[256] The larger iron chains that may have held hounds or slaves were recovered in Hugh Hencken's excavations of Lagore.[257] But this leaves us looking for plausible antecedents to large silver chains that are mentioned in the tales either as human ornament or, more often, restraining dogs. Silver dog chains, naturally, are not found and the best one can do here is note that across the Irish Sea in Scotland large silver chains have been found that date between the 7th and 9th centuries.[258]

Mills

The Ulster tales pay little attention to agricultural pursuits but there are a number of references to the grinding of grain, occasionally in similes, including 'as fish malt is ground in the mill we be ground by Cú Chulainn.'[259] In one instance we find a reference to individuals grinding grain with a quern.[260] Such an image could derive from any period in Ireland's past since the introduction of farming *c.* 3800 BC. On a number

9.7. A beehive rotary quern from Ticooly-O'Kelly, Co. Galway.

of occasions, however, the motion of the millstone clearly indicates some form of rotary quern, and these were not introduced into Ireland until the Iron Age, where we have over 200 such querns from the centuries either side of AD 1 (FIG. 9.7). These have either a flattened disc or a much thicker beehive-shaped upper stone and where no further description is provided could offer a potential match to some of the references in the tales, such as 'the fort [of Cú Roí] revolved as swiftly as a millstone'.[261] But on a number of occasions we encounter characters moving as swift as a mill wheel (*roth búaile*)[262] or Cú Chulainn reduces a monster to feeling like a waterwheel, or in other words giddy.[263] Elsewhere we find that a grinding stone also involves a 'wheel-shaft',[264] spokes[265] and paddles,[266] which provides a clear indication that the authors of the tales were thinking of horizontal water mills that only began to appear in Ireland in the 7th century.

Conclusions

In terms of general material culture, there are very few (if any) objects that we can assign to the historical present of the tales. We know so little about the dress of the people of Iron Age Ireland that it is impossible to make a creditable contrast to what may have existed before we obtain iconographic evidence from medieval Ireland. We can only say that all the dress described in the tales can all be explained with reference to what we know of contemporary dress of the medieval period, and that some of the more exotic materials such as silk and satin are unlikely to have been present in Ireland before the medieval period.

The metal ornaments described in the literature offer a greater archaeological opportunity for determining their dates, although the actual literary descriptions often pose problems. If the brooches are dated by their material of composition, then almost all of them would need to be assigned to the medieval period. Iron Age brooches were made of bronze (or, in a few instances, iron) and there are only about half a dozen brooches described in the tales as being of bronze. If these had all been labelled with the same name, one might have been able to suggest that this evidenced a specific type of archaic brooch but this is not the case at all as a different name was assigned to each bronze example.[267] At least one of these brooches, the *roth* 'wheel', is certainly indicative of a medieval rather than Iron Age brooch, the latter never circular. The brooches described are overwhelmingly gold (or gilded) or silver (silvered), which suggests a medieval date too. In some cases, such as the *casán*, the brooches are exclusively of silver.

In terms of form, only one brooch manages to better resemble an Iron Age brooch than a medieval one: the leaf-shaped brooch. But here we find both an inconstancy of verbal designation and the fact that they are routinely described as of gold or *findruine* rather than bronze, all of which suggests that the leaf-shaped brooch is probably not a poetic relic of the Iron Age but rather another description of a medieval ornament.

A similar argument for a medieval date concerns both the head ornaments and rings portrayed in the Ulster tales. Consider, for example, a tale from the historical period such as *Scéla Cano Meic Gartnáin*, which includes a section of descriptive passages pertaining to dress, ornaments, weapons and games.[268] Here we find descriptions of clothing (green mantle with silver corners, tunic with gold insertion or fringe, tunic of yellow silk), ornaments (golden brooch), a gold neck-ring, gold crown), a *fidchell* board with gold and silver men, and a timpan of bronze/tin. Although these descriptions are all attributed to a historical character of the 7th century (the story was obviously composed more recently),[269] any of these items could also be found in the Ulster tales.

The containers, as we have seen, pose a different set of problems. Our knowledge of Iron Age vessels, other than cauldrons, tends to be minimal and as the cauldron existed from the Late Bronze Age and continued in use through to the medieval period it is impossible to fix a date for the literary allusions. Many of the other vessels carry foreign names, usually Latin, and so we can suspect that they are not native. The silver argument (and precious stones) can also be employed to argue a medieval rather than an Iron Age date for many of the vessels. As the vessels are generally, though not invariably, associated with elite drinking or dining at communal feasts, it is perhaps not that surprising that we lack descriptions of clay vessels, which would have appeared in the early medieval period, at least in the northeast of Ireland.

In terms of date little can be said of the musical instruments or games although all of them were certainly compatible with a medieval date and, at least in terms of the board games, they are often depicted as made of precious metals that may well be fantasy (e.g. silver gaming boards) but probably medieval fantasy, not Iron Age. On the other hand, the very existence of such games, as we have seen in the case of *fidchell*, probably did originate in both Britain and Ireland during the Roman Iron Age. The chains are more certainly a medieval motif (at least until we begin recovering parallels from Irish Iron Age sites). The references to querns, at least those relying on rotary motion, could derive from the Iron Age although they need not be confined to that period. Those that are described as driven by water-power are clearly medieval motifs.

CHAPTER TEN

Burial

...and the days of mourning for the King's daughters came to an end, and they buried them beside the well of Clebach, and they made a round ditch after the manner of a *ferta*, because this is what the heathen Irish used to do, but we call it *relic*.

Tírechán, *c.* 650[1]

Unable to wait for the following day to engage in his duel with Cú Chulainn, the foolishly impetuous Connacht warrior Etarcomol pushed the Ulster champion's patience until he was diced, sliced and his body dragged back to Medb behind Fergus' chariot. He was then buried:

> *Cladar a **fert** íarom. Sátir a **lia**. Scríbthair a ainm n-**ogaim**. Agair a gubae.*

> 'Then [Etarcomol's] **grave** was dug and his **stone** was planted; his name was written in **ogam**. He was mourned'.[2]

We might compare this with the burial of Ferb in the *Tochmarc Ferbe*:

> *Ro claided **úag** do Feirb iarsin, 7 ro tócbad a **lia** 7 ro scríbad ainm oguim, 7 doringned **duma** immon **licc**, conid Duma Ferbi a ainm ri Ráith Ini, aniartuáid atá.*

> 'And they dug a **grave** for Ferb, and a **stone** was erected for her, and her name was written upon it in **ogam**, and a **monument** of stone was made, so that Duma Ferbe is the name that is now for Raith Ini – in the northwest does that monument stand'.[3]

And from an event that allegedly occurred nearly two millennia earlier, we have the account of the burial of Nemed during the First Battle of Mag Tuired (1897 BC):

> Roclaided a **lia** 7 rosaithed a **cairthi** coned **lia** Nemid a ainm
> o sin ale.

'They dug his **grave** and erected a **pillar** for him, and the **Stone** of Nemed is its name to this day'[4]

A comparison of these three passages (and many more could be added) indicates that the Mythological and Ulster cycles both utilized a roughly standard description for burials but with some variation in details or vocabulary. In general we are essentially informed that a grave is prepared, a stone is erected that may or may not have an inscription written along the edge in the ogam alphabet (FIGS 3.1, 3.2), and that the resulting grave might be either an earthen mound or a stone cairn.

Unlike many of the other items discussed so far, the monuments of the dead have been evident across the Irish landscape from the time of the earliest farmers, *c.* 3800 BC, until the present. From the perspective of the Dreamtime, it was in 2958 BC that Bith, one of Cesair's party, was buried under a cairn atop Sliab Betha.[5] And when Medb boasts of the destruction she has wreaked on Ulster towards the end of the *Táin*, Fergus reminds her that 'every mound (*fert*) and every grave (*lecht*), every tombstone (*lia*) and every tomb (*ligi*) from here to the eastern part of Ireland is a mound (*fert*) and a grave (*lecht*), a tombstone (*lia*) and a tomb (*ligi*) for some goodly hero.'[6] Thus, Iron Age Katubutos and his distant medieval descendent Cathbad shared the same mortuary landscape where earlier mounds and cairns were remembered as the graves of past heroes. We have already seen how this led to retrospective burial, with the assigning of mounds and cairns across the Irish landscape to the names of heroes who reputedly died centuries or even millennia after the grave in question was erected. On the other hand, there is probably no more obvious monument that an archaeologist might employ to distinguish between pagan Iron Age and Christian medieval Ireland. This is because the early Christians of Ireland themselves felt that there was 'a necessity to distinguish non-Christian from Christian practices' with respect to mortuary practice.[7] So we will need to break the literary descriptions of burials down into their individual elements to see to what extent they provide relics of Ireland's pagan past. Edel Bhreathnach has discussed a number of the terms under three headings: those associated with pagan burial, those associated with Christian burials, and terms that straddle both cultures.[8]

She concludes that the nomenclature of Christian burials derives entirely from Latin and that such nomenclature is never employed in the Ulster tales.

The burial rite

The basic verb employed in describing the process of burying the dead was *ad-anaig*[9] which means both 'bury' but also 'escorts, conveys'. There is no description of the preparation of the body beforehand or any further reference to the process of burial be it the physical digging of a grave or the erecting of a mound or stone cairn.

But from the many descriptions of burials we can recover a useful list of implicit behaviours. As might be expected where few if any of our characters died peacefully in bed, it was usual for a burial to be erected roughly in the place where the deceased had fallen.[10] The only exceptions to this practice apply to the burial of royalty or a premier hero; the body of Conaire Mór, for example, was brought to Tara[11] for burial as was also the head of Cú Chulainn and Eochaid was buried at Cruachain.[12] While there might be burials in adjacent monuments – three Connacht warriors fall and their three separate tombs are erected[13] – there is little hint that there were actually formal cemeteries (other than Cruachain, which was regarded as a royal cemetery), but again we are dealing primarily with campaign deaths. Most importantly, inhumation is implicit in all the burial descriptions in the sense that there is really no hint of cremation. W. K. Sullivan suggested that the early Irish did practice cremation on the basis of the evidence of one tale from the Kings cycle whose events should be set to the 5th century AD. The translated passage that he employed concerned the burial of Fiachra, one of the sons of Eochaid Mugmedon (the father of Niall of the Nine Hostages):

> His *leacht* was made, and his *fert* was raised, and his *cluiche*
> *caintech* was ignited, and his ogam name was written, and the
> hostages which he brought from the south were buried alive
> around the Fert of Fiachra.[14]

Sullivan believed that this passage indicated that the ancient Irish practiced both cremation and engaged in human sacrifice. While the burying of the hostages alive would certainly provide literary evidence for sacrifice (and I would love to know where this motif was drawn from), there really is no indication of cremation here. The verbal noun *adnad* (or *adannad*) often means 'ignite' but the object of this verb, the *cluiche caintech*, simply means funeral games that (with the exception of the

Hunger Games) are hardly combustible. As *adnad* may also simply mean 'begin', it seems better to translate the enticing passage as 'his funeral games were initiated'.

The tomb

The *scéla* employ three basic terms to designate the 'grave'. The commonest word is *lecht* 'grave, tomb', which is a loanword from Latin *lectus* 'couch, bed, funeral bed, bier' (and may also underlie the Welsh *llaith* 'grave'). It is generally employed in the broad meaning of a 'grave', either in terms of an actual structure or metaphorically in the sense of death, as in 'for I am the one destined to bring you to your grave (*thiglecht*)'.[15] As a structural term it is ambiguous in the extreme as it frequently covers a variety of grave types, including mound,[16] cairn[17] and even stone marker.[18]

Another word for grave is *úag*, common enough in early Irish although its use in the Ulster cycle tends to be very limited. It does occur in a classical description of the burial of Ferb: 'they dug a grave (*úag*) for Ferb...' (see p. 255).[19]

The third word is *lige*, which basically means the 'act of lying down', but as a noun it came to mean 'grave, bed, couch' and, to make matters all the more obvious we have the compounds *lechtluigi* 'grave-bed',[20] *crólige* 'gore/death-bed')',[21] and *otharlige* 'wounded/sickbed'.[22]

Grave goods

There are only two references to grave goods in the Ulster tales. The first is in relation to the burial of Cú Chulainn's head and his right hand, which also included 'the whole panel of his golden shield (*lán lainne a scéith di úir*)'.[23] The other example is with reference to the troop of Mac Irmara who were 'buried standing up with their shields before them, each man in his *duma*' (see below).[24] It is notable that in the only two examples from the tales, both involve the burial of a shield.

Gravestone

If the terminology associated with the grave itself is not instructive, the recurrent motif of an accompanying gravestone can be tested against the archaeological record. There are several terms (*coirthe*[25] and *lía*[26]) that, in the appropriate context, may be loosely translated as 'gravestone' and would appear to be native Irish words.

coirthe 'pillar-stone'

As we have seen above (Chapter Six) the *coirthe* 'pillar-stone' often occurs in contexts where there is no burial indicated, such as standing, sometimes in number, on the green of a fort, or apparently randomly sited across the landscape to provide a perch for war-goddesses who have assumed the form of birds, or as manikins to be dressed as kings to deceive near-sighted warriors. But the same word is also employed to indicate a gravestone, and we are reminded in the *Táin* that 'gravestones (*coirthi*) will be erected over graves (*i llechtaib*)'.[27] The context suggests that every individual would have a headstone (e.g. 'their 29 headstones (*coirthi*) were erected then'[28]) but there is one interesting exception: in the death-tale of Conchobar we find 'a pillar-stone at his head, and another at his feet'.[29]

lía 'stone, standing-stone, pillar-stone, ogam-stone'

By far the most frequent reference to a standing stone over a grave is the *lía*. The *lía* is a standard part of the burial descriptions, and may appear either before or following the construction of the grave: Celtchair's 'stone (*lía*) and tomb (*lecht*) were raised there',[30] 'their tombs (*fert*) and their stones (*lia*) were raised by Cú Chulainn'.[31] Like the *coirthe*, the *lía* was erected for each individual, as can be seen in the *Táin* where we read regarding the 13 men of Ferchú that 'their 13 headstones (*líic*) mark the spot'[32] or in the second recension of the *Táin* where Cú Chulainn 'planted 12 stones for them in the ground and put a head of each of them on its stone *and* also put Ferchú Loigsech's head on its stone'.[33]

The *lía* might also be recalled in place names, such as in the *Táin* when we find that Úalu's 'grave and his headstone (*lía*) are on the road beside the stream, Lia Úalu is its name'.[34] The word is also used to describe the gravestone of Fergus at Enloch in Connacht, from whence Fergus was summoned to recite the *Táin*. Here we learn that 'Muirgen chanted a poem to the gravestone as though it were Fergus himself'.[35]

Occasionally, references to the *lía* mention an ogam inscription (for example with reference to Etarcomol and Ferb above). Also, Conall raised 'the stone and wrote his [Cú Chulainn's] name in ogam and made a funeral song'.[36]

Cairn

The grave itself may be covered by either a cairn or an earthen mound. As the cairn provides fewer problems of interpretation and is identified by only a single word, it will be reviewed first.

The *carn* 'cairn' is an inherited word with a good claim to antiquity.[37] Its use in the Ulster tales is often connected with place names or prominent landmarks rather than directly related to the burial of the recently deceased. For example, the young Cú Chulainn enquires regarding the name of a cairn on his first raid,[38] an army passes by the cairn or an army is advised not to engage in a raid 'until every fair cairn is conspicuous'.[39] That the cairn was employed for burial, however, is obvious: 'then Eochaid was overwhelmed by numbers, not in fair fight, so that his cairn is on Mag Rois';[40] 'corpses shall be in the bed of the cairn'.[41]

Two tales provide some insight into the erection of a cairn. Generally, one might assume that a single individual would erect a cairn (e.g. 'Cet beheaded his nine men and made a cairn and mound over them'[42]), but in two instances the erection is corporate. In one tale we read that 'Celtchair cut off his head, over which a cairn was raised, viz. a stone was placed by every man that came there'.[43] This suggests that the cairn accumulated in size over time as each visitor added a stone to the grave, a custom that continued at least into the 19th century[44] and is somewhat reminiscent of the Jewish custom of placing pebbles or stones on a grave. This practice is reinterpreted in the tale recording the destruction of Da Derga's hostel, where each of the raiders contributes a stone to a cairn before attacking the hostel,[45] and then those surviving remove a stone, the remainder of the stones serving as a visible body count of the casualties.[46]

The single most complicated (and somewhat bizarre) account of burial under a cairn derives from the *De Síl Conairi Móir*, a *scél* more appropriately attached to the cycle surrounding Conaire and Tara. After a battle we read that:

> His [Mac Irmara] *mound* was raised by Mac Con [his maternal uncle] and a *cairn* of stones for each of his men. They [Mac Irmara' men] were buried standing up with their shields before them, each man in his *cairn*.[47]

Setting aside the topos of upright burial with weapons,[48] we may note that the senior figure, Mac Irmara, is buried under an *aibenn* 'mound', while each of his men is placed under a *carn* 'cairn'.

Barrow

There are three words in early Irish that are employed to designate a mound or barrow. The first is the somewhat obscure word *aibenn* or *aimend* 'mound', which only occurs once in the tales in the burial of Mac Irmara cited above.[49]

A commoner term is *duma* 'mound, tumulus, barrow', which may be associated with the word for 'hill' in Gaulish.[50] While the meaning 'barrow' is simple enough there is some evidence that *duma* was not always simply intended to indicate a mound but rather a surrounding bank that, as we will see below, is of considerably more archaeological interest. Such a use might be argued on the basis of several, admittedly difficult, passages. For example, let us return to the burial of Ferb, where A. H. Leahy translated the relevant passage[51] as:

> And they dug a grave for Ferb, and a pillar of stone was erected
> for her, and her name was written upon it in letters of Ogham,
> and a monument of stone (*duma licc*) was made, so that Duma
> Ferbe is the name that is now for Raith Ini – in the northwest
> does that monument stand.

If the descriptive sequence (grave, ogam stone and then stone *duma*) is intended to reflect a sequence of activities, it seems to imply that the grave and the ogam stone were encased in a stone cairn and, perhaps, better sense is made if we translate:[52] 'they made a *duma* about the stone'. Similarly, we find that 'Cet beheaded his nine men and made a cairn (*carn*) and mound over them (*dumbha forra*).'[53] Erecting a cairn and building a mound over it on the same spot is not entirely unheard of: the '40-metre structure' at Navan Fort, for example, was first encased in a stone cairn that was subsequently covered with turves to form a mound, but here it is easier to imagine that 'he built a cairn and a *duma* about them'. Otherwise we may be dealing with a redundant expression, such as 'they built a fort and a *longphort*'.

Less clear is the unique description of the burial of Mac Irmara and his men that we have already cited above, where the translator has interpreted *duma* to designate the cairn that each man was buried in, which seems redundant in that the text has already indicated that there is a cairn for each man. On the other hand, the only mound so far mentioned is the *aibenn* of Mac Irmara himself. If we translate *duma* here as mound, it again implies the encasement of a cairn within a mound and we have no idea how one is to be impressed by the fine standing stone at Mac Gubai's grave if it is buried inside a mound. So there is at least a possibility that we are dealing with an earthen enclosure about the cairn and stone.[54] The *duma* is also a regular place name element, e.g. Duma Ferbe.

The final and most problematic word is *fert* 'a mound or tumulus; glossed *tumulum*, especially a mound over a burial place'. The precise meaning of *fert* has been recognized as a problem, at least since the time of O'Curry.[55] The first issue is distinguishing between a *fert* as a mound associated with a burial and a *fert* as simply indicating a mound without any mortuary connotations. The second problem is whether one should envisage the *fert*, when it is applied to burial practice, as a simple tumulus over the grave or as an enclosure. The one thing we can say for certain is that the word *fert* is at home in Celtic and not a loanword.[56] In the following discussion instances of its usage will be largely confined to the Ulster tales.

Our first problem is that the Old Irish word may indicate both a burial mound and a mound erected for some other purpose, as in 'At once they cast off their garments and dug up a turfy mound (*fert fótmaig*) as a seat for their leader'.[57] In a number of instances, especially in the *Táin*, it is not always clear whether the *fert* is a burial mound or not, although it is invariably locked into the topography, as in 'he [Órlám] is on the mound (*fertai*) yonder'.[58]

It should be noted here that prehistoric mounds, whatever their origin, were also absorbed into medieval social practices as inauguration mounds, high places upon which local kings would be 'crowned'. For example, after the death of Fráech, his body was taken to Cruachain where it was buried in Síd Fráech (identified usually as Carnfree) but this monument was then employed as the inauguration site of the Uí Chonchobair kings who ruled much of the surrounding territory.[59] Indeed, Richard Warner has suggested that monuments such as the Iron Age mound at Navan Fort were prototypes for these inauguration mounds upon which a king might serve as a conduit between his own people and the Otherworld.[60]

The *fert* is often employed in full burial descriptions that describe the digging of the *fert*, the erection of a headstone (sometimes with an ogam inscription) and sometimes the chanting of a funeral dirge.[61] Those buried within a *fert* include Etarcomol, Fer Báeth, Úalu, Deirdre and the Sons of Uisnech, Luaine, Conla, Derbforgaill and Lugaid, Ailill, Fachtna Fáthach, Fergus mac Léti, Fergus mac Roích and Cú Chulainn.

Context at least gives a hint as to whether we are dealing with a mortuary *fert* or some other kind of mound. We might expect an impressive mound when we read that Luaine's '*fert* should be dug, that from it her grave (*lecht*) should be conspicuous'.[62] But consider the following passage from a later version of the Deirdre story: 'Deirdre sat in the tomb (*fert*) and gave three kisses to Noíse, before going into the grave (*uag*)'.[63] Clearly if Deirdre is perched on a mound covering the remains of her *ménage à quatre*, she could hardly dispense kisses to her lover Noíse (nor go herself into the same grave), unless she were a mole or badger. In this case translating *fert* simply as 'barrow' just doesn't do the trick. And here we are aided by a 7th-century bishop, Tírechán, who describes the burial of two recently converted daughters of an Irish king who had just been baptized and were rewarded with instant death: 'and the days of mourning for the King's daughters came to an end, and they buried them beside the well of

Clebach, and they made a round ditch after the manner of a *ferta*, because this is what the heathen Irish used to do, but we call it *relic*.[64] Here the Latin text refers to the *fert* as a *fossam rotundam* 'round ditch' rather than a *tumulus* 'barrow'. This makes far better sense and basically defines an enclosed space, formed by a round ditch and corresponding small earthen bank, from which the mournful Deirdre could view the burial of her lover and his two brothers (albeit with their heads detached). In Irish law the *fert* served as an ancestral boundary and property marker, a claimant to land having to cross the boundary of the *fert* in order to establish his bona fides to the land (guaranteed by the ancestors who permitted him entry into their precinct). The *fert* was also often accompanied by an ogam stone.[65] So it would seem that the *fert* might refer either to a burial mound or a bank and ditch enclosure around a grave.[66]

Lamentation

Other than the frequent mention of a funeral dirge or lamenting (*guba*), there are only a few other indications of mortuary behaviour. In one instance from what might as well have been placed in the Mythological cycle, we read that the livestock of the deceased are killed: 'And Étaín was left with Ailill that his last rites might be paid by her – that is, his grave (*fert*) dug, his lamentation (*guba*) made, his cattle slain'[67] (but it should be noted that reference to the cattle (*coro hortha a chethrai*) is not part of the original text but entered later and not found in other redactions). In the story of the death of Cú Chulainn's son we read that calves were deprived of their cows as part of the lamentation: 'then his cry of lament (*guba*) was raised, his grave (*fert*) made, and his stone (*lia*) set up, and to the end of three days no calf was let to their cows by the men of Ulster, to commemorate him'.[68]

Synopsis

We can now take the various descriptions above and add several more non-lexically defined elements to provide a synopsis of the mortuary practice of the Ulster tales from the point of death until the lament.

Inhumation was the only burial rite practised and there is no creditable trace of cremation. Burial was generally individual rather than collective. If the latter, this was generally motivated by something other than an appeal to tradition. For example, Deirdre is buried in the same tomb as the three Sons of Uisnech while Eochaid Feidlech wished to be buried in Cruachain with the heads of his three sons on one side of him and their bodies on the other.[69] There is no indication of orientation of the burial or that orientation was regarded as something requiring description. Only two tales suggest the presence of any form of grave goods and these comprise shields. The deceased was placed under or within: a) an earthen barrow (*duma, fert?*); b) an earthen enclosure (*duma?, fert?*); c) a stone cairn (*carn*); or d) a simple flat grave (*lige*, etc.). In many instances there is reference to the erection of a headstone (*coirthe, lía*) either within the grave itself or presumably close by, and the stone may or may not have been inscribed in ogam.

Assessment

We may now review how well the literary descriptions can be matched against the archaeological record. As we have reviewed the literary evidence in terms of the discrete features of Ulster cycle burial, we will follow the same course for the archaeological evidence.

Burial

The many victims of Cú Chulainn in the *Táin* and all other tales suggest that inhumation was the burial practice of the Ulster cycle. In terms of archaeology, ever since at least the Middle Bronze Age the basic burial rite in Ireland was predominantly cremation, and this continued up until *c.* AD 400.[70] The only minor exceptions were a small number of flexed inhumations in the area around Tara and the Boyne that date to *c.* 100 BC–AD 200 and which may well be indicative of foreign (Romano-British) settlers. In short, during the Iron Age Katu-butos' descriptions of burials were likely to be confined to cremations which, obviously, fail to match the evidence of the tales.

At some time around the 5th century onwards, extended inhumation becomes overwhelmingly the primary form of burial in Ireland. From the perspective of our potential *filid*, either Cattubuttas or Cathbad could have been composing the burial descriptions involving inhumation.

Grave goods

As we have seen, other than two references to the burial of shields in the tales, there is really no reference to grave goods accompanying the deceased. The earliest (flexed) inhumation burials do tend to have some grave goods, usually of a foreign nature, which helps support the notion that they are intrusive into Irish society.[71] The extended inhumations generally lack any detectable grave goods (perishable goods would not usually survive) and Elizabeth O'Brien has suggested that the lack of grave goods in Ireland might be accounted for by the influence of Wales and Cornwall (where the Irish had established colonies) as these areas also lacked the practice of depositing grave goods.[72] As Early Christian burials also lacked grave goods this makes it impossible to determine whether the inhumation graves are non-Christian or Christian simply because they lacked grave goods.

The two instances of burial accompanied by shields in the Ulster tales, therefore, remain as a topos in search of a source. The earliest and closest physical source would be Anglo-Saxon burials, where, in a survey of the inhumation burials with weapons, about 45 per cent were accompanied by a shield (i.e., about 8 percent of all burials), a figure higher than for their continental contemporaries.[73] These shield burials date from the 5th to 7th centuries (a time during which Anglo-Saxons made occasional raids on Ireland). The upright stance of one of the Ulster tale descriptions is, of course, not part of Anglo-Saxon practice, where the shields are generally placed horizontally on top of the body, and exceptionally set vertical when the body is in a coffin that could not accommodate the width of the shield. Of some interest is the fact that shield burial is not a clear marker of wealth in Anglo-Saxon burials due to its frequency: the prestige markers would have been the seax, sword and axe. As there have been no finds of shields listed among the grave goods of suspected Anglo-Saxon burials in Ireland,[74] one might presume that this feature was borrowed by Irish writers in contact with Anglo-Saxon or continental society. Alternatively, the motif may be somewhat later and relate to Viking burials of the 9th century, with shield bosses reasonably common among the burial goods recovered from Norse burials in Ireland.[75] There is also one potential biblical source. When Ezekiel runs through a list of torments for Israel's enemies, he warns that the warriors of Meshech and Tubal 'do not lie with the fallen warriors of long ago who went down to Sheol with their weapons of war, whose swords were laid under their heads, and whose shields are upon their bones.'[76] Had the Ulster tales included the sword burial along with that of the shield, this would have made a very convincing source for the custom. But without the sword, the routine burial of shields with Anglo-Saxon or Norse graves offers a more plausible source.

Headstone

The Ulster cycle routinely depicts the insertion of a pillar-stone or ogam stone within the grave. We need to distinguish here between the simple standing stone and a stone carrying an ogam inscription, as the latter is temporally much more confined.

Simple standing stones have been found with burials at least since the Early Bronze Age, for example the Longstone, Co. Kildare, or at Drumnahare, Co. Down,[77] but these examples accord in no other way with the descriptions in the Ulster tales as they are associated with cremations, cists and a range of grave goods. Also, it is often difficult to determine whether the stone is actually contemporary with any nearby burials rather than serving as a prior monument that 'attracted' burial; the Longstone, Co. Down, for example, had no evidence for ancient burial at its foot but had managed to attract the modern burials of a pet dog and rabbit near its base – but there was also a Late Bronze Age cremation in a ring ditch 50 m away.[78] Standing stones are also known to be proximate to burials during the Iron Age, such as at Ballykeel South, Co. Clare, which dates to *c*. AD 400.[79]

One of the closest examples to the ritual described in the Ulster tales would be the burial at Kiltullagh, Co. Roscommon,[80] where the body of a mature male was placed in the extended position, possibly covered with timber planks, with a standing stone at his head (FIG. 10.1). Although some animal remains were found within the grave, the excavators suspected that it was merely 'discarded food refuse incidentally included in the backfill'.[81] The burial was radiocarbon dated to AD 406–532.

10.1. Burial from Killtullagh, Co. Roscommon, dating to the 5th/early 6th century AD. The standing stone may not be in its original position.

But there is a problem here in that the standing stone was inserted into a separate pit from that containing the inhumation and it is uncertain whether the stone was in its original place, as there were records of it having fallen and been replaced. In O'Sullivan and Harney's (2008, 148) review of early medieval archaeology,[82] it was presumed that the standing stone 'had become the focal point of later inhumation burials in the 5/6th centuries' which suggests that it existed (long?) before the actual burial. Indeed, O'Sullivan and Harney suggest that the standing stones of the 5th and 6th centuries were essentially earlier monuments that had been reused.[83]

In addition to the standing stone it is obvious that the Ulster cycle regarded the erection of an ogam stone as part of the burial ritual. Ogam inscriptions can be generally confined between the 4th and 8th centuries. Some have argued that the great majority of them had been erected by pagans rather than early Christians,[84] but the jury is still out on this. Damian McManus suggested that there is really too little internal or circumstantial evidence to determine whether an inscription refers to a pagan or a Christian,[85] while Catherine Swift has adduced evidence that many were indeed associated with Christians (Christian symbols on ogams, Latin names).[86]

Key questions here are whether, as in the Ulster tales, the ogam stone was actually erected as part of the burial and do the Ulster tales accurately reflect the behaviour associated with them? Today ogams are generally interpreted as commemorative memorials[87] and boundary markers; whether they ever actually marked burials is a moot question. Nancy Edwards, for example, does not dismiss that possibility but does warn that 'no ogham stone has yet been found in direct association with a grave'[88] (excluding reuse to mark the position of a modern grave);[89] while Harold Mytum asserts that at least some 'marked actual graves' although no direct evidence is provided.[90] The problem here is that *in situ* discoveries of ogam stones are very rare. In terms of dating the historical present of the Ulster cycle burials, the function of the ogam stones is critical. If they were routinely employed as burial markers, then the tales could reflect a past that extended back to the 4th century AD. But if they were not, then the burial descriptions are the products of the imagination of Christian authors who assumed that ogam stones, like standing stones and earthen mounds, must all reflect their pagan past. McManus has reviewed some of the evidence for ogams in early Irish literature and concluded that the references there suggest that either their authors were 'familiar with the practice of erecting stones bearing memorial inscriptions in Ogam', though this may have ceased by the time of their composition or else they have taken their own tradition of writing gravestones in the Latin script and back-projected this with the help of what they knew was an earlier writing system.[91]

10.2. The distribution of ogam stones in Ireland is essentially concentrated in the far south and west with very few located in the north, where much of the action of the Ulster tales occurs.

He also notes that if one wishes to accept the first proposition, it is curious that nowhere in the literature do we encounter the text of an orthodox ogam inscription (although we do have the key to reading ogams in the Book of Ballymote). To this caveat we might also add that most of those who are associated with an ogam stone died and were presumably buried in the northern half of Ireland. This is far from the main distribution of ogam stones, which are largely to be found in Kerry, Cork and Waterford; only one is known from Armagh, two from Antrim and none from Down (FIG. 10.2). This reflects a real discordance between where the Ulster cycle says ogam stones were erected as burial markers and where we actually find them. In fact, from the viewpoint of Catherine Swift, the ogam stones indicate the spread of Christianity in the southern half of Ireland.[92] In short, there does not seem to be a compelling reason to conclude that the Ulster cycle reflects a view of ogam stones that was contemporary with their erection. It could be argued, then, that both the standing stone and the ogam stone are retrospective elements of the Ulster tales involving a reimagining of the prehistoric landscape and the original purpose of its monuments.

Cairn

As with mounds, burials under a stone cairn can be dated from the Neolithic onwards. What is striking is how rare they appear to be in the later Iron Age/early medieval period. At Claristown 2, Co. Meath, a cairn covered an earlier Iron Age burial that had itself overlain features dating to *c.* 300–1 BC.[93] And as with mounds, in some cases later Iron Age burials were inserted into earlier Bronze Age cairns, such as at Ballymacaward, Co. Donegal.[94] It may be noted that cairns are attested in medieval literature. Elizabeth O'Brien[95] cites the example of Tírechán's description of a cairn being erected over the grave of St Patrick's charioteer and Adamnán's reference to the burial of a man under a cairn in the time of Columba. The historical present of these burials would fall in the 5th and 6th centuries. But the archaeological evidence is really meagre and one cannot help but suspect that we are dealing again with a back-projected motif derived from the obvious presence of cairns on the Irish landscape which were serving as beacons for burials in the 5th and 6th centuries.

Barrow

Setting aside for a moment issues concerning the precise meaning of Old Irish *fert*, the Ulster tales make it clear that their heroes were interred in or under barrows, as we have other words (*aibenn, duma*) to describe this as well as *fert*. Burial under a tumulus begins in Ireland at least with the Middle Neolithic and continues in some form through the Bronze Age and Iron Age, where we routinely encounter cremation burials under ring barrows or ring ditches.[96] The cremation burials that appear in the Iron Age up until *c.* AD 400 are routinely found associated with ring ditches, many if not most of which are presumed to have had either a central mound and/or a surrounding bank.[97] The use of mounds continued with the shift to inhumation where, for example, two inhumations under a large mound (*c.* 24 m diameter, 5 m high) were found at Ninch, Co. Meath, that were dated *c.* AD 390–680.[98] And we even have evidence for Viking mounds, such as College Green.[99] So the location of burials under mounds has been so integrated into Irish mortuary tradition that it is difficult to see how one could have avoided ascribing tumulus burial to the characters of the Ulster tales no matter when one sets their date.

But what is striking is that in the 2,000 years before the production of the Ulster tales, the evidence for inhumation burial under a mound is so exceedingly sparse that the case for any accurate recollection of pagan burial in Ireland is suspect. It is far easier to imagine that burial under a mound was simply an imaginative reconstruction of a distant past based on the knowledge that mounds did contain human remains. This would be especially pertinent to the practice of inserting later burials into earlier mounds in an attempt to legitimate one's claim to a given territory.[100] Alternatively, although probably less likely, the motif was imported from contemporary 'pagans' such as the Norse.

Fert

The final issue concerns the *fert*, and we have already seen the difficulties in determining whether this word in the Ulster tales denoted simply a mound or rather a ring ditch and bank. As we have already dealt with mounds, the critical archaeological evidence for the alternative meaning would be some form of bank and ditched enclosure. And if we presume extensive damage of surface features, then we can again refer back to the ring ditch, which has been employed to surround burials at least since the Late Bronze Age. In short, it would have been possible to employ the term *ferta* (or any of its linguistically earlier forms) to monuments from at least *c.* 1000 BC until the time of the tales themselves. Indeed, this is how one of the burials at Ballymacaward, Co. Donegal, is described by modern archaeologists who note how 'an ancestral boundary mound or *ferta* that was erected in the Bronze Age' was later utilized to house Iron Age cremation burials and then inhumation burials from the 5th/6th and 7th centuries.[101] At Collierstown 1, Co. Meath, another *ferta* was only initiated with the burial of a woman in the 5th/6th century that was followed by more than 60 more burials extending into the 8th century.[102] In short, the *ferta*, no matter how envisaged, offers little or no indication of the date of this motif in the Ulster tales.

Conclusions

If one understands the historical present of the Ulster tales to have been around the 1st centuries BC and AD, then it seems fairly clear that the tales do not really preserve a memory of Iron Age burial in Ireland. The complete absence of cremation, the most diagnostic element of the Iron Age burial ritual that we have examined, indicates that the literary descriptions fail to provide the type of privileged information that might have confirmed an Iron Age date for the motif. It is also noteworthy that later burial practices such as slab-lined graves receive no mention either, and it is at least highly questionable whether the Ulster tales provide contemporary descriptions of the erection of ogam stones. If we must go outside an Iron Age source, no matter how defined, then there were probably at least three strands of sources informing the authors of the Ulster tales.

One is clearly the Irish archaeological landscape, where an abundance of prehistoric mounds, cairns and standing stones encouraged the belief that they were the burial places of earlier heroes.[103] If one accepts the idea that burial in a *fert* described in early Irish tradition represented attempts to maintain territorial claims through association with distant ancestors, then the Ulster cycle (and similar 'ancient' tales) were laying down the ancestral dates for such monuments.

The second source derives from the archaeological landscape of the period between the 5th and 7th centuries, when pagan and Christian burial continued side by side or were indistinguishable from one another (e.g. inhumation, absence of grave goods, standing stone). In short, by avoiding obvious reference to established Christian cemeteries, burial descriptions could pass for pagan.

Finally, there is the occasional exotic element, such as burial with shields, in which the Irish may have borrowed from either their pagan neighbours in Britain (Anglo-Saxons), the pagan Norse in Ireland, or just possibly one passage of the Bible. In examining the topos of the 'sentinel warrior burial' in early Irish literature (to which we might perhaps add from the Ulster cycle the upright burials of Mac Irmara's troop in *De Síl Conairi Móir*), Elizabeth O'Brien suggests that the motif may have been lifted by the Irish from their knowledge of Anglo-Saxon burial rites, reasoning that 'if this was acceptable burial practice for pagan or semi-christian Anglo-Saxon warrior-heroes then the Irish must have had the same in their pagan past'.[104] This type of borrowing, I have suggested, helps explain many of the anachronistic items of material culture depicted in the Ulster cycle and raises the interesting possibility that the early Irish frequently turned a blind eye to their own pagan past and sought to reimagine it through the cultures of their pagan neighbours.

Finally, little mention has been made of classical sources here because they are not really convincing. Although the Irish were exposed to descriptions of the burials of great heroes of classical literature, which naturally included mounds,[105] they also routinely describe cremation burials. In the Latin *Iliad*, for example, Hector along with his weapons, chariot, horses and some Greek soldiers, are all burnt on a funeral pyre.[106] The Irish never adopted cremation as an element in their description of the burial rite and so the classical references probably have little to do with the Irish texts other than reinforcing the already well-rooted notion of the burial mound. And when a classical text only mentions the use of a tumulus, such as the one that served for Polydorus, the Irish gave him a proper send off with a *fert*, a stone with his name engraved, and a group of mourners.[107]

Whence the Dreamtime?

The poems which tell of the mighty feats of Cuchulain, and of the heroes whose life-threads were interwoven with his, date back to a purely pagan Ireland – an Ireland cut off from all connection with the splendid and slowly dying civilization of Rome, an Ireland in which still obtained ancient customs that had elsewhere vanished even from the memory of man.

Theodore Roosevelt, 1907[1]

Theodore Roosevelt, sometime American president and always a jobbing writer, clearly believed that the earliest Irish tradition was anchored deep in the Irish past. Having 'tested' the descriptions of the earliest Irish tradition's treatment of the island's cultural history against the archaeological record, it is now time for us to draw the evidence together and attempt to identify the various sources reflected in the Irish Dreamtime. So far we have identified at least five different potential sources:

1. Prehistoric Ireland, the historical 'present' of the tales which, for the Mythological cycle is contemporary with the later Neolithic, the Bronze Age and the earlier part of the Iron Age, c. 2800–100 BC, and for the Ulster cycle, the Irish Iron Age, c. 100 BC – AD 400, more specifically c. 100 BC to AD 100.

2. Early medieval Ireland, c. AD 400–1100, in which we find Irish literature first recorded or created in written form until the time of our earliest surviving manuscripts. Here we might also include the wider cultural environment, both literary and physical, in which the medieval Irish operated, comprising both Britain and Western Europe.

3. The Bible in both its 'Old Latin' edition and St Jerome's Vulgate translation, which was an integral part of the cultural milieu of those who produced the written version of the earliest Irish tradition.

4. Classical literature, exclusively in Latin, that was on the shelves of the Irish monasteries and was not only well known to the literate elite but in a number of instances was translated by monks into Irish.

5. The fundamental encyclopedia of the early medieval period, the *Etymologiae* of Isidore of Seville.

6. The creative world of the scribes who enjoyed fleshing out their own imagined past.

The Mythological cycle

While there has been considerable analysis of the biblical and other potential sources for the characters and major pattern of events in the *Lebor Gabála Érenn* and related works, our concern here is confined to the material culture depicted in the medieval documents associated with the Irish National Origin Legend. While the Bible may have played a central role in structuring the Irish account, as a source for the sequence of cultural innovations, it offers only a rather remote possibility. We have already seen in Chapter Four that despite a few, perhaps 'lucky hits', the sequence of events and inventions indicated in the traditional sources does not make a very convincing case that the Irish actually preserved any recollection, other than perhaps the track-way at Corlea, of the cultural prehistory of Ireland.

Although the Bible may well have prompted the Irish to cast themselves as a lost tribe of Israel, it is probably not the source for the sequence of inventions indicated in the tales. From *Genesis* we learn that Jabal was the ancestor of pastoralism, Jubal was the starting point for musicians who played the lyre and pipes and Tubal-cain made all sorts of bronze and iron tools.[2] Then comes Noah, who planted the first vineyard (and then experienced the first hangover),[3] followed by Nimrod who was the first real warrior.[4] This window of invention was comparatively narrow, covering only a few generations in *Genesis*, and the number and nature of these innovations is hardly of the type that we find in the Irish sources. The same could be said for the *Sex Aetates Mundi*, which revisited most of the same inventions listed in *Genesis* and was also translated into Irish.[5]

Classical literature might offer better parallels but, again, appears (in so far as I have been able to determine) to lack the scale of the Irish inventory of innovation. Lucretius (*c.* 99–55 BC), for example, lumps the invention of copper, gold, iron, silver and lead altogether.[6] In one area, however, he demands our attention. Lucretius is quite definite that horse-riding preceded chariotry and that the use of the two-horse chariot in war preceded both the four-horse version and the use of the scythed chariot.[7] Irish tradition also set the four-horse chariot after the inception of chariotry and while one might regard the sequence of development from two to four horses as evolutionarily natural, the interesting thing is that both sources felt compelled to make explicit mention of the sequence. And, of course, it is always interesting to encounter references to the scythed chariot yet again. Unfortunately, to see Lucretius' hand in anything Irish would require some evidence that his work actually survived in an Irish monastery, as it seems to have largely disappeared from the library shelves of medieval Europe.

But the most likely prompt for the list of Irish inventions originated in the chronological summaries that began with Eusebius and passed to the West in Latin translations such as the *Chronicon* of St Jerome.[8] Here we learn that the vine was discovered by Dionysus (in the time of Moses rather than Noah), Trochilus was the first to yoke a four-horse chariot team in Greece, Phidon the Argive was the inventor of weights and measures, etc. Such chronicles provided the background for the cultural developments in Ireland but these were probably generated from a more immediate source, Isidore of Seville. In his *Etymologiae*,[9] he provides a summary of the Seven Ages of Man, wherein he lists the Anno Mundi dates for the time when the Greeks began to cultivate crops, Atlas discovered astronomy, the Hebrews began to write, the yoking of the first chariot, Apollo's invention of the cithara and Mercury's invention of the lyre, etc. While we do not find exact parallels for the Irish innovations, excepting perhaps the chariot, the basic approach to the presentation of the chronology of cultural innovations may well have encouraged the Irish to ponder the origins of some of their own technology and manufacture their own corresponding sequence of cultural development.

While I do not believe we have been left with a totally accurate description of the great causeway across Móin Lámraige that Midir reputedly built in the Iron Age, I do suspect that some Iron Age *fili* once sang the praises of the highway engineers who constructed the Corlea trackway and he seems to have done such a good job that recollection of this engineering feat survived across the centuries into the Middle Ages.

The Ulster cycle

Although few have regarded the Mythological cycle a worthy pond in which to fish for useful cultural historical evidence, the Ulster cycle has been traditionally regarded by some as a useful source for retrieving the world of the Iron Age Irish. The remaining conclusions are largely confined to the date and sources for the material culture of the Ulster cycle of tales, particularly the *Táin*.

Before Katu-butos?

The attentive or sceptical reader will no doubt have noticed that in Chapter Three, when I introduced our three *filid*, Katu-butos, Cattubuttas and Cathbad, I began my sequence with an amnesiac. Katu-butos was sent out into the field, trailing after the army of Queen Medb, with no prior cultural inheritance. This, of course, would be most improbable as he should have absorbed a long tradition of poems and tales before he was ever accepted into the ranks of the poets. In short, the earliest Irish tradition must have had its own antecedents and it is now time to consider that evidence. The best place to start is with the scholar who stimulated much of this discussion, Kenneth Hurlstone Jackson (1909–1991), who made monumental contributions to the scholarship of the Celtic languages.

After reviewing a number of parallels between classical descriptions of the Gauls and the similar cultural behaviour of characters in the Ulster cycle, Jackson argued:

> That there is no connection between the Gaulish and the Irish
> in all this is more than I, for one, am prepared to believe.[10]

Jackson's attitude is quite understandable. There really are a series of striking parallels between what little we know of the Gauls, much of it gleaned from a lost work of the Greek philosopher Posidonius (135–51 BC), who travelled extensively in Gaul during the 1st century BC and the earliest accounts of the Irish. These drove Jackson to conclude:

> If we want to know what it was to be a late La Tène Celt, and what
> life in the Early Iron Age was like, we can get some notion of it by
> reading the Irish Ulster cycle of hero stories.[11]

Jackson's arguments led to the oft-cited claim that the Ulster cycle provided a 'window on the Iron Age', a thesis that this book has not found convincing. Yet John Koch, another critic of Jackson who also rejected his Iron Age thesis, could nevertheless write: 'I still believe that the Ulster Cycle has preserved some traditions from ancient Celtic Europe'.[12] He went on to list a number of Jackson's parallels which he thought were still convincing, such as headhunting, chariot warfare and contests for the champion's portion. Below I have attempted to assemble a list of some of those parallels, including those made by Jackson and Koch as well as and whatever else struck me as worthy of consideration, especially when it bears some relationship to material culture. I have tried to adopt a best-case scenario to be as fair as possible.

1. The use of the two-horse chariot consisting of a driver and a warrior.[13] The Gaulish and British chariot was used primarily for display, disruption of the enemy ranks, to convey the warrior to the battlefield where he would dismount to fight on foot, and to retrieve the warrior if he was in trouble. In some regions it was also employed in the funeral rite and buried with the deceased. Other than its more overt mortuary associations, this parallels its use as depicted in the Ulster tales.[14]

2. The use of broad slashing swords (in both Gaul and Britain) as opposed to the smaller thrusting swords that the Romans employed to great effectiveness in close combat.[15] Here one might argue that the use of the swords in the Ulster *scéla* had more in common with those of the continental Celts or Britons than the small thrusting swords we find in Iron Age Ireland; in other words the *Táin* may have preserved images of the culture of continental Celts whose narratives had been transplanted to Ireland.

3. The use of spears with very long heads, including one with a notched spiral head that cannot be removed without tearing the flesh apart and making a much worse wound.[16] Reference to this Gaulish spear might be compared with the type of damage done by the *gae bolga*[17] and be seen to provide another continental Iron Age weapon that has been placed into the hands of an Irish hero.

4. Shields decorated with bronze animal ornament.[18] This type of ornament is found on some of the shields described in the Ulster tales.

5. The taking of heads as trophies in battle and their subsequent preservation and display.[19] Recall here the preservation of Mesgegra's brain by Conall and the assignment of one of the structures at Emain Macha to storing heads.

6. The establishment of special banqueting halls to serve the elite but also strangers. Here food would be prepared in large cauldrons or on a spit and the prestige meat was pork.[20] This practice, assigned to either the Gauls or the Galatians, is comparable to the *bruiden* 'hostel' described in the Ulster tales.

7. The Celts would attend at night the tombs of their ancestors in order to obtain special oracles.[21] This has been compared with the vigil at the tomb of Fergus to gain knowledge of the *Táin*.

These parallels are, on the one hand, striking at times and, on the other, problematic since the precise mechanism by which we might connect what has been ascribed to Gauls in the first centuries BC/AD with the material culture and practices depicted in medieval Irish tales has seldom been discussed in any detail. It is easier to claim that the Irish tales 'preserve' ancient Gaulish or Celtic traditions than it is to explain how this process of preservation was carried out. So let's consider the various reasons why the Irish *scéla* might so resemble these fragments of ethnographies, particularly those of Posidonius. I will offer three hypotheses:

1. *The Irish drew on the ethnographies themselves when composing the tales of the Ulster cycle.* This theory, which would have made life ever so much easier, is most unlikely. So far there is no evidence that the Irish had access to these particular classical sources, many of which were written in Greek, nor do we have any reason to suspect that the medieval Irish felt any particular cultural affinity with the Gauls or ancient British.[22] Until someone discovers a Latin translation of Posidonius' long-lost ethnography of the Gauls and can connect it with an Irish monastery, this theory does not have anything going for it.

2. *The Irish inherited a similar 'Celtic' culture to that depicted in the classical ethnographies of the Gauls.* This is the usual explanation for why so many aspects of the Ulster tales resemble descriptions of Iron Age Gauls and, to some extent, also Britons. For example,

John Koch has suggested that passages in the *Gododdin*, an early
Welsh collection of poems, praising the valour of fallen British
warriors engaged in a 6th-century battle, may have included
remnants of epithets or remembrances that pre-dated the Roman
conquest of Britain. These would include the use of the chariot,
the wearing of a laurel wreath and golden torcs.[23] Julius Caesar,
for example, was the first to employ *essedum* to denote the British
chariots he encountered when he invaded Britain, and this word
is continued in the occasional reference to the Welsh *asseδ*
'war-chariot' found in the *Gododdin*.

For Ireland, however, there are issues with this model that
complicate matters, as the notion of 'inheritance' requires that
something is 'passed down' from earlier and this seems to require
us to know *when* the Celtic-speaking Irish arrived in Ireland and,
consequently, separated from their linguistic relations elsewhere
in Atlantic Europe.[24] If we could demonstrate that this only
happened around the beginning of the La Tène in Ireland,
c. 300 BC, we would not be surprised if the Irish shared a number
of the cultural traits found among their Gaulish cousins from
whom they recently separated. But if one argues that the ancestors
of the Irish arrived *c.* 1000 BC, then it is a bit more difficult to have
them inheriting the same culture as 1st-century BC Gauls, much
less preserving a Gaulish legacy in their tales. And if you prefer
a much deeper Irish origin, the Beakers at *c.* 2500 BC, or the
beginning of the Neolithic at *c.* 4000 BC, then the common
inheritance argument becomes ludicrous, e.g., there were no
chariots on the planet earth during the earliest period. In short,
if we must know *when* the Irish arrived in Ireland to run with
this model, we really are not going to get very far with it.

3. *The Irish participated in a West Atlantic cultural world in which
both artifacts and narratives easily circulated.* Here we could shift
the model that requires some form of genetic inheritance between
continental Celts and the earliest Irish and rather emphasize that
the Irish, British and Gauls did speak very closely related
languages, especially at the higher register in which one might
compose a poem or tale about ancient heroes. In this world, no

matter when the Irish originally came to Ireland, it seems clear that by the Iron Age they could have been well aware of at least some of the cultural behaviour of their continental or British neighbours. Tales and artifacts circulated across the Celtic-speaking world and when the Irish began to form a narrative that would later emerge as the *Táin*, it could have been at least partially fleshed out in an imagined world that drew on international *realia* and motifs. Let us recall that the longest poem in Old English, *Beowulf*, has nothing really to do with England (despite decades of archaeologists illustrating it with material from the royal Anglo-Saxon burials at Sutton Hoo),[25] but is entirely devoted to the activities of a Geatish (Swedish) hero who rids the Danes of two monsters and his own land of a dragon. There is no reason to confine the imagined world of *Beowulf* exclusively to Anglo-Saxon England.

Does this 'international' model get us anywhere? It really depends on where we are trying to go in the first place. Some of our striking parallels are admittedly pretty generic. The use of chariots by heroes is embedded in the heroic literature of India, the Near East, Greece and Italy, and the chariot was also found among the Thracians as well as the Celts, so it is difficult to understand precisely what point one is making when its presence in the Ulster cycle is regarded as a Celtic 'legacy'. While we do occasionally find possible remnants of a shared earlier insular Celtic heroic age, for example a tradition involving a hero with a special sword (Irish *caladbholg*, Welsh *caledfwlch*), how much more evidence for this shared 'heroic' horizon is recoverable?

However one chooses to interpret the similarities between the Ulster tales and Gaulish ethnographies, the critical question is whether such comparisons actually impinge on the main issue, dating the cultural motifs described in the Ulster tales. For example, Nicholas Aitchison rejected such parallels as chariot warfare and decap-itations on the grounds that the chariot and head-taking were well enough attested in medieval Ireland so they 'could just as easily have originated from the composition of the epic literature within the early historic period'.[26] Other parallels, such as disputes over the champion's portion, were dismissed as generic traits that one might expect within any barbaric and heroic society.

The key issue here is the precision one requires when attempting to date a cultural motif. If a writer simply indicates that James Bond is driving an Aston Martin, the vehicle could date from 1914 to the present. But if he is depicted driving an Aston Martin DB10, then we know that his vehicle cannot date earlier than 2014 when this model first appeared. It is largely immaterial that an archaeologist or auto-historian can trace the pedigree of Aston Martins back in time through earlier models such as the DB5, which Bond also drove, to models such as the 1934 Aston Martin Ulster or the Bamford and Martin (1914–1925), which predate the existence of James Bond. We also doubt the relevance of the earlier vehicles because of their function: James Bond's employers do not normally issue him a vintage car for his high-tech car chases. The origin and heritage of Aston Martin construction do not really bear on the mental template we recover from the written text. Similarly, when we approach the problem of the Old Irish chariot we involve ourselves in issues of function and date.

The first of these requires a functional analysis of the motif. Raimund Karl has done just such an analysis of all the functions of the chariot described in the texts: how they were employed for travel and battle, built with an open front and rear, employed cognate terminology, etc. This indicated that the chariots described in the *scéla* and those known from the Iron Age (Gaul and Britain) coincide on every point. Moreover, some aspects of these 'Celtic' chariots are not found in those described in classical literature and there were very few parallels with the chariots described in the Bible.[27] This approach provides an answer to the question: is the Old Irish chariot (in its earliest descriptions) derived from the prehistoric past of Britain and Ireland or a transferred literary motif drawn from foreign literature. It does not, however, provide a precise date for the chariot motif.

The second approach is descriptive, comparing the images of the chariot depicted in the *scéla* with archaeological (or literary) sources. Here we found (Chapter Seven) that several non-perishable items presumed to be associated with the chariot (metal yoke-ends, linch pins) or horse-trappings (Y-pieces),however they were employed, are not reflected in the chariot or horse descriptions of the Ulster tales despite the fact that the chariots and horses themselves are described in considerable detail.[28] Such evidence is admittedly slight, but if a decision need be made, it would favour some vehicle other than that presumed to have existed in Iron Age Ireland.

A similar critique might be made of the evidence for headhunting. The archaeological evidence for decapitations exists both for Iron Age Britain and Ireland and we can find ritual manipulation of the human skull from at least the Late Bronze Age. Such evidence when coupled with the archaeology and the ethnographies of the Gauls in southern France has led to the concept of a head-cult as part of the general Celtic package.[29] After reviewing the archaeological evidence for European headhunting in some detail, Ian Armit concluded that 'headhunting in Iron Age Europe had nothing to do with any pan-Celtic belief in the power or divinity of the human head: there was no "Celtic cult of the head".[30] By this I take it that there is so much regional and temporal variation that we cannot ascribe, for example, depictions of headhunting in the Ulster tales as the legacy of a specific Celtic culture (although I find any concept that does not presume geographic and temporal differences as something of a paper tiger). But until someone provides a detailed study as to how headhunting as depicted in the Ulster tales differs from that depicted in the medieval annals and how it can only be derived from specific behavioural motifs found in southern France in the first millennium BC, it will remain another of the vague 'legacies'.

In short, while various objects mentioned in the Ulster tales may be generically preserved in the *scéla*, the only meaningful date for associating any description with an actual object requires a correlation with the archaeological record.

The legacy of Katu-butos (600 BC – AD 400)

The slow changes in the natural environment make it difficult to distinguish appropriate dates for the semantic fields that concern the vegetation and fauna depicted in the Ulster cycle. The trees and plants known to Katu-butos were still known to his later descendants and so we cannot determine if there are any environmental motifs that must have been restricted to the Iron Age. Among the wild animals, there are a number that are not native to Ireland and, at least in some cases, were probably stimulated by classical literature and do not belong to the Irish Iron Age. There is some temptation to make a case for the role in the Ulster tales of the pig which is depicted as the prestige food and whose serving is contested as part of the motif of the 'champion's portion'. As the most numerous animal remains at the site of Emain Macha, the importance of pig in the Iron Age might seem at least part of the alleged 'Celtic' legacy of prestige pork consumption attested for the Gauls. But this could also be a blatant example of 'confirmation bias', since the other major ceremonial sites of Knockaulin and Tara, which also yielded evidence of feasting, revealed cattle and not pig as the dominant species.

There is very little of the built landscape that we can credit to Katu-butos, other than fixing so much of the action of the stories around the main Iron Age ritual centres of Navan, Rathcroghan and Tara, which is one Iron Age relict that I think Katu-butos can claim. In terms of the appearance of the actual monuments, however, it is difficult to assess how much might have survived from the Iron Age. By the 1st century AD the major timber structures at Navan and Knockaulin were already removed from sight and this may indeed have also been the case for the other ceremonial centres. This leaves a major discontinuity in the erection of large circular timber structures until the admittedly disputed evidence of Lissue, perhaps a thousand years later. I have suggested on the slenderest of grounds that I suspect that the mental template for these structures derives from the medieval period, since that would provide a more proximate secular building as depicted in the tales rather than the more elusive Iron Age ceremonial structures. But if future excavations uncover evidence for a missing link between the Iron Age structures and Lissue, this archaeologist will not be disappointed. On the other hand, the meagre evidence of topographical descriptions, such as the mound at Navan Fort, does suggest that the medieval Irish only knew Emain Macha as an ancient ruin, a national monument, but not as a living site.

One line of evidence that we might have expected to find in the tales, had they been created in the Iron Age, is some clear reference to the enormous linear earthworks that were erected in the centuries in which the tales were set. Instead, we only find one statement asserting that such structures did *not* exist at that time and a few others reflecting the type of later folkoric explanations for enigmatic landscape features.

In terms of weaponry, there is at least an argument for regarding the *colg* 'sword' as a lexical relict of the Iron Age. The descriptions of it with its unequivocally organic hilt would also match those of the Iron Age but they could, of course, just as well belong to the subsequent period. The actual size and use of the *colg* is too poorly represented in the tales to utilize as a chronological marker, but there is some evidence that it was treated very much in the same way as a *claideb* (although it may have been regarded as an earlier – more old fashioned and perhaps more appropriate – word). The spears are difficult to place in time although references to those employing precious metals are hardly at home in the Irish Iron Age. The one clear Iron Age association with spears, the metal spear-butts, are missing from the Ulster tales. The shape of the shields, if understood to be oblong or rectangular, would indicate an early date, contemporary with Katu-butos, but in general they would appear to be circular and belong to later periods.

As we have seen above, it is unlikely that we have inherited a completely accurate depiction of the Irish Iron Age chariot, whose descriptions are probably no older than the early medieval period. This is not to say that Katu-butos was ignorant of chariots or that he did not include them in his (hypothetical) account of Medb's great cattle-raid, but those are not the precise descriptions we find in the tales.

There is so little evidence distinctive of the Iron Age that it is difficult to assign much to this period in terms of dress or ornament other than those generic descriptions that could belong to any period, such as dress involving a tunic and a cloak and belt. The ornaments depicted could include those of the Iron Age but they tend to make a much better fit with later periods, either because of their shape (circular pins) or material of manufacture (precious metals). As we have already seen, the clothes ascribed to Iron Age heroes came off the same rails as those employed to dress characters from the historical tales so it is unlikely that the tales retain some sort of Iron Age fashion sense. The only item to pose a problem in terms of form is the 'leaf-shaped brooch', which would accord with a description of an Iron Age brooch far better than any subsequent period.

Given the British cognates for the Irish board game *fidchell* and the probability that it derives from a Roman game, it is at least possible that this motif entered the Irish narrative tradition in the time of Katu-butos.

As for the burials in the tales, Katu-butos could only wonder what had happened to his stirring descriptions of the roar of the flames on the funeral pyres and puzzle as to how the names of heroes might have somehow been embedded in the very stones erected over the graves. The tales do not provide us with a window on Iron Age burial.

The legacy of Cattubuttas (AD 400–700)

It is difficult to identify any particular environmental or economic motif specifically to the time of Cattubuttas although, naturally, almost any of the flora and fauna depicted in the tales could also be set to his period. The motifs that probably derive from classical sources could theoretically be attributed to the final century of Cattubuttas although they could have just as easily been grouped together in the succeeding period, when we are more certain about which classical texts were of most interest to the Irish.

The built landscape of Cattubuttas sees the earliest appearance of ringforts and cashels, monuments that are easily referenced in the Ulster tales, and so much of the rest of the built landscape dates to the later part of the time of Cattubuttas or to that of Cathbad. As Cattubuttas certainly was acquainted with the Bible and at least some classical literature it is entirely possible that the embellishments of the elite palaces began during his time. It is also possible that the most archaic form of the Standard Irish Palace Description was initially developed during this same period.

Cattubuttas lived at the time when the standard name for the sword, the *claideb*, was introduced into Ireland and it is likely that this also coincided with the introduction of sub-Roman swords from Britain. The entire concept of a slashing sword, as depicted in the tales, would also be at home with the types of swords with expanded blades that are encountered in early medieval Ireland as well as the occasional reference to a weapon related to an Anglo-Saxon seax. The frequent references to organic hilts could also fit with the time of Cattubuttas although the same could be said for his predecessor. The spears, which may be described with multiple rivets, may belong to this or a later period. If we take most of the shields to be round or, at least, rounded, then this suggests that they date from the time of Cattubuttas or more recently. The references to archery, armour and helmets may all belong to this period or that of Cathbad as they rely heavily on foreign sources both with respect to language and the objects themselves.

While it is a very close call, what little evidence we have suggests that the basic description of an Irish chariot that we inherit was that of the time of Cattubuttas. The evidence for such a date is slender but the match between literary description and our extremely meagre archaeological evidence suggests that the Ulster cycle does not quite reflect the appearance of an Irish Iron Age prestige vehicle, so a subsequent early medieval vehicle is a slightly more likely source.

In terms of dress, many of the items that were at home in the time of Cathbad actually begin to appear in the archaeological record in the time of Cattubuttas. This would include the possibility of wearing silk or satin garments, the gilding or use of silver in brooches, and the shift towards penannular brooches. The similarity of the depiction of the lyre played at Cruachain and those found in Anglo-Saxon burials could also be set to the time of Cattubuttas, although the instrument itself could derive from an earlier time. And the references to water-powered mills might have begun in the later part of Cattubuttas' period.

The burials described could date from the time of Cattubuttas or his successor. There is some evidence to suspect that because the ogam stones were being routinely described in the tales as engraved headstones which were thought to be ubiquitous across the Irish landscape, this is not a motif directly generated by the same people who were actually erecting and engraving memorial inscriptions on the stones. This suggests that while the ogams were erected in the time of Cattubuttas, a misunderstanding of their function and distribution were products of the later period of Cathbad. All of the other elements of the burial rite, however, could derive from Cattubuttas.

The legacy of Cathbad (AD 700–1000)

Cathbad lived at a time when Latin literature was very much a part of the education of those who worked in the scriptoria of the monasteries. So it is to this period that we probably derive most of the exotic wild animals (such as lion, tiger, bear and possibly the motif of the poisonous snake). The hedgehog, assuming that the reference to this animal has been correctly translated, would seem to be an (unaccountably) even more recent motif. By the time of Cathbad a more diversified livestock economy also emerges and this system probably provides a more realistic source for the very occasional listing of livestock that indicates a greater parity of sheep or goat compared to that of cattle and pig.

Much of the built landscape of the Ulster cycle derives from the time of Cathbad, although it may also have begun during the last century of his predecessor. The frequent reference to heroes in their forts, including the trivallate forts of the elite, would have been commonplace in the time of Cathbad. The evidence for stone-walled forts also would appear to reference medieval cashels rather than Late Bronze Age sites. Also, the toponomy of much of the landscape is generally anchored on sites that appear to have been occupied only during the medieval period. If the references to souterrains be accepted, we again have another architectural feature set to the medieval period unless there was some rather unlikely confusion with the Iron Age landscape of neighbouring Scotland.

As for the Standard Irish Palace Description, the evidence is not conclusive in providing a start date. That the world of Cathbad recognized the existence of large elite halls in their annalistic records, as argued by Warner, seems secure enough. As for the archaeological evidence, the site of Lissue does stand both alone and in a controversial position, but it certainly offers a possible template for the large halls indicated in the tales. But how much earlier such structures appeared remains entirely unsettled. The furnishing of the palaces with features decorated in precious metals appears to be a product of Cathbad's acquaintance with the Bible and classical literature.

In terms of weaponry, the imagined world conjured up by Cathbad is strongly represented in the description of both the size of swords and their metal hilts, which were occasionally decorated with precious metals. And while we cannot be too precise in indicating at what time classical descriptions of chariots from Latin literature crossed with native Irish depictions of their own vehicles, it seems fairly certain that by the time of Cathbad those built out of precious metals did have a classical source.

The characters of the Ulster cycle appear to have worn clothes that would certainly have been familiar to the contemporaries of Cathbad, although they may well have also been recognizable to those of his predecessor as sartorial fashion does not seem to have changed at such a rate (or we simply do not have sufficient evidence) that we can employ it for the purposes of fine dating. The references to the use of silk and satin would fit easiest into the time of Cathbad but could just possibly derive from the time of his predecessor. The absence of trousers in the tales does pose an interesting problem. It may have been because such apparel was regarded as lower class or, perhaps, as it was never encountered in biblical or classical literature (outside of references to such barbarians as the Celts or Scythians), it was regarded as unsuitable for elite warriors. This latter argument does involve the irony that the Irish never saw themselves as related to the trouser-wearing continental Celts in the first place, but they did believe that they shared an origin with the trouser-wearing Scythians.

The ornaments that fastened the garments or that were worn to decorate the body are almost entirely congruent with contemporary fashion in the time of Cathbad. The same type of sartorial anachronisms that we regularly encounter when we view medieval and Renaissance paintings of biblical scenes appears in the Ulster tales. Heroes wear silver(ed) and gold/gilded penannular brooches, brooches with zoomorphic ornament, a silver torc, large silver chains resembling those of their Pictish neighbours, and other items that would be at home in the time that the tales had assumed written form, but would have been unknown at the time of their 'historical present'.

The vessels out of which the characters of the Ulster tales ate and drank are also largely assignable to the medieval period, given the frequent references to silver vessels and the number of vessels whose names derive from Latin. The one problematic area is that during the time of Cathbad, any monk working in the northeast of Ireland, where so many of the tales are centered, would have been well aware of clay vessels, yet these appear nowhere in the tales. Probably, they have been excluded as too plebeian for the warrior elite depicted in the tales.

As for the board games so often encountered in the Ulster tales, while we cannot be certain as to when they were introduced to Ireland, it seems clear that medieval audiences would have been wholly familiar with the type of tablut or tafl games that the Irish enjoyed before the spread of chess. As we have also seen, *fidchell* may have entered the gaming world much earlier.

The burial rituals described in the tales could have been formed either in the time of Cathbad or his predecessor. If all of the ceremony involved was merely a back-projection of an assortment of traditions regarding mounds, cairns and standing stones being associated with ancient heroes, then Cathbad could have generated such descriptions on his own. Moreover, the probably mistaken references to ogam grave-stones in the tales actually make a better fit with the time of Cathbad, when the purpose of the stones had been forgotten, than the time of Cattubuttas when the stones were originally erected.

Colophon

As we have seen, the second recension of the *Táin* concluded with two colophons – one in Irish calling down a blessing on everyone who accepted the text verbatim and a second in Latin warning that much (although not all) of the account was fabulous stories unworthy of any credence. Did the medieval Irish actually believe that they were recording history in a sense that we can understand today?

Gregory Toner has tackled this issue and concluded that the authors of the Ulster *scéla* did believe in the 'historicity' of the material they dealt with.[31] But this conclusion must be qualified as he also argued that:

> 'truth and falsehood did not relate to the factual accuracy of an account but to the logical coherence of the text and the reliability of its sources.'[32]

He ably supported this statement by demonstrating how the 'editor' of the first recension of the *Táin* employed traditional medieval historiographic techniques to compare the various accounts of the great cattle-raid and evaluate which versions he regarded as the most likely. This is fine as far as it goes but for the purposes of this book I think we need to go further. The authors/editors of the different versions of the *Táin* were not shifting through a pile of verbatim transcripts from elated or trau-matized Iron Age warriors who had engaged in Medb's raid or the defence of Ulster. They were involved in comparing and generating a series of tales that depicted events played out in an imagined world.

The monks who have left us the Ulster cycle inhabited a Primary World of around the 9th century AD. This was a Christian world with a literate elite whose lives centred on monasteries and, presumably, the centres of a secular elite who dwelt in ringforts. In order to depict a past world they created a Secondary World and the only way this world was going to convince or, at least, provide an immersive experience for those who read or listened to the tales, was for it to meet certain basic criteria.[33] It had to relate to the Primary World but it had to change it so that the audience experienced something different. Their Secondary World was one where the elite lived in large halls decorated in precious metals and where travel was almost exclusively undertaken by chariot. Its characters feasted on the choicest meats, drank from vessels made out of precious metals, dressed in the finest garments and fought with the best weapons. The world of the Ulster tales was relatively consistent: similar descriptions of chariots, weapons and dress are found across most of the tales and while there are always lapses, it is still quite impressive that so many different authors over a period of centuries could produce so many culturally interrelated tales without access to the type of 'continuity database' (30,000 plus entries) employed by the *Star Wars* franchise.[34] And just like a modern franchise, we not only find the basic stories but also prequels and sequels built around the *Táin*, filled with characters who appear in multiple tales and even in crossovers, making guest appearances in other cycles. And, as Mark Wolf reminds us: 'imaginary worlds are enjoyed not only by those who visit them, but also by those who invent them.'[35] We would not have so many tales if the scribes had not enjoyed producing them.

If we return to the subject of historicity, we should realize by now that while we might argue that medieval scribes may have believed that they were recording history, it is probably fairer to say that at very best they imagined they were writing stories 'based on actual events.' When they reached either within their memory or on the shelves of their scriptorium for a choice simile from classical literature or wanted to gild their descriptions of their Secondary World with material drawn from the Bible, Latin literature, or what brother Brendan had seen in one of the palaces of the Merovingians, they knew full well they were not writing out eyewitness accounts of past events. After all, in their translations of Latin literature they did not hesitate to occasionally Hibernicize their descriptions of weapons, clothes and burial.

In the end the early medieval Irish literati created a Secondary World that they passed off as the Irish Iron Age. That they did a superb job is evident in the centuries of scholars who have argued whether this imagined world was a real document from Ireland's prehistoric past. In a way, although remaining anonymous, these medieval Irish world-builders managed to accomplish what another Irishman sought to do a millennium later. Speaking of *Ulysses*, James Joyce once wrote:

> 'I've put in so many enigmas and puzzles that it will keep
> professors busy for centuries over what I meant, and that's
> the only way of insuring one's immortality.'[36]

Notes

PREFACE (pp. 6–8)

1 Waddell 2014.
2 Dooley 2006.
3 O'Connor 2013.

INTRODUCTION (pp. 9–12)

1 Which makes an impossible fit with the story itself where the children spend 900 years in the form of swans before they hear a church bell.
2 At least one Celticist accepted the legitimacy of this comparison, see Ford 2000.
3 The Indians are not included as they didn't play by the same rules in reckoning historical dates.

CHAPTER ONE (pp. 13–32)

1 O'Flaherty 1793, 34.
2 O'Meara 1982 provides the standard English translation of this work but see also Forester 2000.
3 Butler 2005, 97.
4 *Expugnatio Hibernica*, pref. (Forester 2001, 6).
5 *Topographia* 20.
6 Latin would have been largely confined to the church and learned classes with the gentry speaking Norman French and the vulgar illiterates speaking something between Late Old English and early Middle English. Giraldus remarked that the scholastic style of his book 'obtained uniform praise from all quarters' (Forester 2001, 1).
7 Carey 1994.
8 *Historia Britonum* 8–11.
9 Carey 1993, 3.
10 Carney 2005, 462.
11 McCarthy 2008, 183–85.
12 Charles-Edwards 2000, 9.
13 The Anglo-Saxons of Northumbria even adopted the Irish word *bratt* for 'cloak'.
14 Bede, iv.26.
15 *Topographia* 71, 84.
16 An enjoyable popular account of the major Irish manuscripts can be found in Slavin 2005.
17 Carey 2009; Cunningham 2010, 57.
18 It is very likely that a copy of the *Lebor Gabála* was lost with the opening leaves of the LU; Scowcroft 2009, 23–24.
19 The critical edition is Macalister 1938–41, but the reader would be advised to spare his or her sanity and consult the far more readable translation by John Carey (1995).
20 Mac Cana 1980.
21 The spelling of names of literary/ mythological characters and places tends to vary considerably and so this book will follow those provided in MacKillop 1998 whenever possible.
22 Already by the 11th century there were those that claimed the Ulster tales were composed by lying poets to ingratiate themselves with the Ulstermen, possibly because it was an Ulster king who provided hospitality to the poet class who had recently been banished elsewhere (Byrne 1973, 106).
23 Siewers 2009, 83.
24 Mallory and Ó hUiginn 1994; Tsvetoukhina, Mikhailova and Bondarenko 2013.
25 See Dillon 1994.
26 One of the approaches to this history, adopted from St Augustine, was to divide human history into six (or seven) ages, beginning with Adam down until the end of the World. The first age ran from Adam to Noah, the second from Noah to Abraham, and so on. The medieval Irish also bought into this system; see *Sex Aetates*.
27 McCarthy 2008, 119.
28 AFM AD 266.
29 Keating 1902, intro, ix, p. 86, 74–80.
30 Cunningham 2010, 57, 71.
31 Cunningham 2010, 74–76.
32 Cunningham 2010, 79–81.
33 The first actual book to be published in Irish was a translation of John Knox's *Liturgy* that was printed in 1567 (Tristram 1989, 17).
34 George Petrie bought a copy of the manuscript for £35 and sold it for same to the Royal Irish Academy. The deluxe seven-volume edition that sold for 14 guineas did not do as well as was hoped and O'Donovan, speaking of the publishers who were also booksellers, related that they 'can hardly bear the sight of me in their shop' (Cunningham 2007a, 70).
35 Keating 1902, vol. 1, intro, preface.
36 Keating 1902, vol. 1, intro ix, p. 74, 11–28.
37 Keating 1902, vol. 1, intro ix, p. 76, 40–42.
38 Keating 1902, vol. 1, intro ix, p. 74, 17–18; a fuller critique is in vol. 1, bk 1, iv, p. 146, 5–85.
39 Keating 1902, vol. 1, intro vi, p. 50, 1–12.
40 Keating 1902, vol. 2, bk I, xxx, 2708.
41 Keating 1902, vol. 2, bk I, xxxiii, 3170–86; Keating had Conchobar die after hearing a prediction of the death of Christ by a druid.
42 Toner 2000, 6–12; 2009, 10–11.
43 There was another tradition that Fintan, unable 'to satisfy the lust' of all 50 women fled, and that the randy women collapsed dead in groups while in pursuit (Smith 1958, 211).
44 *Antiquities* 1.70–71.
45 Campion 1809, 29–34.
46 Campion 1809, 103. This is the story of the son of Gulguntius, a British prince, who supposedly aided Partholón and his company, granted the deserted Ireland to him for which Partholón agreed to pay an annual tribute. This provides the basis for a claim, repeated in the 11th act of Elizabeth I, that supports the 'ancient and sundry strong authentique tytles for the kings of England to this land of Ireland', Cusack 1868, 35.
47 Hanmer 1809, 2–4.
48 Hanmer 1809, 8.
49 Spenser 1633, 1135.
50 Spenser 1633, 1196–1215.
51 Spenser 1633, 1233–48.
52 Spenser 1633, 1515–1840; in 1835 G. Hansbrow expanded on the 'Asiatic' customs that have been retained by the Irish including simple greetings, hospitality, shaking hands to conclude a contract and fire cults (Hansbrow 1835, 20).
53 Spenser 1633, 1882–1907.
54 George Buchanan (1506–1582) was the first to assert the linguistic affinity of the different Celtic languages of Gaul, Britain and Ireland. His theory of the former unity of the Celtic-speaking peoples was well known to Spenser.
55 Spenser 1633, 1326–27.
56 Cox 1689.
57 Hill 1988, 102–103.
58 Leland 1784, 1.

59 Plowden 1831, 3.
60 Keating 1902, intro 1.24–25; Keating distinguished *bualtrach bó* (cow shit) and *otrach capaill* (horse shit).
61 Mac-Geoghegan 1844, 13.
62 Mooney 1845, iii; cf. also James Mac-Geoghegan (1844, 12), who complains of Giraldus's 'poisoned darts' that have provided the basis for centuries of abuse regarding the manners and customs of the Irish.
63 For a major account on the role of the Milesian debate and its social and political context, see O'Halloran 2004, 13–70. For the attitude of British writers regarding the Irish in this period see Leerssen 1996, 32–76.
64 Cusack 1868, 45.
65 The 'other-side' could also include Thomas Innes, a Scottish Catholic priest (Hill 1988, 107–108).
66 O'Flaherty 1793, 149. Similarly, we know that Cú Chulainn died in AD 2 at the age of 27 'by the unanimous consent of different authors' (p. 186).
67 O'Flaherty 1793, vii.
68 Cusack 1868, 20, 44–48.
69 This argument was lifted from Thomas Leland (1784, 24–25).
70 Hyde 1899, 68–71.
71 Ní Mhaonaigh 2005, 46.
72 Schlüter 2010, 221. See also Schlüter 2009, 29.
73 Ó Néill 1999.
74 Translation by O'Rahilly in TBC², 272.
75 One of the three wonders of the *Táin* is that it granted 'a year's protection to him to whom it is recited' (Bondarenko 2009, 24).
76 Ó Néill 1999, 273–74.
77 O'Flaherty 1793, 5.
78 O'Flaherty 1793, 16.
79 For example, Elizabeth (1844, 11–12).
80 Cusack 1868, 21.
81 Cusack 1868, 51.
82 Joyce 1903, I, 131.
83 O'Curry 1861, 437.
84 O'Curry 1861, 441.
85 O'Curry 1861, 443–45.
86 O'Curry 1861, 447–49.
87 O'Curry 1873, II.50.
88 O'Curry 1873, II.235–46.
89 O'Curry 1873, I.lxxvi.
90 O'Curry 1873, I.lxxi.
91 Waddell 2005, 51.
92 O'Curry 1873, I.235–47.

CHAPTER TWO (pp. 33–58)

1 Cox 1689.
2 Arbois de Jubainville 1903.
3 All dates in this chapter derive from the AFM (-5200 years).
4 In one version (DGE 9–11) Cesair convinces the men to worship a pagan idol who advises them to build a ship and sail to Ireland as God was not letting them on board the Ark. There is also a variant account claiming that Banba arrives with 150 women and three men, who all drown.
5 O'Donovan argues (AFM 3, ft. c.) that Cesair's landing place was really in Bantry Bay.

6 There is an alternative account where the women are not drowned but because the last surviving male, Fintan, found it impossible 'to satisfie the lust of their bodyes', he fled and the randy women dropped dead from exhaustion while chasing him (Smith 1958, 211).
7 STT.
8 To make matters even weirder, a later section of the *Lebor Gabála* [104] claims that Fintan, who was Cesair's husband, was only born seven years before the Flood. Accounts of how he survived the Flood range from transforming himself into a salmon to simply falling asleep in a cave.
9 LG III, 168, 173, and poem xxii.
10 SC [ST – a 9th century tale] where the survivor was rejuvenated as a stag, a boar, a hawk and a salmon, which was eaten by a woman who gave birth to Tuan son of Cairell. The tale claims that 'whatever history and genealogy there is in Ireland, its origin is from Tuan son of Cairell' (ST 79–80).
11 CMT1.
12 TEt.
13 In the DGS it is the Dagda who is tricked out of his home.
14 ATDM. This tale largely concerns the daughter of Oengus' steward going off her 'pagan' feed and subsisting on a diet of milk for centuries until converted by St Patrick.
15 AO.
16 LG 319.
17 OCT. The other two 'sorrows of storytelling' are the story of Deirdre (LMU, OMU) and the Children of Lir (OCL).
18 CMT2.
19 The Second Battle of Mag Tuired is generally interpreted as an Irish version of the Indo-European End-of-the-World battle, also found in ancient India and among the Norse (see O'Brien, S. 1976).
20 OCL.
21 CU.
22 ODR. The chronology conflicts with a poem at the end of the tale that claims that these events occurred 300 years before the birth of Christ. Moreover, the tale itself is generally regarded as part of the King's cycle and should be later than the Ulster tales.
23 There is no way one can hold to the annalistic dates summarized in Kelleher 1971, 109 and tell a coherent story, but they will be indicated, where appropriate, in the footnotes.
24 CLR; the political situation depicted in this tale deviates from the standard picture in that it fragments the province under six rulers (Fergus mac Róich as half-king, Fintain, the son of Niall of the Nine Hostages (who rules centuries later!) at Dún Dá Benn in the north, Léite, son of Fergus mac Léti in north-Ulster, Conall in Caile Conaill and Subaltach in Muirthemne and the Sons of Donn in Farney). As for Fergus, this places his reign

nearly a century earlier than is usually indicated in the Ulster tales.
25 Elsewhere this event is set to AD 44 (Kelleher 1971, 110).
26 DSCM.
27 TBDD.
28 Another tale (DMC) attempts to relate an account of the vengeance of the sons of Conaire but this appears to belong to a very different tradition than the other tales and is not summarized here.
29 EF-A: this tale places the event during the reign of Conn Cétchatach ('of the hundred battles') for whom the AFM date of AD 157–165 is totally out of synch for the story of a king who should have reigned *before* rather than *after* his 'doublet', Fergus mac Róich. Other annals set the date to c. 39 BC, which makes a lot better narrative sense (Kelleher 1971, 109).
30 EF-B.
31 CCon; SCMN 1–3.
32 Conchobar supposedly began his reign in 30 BC.
33 SCMN. Specific seating arrangements are presented in LTRR.
34 CB.
35 CCC.
36 Sétanta was born in 34 BC (Kelleher 1971, 9).
37 The childhood deeds comprise a section of TBC.
38 TEm, FC overlap in the main essentials.
39 VS.
40 AG.
41 CCS.
42 FB.
43 FBL.
44 AD.
45 Ruled as high king for only one year, 9 BC.
46 CE.
47 SMMD.
48 LMU. A later and much extended version, the OMU, relates essentially the same plot but with many additional or different details, e.g., in OMU the son of Fergus who defends Deirdre and her trio of men is Illann who is accidentally killed by Conall Cernach. Otherwise, Illann dies among the Ulstermen much later in Da Derga's hostel in TBDD.
49 CF.
50 TF.
51 IDT.
52 TBFr.
53 TT.
54 TBD.
55 TBR.
56 EN.
57 In another fore-tale (TBRa) Cú Chulainn encountered a very hostile war-goddess, the Mórrígan, driving a single cow to mate with the Brown Bull of Cuailnge and produce a calf. She predicted that as long as the calf remained a yearling, Cú Chulainn would survive, and she described the various animal adversaries she would transform herself into to oppose Cú Chulainn when they met again during the Táin.

58 DCDM.
59 TBC¹; TBC²; TBC³.
60 Kelleher 1971, 110.
61 A separate description of Cú Chulainn in his scythed chariot is given in CS. The word indicating a 'scythed' chariot (*serda*) might also mean 'Serian' or 'oriental', see Chapter Nine.
62 CRR.
63 SCC.
64 AE.
65 MU – the temporal placement of this tale is nearly impossible as it has characters from the Mythological cycle (Tuatha Dé Danann), the Ulster cycle and the King's cycle (the son of Niall of the Nine Hostages). That the three Sons of Uisnech are alive in the tale has determined its placement before the story of Deirdre.
66 AAA.
67 CCL. In this version Cú Chulainn defeats his son on sea with the *gae bolga* as he was unable to better him on land.
68 The fortress of the Men of Falga, Dún Scáith, is generally regarded as belonging to the Otherworld (Ó Béarra 2009). See also FFF.
69 ACR.
70 BF 11.
71 AmCR.
72 BM.
73 Kelleher 1971, 110.
74 ACMU.
75 ALB.
76 ACon.
77 Kelleher 1971, 110.
78 This scene may have been prompted by a 7th-century Frankish source where the king, hearing of the crucifixion, claimed that if he had been there with his Frankish troops, he would have avenged Christ (Chekhonadskaya 2001).
79 CA.
80 AFMR.
81 ACMM.
82 GCC.
83 AM.
84 SC.
85 STT.
86 FTBC.

CHAPTER THREE (pp. 59–83)

1 Powell 1950, 178.
2 Knott and Murphy 1966, 114.
3 Byrne 1964; Ford 2000; Clarke 2009.
4 Bowra 1970, 9.
5 Haslam 1997, 56.
6 TBC¹.
7 Turner 1997, 137.
8 Mac Cana 1980, 87.
9 Toner 2000; 2009.
10 Tristram 1988.
11 Mac Eoin 1989, 182–83.
12 Herbert 2009.
13 For example, Mac Cana 1989, 129.
14 Mac Cana 1989.
15 MacEoin 1989, 160.
16 Corthals 1989, 216.
17 Tranter 1989.
18 O'Rahilly 1976, 196.

19 Haslam 1997, 81.
20 Bennett 1997, 530.
21 Johnston 2013, 131–76.
22 Ó Cathasaigh 2006, 20.
23 Page 1959, 223.
24 Page 1959, 232.
25 See O'Nolan 1968 for a comparison of oral formulae in Homeric and Irish literature.
26 Stubbings 1962, 517; Bowra 1970, 14; Foltiny 1980, 237.
27 O'Curry 1873, 2, 329 relates an Irish tale that indicates that each Ulster warrior was required to have a different form of ornament on his shield.
28 Morris 1997, 623.
29 See, for example, Sayers 1996; Clarke 2009, 240.
30 Berschin 1982; Miles 2011, 34–36.
31 Quoted in Stanford 1970, 38.
32 Kennedy 1998, 7–11.
33 *Ephemeridos*.
34 Miles 2011. See also Clarke 2009.
35 Stanford 1970, 37.
36 *Aeneid* 3.63.
37 *Imtheachta Æniasa* 87–89.
38 *Merugud Uilixis*; see also Hillers 1996–97.
39 *Merugud Uilixis*.
40 Page 1959, 219.
41 Foley 1997, 149.
42 Bennet 1997, 524 does acknowledge one archaism in Homer that is also found in the Linear B tablets, i.e. the use of tmesis where a verb can be separated from its preverb.
43 Buchholz 2010, 110.
44 Leaf 1892, 11–12.
45 See Thomas 1970 for an example of how the debate concerning the antiquity of Homer's poems is presented as an (insidious) dichotomy.
46 Bennet 1997, 512.
47 Raaflaub 1997.
48 Donlan 1997.
49 van Wees 1997; Lakovides 1977.
50 Page 1959, 218, 233; Bowra 1970.
51 Buchholz 1980, 236–37.
52 Sherratt 1990, 810–11.
53 O'Curry 1873, II.240.
54 O'Curry 1873, I ccccxxxviii-ix.
55 Joyce 1903.
56 Pflug-Harttung 1892.
57 Ridgeway 1905–6.
58 Dobbs 1912; Dobs 1917, 79–86.
59 Bauersfeld 1933.
60 Powell 1950, 189.
61 Jackson 1964.
62 Hamilton 1968.
63 Hamilton 1968, 108.
64 Mallory 1981.
65 Mallory 1994.
66 Mallory 1992; 1993.
67 Whitfield 2004; 2006.
68 McCone 1990; 1991.
69 Aitchison 1987, 96.
70 McCone 1991, 69–70.
71 Aitchison 1987, 109; Bruford 1994.
72 Lamberton 1997, 35.
73 Cornill 2011–12, intro.
74 Aitchison 1987, 90.
75 For the Rig Veda, e.g, Rau 1983; for the Avesta, D'yakonov 1961.
76 Aitchison 1987, 93.

77 In the case of the word for gold, it is possible that gold production fell so low after the Late Bronze Age that most of the gold the Irish encountered was from the Roman world and hence they borrowed a new word for it. (R. Warner, pers. comm.).
78 AmCR 3.
79 BDC 46: 353.
80 TBC I 331.
81 Mallory 1992, 139–42. Bhreathnach (2014, 66) cites evidence that 7 people were beheaded among the 79 burials known from Owenbristy, Co. Galway, that date from the 6th–10th centuries.
82 At least somewhere between 19 and 8 BC (Kelleher 1971, 110).
83 TBC II 4919–20.
84 Vansina 1961, 53.
85 Carney 2005, 458.
86 Carney 1966, 15.
87 This is the genitive form of an unattested 'Cattubus', but later in Old Irish it could also be taken as the underlying nominative form of an Old Irish Cathbad, a name well known in the Ulster tales. For this reason I have opted for Cattubuttas rather than the more accurate Cattubus.
88 MacManus 1983, 154–63.
89 Macalister 1928, 215–16.
90 We do have a key to reading it written in the Book of Ballymote.
91 Ní Bhrolcháin 2009, 12: a poem on the death of Colm Cille by Eochaid Dallán Forgaill.
92 Carney 2005, 477; Olmsted 1992.
93 Carney 2005, 468–69.
94 Technically, apocope (the loss of the final syllable of a word) and syncope (the loss of internal syllables). Hence a loanword such as Latin *apostolus* 'apostle' in Old Irish first underwent apocope to *apostol* and then syncope to *apstal*.
95 Koch 1994, 233–34.
96 McManus 1983; Koch 1994; 1995, 44–45.

CHAPTER FOUR (pp. 85–100)

1 Mcalister 1928, 208.
2 Carey 1994.
3 Mallory 2013, 201–14; Baillie and Brown 2013, 69.
4 Commerford 2003, 81.
5 Ó Maolfabhail 1973, 7.
6 AFM ᴀᴍ 2242 = 2958 ʙᴄ.
7 LG 225.
8 AFM ᴀᴍ 2520.
9 LG 219.
10 ASCD 85–86; Moore 2012, 18–31.
11 AFM 3–4, ft. g.
12 AM.
13 LG 212.
14 LG xxxiv 1203.
15 Gen 9.20–21.
16 Even worse would be the acceptance that oxen were first yoked by Eochaid Airem (TEt III 8) in 129 ʙᴄ.
17 LG 224; xxxi, 999; DGE 24 lists the names of the four oxen (Lee, Lecmagh, Iomaire and Eterche). The medieval Irish regarded the four-oxen team as standard (Kelly 1997, 474).

18 LG 225.
19 LG 225; in DGE 24, Biobal, a merchant of Partholón, is the first to bring gold to Ireland.
20 AFM ᴀᴍ 2820.
21 AFM ᴀᴍ 2850.
22 AFM ᴀᴍ 2859. The two forts are Ráth Cinnech, which was located in north Armagh near the southwest corner of Lough Neagh, and Ráth Cimbaeth, which was situated in east Antrim near or on Island Magee (another Ráth Cimbaeth is located near Emain Macha in Armagh). Ráth Cinnech was supposedly dug by a party of four in one day.
23 AFM ᴀᴍ 3266.
24 LG 282, 299, etc.
25 LG 296, xlvii; and the Gaileoin were named after their javelins (*gai* + *lin*), LG 295.
26 LG 310.
27 LG 305.
28 LG 316.
29 LG 307, 316; in the AFM they are mentioned for ᴀᴍ 3817 (1383 ʙᴄ).
30 Raftery 1993, 175–77.
31 AFM ᴀᴍ 3656.
32 AFM ᴀᴍ 3817.
33 AFM ᴀᴍ 3872.
34 AFM ᴀᴍ 3991.
35 AFM ᴀᴍ 4176.
36 Warner 1990; with a critical rejoinder in Mallory 1995.
37 Gen 2.12–13.
38 Kelly, E. 2002, 58.
39 Eogan 1994, 47; Warner (pers. comm.) suggests cast gold by *c.* 1500 ʙᴄ.
40 Cahill 2002, 87.
41 Cahill 2002, 98–99.
42 Warner 2014.
43 Edwards 1990, 92.
44 Warner 1990, 31–33.
45 Brown and Baillie 2007, 30.
46 Warner 1990, 32–33.
47 *Clon* 36.
48 AFM 3942.
49 AFM 4319.
50 O'Connor (1822, vol. 1, cxlix-clx) provides lists of stomach churning etymologies where Phoenician, Hebrew and other Near Eastern words are explained by Irish, e.g., Mel-chi-ze-dek < Mulloc-ce-saoi-deag 'good and well instructed chief of the land'.
51 O'Connor 1822 (and available online on the Internet Archive); see also Macalister 1941 for an apoplectic review of a reprint.
52 AFM ᴀᴍ 4532.
53 Mallory 1997, 199.
54 Mallory and Baillie 1999.
55 AFM 3502.
56 Roche 2002, 74.
57 Hicks 2007, 185.
58 Waddell, Fenwick and Barton 2009.
59 Mallory 1988.

CHAPTER FIVE (pp. 101–32)

1 Matasović 2009, 97.
2 FBL 19.
3 This system is not universally agreed.
4 Plunkett 2008.

5 Coyle McClung 2013.
6 Baillie and Brown 2013, 68–69.
7 Corlett and Potterton 2013.
8 Coyle McClung 2012, 200–211.
9 Coyle McClung 2012, 212–25.
10 FB 29; TBDD 35:332.
11 MU 426.
12 EF-B 245.
13 ACMU 10.
14 TBC¹ 1415–16 = TBC² 1698.
15 TBC¹ 1776=TBC² 1898 = TBC2I 37, 40.
16 TEt I 9.
17 TBC² 1221–22.
18 EF-B 245.
19 BM-A 11.
20 TEt I 16.
21 TBFr 17: 194–95; EF-B 241, 245.
22 TBC² 1255.
23 BM-B 49; see also IT 70.
24 TBC² 4003, 4027.
25 TBC² 1492.
26 TEt I 6.
27 LMU 17: 212; FBL 166.
28 IDT 10/24 and 270.
29 EF-B 245.
30 AACC 104: 16; TBFl II 2–228; TBFl 2–312.
31 CE 62.
32 BDC 13:66.
33 EF-B 245.
34 TBR 4:74; and from the *Dindshenchas*, D (ACM) 26, BD (ACM) 3–492.
35 TBC² 2269=TBC² 2286=TBC2I 151.
36 TBC¹ 1654; SCMN 20.
37 EF-B 245.
38 TBC¹ 112.
39 TBR 4: 74; D (ACM) 26; BD (ACM) 3, 492.
40 TBDD 60: 531.
41 TBC³: 68, 70. The juice of the berry or 'sea tangle' (*smertan*) is employed in TBC¹ 1901=TBC² 1974.
42 ACR II 5; MU 913–14; FB 55.
43 If one follows Windisch's reading of *saire* as *daire* in his edition of TEt III 158.
44 CRR 37; FB 81.
45 SMMD 18.
46 TF 313; BDC (Stokes, Version B) 57. In very late tales such as CRR-B 35, 39 and TBFl II 4–216 *rail* is the word used for 'oak', while TBFl II 4–22 also uses *omna* 'oak' to describe Fergus and Ailill.
47 *Ilias Latina* 180.
48 *Aeneid* 3.680 = Imtheachta Aeniansa 187.
49 TBC² 457.
50 TBC¹ 827.
51 TBC² 3307; AG 19.
52 AG 9; the late CRR-B 29 also speaks of towering oaks.
53 E.g., TBDD 184, 610; TEm III 1.
54 FB 55; TBFr 7:67; SCMN 21.
55 MU 914–15.
56 TEt-E 18.
57 EF-B 238, 245.
58 TEm 78; TEm III 70.
59 TBFr 7: 69–70.
60 http://www.pbs.org/wgbh/nova/transcripts/3304_bog.html
61 Six small pieces of pine branches, the longest of which was 15 cm, were uncovered at Deer Park Farms in 7th

and 8th century contexts. They could have derived from small stands or, alternatively, been pulled from a bog (Neill 2011, 464–65).
62 Mallory and Baillie 1988, 29.
63 *Cogadh Gaedhell re Gaill*, Todd 1867, 142, ln. 2.
64 Murphy 1956, 10.
65 Lucas 1954.
66 *Aeneid* 3.659 = Imtheachta Aeniansa 173.
67 *Thebaid* II.598; IV.155; IX.552
68 *Song of Solomon* 1.17.
69 CE 56 where the word nut (*cnú*) was glossed *ind airme* 'of the sloe of a blackthorn'.
70 FB 9.
71 TBFl II 3–212.
72 TBC² 3888; FB 24.
73 TBC¹ 2586.
74 TF 74; see also IDT 10, 154.
75 FB 42; TBC¹ 26.
76 TBC¹ 2269–71; TBC³ 151; BM-B 34; also Conaire's steward in TBDD 85: 789.
77 TEm 55; TEm III 65.
78 TBDD 1166–67. *Proverbs* 25:11 also refers to golden apples.
79 ACR I, 10.
80 EF-B 245.
81 EF-B 245.
82 VS 8.
83 EF-B 245.
84 TF 65–66.
85 TBC² 1203–4.
86 EF-B 245.
87 EF-B 245.
88 FB 97:961; BDC 45:342; TE-E 4.
89 LMU 4:34.
90 TE-E 4; TEt III 10; TBDD 2:21.
91 TBDD 97: 960–61; TF 42; in MU 589 the word is *luss liach*.
92 BM-B 32.
93 FC 19; bees would collect from the head of white flowers – FC 35.
94 TBDD 109:1164.
95 TEt III 10.
96 TBFl II 4–108; EF-B 251.
97 MU 721.
98 AG 9.
99 AG 30.
100 TBC¹ 4099; TBC² 3305, 4802.
101 TBC¹ 3176; TBC² 3122; AG 28; TF 65–66. There were other terms for rushes, such as *bo(i)csimin* (TBC² 2264=TBC² 142; TBDD 105:1128–29), and *curcas* (TF 44).
102 FBL 216–17.
103 SCMN 10.
104 IDT 10/198.
105 TBDD 94:921, 101:1056; DCDM-E 236; CLR 15; DGS 55; IDT 10/115; cf. the modern *prátaí agus bainne* 'potatoes and milk'.
106 TT 167:21.
107 CLR 15.
108 TEt I 1.
109 TBC¹ 1314; TBC² 1598; in TBC¹ 1173 'seaweed' is used to translate *trechlam* as well.
110 TBC¹ 1173, 1314, 2730–31; TBC² 1598.
111 TBDD 1385.
112 OMU 162.
113 FB 46.
114 MU 665–66; IDT 4; BM-B 3.

115 FB 63.
116 FB 9.
117 EF-B 247.
118 CCC II (LU) I; DS CCC I.
119 TBC¹ 1904; also IDT 10/4.
120 FB 9 *luigfér* and 'meadow-hay' (*glasfeoir*).
121 FB 9; other references to heather in SMMD 20; SCC 45:787; TF 266.
122 TBC¹ 2143=TBC² 2164=TBC³ 126.
123 EF 4.
124 EN 10: 95.
125 BM-A 298.
126 IT 56.
127 EF-B 245.
128 FC 54
129 BM-B 20 and MU 649.
130 IT 52.
131 *dega*: TBDD 44: 407, 55:518, etc; *doél*: SCC 37: 625; BDC 33:237.
132 LMU 18: 280; TBDD 2:22; TE-E 4.
133 TBDD 97: 962.
134 TBFr 3:18.
135 CA 16; TBFl II 224.
136 AmCR 3; also IDT 10/150.
137 TBC¹ 2964; see also TBDD 1169; FC 35; IT 30.
138 Pompelius Mela, *Collectanea rerum memorabilium* 22.2–5, cited in Freeman 2002, 79.
139 Raftery 1994, 126.
140 TBDD 162:1505–6.
141 TBC² 1235.
142 FB 98.
143 TEt I 17.
144 SCC 25:267.
145 Tem III 31; TBDD 17:185–86; see also vessels filled with fish in FBL 8.
146 TBC¹ 1312–13.
147 EN 13: 126–27;
148 TBC² 1708.
149 TEm III 31.
150 TBC¹ 1312–13; TBC² 1597.
151 FB 24, 51, 87; TEm 77; TEm III 15.
152 MU 59.
153 TBFr 16:189.
154 IT 72: here the word is *bratán*.
155 IT 18.
156 CU-A 120.
157 FB 48.
158 FC 16.
159 TBC¹ 1857=TBC² 1998=TBC³ 81 etc.; TBRa 6:64.
160 CRR 10.
161 ACon D-2; TBC¹ 1087; CRR-B 22, 33; TF 309; CLR 11.
162 DCDM-E 109.
163 TBC¹ 1087, 3767; TBC² 245, 3312, 4476; FB 46; OMU 595; TBDD 1238.
164 DCDM=L 63.
165 *Topographia* 21.
166 TBDD 56: 502–3.
167 EF 6.
168 EF-B 250.
169 SC 386.
170 TBC³ 112.
171 BM-B 40.
172 BM-B 14, 42.
173 TBRa 5:46.
174 DCDM-E 47.
175 TEt III 15.
176 AD 2–3.
177 FFF 1.
178 SCC 35:585.
179 TE III 156.

180 TT 169–14; in BDC 6:28–29 Cormac Connloinges was forbidden to swim with the birds of Loch Ló.
181 EF-B 241.
182 TBC¹ 787–88. Other instances: CU-A 120; BM-B 8; CCC-II (Eg) 143 (8); *foram* : TBC² 552.
183 TBC¹ 925–27; TBC² 1274. For birds perched on shoulders see also SCC 4:28–29.
184 TBC¹ 1583.
185 BDC 6:27.
186 TBC² 1706–9; FBL 8.
187 IT 74.
188 TBC¹ 3075=TBC² 3012.
189 TBC² 1596.
190 TBC¹ 1171, 1313; TBC²; IT 70.
191 MU 467; BM-B 14–40.
192 Hamilton-Dyer 2007, 106–7.
193 MU 467.
194 TBC¹ 2257=TBC² 2274=TBC³ 145; SCC 5:45; AG 9. See also FB 100, where it involves stretching one's neck as long as a crane.
195 McCormick and Murray 2007, 74.
196 TBC¹ 741–42; TBC² 1135.
197 MU 469.
198 TBC¹ 781=TBC² 1160.
199 AO 13.
200 AG 32.
201 OMU 176.
202 IT 24, 40.
203 MU 465–66.
204 *ainnel*: CS 196; *fannall*: TBC¹ 2285; TBC² 424, 3311–12.
205 TBC¹ 741–42=TBC² 1135.
206 TBC¹ 4086=TBC² 4791.
207 FFF 1.
208 TF 637.
209 AmCR 4.
210 TBC¹ 2927=TBC² 2870; see also TBC² 2921.
211 TBC¹ 2351=TBC² 2355=TBC³ 174.
212 OMU 600, 647.
213 BDC 14 (Stokes).
214 *séig*: TBC² 3308, 4804; *sebac*: CRR-B 21; CCC 25. There is also a possible reference to a kite as a *serech* in TEm III 79.
215 TBC¹ 960.
216 CRR-B 29,35; TBFl II 2–310, 4–16.
217 For example, *bran*: TBC¹ 3878; TBC² 2384, 2427; FB 68; CRR-B 29, 35; TBDD 35:331; TBFl II 3–204; *fiach*: TBDD 35:331; TEm III 79.
218 BM-A 381.
219 A fragment of a bear bone was recovered from the Beaker layer at New Grange (McCormick and Murray 2007, 143). A probable bear tooth was recovered from an early medieval site, but is presumed to have been an ancient curiosity carried onto the site from elsewhere, McCormick and Murray 2007, 248.
220 McCormick 1999, 359.
221 TBC² 4503.
222 CRR-B 33; this same text also uses *mathgamain* in CRR-B 40.
223 OMU 607.
224 DCDM(LL) 87.
225 TBFl II 4–22.
226 FB 52.
227 TBC¹ 2265; TBC² 4555; TBC³ 149. In the Bible bears and lions are also

found together, although not fighting one another, e.g. 1 Sam 17:34, 36, etc.; Prov 28:15.
228 TBFl II 4–22.
229 *Thebaid* IV.272; VII.661, etc., refers to the use of the hides of the lynx = *Togail na Tebe* 1549–52. Lynxes are also present in the *Scél Alexandair* 494b 22–32, along with lions, tigers and panthers.
230 TBC¹ 385.
231 TBC¹ 1088.
232 TBC¹ 3731.
233 TBC¹ 3757=TBC² 4502.
234 TBC² 3576.
235 OMU 36–37, 608. Other such references would include CRR-B 35, 39; TBDD 92:894; DCDM-L 90: TF 733; TEm 43; TEm III 63.
236 CRR 40, 41, 42, 43, ft. 4.
237 CCC 26.
238 DCDM-L 59–60 (*os(s)*).
239 SC 380.
240 AFMR 3.
241 *Topographia* 18.
242 TBC¹ 770, 778. The motif of a warrior being swift enough to catch deer 'leaked' into the Irish translations of classical works, where we find similar references to Achilles (Irish *Achilleid* 18) and Parthenopaeus (*Togail na Tebe* 2430–35).
243 TBC¹ 793–94.
244 TBC² 1149.
245 TBC² 1709; in Scotland, Deirdre and the Sons of Uisnech also dine on venison (*sideng*)(OMU 160).
246 TEm III 89.
247 Kelly 1997, 673–74.
248 Waterman 1997, 120.
249 McCormick and Murray 2007.
250 TBFr 5: 55; TBDD 135: 1340.
251 McCormick 1999, 363. I once mistakenly referred to a foul tasting beer as 'weasel piss', but was informed that in south Armagh one says 'stoat's piss'.
252 BM-B 32.
253 TBFr 5:55 (here it is known as the *míl maige* 'animal of the plain'; see also a russet clad hare (*míl*) in EF-B 242.
254 TBFr 5:57.
255 TBFr 9:91.
256 BM-B 41.
257 MU 724.
258 TBC¹ 920, 923 = TBC² 1276.
259 McCormick 1999, 363.
260 CRR 10.
261 FB 52.
262 IT 96. One was also cast up on shore in AD 752 according to the *Annals of Ulster*.
263 TBFr 5: 54.
264 MU 335.
265 TBC¹ 4051.
266 McCormick 1999, 362.
267 GCC 105:11 where *cú* underlies what the translator has rendered 'The Three Wolves of Martin'.
268 CRR-B 21; TF 743.
269 IT 48.
270 TBC² 724.
271 McCone 1987.
272 TBDD 66:601–4.

273 TBC² 2001, 2061; TBC³ 80, 94–11; TBRa 7:69.
274 TBC² 1136.
275 McCormick and Murray 2007.
276 McCormick and Murray 2007.
277 Mallory 2013, 42.
278 McCormick 1999, 365.
279 TBC¹ 2352=TBC² 2356=TBC³ 174. Its occurrence across all recensions makes it more difficult to explain away as a typo for *gríb* 'griffin' (see O'Rahilly 1976, 272 for discussion), which is well known for its talons, e.g., *Achilleid* 10.
280 *Topographia* 20.
281 McCormack 1991, 49. See Mallory 1992, 117 for fuller discussion.
282 Mac Coitir 2010, 131–33.
283 E.g., TBC² 1413, 1417, 1426.
284 DCDM-E 148–49.
285 CRR-B 46; TBFl II 4–114.
286 McCormick 1991, 31.
287 McCormick and Murray 2007, 98.
288 OMU 647, 651.
289 BF 1.
290 TBDD 43: 396.
291 SMMD 1.
292 AG 29.
293 TBDD 28: 274.
294 *cú*: BDC 45:342–43; IT 52; *mílchú*: TF 45; TBFr 3: 31, 5:53; *sod*: AmCR 3.
295 LMU 10:132.
296 BDC 7:33.
297 IT 38.
298 SMMD.
299 NC 59.
300 TF 707.
301 RD (DS) 15:471.
302 SC 380.
303 TBC¹ 3166. Seriously wounded but in denial, Cethern kills every physician who gives a negative prognosis.
304 ACMU 10–12.
305 TBC¹ 572(M); TBC² 862; MU 611 speaks of the bay of a foreign hound.
306 McCone 1984.
307 TBC¹ 861.
308 MD (Boand I) 83 (MD vol. 3, 32).
309 McCormick and Murray 2007, 99–100.
310 AmCR 3.
311 TBFl II 4–216.
312 TEt 3–20.
313 BM-A 11:235. Here the word *oirce* is used, generally for a pet or lap dog.
314 McCormick 2002.
315 McCormick and Murray 2007, 231.
316 TBC¹ 3085, 4100.
317 TBC² 1840.
318 FB 30.
319 FB 57.
320 MU 732.
321 IT 80.
322 McCormick 1988.
323 TBC¹ 3789; TF 647; SMMD 15.
324 AG 19.
325 *blichtach*: TBC¹ 1270; cf. also CRR-B 3.
326 *bó*: TBC¹ 1275–76 = TBC² 1508.
327 TBC¹ 2041= TBC³ 106.
328 AAA 13.
329 IT 56.
330 McCormick 1992.
331 Smyth and Evershed 2015.
332 TBC¹ 1202.
333 TBF 2: 9; TBDD 94:923–24; SMMD 6.

334 *lóeg* 'calf': TBDD 54: 490; cf. LMU 7:90.
335 FBL 5.
336 *dam*: AmCR 4; IT 82.
337 ACMU 1.
338 FB 91.
339 TBC¹ 1492=TBC² 1320.
340 TBFr 1:5.
341 TBFr 14:164–65.
342 *Crith Gablach* 87.
343 *Crith Gablach* 90.
344 TBD 1:6–7.
345 ACMU 1.
346 TBDD 28:267.
347 SMMD 2.
348 CE 54:5.
349 TBR 5:83–85.
350 TBF 6:82–84.
351 TBF 82–84.
352 Lucas 1989, 150–51.
353 TBC² 69.
354 TBR 3:55.
355 AmCR 3.
356 *Cogadh Gaedhel* 77.
357 *Cogadh Gaedhel* 90.
358 Kelly 1997, 8–9.
359 CE 54:5.
360 TBD 1:607.
361 TBDD 11:123; SCC 23.
362 TBC² 1993=TBC³ 84; IT 54; Mac Coitir 2010, 77–78.
363 Kelly 1997, 33–34.
364 TBC¹ 1866; TBFl II 2–24; for discussion of hornless cows, see Kelly 1997, 35–36.
365 CCC 15.
366 BF 4, 34.
367 LMU 9:111.
368 TEm III 42.
369 TBC¹ 3026, etc.
370 AmCR 4 (glossed 'old boar'), etc.
371 CRR 57.
372 TBC¹ 1202, etc.
373 FB 68.
374 *Ilias Latina* 595.
375 TBC² 66.
376 TEm III 89.
377 TBR 3:55.
378 TBDD 28:269.
379 AmCR 4.
380 SMMD 17.
381 TBC¹ 513.
382 SCMN 13.
383 EF-B 249; DGS (LL) 56. Cf. the Norse god Thor who had a re-usable goat.
384 TBDD 38:352–53, 39:362; 136:1351–52.
385 TBC¹ 1202; TBDD 94:923–24; SMMD 1.
386 TBDD 54:490.
387 TBDD 51:463.
388 TBC² 3902; cf. also CRR 15 where an old horse is yoked to an old chariot.
389 TBC¹ 3863–64.
390 TBC¹ 4123; cf. also TBC² 4850.
391 CRR-B 21.
392 Sayers 1994, 236.
393 FB 69; Ercol's horse is later killed by Cú Chulainn's.
394 BM 23.
395 MD (CC) 24.
396 RD (AM) 16–45; cf. MD (RC) 24.
397 TBDD 28: 275.
398 TBC² 2657.

399 AmCR 3.
400 Ní Chatháin 1991, 123–24.
401 McCormick 2002, 106–7.
402 TEm III 5.
403 AmCR 4.
404 TBC² 60.
405 TBC² 62–63.
406 TBR 3:55.
407 TBFr 27:338.
408 TBC¹ 2262–63.
409 TF 743; CRR-B 21.
410 OMU 746.
411 TBFr 9:93. The word may also designate the roe, but this animal is not native to Ireland.
412 BM-B 30.
413 AmCR 4.
414 McCormick 1991, 31.
415 For example, 2 Sam 5:11, 7:2, 7:7; 1 Kings 6:9, 6:10, 6:15, 6:16, 7.2, etc.
416 Coughlan 2012, 73–75.
417 Whitty 2012, 316.
418 Num 21:6–9; Deut 8:15; Psalm 58:4, etc.
419 Van Wijngaarden-Bakker 1989, 127.

CHAPTER SIX (pp. 133–74)

1 LL 21477–80.
2 CCC I (LU) 2.
3 Newman 1997; Roche 2002.
4 Waterman and Lynn 1997.
5 Johnston and Wailes 2007.
6 Waddell, Fenwick and Barton 2009.
7 Clutterbuck 2013.
8 Danaher 2013.
9 McCormick 2008, 215–18.
10 TBC¹ 3906.
11 CCI-LU 2.
12 *Aeneid* vii, 157–59; *TogTr* 1242–43, 1269–72; *De Excido Trojae* xxvi; *Pharsalia* iv.168–69; *In Cath Catharda* 365.
13 TBC¹ 1530, 1968; TBC³ 74.
14 TBC¹ 1530.
15 O'Sullivan et al. 2014, 121–23; Kelly 2015.
16 TBC² 170, 319–20, 332, 1341, 1372, 1464, 1796; the same expression occurs in the Irish version of the Troy story (*Togal Troí* 604).
17 TBFl II 3–124.
18 TBC¹ 2087; TBC² 3822–23, 3848.
19 TBC¹ 1731; the *sosad* could also be applied to a 'hut' which was generally paired with the *pupall* 'tent' (TBC² 518–19, 685, 1465–66).
20 CRR 14, 20, 23; CRR-B 19.
21 TBR 3: 56.
22 Also borrowed into Welsh as *pebyll*.
23 AmCR 4.
24 BM-B 44.
25 CRR 11.
26 TBC¹ 3938.
27 TBC¹ 140–42.
28 TBC¹ 2866.
29 TBC² 320–1.
30 TBC² 320–1.
31 TBC² 518–19.
32 OMU 86–88; TBFl II 1–104.
33 TBC¹ 1017.
34 AG 56.
35 TBC¹ 1023; TBC² 1375–77.
36 FB 91.
37 Raftery 1996, 113.

38 Cessford (1995) believes that this word along with an assortment of other military words borrowed into Welsh suggests that ancient Britons may have served with the Roman cavalry. The problem with this is that almost the same borrowed vocabulary is found in Old Irish and whose ancestors had a relationship with the Romans that was not so intimate. Also, a word like *pupall* (which retains the Roman initial 'p' sound that did not exist in the earliest Irish) can hardly be a very early loanword.

39 *Pharsalia* 1.514–18. See *In Cath Catharda* 2346 for use of *pupall*. But in the *Scél Alexandair* we find *scor* used to translate Latin *tentoria*, e.g. 490b 38, 494b 24.

40 Ex 26:36.

41 Bede xix.

42 AFM AM 2859.2.

43 AFM vol. I, 9, notes h and i.

44 AFM AM 3529.2.

45 AFM vol. I, 37, notes e–i

46 In the *Táin* I, for example, one might be killed in a *dún*, *dúnaid*, *daingen* or *din*.

47 In the Ulster cycle *borg* is used in TF 842 and FB 53:20.

48 FB 80: 8–9.

49 ACR II 4; Thurneysen 1921, 440 for date of tale.

50 McKay 1999, 66.

51 TBC² 1793–94; TBC³ 18.

52 TEm III 85.

53 TBC² 221.

54 TEt-E 1.

55 TBC¹ 672.

56 TBFr 5: 50.

57 TBC¹ 700–702; TBC² 1055.

58 FBL 239.

59 TBFr 5:56.

60 TT 168:9.

61 Mallory 1987, 15, e.g., TBC¹ 419, 455, 471–72; TBC² 751, 928, etc.

62 TBC¹ 1069; AG 44; MU 376–79, 815–16; FBL 77; BM-B 13.19; TBFl II 3–118: 32.

63 TBC² 1581.

64 BD (BI) 3–500. In TEm III 41 the well of Nechtan was situated at the bottom of the *dún*.

65 *Togail na Tebe* 2941; *In Cath Catharda* 1833.

66 TBC¹ 2299–302; TBC² 2307; TBC³ 160.

67 *dún drech-solus Delgga* – CRR 9.

68 ACR II 4–5.

69 TF 235–39.

70 TBC² 1146–47.

71 CRR 3, 15.

72 MU 362, 451, 502–5.

73 LMU 8:101–2.

74 FB 88.

75 TBC¹ 3518.

76 TEm 147–52.

77 TBC¹ 3836; TBC² 2314; in TBC² 4556 there are four ramparts and we find seven walls surrounding Dún Scáith (SC 386: xi).

78 FB 17–20; Fedelm also leaps over three ridges (ramparts?) from the hall of Briccriu (FB 17:10–11).

79 TBDD 149.5; also 147.3.

80 BDC (Stokes) 52.

81 FB 17: 10–11.

82 Mac Mathúna 1976.

83 TBC² 890.

84 TF 235–39.

85 SC 386: xi.

86 FBL 144.

87 *Thebaid* II.454–55, 848.

88 *Aeneid* vi.549.

89 FBL 71.

90 TBC¹ 588–89.

91 AmCR 4.

92 CMT I: 87–88.

93 TEt-E 11.

94 TEm III 10.

95 EN 8:78.

96 CCon II 38.

97 TBC² 216.

98 FC 32.

99 TBFl II 3–210; CCC 4 (*ráth* of the door-keepers).

100 CE 54:5.

101 TBF 82–84.

102 TBFr 361.

103 McCormick 1995, 34.

104 TBC¹ 572–74. Problematic as when the hound attacks, the Ulstermen climb over the palisade in their attempt to rescue the young Sétanta.

105 ACMU 10; see also SC 380: 24.

106 FB 25.

107 FB 82.

108 McCormick 1995, 34.

109 TBR 2:27; TEt III 13; TL 22.

110 TBC¹ 531.

111 CF 7 [E IV.3].

112 FBL 165.

113 TBC² 3512–24.

114 AG 24.

115 SMMD 5:6.

116 TBF(LU) 4:34.

117 SMMD 18:6–10.

118 TBF 5: 45–48, 6:45.

119 MU 1025.

120 CCC 2; TBFl II 4–12.

121 TBCI 1525–26; see also ACR I 3; TBFl II 2–20: 17.

122 BM-A 24:389.

123 O'Sullivan et al. 2014, 82; Stout 2000.

124 Meyer 1895, I 47:17–18.

125 TBC¹ 700.

126 Mallory 1992, 126–27.

127 Why Mongán.

128 There are a series of other terms, generally only appearing once, that designate either some form of structure or compartment within a house, e.g., *áitt* 'apartment' (CRR 13); *carcar* 'prison' (BDC 70:638); *etsad* 'chamber' (MU 343); *mennat* 'dwelling; (TBC¹ 3343); *adba* and *dadb?* 'abode' (IDT 10/118); and *treb* 'dwelling' (DGS 56).

129 E.g., CúRoí (TBC¹ 1623); the Mac Oc (TEt I 20).

130 E.g. Daire (TBC² 88); Bricriu (FB 1); Cú Chulainn (TBC¹ 3002); Da Derga (TBDD 29:280).

131 TBC² 856.

132 TBC¹ 2890.

133 FC 24, 26.

134 MU 199; CRR 13; CCC 3, 7.

135 MU 202.

136 ACMU 1; TBDD 27: 260.

137 *Laechthech*: TF 84–85; *slogthech*: MU 202.

138 *Tech n-óla* (CRR 11; IT 12; CCC 3; TBFl II 304); *tech tremmeda* 'strong-mead house' (AG 45). *Tech midchúarta* is variously translated as mid-court or mead-court, e.g., FB 22, 68; TBDD 87: 824; CF 8.

139 Stokes (Joyce 1903, II.174) compared these with the six Jewish cities of refuge, e.g. Num 35, but other than the number, they really are not that comparable, the Jewish cities serving as sanctuaries for unintentional murderers.

140 SMMD 1.

141 MU 203–4; also Dun Atha Fen in TBFl II 1–304, Dun Atha Deirg in TBFl II 2–114, etc.

142 SMMD 3; SCC 10:881; FB 44, etc.

143 ACMU 2; see also FB 64; TBFl II 2–102.

144 TBFl II 2–104.

145 FB 64.

146 SMMD 18.

147 MU; see also ODR for a similar incident, and the later Welsh version in *Branwen verch Lyr*.

148 Warner 1994. His discussion proposes a possible ritual involving the burning of nobility in a house that is attested in the Irish annals.

149 Lynn and McDowell 2011, 105–7.

150 Dan 3:19.

151 Orosius 1.20.

152 FB 80 (the entrance to Cú Roí's fort).

153 TBDD 6: 80–81.

154 SMMD 5 (Rawlinson).

155 FC 17.

156 EF-B 249.

157 TBDD 102: 1088.

158 TBDD 29:280–84.

159 BDC 31:228.

160 MU 203–4.

161 BDC 44–46:336–60.

162 MU 880–81; SC 386.

163 MU 913–16.

164 EF-B 249; and the lintel was of *findruine*.

165 FB 21; MU 866; TEm 60; TBFl II 4–12; EF-B 249.

166 TBDD 29:281–84.

167 TBC² 713.

168 MU 923; FC 65; IT 112.

169 TBDD 135:1345; BDC 33:239; EF-B 238; CCC 4; TBFl II 713.

170 FB 1.

171 ALB.

172 Lynn and McDowell 2011, 113–14.

173 FB 88.

174 TBFl II 2–100, 2–104.

175 FB 3.11.

176 TEt I 20; also *forlés* 'roofwindow' in TEt III 161.

177 FC 17; see also TBFl II 2–208.

178 CRR-B 46; TBFl II 2–102, 3–118.

179 *tuir*: SCC 31: 451–52.

180 FBL 146.

181 FBL 18–19.

182 SCC 31: 451–52.

183 Gold: Ex 26:32; silver: Song 3:10; brass: 1 Kings 7:15, 16, etc.

184 FB 101.

185 FB 98.

186 TBDD 122; see also TEt I 21; MU 953–54.

187 FB 64.
188 *ochtach*: FBL 145; *féicce*: BM-B 22; TBFl II 2–102.
189 FB 57.
190 MU 497.
191 E.g., CRR 17, 19; SCC 44: 739, 776; TF 69; TT 167: 27.
192 BM-B 9
193 MU 201.
194 TEt 1, 20,
195 FC 17.
196 FB 3.
197 *Etymologiae* XV.iii.11–12.
198 *Togail na Tebe* 40. *Thebaid* I.534 does mention a *thalamus* 'bower, bedchamber'. Cf. also *In Cath Catharda* 243.
199 E.g., TBC¹ 475–76, TBC² 330; FB 21; TBRa 1:4, etc.
200 FB 2.
201 SMMD 5 (Rawlinson).
202 FBL 24.
203 TBFl II 2–100, 2–102.
204 FC 17, here 294 compartments with 150 girls in each one!
205 SCC 16:164.
206 *Iliad* 6.243–50.
207 E.g., TBC¹ 1275; TBC³ 22; TBD 9:121; TBDD 11:125.
208 E.g., TEt-E 9; VS 29.
209 E.g., TBC² 1, 1294, 2940; LMU 1:6; ACMM 8: MU 814; TBDD 63:573.
210 TF 701.
211 TEm 65; EF-B 249.
212 TBC¹ 3176; TBC² 3122.
213 TBC² 98–99, 1941–42; TEm III 88.
214 TBC¹ 140–42.
215 FB 4.
216 AG 28.
217 SCC 33: 486.
218 BF 9, 10; ACR II 6.
219 AA 1; but TBDD 112, 115 are problematic.
220 TBC² 2; also FB 4; CCC 5.
221 TF 592; AG 8; *frithadart*: TBC¹ 3176.
222 FB 4; FBL 162–63.
223 TBC¹ 140–42; FB 4; MU 917; FBL 162–63.
224 TF 407.
225 Lynn and McDowell 2011, 127–28, 422–23.
226 *rígsuide* (CCon I 50; TBFl II 2–210).
227 TBDD 105:1121.
228 CCC 5.
229 AG 19.
230 TF 92, 402–3.
231 MU 495; AmCR 5: AG 47; BM-A 13776–7; TF 91. Also *alchaing* (MU 495–96).
232 MU 495–96.
233 MU 495.
234 TF 91; AG 47.
235 TBC¹ 3178; TBC² 505–6.
236 TBC² 3637.
237 TEm III 45.
238 Moffat 2005, 206.
239 *Columa* from Latin *columen* or *columna*; *gallán*.
240 TBC¹ 585; TBC² 884.
241 TBC¹ 2544.
242 TBC¹ 1441.
243 TBC¹ 3317–19; TBC² 3799–3800.
244 CU-A 120.
245 TBC¹ 711–14; TBC² 460, 1069–70.
246 TBC¹ 956; TBC² 1304.

247 BM-A 22:371; BM-B 41.
248 *coluna* (MU 379).
249 BM-B 13.
250 MU 646–48.
251 FBL 77.
252 AG 44.
253 TBDD 157:1478–80.
254 AAA 11; TBC¹ 1602–4; figuratively in TBFl II 4–22; and one on each side of an island between which a giant lies in FBL 193–95.
255 MU 815–16.
256 TBDD 67:623–24.
257 Why Mongán, 156.
258 MU 308–9.
259 SCM 25.
260 SMMD 20.
261 FC 15, 16; TEm III 67.
262 MU 911–12.
263 CCC-I (LU) 2.
264 TBDD 103:1107.
265 D(ACM)4; RD(ACM) 15–459; BD(ACM) 3–492; and with *fál* (BD(BI)3–500; RD(ACM) 15–459.
266 TBC² 2230.
267 Walsh 1987.
268 Williams 1987.
269 Lynn 1981; 1989.
270 Condit and Buckley 1989.
271 Raftery 1994, 83–97; Lynn 2003, 61–62.
272 Dobbs 1912.
273 Or the tale originally envisaged a raid emanating from Tara.
274 Muhr 2009, 122–23.
275 CMT2 93:296.
276 For a discussion of the myths centered on the Boyne, see Waddell 2014, 15–32.
277 Joyce 1903, II.172.
278 Frazer 1879–88.
279 O'Brien, E. 1992b.
280 MacNeill 1983, 109.
281 McErlean 2013, 11–14.
282 Warner 1985; McErlane 2013, 4–8.
283 Macdonald 2014a and pers. comm.
284 Macdonald 2014b; cf. also Muhr 1996, 27–28, 58–59.
285 Waddell et al. 2009, 27–32.
286 Ó hUiginn 1988, 21; MD (Ráth Cruachain) 2 (MD vol. 3, 348).
287 Ó hUiginn 1988, 21–22.
288 Waddell 2009, 237–48.
289 CRR 16; EN 8:78; AACC 103:23–24; etc.
290 TBFr 4:41, 19:221; EN 6; FB 55.
291 EN 6.
292 Waddell et al. 2009, 79–89.
293 TBFr 20:242; EN 6; TBRa 5:53.
294 TBFr 16:177.
295 AACC 103:31–104:14–15.
296 MD(Carn Fraích)42 (MD vol. 3, 358).
297 FBL 71.
298 FB 44; BM-B 3.
299 FB 54.
300 *tech n-immacallamae* (TBFr 12:136).
301 TBFr 19:225.
302 TBC² 1138.
303 TBC¹ 745.
304 Mallory 1997, 203; Warner 1988.
305 TBC² 769; OMU 560; etc.
306 TBC¹ 436.
307 TBC¹ 803.
308 LMU 8:100–1; BM-B 44.
309 TBC¹ 3426–27.

310 TBC¹ 3426–27.
311 TBC² 4010–18.
312 IDT 5; CLR 3.
313 TEm 2.
314 SCMN 15.
315 Mallory 1997, 205.
316 FB 55.
317 TEm.
318 Hessen 1912; see also Mallory and Baillie 1988.
319 TBFr 7:51–55.
320 Alternatively, Sayers describes the king's hall as 'running along an east-west axis' with two outer and two inner rows of dining compartments (Sayers 1991, 25).
321 FB 2.
322 1 Kings 7.
323 *Aeneid* 1:448–49.
324 Waddell et al. 2009, 175–77.
325 There are actually seven rings, but the outermost ring is merely a series of post reinforcements to the 6th ring and there is no intervening space between the two rows.
326 Aitchison 1994.
327 Warner 2000 argues that the hengiform enclosure was designed to protect the outside world from the potent Otherworld forces of the major ceremonial sites.
328 O'Connell 2013.
329 Hammerow 2012.
330 O'Sullivan et al. 2014, 90.
331 AI 972.
332 For example, Edwards 1990, 26–27.
333 Warner, in press.
334 Aitchison 1994, 50–130.
335 Aitchison 1994; Bruford 1994.
336 Lakovides 1977; Raaflaub 1997.
337 If one follows T. O'Rahilly (1946, 175–81) the original horizon of political opponents was Tara versus Emain Macha and Cruachain was introduced to the story later.
338 Chris Lynn offers an interesting but highly speculative attempt at linking the '40-metre structure' to the Ulster heroes by tying the 34 post-pairs of the building to a catalogue of about 34 Ulster chieftains mentioned in the *Táin* (Lynn 1994).

CHAPTER SEVEN (pp. 175–205)

1 CMT2 778–80.
2 CMT1 24–26.
3 CMT1 31 attempts to correct this by alluding to the introduction of pointed weapons during the reign of the previous Fir Bolg King, Rinndal.
4 O'Curry 1873, II 240–47.
5 O'Curry 1873, I ccccxxxvii–ccccxl.
6 Mallory 1995, 11.
7 Raftery 1983, 83–106.
8 The quote (*dentibus marinarum belluarum*) occurs in the 'second' edition of Solinus' work which may have been written by Solinus himself (Walter 1969, 61–63).
9 Raftery 1983, 109–10. Two spearheads from Lisnacrogher measured over 40 cm long.
10 Rynne 1981, 93.

11 Halpin 2015. The Anglo-Saxons and Franks also employed archery and could have introduced it to the Irish (in fact, Old English *boga* is identical to the Old Norse form – Sandberg-McGowan 1996, 227) but I am going with the supposed Norse etymology of the Irish archery terms and its identification as 'a definitively Viking artefact'.
12 Halpin 2005, 128–29.
13 Halpin 2005, 126
14 FB 67.
15 CCon II 30.
16 TBFI II 1–314.
17 O'Rahilly, T. 1946, 67; in some versions Nuadu possessed a special spear, while it was Lug who carried the special sword.
18 Brady 1979, 98.
19 Also *Caladcholg* as it is known in TBC¹ 4027 and elsewhere which O'Rahilly (1946, 68–69) regarded as a folk etymology ('hard-sword') that replaced a misleading reading of the original *Caladbolg* as 'hard-bag' rather than 'hard-lightning'.
20 O'Rahilly, T. 1946.
21 EF-B 251.
22 TBC² 4759–60.
23 AG 20, 38.
24 OMU 549–50.
25 TBC¹ 3798–99, 3853–54; TBC² 2365–66, 3258–60, etc. A late version of the death of Cú Chulainn suggests that he was right-handed (BM-B 43).
26 TBC¹ 1934, 3279; TBC² 4500, 4542; TBC³ 73.
27 TBC¹ 2361–62; TBC² 3730; BDC 10:44; TF 4–5, FBL 14; etc.
28 TBC¹ 3599, 3635; TBC² 1641–42; etc
29 AG 10.
30 TBC¹ 4037, 4053–54.
31 The word 'blade' *faebar* was also used on occasion, e.g., TBC¹ 2769; TBC² 2762; etc. and there are also unique words for sword, e.g., *coire* and *sathach* in AmCR 3. We also have *foga* for a 'dagger' (TBC1 3698) whose description in TBC² (2366–67) includes thongs and rivets. If the translation of *maeldorn* as 'sword' be correct, then we also have mention of a weapon made out of white-silver (TBC¹ 3619; TBC² 4336–37; MU 748).
32 Kelly 1971.
33 McManus 1983, 33–34.
34 Mallory 1981, 110–12.
35 AmCR 3.
36 TBC¹ 3635.
37 *ruise* (SCC 630); *derg* (BM-A 13:276; SCC 430; TBC² 2845). Bauersfeld (1933, 336) sought to interpret the use of *derg* as referring to a bronze sword.
38 TBC² 3226, 3230; MU 592; etc.
39 MU 542; TBDD 82, 128, 137; etc.
40 TBC² 3226, 3230; MU 592; etc.
41 TF 533; CS 197; etc.
42 CS 197; TT 175:22–23; etc.
43 TBDD 87:822–23.
44 TBDD 128:1128–29.
45 1 Sam 17:7; 2 Sam 21:19; 1 Chron 11:23.
46 West 2013.

47 TBDD 128: 1228–29 *claideb duba dímóra* (without the comparison with a 'weaver's beam') also occurs at 82: 748–49 and 137: 1365.
48 TBC¹ 1360.
49 SCC 2:14–17.
50 AAA 10.
51 TBC¹ 1357–58.
52 TBFr 11: 116–17.
53 TBC² 3338; MU 541–43.
54 TBC¹ 1476; TBC² 1743–44.
55 SCC 6:48–49. There are also accounts in Norse sagas of throwing swords (Mallory 1980, 106) and in ancient Indian epic a sword was as likely to be thrown as to be held in the hand of a warrior (Singh 1965, 110).
56 TBC¹ 3318–19.
57 MU 888–89.
58 TBDD 76:684–87.
59 TBC¹ 1069–70.
60 TBC¹ 2750–51.
61 TBC² 1492.
62 TBC³ 120.
63 TBC¹ 2361, 3279, etc; TBC² 2365, 3753, etc.; TBC³ 178; MU 536; TBDD 75, 97; etc.
64 TBC¹ 2361; TBC² 2365; MU 536; etc.
65 TBC¹ 3784; TBC² 159: etc.
66 TBC¹ 3662; TBDD 95; etc.
67 TBC¹ 3273; TBC² 159, 3730; MU 725.
68 TBC² 1492, 4322; TF 4–5; etc.
69 4 swords (TBC¹ 87, 3853; TBC² 252); 8 swords (TBC¹ 2230; TBC² 2247).
70 Tacitus *Agricola* 29–33.
71 FB 23.
72 MU 541.
73 FB 45.
74 *Dét*: TBC¹ 90, 1250; BDC 9:41; etc.; *co n-imdurn diad* (TBC¹ 3661–62). Sullivan (O'Curry 1873, I ccclvi) believed that *colg ndét* indicated a 'tooth-hilted-dagger', i.e., that the reference to 'tooth' was not to the material of the hilt (?) but the manner in which the sword was hafted. But all swords prior to the Vikings in Ireland bore organic hilts and it is unlikely that one would regard the hafting mechanism itself as requiring mention in describing parade dress.
75 TBC² 3339–40.
76 VS.
77 TBC¹ 1250–51, 3606–7; TBC² 4405–6; CRR-B 23.
78 TBC¹ 3214; TBC² 4371–72, 4486–87.
79 Rynne 1981, 95.
80 Harrison and Ó Floinn 2015, 78–86.
81 Bone 1989.
82 Harrison and Ó Floinn 2015, 76.
83 2 Maccabees 15:15. Also, the only reference to a sword hilt is in Judges 3:22 which is not described.
84 *Aeneid* ix:303–5.
85 *Ilias Latina* 628–29.
86 *Aeneid* xi:11.
87 *Aeneid* xii:389.
88 For example, *Imtheachta Aeniasa* 769–70 where Vergil's 'sword with tawny jasper' (iv. 261–62) became 'a sword, gold-hilted, gemmed with carbuncle'; also 1916–18, 1930–34, 2491–92 (where the Irish *colg nded* appears); and in 2847–48 Turnus has

a 'sword, gold-hilted, inlaid with silver'. The Irish *Togail Troi* (895–96) and the *Togail na Tebe* (4525) have the Greeks bearing Irish swords as well.
89 *In Cath Catharda* p. 387.
90 Riddler and Trzaska-Nartowski (2009).
91 Among the legacy of Cú Roí in AmCR 3 is the *sathach*, presumably a sword or dagger, whose name is derived from *sáthaim* 'I thrust'.
92 TBC¹ 3280=TBC² 3753–54.
93 TBC² 2565, 2573; TBC³ 226; etc.
94 TBC¹ 2718–19; also interlaced design in CS 197; white silver in TF 36.
95 FC 37; CS 197; CRR-B 27.
96 Mallory 1986, 46–47.
97 TBC¹ 105.
98 BM-A 23; BM-B 43.
99 BM-A 29:478–79; cf. also Iliach in TBC¹ 3384–85.
100 CRR 51; CRR-B 43.
101 TBC¹ 3076; TBC² 3013; BM-B 49, 58.
102 TBC¹ 334.
103 TBC² 2527.
104 FC 32; FBL 10.
105 SMMD 16.
106 ACon-A 1; CE 62.
107 Raftery 1992, 195–97.
108 See Armit 2012 for examples of headhunting throughout the Iron Age in Atlantic Europe.
109 Mallory 1992, 139, 142.
110 *Togail Troí*, 1312–13, 1889.
111 Armit 2012, 31.
112 The Fir Bolg has the *cruísech* and *fiarlan*; the Tuatha Dé Danann fought with the *goth manais* and *sleg*; the Sons of Mil employed the *fogad*, *fogue* and *gae*; the Laigin (Lenstermen) introduced the *laigen*, a 'Gaulish lance' (O'Curry 1873, I ccccxxxvii-viii).
113 TBC¹ 415–17, 578; TBC² 578, 760, 786. Note that in the Irish version of Statius' 'Achilleid' (18), Achilles could shoot an arrow and reach the spot where the arrow landed as fast as the arrow itself.
114 TBC¹ 1512; TBC² 1806–10; TBC³ 216; etc.
115 TBC¹ 1504–5; TBC² 1780, 3349–50.
116 TBC² 1780.
117 TT 13911; CS 196.
118 CRR 51.
119 ACMU 12.
120 MU 739–41; TBDD 128–29.
121 MU 726–33.
122 O'Curry 1873, I ccccxxii.
123 TBC¹ 3608–10; TBC² 4317–21.
124 TBC¹ 19, 3725; 3810–11; TBC² 4337; TBDD 88: 847–50.
125 BM-B 53.
126 TBC¹ 3235–36; 3246–47; TBC² 3696–97.
127 TBC¹ 1503–5.
128 TBC¹ 1512–18; TBC² 1810; TBC³ 216.
129 TBC¹ 1465.
130 TBC¹ 1945–46; TBC³ 73.
131 TBC³ 3099.
132 TBC¹ 3649–50, 3685; TBC² 4403–4
133 TBC¹ 3649–50, 3698; TBC² 2366, 4429, 4382–83.
134 TBC² 4382–83.
135 TBC¹ 3685.
136 TBC¹ 3737; TBC² 4488.
137 TBC¹ 2362.

138 TBC¹ 3330; TBC² 3816–18. There is also the possibility that the spearhead may be 'perforated' (súilech) as in TBC¹ 3660–61; TBC² 4391 although the Stowe version would read 'blood stained' (fulech). If súilech was the intended word, it would literally mean 'eyed' (from súil 'eye') and might suggest a spearhead with one or two open areas, i.e. perforations.

139 For example, SCC 38: 662; TF 240–41, 418–20; SCM 83–84; etc.

140 TBC¹ 2081; TBC² 2130–31; TBC³ 119; etc.

141 TBC² 1780.

142 OMU 488; other spear thrusts in TBF 3–4 (19–25); MU 1023; CRR-B 35–36; etc.

143 TBC¹ 3776; MU 609–10; TBDD 749–50; TBFl II 3–116.

144 TBC² 3679–80, 4454; TBDD 76: 682, 97: 968–69, 979.

145 TBC² 3326.

146 TBC¹ 3214.

147 TBC² 3907.

148 TBC¹ 2719–20.

149 TBC² 4522.

150 TBC² 3108, 3110–11.

151 Etimologia 18; In Cath Catharda 2126–27; Togail na Tebe 2085, 4498

152 TBC¹ 14–15; TBDD 75: 674–75; BDC 9:41; TBFl II 3–14; etc.

153 FC 38.

154 TBC¹ 3221, 3732.

155 TBC² 4530; TEt I 22.

156 DCDM-E 106–8.

157 TF 28–34.

158 Bauersfeld (1933, 319–20) didn't get far with this weapon either (a 5 pointed trident?).

159 Quoted in O'Curry 1873, I ccccxlviii.

160 TBC¹ 2231; TBC² 2248; FBL 22, 27.

161 TBC¹ 2096, 3635; TBC² 2145, 3669; TBC³ 117.

162 TBC² 2363.

163 TBC² 4429–30.

164 TBDD 128: 1230–34.

165 TBDD 1249–52.

166 TBC2 3139–44.

167 TF 421; cf. also TBC³ 2.

168 TBC² 1122–27; TBFl II 4–116.

169 TBC¹ 12, 3264–65, 3600.

170 TBC¹ 3799–800; SC 376.

171 TBC² 3746.

172 TBC¹ 3755 where TBC² 4500 reads murnech 'large' instead of muincech 'neck-rings'.

173 TBC² 1121–22. In TBC¹ 3246, warriors carry a handful of javelins suggesting here that they are not particularly massive (or the three champions of Irúath are really big).

174 TBC¹ 3208.

175 Raftery 1984, 108–10.

176 Hencken (1950, 95) describes a number of medieval spears where ash has survived.

177 Mallory 1992, 137.

178 Raftery 1983, 108–9.

179 Swift 2015, 458–59. This article details many other Norse loans, linguistic and material, in medieval Irish literature.

180 Harrison and Ó Floinn 2015, 98, 107.

181 Harrison and Ó Floinn 2015, 113–14.

182 TBC¹ 2232; TBC² 2249–50.

183 TBC¹ 750–52.

184 TBC² 1102–6.

185 TBC¹ 2025–27.

186 TBC¹ 3095–98.

187 FBL 41.

188 FFF V.

189 AAA 11; FC 52.

190 TBC¹ 2025–27, 3095–98.

191 The anal entry has been interpreted as an act of sodomy, Cú Chulainn effectively feminizing his foster-brother (Sheehan 2009, 61).

192 TBC² 2003–4, 3344–47.

193 FBL 41.

194 TBC¹ 3095–98=TBC² 3344–47.

195 The only artist to come close to depicting its use as described in the tales is Paddy Brown in The Cattle Raid of Cooley, Issue 8, 26–27 where a thin shafted gae bolga is clenched between Cú Chulainn's big and second toe and is directed at an angle back towards himself. Facing Fer Diad in the river, he thrusts his foot between the legs of Fer Diad and kicks upwards, driving the gae bolga through his victim's anus and out his chest.

196 O'Curry 1873, 309–12. Sullivan does not mention the weapon.

197 O'Rahilly 1946, 62–63.

198 Pokorny 1918, 195–204.

199 O'Rahilly 1946, 59–60.

200 Togail na Tebe: XII.4892–94.

201 Thebaid XII.774–76.

202 As interpreted, for example, by Davidson 1989, 20.

203 For example, Hines 1989, 30–31.

204 TBC¹ 680.

205 Taball (TBC¹ 1236; TBC² 2099–100, etc.); tailm (TBC¹ 901, 1182–83).

206 TBC¹ 922–23.

207 TBC² 1344–45.

208 Taball (TBRa 7: 77); tailm (TBC¹ 1864, 2000).

209 AM (LL 14431).

210 AAA 7.

211 AC A6.

212 1 Sam 17:15.

213 Statius' Aeneid (20) indicates Achilles was trained in the sling along with the chariot and archery.

214 Sling stones were recovered from the medieval royal site of Clogher, Co. Fermanagh (R. B. Warner, pers. comm.).

215 Topographia 93.

216 CRR-B 29; TBFl II 1–212; EF-B 242.

217 TBC² 2222; TBC² 2238–39; TBC³ 138.

218 CS 197.

219 Halpin 1997, 51.

220 Expugnatio Hibernica xxxiii (Forester 2001, 77).

221 To the discussion might also be added the mátán wielded by CúRoí (FB 37–38) and the mell (EF-B 248).

222 VS 8.

223 TBC¹ 913.

224 TBC² 1255.

225 CRR 37.

226 TBDD 60: 531–32.

227 TBC¹ 3259–60; MU 628, 775; etc.

228 TBDD 130: 1280–83.

229 CRR 46.

230 In Cath Catharda 241, 389, 429, 431.

231 Topographia 100.

232 FB 76–78, etc.

233 FB 101.

234 TBC¹ 4045–48; TBC² 4740–47; SCMN 17.

235 OMU.

236 TBDD 98: 975–77.

237 SCMN 17.

238 TEt I 22; CCC 10; CRR 17.

239 For example, Page 1959, 232–34; Bowra 1970, 14; but sceptical – Carpenter 1970, 46.

240 The giant Goll pulls the same stunt on Cú Chulainn in AG 20.

241 TBC² 3295–3. A similar gambit is seen when Cú Chulainn does much the same thing against Cairbre in CRR-B 43.

242 TBC² 3348–58.

243 TBC¹ 3611–12; TBC² 4326.

244 TBC¹ 971; TBC² 1136, 2369–70; cf. also TBC¹ 3333; TBC² 3821.

245 OMU 521–22.

246 BM- A 13:272.

247 CRR-B 30. The Irish would also have been acquainted with the Roman tortoise (testudo) formation as it occurs in Lucan's Pharsalia III 474.

248 TBC¹ 3648, 3810, etc.

249 TBC¹ 3323–25; TBC² 3807–8.

250 TBC¹ 3443–44; TBC² 4037–38.

251 TBC² 2561–63.

252 TBC² 2372.

253 TBC¹ 2095; TBC² 2144; TBC³ 120, etc.

254 TBC¹ 3684, 3799.

255 TBDD 51: 460.

256 FB 15.

257 LMU 18: 293–94.

258 For example, fotalscíath (TBC¹ 11, 3219–20); lebar 'long' (TBC² 3229); the woman warrior Scáthach was nicknamed Scíathlethan 'shield-broad' (TBC² 3526).

259 cetheóra benna 'four points' (TBC¹ 4045–48); cethri óeib 'four edges' (TBC² 4740–47). See also TBDD 120 where the conjurers also have four-cornered shields and Eochu Rond carries 'a shield with eight edges of findruine' (sciath co n-ocht n-aislib findruine) FBL 92.

260 cromm (TBC¹ 18–19, 1303–4, 3213–14, 3736; TBC² 4370–71; TBDD 116, 125; TBFl II 2–300); cúar (TBC¹ 3697; TBDD 76: 681–82); cruinn (TBC² 4402–3).

261 O'Curry 1873, I ccccxlv.

262 TBC¹ 3723 does not actually mention a shield but the same passage in TBC² 4452 clarifies that the description does relate to a shield. See also TBDD 75: 674, 91: 882. FB 36 depicts seven bosses about a central boss that is also suggestive of a round shield.

263 TBC¹ 3323–25; TBC² 3807–8.

264 Raftery 1994, 146.

265 Beowulf 2566b.

266 CS 197.

267 Aeneid viii.661–62.

268 TBC¹ 18–19, 3213–14, 3264, etc.

269 TBC¹ 3810; TF 26–28.

270 TBC² 2364–65, 3904–5.

271 TBC¹ 1303–4, 2360–61, etc; FB 45.

272 FB 47.

273 TBC¹ 3745; TBC² 1584–85; TBDD 120, etc.
274 TBC¹ 3219–20, 3684, etc.
275 TBC¹ 2095; TBC² 2144; TE2–300.
276 TBC¹ 3660; FB 45.
277 AG 10.
278 BDC 46:352.
279 TBDD 51:460.
280 TF-E 29.
281 TBC² 3904–5.
282 TBC¹ 2360–61; TBDD 75:674.
283 TBC¹ 3272–73, 3762, etc.
284 TBC² 3093–94.
285 TF 26–28. There is also a shield with rivets of *findruine* and plates of gold (TBDD 97:966–68).
286 *Aeneid* x.243, 271
287 *Aeneid* xi.11
288 *Aeneid* x:479–83.
289 2 Sam 8:7; 1 Kgs 10:16–17, 14:26; etc.
290 1 Kgs 14:27.
291 TBC¹ 2196–98=TBC² 2212–13=TBC³ 136; also TBC¹ 2238; TBC³ 138; CRR-B 27; CS 197; etc.
292 Miles 2011, 202–3.
293 TBC¹ 2196–98; TBC² 2212–13; TBC³ 136; CRR-B 27.
294 TBFl II 2–160.
295 TBC² 3254–57; TBFl II 3–302; TT 170:34–35.
296 CS 197.
297 BM-B 37.
298 FBL 41.
299 *cennide* (SMMD 15); *celbarr* (TF 8); *eobarr* (AmCR 3) 'boar-helmet'?
300 TBFr 3:32.
301 CRR-B 27; TBFl II 2–208, 2–308, etc.; TEm III 79; BM-B 33.
302 TBC¹ 2204–6; TBC² 2220–23.
303 FBL 41.
304 TBC¹ 2027.
305 ACMU 8; SMMD 7.
306 TBC¹ 2571; TBC² 2614–15, 2749, 3034.
307 TBC² 3350–51.
308 CMT1 48.
309 CMT1 48.
310 CMT1 35 (*clasaib comarthacha na cloidem*).
311 CM1 35 (*brecclann*).
312 Sandberg-McGowan (1996, 220) emphasizes that pattern-welded blades are not exclusively Viking but rather Germanic, manufactured by the Franks and exported to the rest of Europe.
313 O'Curry 1873, ii, 236.
314 CMT1 25; *maela troma tiubremra uille eochairgera*
315 CMT1 31.
316 CMT1 24, 35, 48.
317 CMT1 48.
318 CMT1 36.
319 CMT1 57 (*sceth drolacha*).
320 CMT1 31.
321 CMT2 16.
322 CMT2 34.
323 CMT2 122; *colg ndét* in CMT2 131.
324 CMT2 162.
325 CMT2 97.
326 CMT2 101.
327 CMT2 103.
328 CMT2 127.
329 CMT2 135.
330 CMT2 131.

331 CMT2 77.
332 CMT2 142–45.
333 CMT2 105.
334 Laing 1975, 287.

CHAPTER EIGHT (pp. 207–28)

1 DBG 4.33.
2 DBG 4.33; Dio Cassius 76.12.
3 *Agricola*, 1.35–36.
4 O'Curry 1873, I cccclxxv. Sullivan mistakenly believed that the Irish word for chariot was a loanword from Latin when it actually continues the earlier Celtic word for 'chariot' and it is Latin that has borrowed the word from the continental Celts. Welsh *cerbyd* 'chariot' was borrowed from Irish (Greene 1972, 61).
5 For example, Ridgeway 1905–6; Jackson 1964:35.
6 Raftery 1984, 15–16.
7 Jope 1955; Haworth 1971.
8 Raftery 1994, 107.
9 Raftery 1993, 176.
10 Mäder 1995–96, 38–40.
11 Maguire 2014.
12 Mäder 1995–96, 36.
13 Laing 1975, 258–59.
14 De Leeuw 2008.
15 Kelly, F. 1997, 538.
16 Stifter 2009, 283.
17 Kavanagh 1991, 98–119.
18 Stifter 2009, 285.
19 There is also a much discussed word *cul* which has been taken to be a more archaic word for chariot by some (see Sayers 1991, 19) but this interpretation has been challenged by Stifter 2009, 280, who only allows it to be associated with the semantic field of 'chariot'. The few instances in which it occurs does not offer any basis for archaeological discussion.
20 TBRa 2: 15–16.
21 Sayers 1981.
22 CMT2 711–23; see Sayers 1991, 29–35 for a list and an attempt to recover the meaning of each name.
23 LTRR 14.
24 CRR 30, 32; TT 168–28.
25 TBC¹ 2204 etc; TBC² 2220 etc; TBC³ 136.
26 Sayers 2014, 86–87.
27 Lucian in his *Zeuxis* 8 mentions the Celtic tribe of the Galatians employing chariots with sickles. Dismissal of the Irish evidence as borrowed from such sources can be found in Greene 1972, 59–60. In TEm III 85 it is suggested that the scythed chariot might be named after its inventors, the Serians; it also occurs in BM-B 35 and although this appears to be Cú Chulainn's special vehicle, there is a remark that Eógan would not have travelled without thirty such scythed chariots (TBC¹ 368–69; TBC³ 133). For classical sources see Statius' *Thebaid* (vii.712) which the Irish certainly knew but curiously enough did not include in their own translation and the descriptions of Darius' scythed chariot in the story of Alexander.

28 TBC¹ 3310–14.
29 CCC 1 – see Chapter 2. Cf. *Aeneid* xii.918 where the chariot of Turnus was driven by his sister.
30 Sayers 1991, 18.
31 TBC¹ 137–38; the warriors of Irúath (Norway?) also travelled in a squadron of nine chariots (TBC¹ 3999–4000).
32 TBC² 580–85.
33 TBC¹ 648–55; TBC² 964–77.
34 TBC¹ 1877–89, 2594.
35 TBC¹ 2594; see also TBC² 41, 86.
36 TBC² 2360; see also 1970.
37 TBC¹ 27–28.
38 TBC¹ 806.
39 SCM 25–27.
40 SCM 19–22.
41 FB 45, 47, 50; TEm 14; TBC¹ 2707f; TBC² 2944f; CS; BM-B 32; SC; see Mallory 1998.
42 Watkins 1963, 231–32.
43 FB 47.
44 TBC¹ 2944–47.
45 For example, the precise meaning of *fertas* which is taken to indicate 'swingle-tree' in Sayers 1984; but challenged in Kelly 1997.
46 Stifter 2009, 281–87.
47 Greene 1972, 65. Note that there are many other terms associated with the chariot such as *essi* 'reins' (TBC¹ 727 etc); *anbluth* 'awning'? (FB 45, 47); *pupall* 'tent' (TBC¹ 3850, etc.); *forgaimen* 'rug in chariot' (TBC¹ 3371–72, etc); *fortche* 'rug in chariot' (TBC¹ 3371–72; FB 24, etc); *suide* 'seat' (TBC¹ 1054–55, etc.); *fochla* 'champion's seat in a chariot' (AG 48); *sosad* 'seat' (TBC¹ 2948).
48 Karl 2003, 20.
49 Sayers 1991, 26 takes this more as a metaphor for 'brilliance' rather than a reference to material of construction; see also Sayers 1991 where *lungeta* is possibly interpreted as one of the horse-trappings that range from bits to terrets.
50 The other tales are BM-A 12; BM-B 35; MU 271; SMMD 20; TF 1151; and non-formulaic descriptions in TBC¹ 1151, 2306, 2918, 2956; TBC² 2861; TBFl II 1–308, 2–26.
51 FB 45, 47, 50.
52 TBC¹ 2944–56; TBC² 2916.
53 TF 16–20; CCC 196; TBF II 1–308, 2–26; BM-B 32; CS 196.
54 TBC¹ 1151–52.
55 FB 47; TEm III 11.
56 FB 50.
57 CCC 196.
58 TBC¹ 792; 2299–301; TBC² 1170, 2306–8; TBC³ 160; MU 271; BM-B 35; AG 32.
59 TBC² 1221.
60 SC 376; FB 47 (mountings), 50; TEm III 14.
61 TEm III 14; SC 376 (ring or mounting of *findruine* on pole).
62 TBC¹ 2956; FB 50 (bronze mounting on silver pole).
63 CS 196.
64 TBC¹ 2708–9, 2944–47; TBC² 2916.
65 BM-B 32.
66 TEm III 14.

67 TBC¹ 2707, 2944–45; TBC² 2916; FB 50; TEm III 14; SC 376.
68 TBC¹ 1151–52, 2918; TBC² 2861; FB 45.
69 TBC¹ 2956–57; SMMD 20.
70 TBC¹ 2978.
71 TBC¹ 2944–47; TBC² 2916.
72 TBFr 3:27–28, 14:164; TF 12–16; FBL 97; TBD 3:39.
73 TBD 3: 39, 4:58; TF 12–16; DCDM-E 97.
74 TBC¹ 2708–9, 2944–47; TBC² 2916.
75 TBC¹ 2970–71.
76 BM-B 32; CS 197.
77 The best comparisons from the Bible are: 'The wheels were designed like chariot wheels: their axles, fellies, spokes and naves had all been cast' (1 Kgs 7.33) and a description of Solomon's palanquin with 'posts made of silver, the canopy of gold, the seat of purple; the centre is inlaid with ebony' (Cant 3.9–10), Mallory 1998, 460. Sayers (1991, 20) suggests that the Bible may have provided a template for describing how the charioteer 'levelled' the plain (Isa. 30: 4–5).
78 *Iliad* 5.721–32.
79 *Metamorphoses* 2.107–9.
80 Sidonius (XI. *Epithalmium* 93–107).
81 TBC¹ 2944–56.
82 Clarke (2009, 240) also remarks that the *Táin* resembles the *Iliad* better than the usual Latin sources despite the lack of a serious knowledge of Greek among the Irish.
83 Greene 1972, 70.
84 Karl 2003, 13.
85 We also have *bélbach* 'bridle' (MU 285); *bellec* 'bridle-bit' (TBFr 3:27–28, 14: 164; FBL 97 [all described as of gold]; *glomraige* 'bits' (TBC2 4207; MU 285, etc.); *pellec* 'bridle-bit' (TBD 4: 58 [of silver]).
86 Greene 1972, 69.
87 Raftery 1983, 12, item 8.
88 Kavanaugh 1991, 98–100; Harrison and Ó Floinn 2015, 189.
89 Raftery 1993, 176.
90 TEm III 27.
91 TBC¹ 2707, 2944–45; FB 50; TEm III 14; SC 376.
92 TBC¹ 1151, 2918; TBC² 2861; FB 45.
93 Sayers 2014, 85.
94 Karl 2003, 20.
95 Sidonius (XI. *Epithalmium* 94–96).
96 Watkins 1963, 219–20.
97 TBC¹ 1405, 1443.
98 TBC¹ 1755; TBC2 1880.
99 SMMD 17 (Rawl.).
100 TBC² 183, 1944.
101 TBC² 2915.
102 CRR 13.
103 *Aeneid* viii 642, x 571, xii 162 and then reintroduced into translations of classical literature such as Statius' *Achilleid* which, though the Latin version lacks any reference to chariots, the Irish felt compelled to insert references to two and four-horse chariots (*Achilleid* 18). See also *Ephemeridos* iii.17; *In Cath Catharda* 20, 245.
104 Greene 1972, 61.

105 Greene 1972, 61.
106 Matasović 2009, 256–57.
107 TBC¹ 1166, 1169.
108 TBC² 3400.
109 FBL 94–96; see also 219, 224.
110 TBD 3: 36.
111 AC-A 10.
112 TBDD 30: 228, 291; on some occasions one might also treat the references to 'horsemen' as teams of horses (see Sayers 1991, 20).
113 TEt I: 131 (14–15); etc.
114 TBFr 3: 26–27; see also TT 170: 18.
115 E.g., TBC2 4009; BM-A 14120; BM-B 44, 48.
116 CE 50; RR-B 23; TBFl II 3–16; DCDM-E 96, 145–46; etc.
117 TF 18.
118 *Agricola* 35–36.
119 Raftery 1993, 177.
120 Kelly, F. 1997, 390.
121 For example, *conar* 'way, road, path' (TBC¹ 2972); *fordul* 'road, path' (TBC¹ 249, 253); *raite* 'road/path?'; *roit* 'path, way' (TBC¹ 3801–2); *rót* 'road' (TBDD 14: 157).
122 TBC¹ 1008–10; see also TBC² 1369.
123 TBDD 27: 157.
124 SCC 47:831–32.
125 BDC 28:195.
126 TBDD 13:151, 14: 157.
127 BDC 31:228.
128 CRR 5; cf. CRR-B 5.
129 TBC¹ 3801–2.
130 TEt 7–8.
131 Warner 1990.
132 Warner 1990, 31.
133 Ó hÓgain 1996, 366. Although the best attested location for Móin Lámraige would be further north in Fermanagh-Monaghan, the other tasks accomplished by Midir were in Longford in the vicinity of Corlea as well as the seat of Midir at Brí Leith near Ardagh, only a few miles from Corlea.
134 Raftery 1996, 418.
135 Ó hÓgain 1996, 359.
136 Although the RIA dictionary compares *curach* with Lat *curūca*, the word is probably native Celtic as we also have Welsh *corwg* 'coracle' and the word is reconstructed to Proto-Celtic by Matasović 2009, 217.
137 BF 5.
138 CCL 124.
139 LG xxiv.802.
140 TBDD 53: 475, 55: 497–98, 87: 816–18.
141 AG 9, 41.
142 BF 35.
143 FBL 128, 141.
144 IT 26; some other references are TBDD 17:183, 56: 503, 58: 514; DCDM-E 215; CCC 27.
145 CRR 8; EF-B 250; CCC 27.
146 OMU 139.
147 TBC¹ 2275; TBC² 2291; TBC³ 153.
148 CRR 11; IT 118.
149 TBDD 65; TL 6; CRR-B 12.
150 AAA 2 (with gilt oars).
151 CCS 4.
152 SCC 15:152.
153 For example, bronze ship (*Aeneid* viii 675); bronze prow (*Aeneid* i.35, x 223).

154 TEm III 46.
155 ACR I 9; TEm III 46.
156 AG 10; CCC 27.
157 OMU 309.
158 AAA 2.
159 AG 9.
160 TBC¹ 1306.
161 TBC¹ 2275; TBC² 2291; TBC³ 153; FC 16; BM-B 34; NC 60.
162 TBDD 48:434, 53: 476.
163 CRR 11; FBL 141.
164 O'Sullivan and Breen 2007, 137–49.

CHAPTER NINE (pp. 229–53)

1 Owen-Crocker 2004, 20.
2 TBC¹ 10–17.
3 Whitfield 2006, 11. St Boniface, however, attributed the wearing of purple among monks as a sign of homosexual proclivities (Owen-Crocker 2004, 172).
4 Whitfield 2006, 12. The loan could even be earlier.
5 Which might be worn over the *léine* according to Dunleavy (1989, 21), although often enough it occurs in place of the *léine* in many of the Ulster cycle descriptions. Fitzgerald (1997, 259) treats it as a shorter tunic that was introduced by the Vikings.
6 It is described as next to the skin of its wearer, e.g., TBC² 4427, 4471, etc.
7 Dunlevy 1989, 17–18.
8 TBC¹ 13–14, 17–18, 30–31, etc.
9 DCDM-E 137–38.
10 TBFr 3:19–20.
11 For example, TBC¹ 17–18; TBDD 132: 1304–5; TEm III 15; etc.
12 TEm III 27.
13 TBC² 3730.
14 TEt-Eg 3; TBDD 1:8–10 (Étaín wears green silk).
15 Another word for tunic was *cliabnar* and Cú Chulainn wore a silky satin one in TBC¹ 2358.
16 Owen-Crocker 2004, 133 quoting Bede.
17 TBC² 2361–64; TBC³ 176.
18 LMU 18:287–90; TBC¹ 2358; BDC 10:42; CRR-B 27.
19 TBC¹ 2190–92; TBC² 2206–8; TBC³ 194.
20 TBFr 16: 185.
21 BDC 10:43–44.
22 SMMD 16; CE58.
23 AC-A 4.
24 ACR II 3.
25 TBC² 2235–38.
26 Cf. also *Aeneid* v 404–5, xii 925; *Ilias Latina* 293.
27 *Ilias Latina* 293. We also find boxing gloves of seven oxhides (v 404–5) and shields (xii 925) in the *Aeneid* and a similar shield in the Irish version of Statius' *Achilleid* (17).
28 SCMG 28–29.
29 TBC¹ 3659, 3796–98; TBC² 4392; TBDD 61: 539.
30 TBDD 28: 268' cf. also TT 175–20. In the very late TBFl II 2–106, Fergus promises his retinue 300 mantles.
31 CCC I (LU) 3.
32 Owen-Crocker 2004, 179.
33 TBC¹ 2969–70; BDC 8:36.

34 CS 197; BM-B 32.
35 TBDD 114, 120, 121, 124, 166; AmCR 5.
36 E.g., TBC¹ 2224–28, 2358–60; TBC² 2241–45, 3356; TBC³ 138; MU 20:644–45; TBDD 123, 126, 127, etc.
37 TBC² 3356.
38 Bender Jørgensen 1992, 19; a sample of horsehair has also been recovered from Iron Age contexts (20).
39 Ó Floinn 1995.
40 Doyle 2015, 90.
41 Owen-Crocker 2004, 19.
42 Whitfield 2004, 70; 2006, 11.
43 Whitfield 2004; 2006.
44 Whitfield 2006.
45 TBC¹ 1302–3.
46 Bender Jørgensen 1992, 22.
47 Bender Jørgensen 1992, 145.
48 Whitfield 2006, 9; Bender Jørgensen 1992, 36, 39, 40; Dunleavy 1989 22.
49 Doyle 2015, 90.
50 Whitfield 2006, 25.
51 Fitzgerald 1997, 259.
52 Mallory 1992, 141.
53 Raftery 1994, 127–28.
54 Hawkes 1981, 70.
55 Fitzgerald 1997, 260.
56 Doyle 2015, 90.
57 TBC² 187.
58 TBC¹ 3595, 3723–24, 3808–9; TBC² 1204, 4393; MU 586; TBDD 91:877, 124; TBD 4:53–54.
59 TBC¹ 3659–60; TBC² 4520.
60 TBC¹ 3695–96.
61 TBD 4:53–54.
62 TBC¹ 2598–99, 3617; TBC² 3719, 4334–35.
63 TBC¹ 2674; TBC² 2704.
64 TBC¹ 31, 2598–99, 3774, 3797; TBC² 166–67, 44381, 563–64; TBDD 27:270–71 (gilded); 119; CE 50; TEt I 6; FBL 149, 170; SCC 33:508; CCC 5.
65 TBC¹ 819, 3215, 3683, 3822; TBC² 158, 3668, 3688–89, 4369; TBC³ 175; AmCR 5; TBDD 125; CCC 5.
66 TBC¹ 3617; TBC² 3719, 4334–35.
67 TBDD 107:1149.
68 TBDD 137:1364.
69 TBC² 166–67, 1583.
70 TBC¹ 1302–3, 3605, 3636; TBC² 2634, 3470, 4306, 4539–40; TBC³ 120; FB 51 (inlaid gold); TEm III 15, 30; TEt I 22; BM-B 22.
71 CRR-B 23; TBDD 114, 118; TT 175–21–22.
72 TBC² 4404.
73 DCDM-E 99–100.
74 TBC² 1490.
75 TBC² 2093; TBC² 2142, 3708, 3729, 4315, 4470; TBFl II 2–208.
76 TBC¹ 3735.
77 TBDD 1:7.
78 SC 376.
79 MU 490–91.
80 BDC 10:45; TF 24–25; TBFr 3:19; TEt-E 3; CS 197; MU 533–34.
81 TBDD 75:673; BDC 8:15, 10:45, 46:357.
82 BDC 9:40.
83 MU 533–34.
84 AmCR I 3.
85 TBDD 99:999–101.
86 TBC¹ 3783.
87 TBC¹ 3754; TBC² 4499.

88 TBFr 3:29–30.
89 TBFr 3:29–30.
90 TBFr 3:29–30.
91 TBDD 681.
92 TBDD 1:10–12; TEt-E 3.
93 TBDD 1:10–12; TEt-E 3.
94 TBDD 137: 1364.
95 TBC¹ 3735.
96 Whitfield 2004, 73.
97 See Mallory 1986; Whitfield 2006, 13.
98 Whitfield 2006, 13–14.
99 Whitfield 2006, 18.
100 The precise meaning of this word is not secure, but suggests a curved (túag) ornament.
101 Raftery 1994, 138.
102 Whitfield 2004, 94.
103 Doyle 2015, 94.
104 Whitfield 2004, 73.
105 TBC¹ 3783; TBDD 99:999–101.
106 cred 'tin; bronze': TBC¹ 3754; TBC² 4499.
107 Medb: TBC¹ 2598–99; Sencha: TBC¹ 3617; TBC² 4334–35; Cormac: TBC² 3719; Cú Chulainn: SC 376.
108 Ridgeway 1905–6.
109 Jackson 1964, 17.
110 Hawkes 1981, 70.
111 These also date from the 9th to 12th centuries (Doyle 2015, 94).
112 TBC¹ 3279.
113 TBC² 2462, 2464.
114 TBC¹ 1593, 2150, etc.
115 TBC² 584, 1344–45.
116 TF 50.
117 TBFr 3:35–36.
118 CS 197.
119 TBC¹ 2199–200; TBC² 2215–16; TBC³ 136; TEm III 16; SC 376; BM-B 32.
120 TBC¹ 2199–200; TBC² 2215–16; TBC³ 136.
121 TBDD 113.
122 TBDD 124.
123 DCDM-E 102–3.
124 Raftery 1984, 268–75.
125 Dobbs 1912, 11.
126 Cóir Anman 256: dá bheinn airgit ⁊ beann óir robhói asa chathbharr.
127 TBC¹ 3279.
128 I am sure that Richard Warner will offer a different interpretation.
129 Whitfield 2006, 28–29.
130 EN 8:70–71.
131 TBC¹ 3279.
132 BDC 19:96.
133 TBFl II 2–208.
134 DCDM-E 102–3; also rígbarr 'royal head covering' as gloss in AmCR 5.
135 CS 197.
136 BM-B 32.
137 TBC¹ 2199–200; TBC² 2215–16; TBC³ 136.
138 TEm III 16; SC 376.
139 TBC² 2462, 2464.
140 TBC¹ 2199–200; TBC² 2215–16; TBC³ 136; TBDD 113, 115, 124.
141 TBC¹ 2150, etc.; TBC² 2172; TBC³ 129.
142 TF 50 (druids); TBFr 3:35–36 (jesters).
143 TEt I 22.
144 Raftery 1984, 198.
145 Owen-Crocker 2004, 127, 147.
146 TBC¹ 2622; TBC² 2638.
147 DCDM-E 105.
148 MU 705–6.

149 TBDD 119.
150 Raftery 1984, 194–97.
151 Whitfield 2006, 31–33.
152 AmCR 4.
153 TBC¹ 3245.
154 Raftery 1984, 192–94.
155 Whitfield 2006, 18–20.
156 Cessford 1995, 237.
157 TBC¹ 2622; TBC² 2638; DCDM-E 105.
158 MU 705–6.
159 TBDD 119.
160 TBFr 20:236.
161 TBC¹ 3245.
162 ?AmCR 4 but glossed foilge 'arm-ring?'
163 CCL 124.
164 TEm III 76; CCL 124.
165 TBC² 58.
166 TBDD 119; AAA 1; FBL 188–89.
167 TBC¹ 3114–15.
168 Mallory 2009.
169 AG 48.
170 TEt I 21.
171 AmCR 4; glossed uma.
172 TBFl II 2–104.
173 TBFl II 2–104.
174 AmCR 4.
175 SMMD 1; FBL 176; TBDD 87: 813.
176 SCC 4:46; TBDD 128:1234–35.
177 AG 10.
178 FB 91.
179 EF-B 244.
180 ACR I 2; CRR-B 26.
181 TF 405–6.
182 TF 405–6.
183 FBL 162; AG 30.
184 EF-B 241.
185 TF 405 (with gold and silver engraving).
186 FB 62, 73.
187 TBDD 139: 1384–85; CCon II 42.
188 TBDD 148: 1449–50.
189 FBL 166; AG 30.
190 TBC¹ 3235; AG 9.
191 FB 59 with bird chased in findruine on base; glossed brazen.
192 FB 60 with bird chased in gold.
193 FB 62, 73 with base chased in precious stones; TBDD 148: 1449–50, 154: 1457–58.
194 TEm III 60.
195 TBC¹ 815–16; TBC² 1193–96; FB 53, 54; SCC 36:596–99; BM-A 1:4.
196 FB 9; TF 196–99.
197 SCC 33:510.
198 TF 748.
199 TF 196–97, 847, etc.
200 EF-B 238 (colour of red yew).
201 TF 403–4 (silver rims).
202 TBFl II 2–104.
203 AG 30.
204 TBC² 57; cf. MD (Bend Etair II) 32 (MD vol. 3, 112).
205 DCDM-E 185–86; CCI (LU); CCI (Eg) 5.
206 AG 48.
207 TBDD 1:4–6.
208 TBDD 1:4–6; TEt-E 3.
209 TBFr 23:285.
210 It is later described as a silver bird in FB 73, 74.
211 FB 59, 60, 62, 73.
212 TF 405.
213 Matošović 2009, 126.
214 There are a few other inherited words for vessels in early Irish that are not in

the Ulster tales that are discussed in Mallory 2009.

215 Gen 44:2; Num 7:13, 19, 25, etc; 2 Kings 12:13; etc.

216 Raftery 1984, 222–23.

217 *Thebaid* I.540–41.

218 *Togail na Tebe* 486.

219 Raftery 1995.

220 Campbell 2007.

221 Mallory 2009, 185–87. A possible exception is reference to *brisc brúar* in BDC which Toner (page 199) translates as something like 'broken pot sherds', and he also calls attention to Adamnán dropping a *ballán* of milk which falls and breaks into pieces. But in both cases, a wooden bowl could fracture very much the same way.

222 McSparron, in press.

223 CE 54:5.

224 ATDM 6:33. St Brigit was also reputedly sustained from the milk of a white cow with red ears.

225 E.g., TBDD 119.

226 E.g., LMU 17:225; TEm III 92.

227 TEt I 17.

228 E.g., TBC² 4339–40.

229 TBF II 4–112.

230 TBFr 91–96.

231 http://www.bbc.co.uk/news/uk-scotland-highlands-islands-17537147

232 TBC¹ 415–16, 501–2, 534–35, etc.

233 TBC² 758–59.

234 TBC¹ 552–56.

235 TBC¹ 758–59.

236 TBC² 882.

237 http://www.ancient-origins.net/news-history-archaeology/archaeologists-china-unearth-2400-year-old-polo-sticks-and-balls-003066

238 TBC¹ 471–72, etc.

239 TT 168:809.

240 Ó Maolfabhail 1973, 2.

241 MacWhite (1945) is usually regarded as the first major study while Niehues (2011) provides the most recent survey of the literature.

242 TBFr 8:83–85.

243 TEt III 152.

244 Niehues 2011, 51.

245 CMT2 69:281–85. Note that *fidchell* is also ascribed to the Trojan War in *Togail Troi* 218–19.

246 Niehues 2011, 54.

247 Hencken 1938; Niehues 2011, 48–50; Harrison and Ó Floinn (2015, 201) describe four Viking whalebone gaming pieces that may have been employed in *hnefetafl*, the main Viking tablut-type game and most likely relative of *brandub*.

248 *slabrad* on a hound (TBC¹ 572–73; TBDD 28:274; BDC 45:343; TF 45–47; TBFr 3:31–32; AmCR 3); *conarach* on a hound (TBC² 867); *rond* on a heifer (TBC² 1993–94).

249 *Rond* (TBC¹ 3241); *cengal* (TEm III 30; MU 659); *slabrad* (TBFl 3–10).

250 SCC 7:59–60; AD 3; TBFl II 2–102.

251 CC1 Lu2; AA 8.

252 Raftery 1994, 115.

253 Isaiah 40:19.

254 Mahr and Raftery 1932–41, 126.

255 Gold: SCC 7:59–60; AD 3; silver: CCC I (LU) 2.

256 Bøe 1940, 73.

257 Hencken 1950–51, 115–17.

258 Stevenson and Emery 1963–64, 209; Henderson 1967, 212.

259 FB 52; see also TBC² 3306, 4801–2; FB 52.

260 TBC¹ 1269–70.

261 FB 80.

262 TBDD 107:1151; 127:1216.

263 FB 87.

264 FB 37; TBDD 85:794–95.

265 FB 52.

266 TBDD 85:794–95.

267 *eó* (TBC² 4404); *brotga* (TBC² 1490); *roth* (TBC¹ 3754=TBC² 4499); *muirnech* (ACR I 3).

268 SCMG 28–37.

269 Daniel Binchy regarded it as a later re-editing of a tale from around the 9th century (SCMG xiv-xvi).

CHAPTER TEN (pp. 255–72)

1 Cited in O'Brien, E. 1992a, 133.

2 TBC¹ 1385–86.

3 TF 756–58.

4 CMT1 39.

5 AFM AM 2242.

6 TBC² 4581–82.

7 Bhreathnach 2010, 24.

8 Bhreathnach 2010, 24–28.

9 TBDD 164.

10 For example, 'Dumhadh Daigh is the name of the place where he [Daigh] was slain, and there he was buried' (CRR-B 72).

11 TBDD 164.

12 CF 19.

13 CLR 9.

14 O'Curry 1873, I cccxx-cccxxi.

15 TBC² 3030.

16 BDC 65:523; TL 27.

17 CLR 9; OMU 584–85.

18 TBC¹ 1005–6; ACMU 12.

19 TF 756–57; also OMU 637.

20 BDC 57:467.

21 TF 699.

22 BM-A 24:87.

23 BM-A 24:87–88.

24 DSCM 87–90.

25 This word lacks a solid etymology but the *Lexique étymologique de l'irlandais ancien* (C-154) hazards a guess that it may derive from *cor* 'putting, placing, setting up', i.e., something that has been erected.

26 The ancient word derives from a Proto-Celtic *līwank-* 'stone, pillar' (Matasović 2009, 242) from a Proto-Indo-European root *leh₁w- 'stone' with cognates in Greek *lâas* 'stone' and Albanian *lerë* 'rubble' (Mallory and Adams 2006, 122). Although the word has a possible cognate in Gaulish (*lawā* as in Gallo-Latin *lausiae* 'pebbles in a quarry') there is no evidence that it indicated a stone pillar or was associated with burials in any other language than Irish.

27 TBC¹ I; TBC² 2385.

28 TBC¹ 2566.

29 ACon A-6.

30 ACMU 12.

31 AD 122.

32 TBC¹ 2522.

33 TBC² 2528–29.

34 TBC¹ 1005–6; cf. TBC² 1357–58.

35 FTBC LL 32887.

36 BM-B 58.

37 It derives from Proto-Celtic *karno-* 'heap of stones, tomb', and is also found in Brittonic, e.g., Middle Welsh *carn*, Middle Breton *Pen karn* (place name).

38 TBC¹ 696–97. Bhreathnach (2010, 24) identifies this cairn with Fincarn Hill, Co. Monaghan.

39 CRR-B 5.

40 BF 18.

41 TF 105.

42 CF 17.

43 ACMU 9.

44 O'Curry 1873, I cccxxix.

45 TBDD 67.

46 TBDD 168.

47 DSCM 87.

48 See O'Curry 1873, I cccxxxix-xl; O'Brien, E. 2008b.

49 O'Mulchrony's glossary defines it as a *tulach*, i.e., 'mound, hillock' while *aiminn* is glossed in the laws as a *suide dála* 'convention seat, judgement seat'.

50 There is a Gaulish *dumio-* 'hill, barrow' which appears as the by-name of Mercury (*Dumiatis*) and also a place name in Spain (*Dumium*) and may be derived from the same root that gives Old Irish *dóe* 'rampart, circumvallation' (Delamarre 2003, 154).

51 *Ro claided úag do Feirb iarsin, 7 ro tócbad a lia 7 ro scríbad ainm oguim, 7 doringned duma immon licc, conid Duma Ferbi a ainm ri Ráith Ini, aniartuáid atá.* (TF 756–58).

52 The clause *doringned duma immon licc* is translated by E. Windisch (1897) in the critical edition as 'und ein Wall wurde um den Stein gemacht'.

53 CF 17.

54 There are some remaining examples that derive from the very late version of the *Tochmarc Flidaise* where the *duma* occurs in the same context as *fert*, e.g., 'his [Torna's] tomb (*fert*) was dug and his lament made. And they made a very great mound (*dumha mór*) over [his grave] which is called the mound of Torna (*duma Torna*) since' (TBFl II 3–116; cf. also 3–122).

55 'There is some doubt about the true meaning of …*Fert*', Sullivan (1873, cccxxix).

56 It derives from Proto-Celtic *wertyā* 'mound', and is built on the same root that provides Middle Welsh *gweryd* 'earth, soil, grave' although that word derives from *wereto-*. Ultimately, these words come from the Indo-European root *h₂wer-* 'cover' (Matasović 2009, 415).

57 TBC1 3591. But the same description is also employed elsewhere in the meaning of burial mound, e.g., 'do thou see his burial mound (*fert fodbuigh*) be heaped for him' (TE II (Edgerton) 8) or in a very late tale, e.g., 'they built a turf grave (*fert fodbaidh*) over him [Donald

303

Yellowlocks]' (TBFl II 4–212; see also TBFl II 3–312 verse).

58 TBC¹ 894. Also, 'Cú Chulainn took up position at the mound (*fert*) in Lerga' (TBC¹ 2076), 'to Fiachna at his mound (*fert*)' (TBC¹ 3464).

59 Fitzpatrick 2004, 48–49.

60 Warner 2004.

61 TBC¹ 1385–86; TBC² 1357–58, AD 122*, TE II (Edgerton) 8, EF-B 252.28–31, SCMN 14; AAA 13; TBFl II 3–20 and in reverse order TL 27.

62 TL 25.

63 OMU 675–76.

64 O'Brien, E. 1992a, 133.

65 Bhreathnach 2010, 27–28.

66 Unfortunately, most of the instances where a *fert* is described in the Ulster tales merely indicates that a *fert* has been made, not how it was made. The commonest verb to describe its creation is *claidid* which can mean 'digs, excavates' where the attention is on the removal of earth (see also *clad* 'ditch, trench' and *claide* 'digging out, trenching') which all might well support the idea of a ditched enclosure (see also O'Brien, E. 2008a, 297). But *claidid* also means 'builds, constructs (a grave mound, rampart)' and *clad* can also mean earthen rampart' while *claide* can also refer to 'building an earthen rampart' (DIL C 214). We can only note that there is only one very late text in the Ulster cycle that employs both *duma* 'mound' and *fert* in the same context: 'his tomb (*fert*) was dug and his lament made. And they made a very great mound (*dumha mór*) over [his grave] which is called the mound of Torna (*duma Torna*) since' (TBFl II 3–116; see also TBFl II 3–122). It is very unlikely that this conserves an archaic description (they first dig an embanked enclosure (*fert*) and then build a mound (*duma*) in the centre) as the two are not so juxtaposed in any of the earlier sources nor is the sequence of monuments likely. Rather, it is more likely that *fert* here simply means 'grave'.

67 TEt II 4.

68 AAA 13.

69 CF 19.

70 McGarry 2010, 176–77.

71 O'Brien 1992, 131; 2009, 138.

72 O'Brien, E. 1999, 27.

73 Dickinson and Härke 1992, 63.

74 O'Brien, E. 1993.

75 Bøe 1940, 33–38; Harrison and Ó Floinn (2015, 116) record 34 shield bosses from Viking graves in Ireland.

76 Ezekiel 32:27.

77 Collins 1957.

78 Mallory 1984.

79 O'Sullivan and Harney 2008, 150.

80 McCormick et al. 1995.

81 McCormick et al. 1995, 93.

82 O'Sullivan and Harney 2008, 148.

83 O'Sullivan and Harney 2008, 150.

84 Ó Cróinin 1995, 34–36.

85 McManus 1991, 55–61.

86 Swift 1997.

87 Ogam stones in Wales, erected by Irish colonists, date back to the 5th

century at least and are bilingual (ogam Irish and Latin) and indicate their function as memorial stones.

88 Edwards 1990, 103.

89 McManus 1991, 49.

90 Mytum 1992, 96.

91 McManus 1991, 155.

92 Swift 1997.

93 Russell et al. 2002; Russell 2012.

94 O'Sullivan and Harney 2008, 152.

95 O'Brien, E. 1992a, 134–35.

96 O'Brien, E. 1992a, 130.

97 Eogan, J. 2012, 107; Delaney et al. 2012, 93.

98 Sweetman 1982–83, 67.

99 Edwards 1990, 188.

100 See O'Brien, E. 2009, for examples of this practice.

101 Wilson, Standish and O'Brien 2012, 138.

102 Wilson, Standish and O'Brien 2012, 140.

103 See O'Brien, E. 2008a, 288–89 for examples from outside the Ulster cycle.

104 O'Brien 2008b, 325.

105 *Aeneid* iii.63, vii.6, xi.103, xi.853.

106 *Ilias Latina* 1048; also *Ephemeridos* ii.41, iii.12, iv.8, iv.18

107 *Imtheachta Aeniasa* 87–89.

CHAPTER ELEVEN (pp. 273–89)

1 Roosevelt 1924, 387.

2 Gen 4.20–22.

3 Gen 9.20.

4 Gen 10.8.

5 *Sex Aetates*

6 *De Rerum Natura* 5.1240–50.

7 *De Rerum Natura* 5.1300.

8 http://www.tertullian.org/fathers/jerome_chronicle_00_eintro.htm

9 http://ebooks.cambridge.org/chapter.jsf?bid=CBO9780511482113&cid=CBO9780511482113A041&tabName=Chapter&imageExtract=

10 Jackson 1964, 38.

11 Jackson 1964, 55.

12 Koch 1994, 229.

13 Diodorus Siculus (citing Posidonius), 5.29 (Tierney 1960; Freeman 2002, 11).

14 It may have been employed as a bier (Dobbs 1912) but the literary evidence that it was used in the actual burial is unconvincing.

15 Polybius, *Histories* 2.28–31 (Freeman 2002, 10); Diodorus Siculus (citing Posidonius) 5.30 (Tierney 1960; Freeman 2002, 12); Tacitus, *Agricola* 35–38 (Freeman 2002, 73).

16 Diodorus Siculus (citing Posidonius) 5.30 (Tierney 1960; Freeman 2002, 12).

17 Jackson 1964, 32.

18 Diodorus Siculus (citing Posidonius) 5.30 (Tierney 1960; Freeman 2002, 12).

19 Diodorus Siculus (citing Posidonius) 5.29 (Tierney 1960; Freeman 2002, 11).

20 Athenaeus, *Deipnosophistae* 4.34 (Freeman 2002, 24); Diodorus Siculus (citing Posidonius) 5.25 (Tierney

1960; Freeman 2002, 27); Strabo, *Geography* 4.4.3 (Freeman 2002, 27).

21 Tertullian, *De anima* 57.10 (Freeman 2002, 35). See also Freeman 1994 for a fuller account of some of these parallels.

22 Mallory 2013, 244–47.

23 Koch 1987; 1997, 157.

24 See Mallory 2013 for a detailed study of the problems involved.

25 Frank 1992, 55 even shows how the archaeological finds from Sutton Hoo, e.g., silver artifacts, have influenced translations of *Beowulf* despite the absence of any reference to silver in the Anglo-Saxon poem.

26 Aitchison 1987, 92.

27 Karl 2003, 19.

28 And even before the ostensible introduction of precious metals from classical sources we should probably include the awning (*pupall*), a clear Latin loanword.

29 Armit 2012, 18. See this work for a description of headhunting throughout Iron Age Atlantic Europe in the context of other headhunting societies in the world.

30 Armit 2012, 224.

31 Toner 2000.

32 Toner 2000, 6.

33 Here I follow Wolf 2012 on what makes a satisfactory imagined world.

34 Wolf 2012, 44.

35 Wolf 2012, 3.

36 Cited in Wolf 2012, 60.

Bibliography

Literary Sources

AAA = *Aided Aenfir Aife*
Meyer, K. (1904) The death of Conla.
Ériu 1, 113–21.

Achilleid = Achilleid of Statius
Mozley, J. H. (1967) *Statius*, vol. 2,
508–95. Cambridge, Massachusetts
and London, Harvard University and
William Heinemann.

ACMM = *Aided Ceit maic Mágach*
Meyer, K. (1906) The death of Cet mac
Mágach, *The Death-tales of the Ulster
Heroes* = Todd Lecture Series 14, 36–45.

ACMU = *Aided Cheltchair maic Uithechair*
Meyer, Kuno (1906) The death of
Celtchair mac Uithechair. *The
Death-tales of the Ulster Heroes* = Todd
Lecture Series 14, 24–31.

ACon = *Aided Chonchobuir*
Meyer, K. (1906) The death of
Conchobar. *The Death-tales of the Ulster
Heroes* = Todd Lecture Series 14, 2–21.

ACR-I = *Aided Conroi I*
Thurneysen, R. (1913) Die Sage von
Curoi. *Zeitschrift für Celtische Philologie*
9, 190–96.

ACR-II = *Aided Conroi II*
Best, R.I. (1905) The tragic death of
Cúroí Mac Dári. *Ériu* 2, 18–35.

AD = *Aided Derbforgaill*
Marstrander, C. (1911) The deaths of
Lugaid and Derbforgaill. *Ériu* 5, 201–18.

AE = *Aithed Emere*
Meyer, K. (1883–85) The elopement of
Emer with Tuir Glesta, son of the King
of Norway. *Revue Celtique* 6, 184–85.

Aeneid = Vergil's Aeneid
Fairclough, H. Rushton (1978) *Virgil*.
2 vols. Cambridge, Massachusetts and
London, Harvard University and
William Heinemann.

AFM = *Annála Ríoghachta Éireann* or
Annals of the Four Masters
O'Clery, M. et al. (1990 [1856]) *Annals
of the Kingdom of Ireland : from the
earliest times to the year 1616*. 7 vols.
Dublin, de Burca.

AFMR = *Aided Fergusa Maic Roig*
Meyer, K. (1906) The death of Fergus
MacRóich. *The Death-tales of the Ulster
Heroes* = Todd Lecture Series 14, 32–35.

AG = *Aided Guill Meic Carbada ocus Aided
Gairb Glinne Rige*
Stokes, Whitley (1893) The violent
deaths of Goll and Garb. *Revue Celtique*
14, 396–449.

Agricola of Tacitus
Hutton, M. and W. Peterson (1914)
*Agricola. Germania. Dialogue on
Oratory*. Harvard, Loeb Classical
Library.

ALB = *Aided Láegairi Buadaig*
Meyer, K. (1906) The death of Lóegaire
Búadach. *Death-tales of the Ulster
Heroes* =Todd Lecture Series 14,
22–23.

AM = *Aided Meidbe*
Meyer, Kuno (1887) The Edinburgh
Gaelic Manuscript XL. *The Celtic
Magazine* 12, 211–12.

AmCR = *Amra Conroi*
Stokes, Whitley (1905) The Eulogy of
Cúroí (*Amra Chonroí*) *Ériu* 2, 1–14.

Antiquities = Jewish Antiquities of Josephus
Thackeray, H. S. J. (1930) *Jewish
Antiquities, volume I*. Harvard, Loeb
Classical Library.

AO = *Aislinge Aenguso*
Muller, E. (1876–78) Two Irish tales.
Revue Celtique 3, 344–50.

ATDM = *Altrom Tighi dá Medar*
Dobbs, M. E. (1929) Altrom Tighi dá
Medar. *Zeitschrift für celtische Philologie*
18, 189–230.

BDC – *Bruiden Da Chocæ*
Stokes, Whitley (1900) Da Choca's
hostel. *Revue Celtique* 21, 149–65,
313–27, 388–402.
Toner, Gregory (2007) *Bruiden Da
Chocæ*. London, Irish Texts Society 61.

Beowulf
Klaeber, F. (1950) *Beowulf and The Fight
at Finnsburg*. Lexington, D. C. Heath.

BF = *Brinna Ferchertne*
Meyer, Kuno (1901) Brinna Ferchertne.
Zeitschrift für Celtische Philologie 3,
40–46.

BM-A = Brislech Mór Maige Muirthemni
Kimpton, Bettina (2009) *The Death of
Cú Chulainn. A Critical Edition of the
Earliest Version of* Brislech Mór Maige
Muirthemni *with Introduction,
Translation, Notes, Bibliography and
Vocabulary*. Maynooth, Maynooth
Medieval Irish Texts 6.

BM-B = *Brislech Mór Maige Muirtheimne
(Aided ChonChulainn)*
Van Hamel, A.G. (1933) Aided Con
Culainn, in *Compert Con Culainn and
Other Stories*, 72–133. Dublin, Medieval
and Modern Irish Series 3, Institute for
Advanced Studies.

CA = *Cath Airtig*
Best, R.I. (1916) The Battle of Airtech.
Ériu 8, 170–90.

CB = *Cath Boinde*
O'Neill, Joseph (1905) Cath Boinde.
Ériu 2, 173–85.

CCC = *Compert Conculainn*
Van Hamel, A. G. (1968) Compert
Con Culainn, in *Compert Con Culainn
and Other Stories*, 3–8. Dublin,
Mediaeval and Modern Irish Series 3,
Dublin Institute for Advanced Studies.
Kinsella, T. (1969) How Cúchulainn
was begotten, in Kinsella 21–25.

CCI = *Compert ConCulainn*, version 1
Windisch, Ernst (1880) *Die Geburt
Couchulainn's. Irische Texte I*, vol 1,
134–45.

CCL = *Cuchulinn ⁊ Conlaech*
O'Keeffe, J.G. (1901) Cuchulinn and
Conlaech. *Ériu* 1, 123–27.

CCon = *Compert Conchobuir*
Meyer, Kuno (1883–1885) The
conception of Conchobur. *Revue
Celtique* 6, 178–82.

CCS = *Comracc ConCulainn re Senbecc*
Meyer, Kuno (1883–1885) The combat
of Cuchulind with Senbecc. *Revue
Celtique* 6, 183–84.

CE = *Cath Etair*
Stokes, Whitley (1887) The siege of
Howth. *Revue Celtique* 8, 47–64.

CF = *Cocad Fergusa ⁊ Conchobair*
Dobbs, M. (1923) La Guerre entre
Fergus et Conchobar. *Revue Celtique*
40, 404–23.

CLR = *Cath Leitrech Ruide*
Dobbs, M. (1922) La Bataille de Leitir
Ruibhe. *Revue Celtique* 39, 1–32.

Clon = Annals of Clonmacnoise
Murphy, Denis (ed) (1896) *The Annals
of Clonmacnoise being the Annals of
Ireland from the earliest period to A.D.
1408*. Dublin, University Press.

CMT1 = *Cath Maige Tuired I*
Fraser, J. (1915) The First Battle of
Moytura. *Ériu* 8, 1–63.

CMT2 = *Cath Maige Tuired II*
Gray, Elizabeth A. (1982) *Cath Maige
Tuired: The Second Battle of Mag Tuired*.
Naas, Irish Texts Society 52.

Cogadh Gaedhel re Gallaibh
Todd, James Henthorn (1867) *Cogadh
Gaedhel re Gallaibh: The war of the
Gaedhil with the Gaill, or, The invasions
of Ireland by the Danes and other*

Norsemen : the original Irish text.
London, Longmans, Green, Reader,
and Dyer.

Cóir Anman
Stokes, Whitley (1897) *Cóir Anman*
(Fitness of Names), in Stokes, Whitley
and Ernst Windisch (eds) *Irische Texte*,
3rd ser, vol. 2. Leipzig, S. Hirzel.

Crith Gabhlach
Binchy, D. A. (1941) *Crith Gablach*.
Dublin, Stationery Office.

CRR = *Cath Ruis na Ríg*
Hogan, Edmund (1892) *Cath Ruis
na Ríg* [=*Todd Lecture Series* 4, 1–59].
Dublin, Academy House.

CRR-B = *Cath Ruis na Ríg*
Hogan, Edmund (1892) *Cath Ruis na
Ríg for Bóinn* [=*Todd Lecture Series* 4,
60–107. Dublin, Academy House.

CrSl = Cross and Slover
Cross, Tom Peete and Clark Harris
Slover (1969) *Ancient Irish Tales*. New
York, Barnes and Noble.

CS = *Cathcharpat Serda*
O'Rahilly, C. (1976) *Cathcharpat Serda*.
Celtica 11–12, 194–202.

CU = *Ces Ulad* or *Noínden Ulad*
Hull, V. (1962–64) *Ces Ulad*. The
affliction of the Ulstermen. *Zeitschrift
für Celtische Philologie* 29, 309–14.
Hull, V. (1968) *Noínden Ulad*: The
debility of the Ulidians. *Celtica* 8, 1–42.

DBG = *De Bellum Gallico* of Julius Caesar
Edwards, H. J. (1917) *The Gallic War*.
Harvard, Loeb Classical Library.

DCDM = *De Chophur in Dá Mucado*
Windisch, E. (1891) De Chophur in
dá muccida. *Irische Texte*, ser 3, vol. 1,
230–75. Leipzig, S. Hirzel.

De Bello Civili of Lucan
Duff, J. D. (1962) *Lucan*. Cambridge,
Massachusetts and London, Harvard
University and William Heinemann.

De excidio = De excidio Trojae historia of
Dares the Phrygian
Frazer, R. M. (1966) *The Trojan War.
The Chronicles of Dictys of Crete and
Dares the Phrygian*. Bloomington,
Indiana University Press.
Cornill, Jonathan (2011–12) *Dares
Phrygius' De Excidio Trojae Historia:
Philological Commentary and
Translation*. Universiteit Ghent. http://
lib.ugent.be/fulltxt/
RUG01/001/891/500/RUG01-
001891500_2012_0001_AC.pdf

De Rerum Natura of Lucretius
Smith, Martin F. (1924) *On the Nature of
Things*. Harvard, Loeb Classical Library.

DGE = *Do Ghabháil Érend*
Macalister, R. A. S. and J. MacNeill (eds)
(1916) *The Book of Conquests of Ireland.
The Recension of Michael O' Cleirigh*.
Dublin, Hodges, Figgis and Company.

DGS = *Da Gabáil int sída*
Hull, V. (1933) De Gabáil in t-sída.
Zeitschrift für Celtische Philologie (19,
53–58.

Dio Cassius = Dio Cassius Roman History
Cary, Earnest and Foster, Herbert B.
(1927) *Roman History*, Vol. IX, Books
71–80. Harvard, Loeb Classical Library.

DMC = *De Maccaib Conairi*
Gwynn, Lucius (1912) De Maccaib
Conaire. *Ériu* 6, 144–53.

DSCM = *De Šíl Conairi Móir*
Gwynn, Lucius (1912) De Síl Chonairi
Móir. *Ériu* 6, 130–43.

EF-A = *Echtra Fergusa Maic Léte*
Binchy, D.A. (1952) The saga of Fergus
Mac Léti. *Ériu* 16, 33–48.

EF-B = *Imthechta Tuaithe Luachra ⁊ aided
Fergusa*
O'Grady, Standish H (1892) The king of
the Lepracanes' journey to Emania, and
how the death of Fergus mac Léide king
of Ulster was brought about. *Silva
Gadelica* II, 238–52, 269–85. New York,
Lemma [reprinted 1970].

EN = *Echtra Nerai*
Meyer, Kuno (1889) The Adventures of
Nera. *Revue Celtique* 10, 212–28. [=
CrSl 248–53].

Ephemeridos = Ephemeridos belli Trojani
of Dictys Cretensis
Frazer, R. M. (1966) *The Trojan War.
The Chronicles of Dictys of Crete and
Dares the Phrygian*. Bloomington,
Indiana University Press.

Etymologiae = Etymologies of Isidore of
Seville
Barney, Stephen A. et al. (2006) *The
Etymologies of Isidore of Seville*.
Cambridge, Cambridge University
Press.

FB = *Fled Bricrenn*
Henderson, George 1899. *Fled Bricend*.
London, Irish Texts Society.

FBL = *Fled Bricrenn ocus Loinges mac nDuíl
Dermait*
Hollo, Kaarina (2005) *Fled Bricrenn ocus
Loinges mac nDuíl Dermait*. Maynooth,
Maynooth Medieval Irish Texts II.

FC = *Foglaim ConCulainn*
Stokes, Whitley (1908) The Training of
Cúchulainn. *Revue Celtique* 29, 109–52.

FFF = *Forfes Fer Fálchae*
Thurneysen, R. (1912) Forfess Fer Falgae
nach der Handschrift von Druim
Snechta. *Zu irischen Handschriften und
Litteraturdenkmälern*, 53–58. Berlin,
Weidmann.

FLFMR = *Fochonn Loingse Fergusa Meic
Roig*
Hull, V. (1930) The cause of the exile
of Fergus Mac Roig. *Zeitschrift für
Celtische Philologie* 18, 293–98.

FM = *Ferchuitred Medba* (Cath Boinne)
O'Neill, Joseph (1905) Cath Boinde.
Ériu 2, 173–85.

FTBC = *Failsigud Tána Bó Cuailnge*
Murray, K. (2001) The Finding of the
Táin. *Cambrian Medieval Celtic Studies*
41, 17–23.

Gantz = Early Irish Myths
Gantz, Jeffrey (1981) *Early Irish Myths
and Sagas*. London, Penguin.

GCC = *Goire Conaill Chernaig ⁊ Aided
Aillela ⁊ Conaill Chernaig*
Meyer, K. (1905) The cherishing of
Conall Cernach and the death of Ailill
and Conall Cernach. *Zeitschrift für
Celtische Philologie* 1, 102–11.

Hull = Cúchullain saga
Hull, Eleanor (1898) *The Cúchulainn
Saga in Irish Literature*. London, David
Nutt.

IDT = *Immacaldam in dá thuarad*
Stokes, W. (1905) The colloquy of the
two sages. *Revue Celtique* 26, 4–64.

Ilias Latina = Latin *Iliad*
Kennedy, George A. (1998) *The Latin
Iliad. Introduction, Text, Translation,
and Notes*. Fort Collins, Colorado.

Imtheachta Æniasa
Calder, George (1907) *Imtheachta
Æniasa. The Irish Aeneid*. London,
David Nutt.

In Cath Catharda
Stokes, Whitley (1909) *In Cath
Catharda: The Civil War of the Romans,
an Irish Version of Lucan's Pharsalia*, in
Windisch, E. and W. Stokes (ed) *Irische
Texte* 4, part 2. Leipzig, S. Hirzel.

Irish Achilleid
Ó hAodha, D. (1979) The Irish version
of Statius' 'Achilleid'. *Proceedings of the
Royal Irish Academy* 79, 83–138.

IT = *Imthecht na Tromdáime*
Connellan, Owen (1857 [1860]).
Imtheacht na Tromdháimhe.
Transactions of the Ossianic Society 1857,
vol. 5; 2–132.

Kinsella = *The Tain*
Kinsella, Thomas (1969) *The Tain*,
translated by Thomas Kinsella. London,
Oxford University Press.

LG/LGE = *Lebor Gabála Érenn*
Macalister, R. A. S. (1938–56) *Lebor
Gabála Érenn*, 5 vols. London, Irish
Texts Society.

LL = *The Book of Leinster*
Best, R. I. and M. A. O'Brien (eds)
(1954–67) *The Book of Leinster, formerly
Lebar na Núachongbála*. Dublin, Dublin
Institute for Advanced Studies.

LMU = *Longes mac n-Uislenn*
Hull, V. (1949) *Longes mac nUislenn:
The exile of the Sons of Uisliu*. New York,
Modern Language Association of
America.

LTRR = *Lánellach tigi rích ⁊ ruirech*
Ó Daly, M. (1962) *Lánellach tigi rích ⁊
ruirech. Ériu* 19, 81–86.

LU = *Lebor na hUidre*
Best, R. I. and O. Bergin (eds) (1929)
Lebor na hUidre. Book of the Dun Cow.
Dublin, Royal Irish Academy.

MD = Metrical Dindshenchas
Gwynn, E. (1903–1935) *The Metrical
Dindshenchas*. 5 vols. Dublin.

Merugud Uilixis = Merugud Uilixis Mhaic
Leirtis
Meyer, Kuno (1886) *Merugud Uilix
Maicc Leirtis: The Irish Odyssey*. London,
D. Nutt.

Metamorphoses of Ovid
Miller, Frank Justus (1916)
Metamorphoses, Volume I, Books 1–8.
Harvard, Loeb Classical Library.

MU = *Mesca Ulad*
Watson, J. Carmichael (1967) *Mesca
Ulad*. Dublin, Mediaeval and Modern
Irish Series 13, Dublin Institute for
Advanced Studies.
Watson, J. C. (1938) *Mesca Ulad. SGS* 5,
1–34.

NC = *Nede ⁊ Caier*
Meyer, Kuno (1912) *Sanas Cormaic. An
Old Irish Glossary* = *Anecdota from Irish
Manuscripts* IV, 58–60. Halle, Niemeyer.

OCL = *Oidheadh Chlainne Lir*
O'Duffy, R. J. (1883a) *Oidheadh
Chlainne Lir, the Fate of the Children
of Lir*. Dublin, Gill.

OCT = *Oidheadh Chlainne Tuireann*
O'Duffy, R. J. (1883b) *Oidheadh Chlainne Tuireann, the Fate of the Children of Tuireann*. Dublin, Gill.

ODR = *Orgain Dind Ríg*
Stokes, Whitley (1901) *The Destruction of Dind Ríg. Zeitschrift für Celtische Philologie* 3, 1–14.

OMU = *Oided Mac n-Uisnig*
Stokes, Whitley (1887) Death of the Sons of Uisnech. *Irische Texte*, 2 ser, vol. 2, 109–84. Leipzig, S. Hirzel.

Orosius = *Historiarum Adversum Paganos Libri VII*
Deferrari, Roy J. (1964) *The Seven Books against the Pagans*. Washington, Catholic University of America.

RD = *Rennes Dindshenchas*
Stokes, Whitley (1894–95) The prose tales in the Rennes Dindshenchas. *Revue celtique* 15, 277–336, 418–84; 16, 81–83, 135–67.

SCC = *Serglige ConCulainn*
Dillon, Myles (1953) *Serglige Con Culainn*. Dublin, Mediaeval and Modern Irish Series 14, Dublin Institute for Advanced Studies.
Dillon, M. (1953) The wasting sickness of Cú Chulainn. *SGS* 7, 47–88.

SC = *Siaburcharpat ConCulainn*
O Beirne Crowe, J. (1870) *Siabur-charpat Con Culaind. Journal of the Royal Historical and Archaeological Association of Ireland*, ser 4, vol. 1, 371–401. [=Hull 275–88; CrSl 347–54].

Scél Alexandair = Irish Alexander story.
Peters, Erik (1967) Die irische Alexandersage. *Zeitschrift für celtische Philologie* 30, 71–264.

SCMG = *Scéla Cano Meic Gartnáin*
Binchy, D. A. (1963) *Scéla Cano Meic Gartnáin*. Dublin, Dublin Institute for Advanced Studies.

SGS = *Scottish Gaelic Studies*

SCMN = *Scéla Conchobair Maic Nessa*
Stokes, Whitley (1910) Tidings of Conchobar Mac Nessa. *Ériu* 4, 18–38.

Sidonius = Poems of Sidonius
Anderson, W. B. (1936) *Sidonius Poems and Letters*. Vol. 1. Cambridge, Mass, Harvard University Press.

SMMD = *Scél Mucce Maic Dathó*
Thurneysen, Rudolf (1935) *Scéla Mucce Meic Dathó*. Dublin, Mediaeval and Modern Irish Series 6, Dublin Institute for Advanced Studies.
Gantz, J. (1981) The tale of Macc Da Thó's pig. Gantz 179–87.

ST = *Scél Tuáin Meic Chairill*
Carey, John (1984) Scél Tuáin Meic Chairill. *Ériu* 35, 93–111.

STT = *Suidigiud Tellaig Temro*
Best, R. I. (1908–10) The settling of the manor of Tara. *Ériu* 4, 121–72.

TBC¹ = *Táin Bó Cuailnge*
O'Rahilly, C, (1976) *Táin Bó Cúailnge: Recension I*. Dublin, Institute for Advanced Studies.

TBC² = *Táin Bó Cuailnge II*
O'Rahilly, C, (1970) *Táin Bó Cúalnge from the Book of Leinster*. Dublin, Institute for Advanced Studies.

TBC³ = *Táin Bó Cuailnge III* [TBC III]
Nettlau, Max (1894) The fragment of the *Táin Bó Cuailghni* in MS Egerton 93.

Revue Celtique 14, 256–66; 15: 62–78, 198–208.
Thurneysen, Rudolf (1912) *Táin Bó Cuailghni. Zeitschrift für Celtische Philologie* 8, 525–54.
Ó Béarra, Feargal (1996) Táin Bó Cuailnge: Recension III. *Emania* 14, 47–65.

TBD = *Táin Bó Dartada*
Windisch, E. 1887. *Táin Bó Dartada. Irische Texte*, ser 2, vol. 2, 185–205. Leipzig, S. Hirzel.
Leahy, A. H. (1906) The raid of Dartaid's cattle. *Heroic Romances of Ireland* II, 73–81. London, D. Nutt.

TBDD = *Togail Brudhe Ui Dergae*
Knott, Eleanor (1936) *Togail Bruidne Da Derga*. Dublin, Mediaeval and Modern Irish Series 8, Dublin Institute for Advanced Studies.
Stokes, W. (1902) The destruction of Dá Derga's hostel. Paris [=*Revue Celtique* 22, 9–61, 165–215, 282–329, 390–437].

TBFl I = *Táin Bó Flidais*
Windisch, E. (1887) *Táin Bó Flidais. Irische Teste*, ser 2, vol.2, 206–23. Leipzig, S. Hirzel.
Leahy, A. (1906) The driving of the cattle of Flidais. *Heroic Romances of Ireland* II, 101–25. London, D. Nutt.

TBFl II = *Táin Bó Flidaise II*
MacKinnon, D. (1905–8) The Glenmasan manuscript. *The Celtic Review*. I, 3–17, 104–31, 208–29, 296–315, II, 20–33, 100–21, 202–23, 300–13; III, 10–25, 114–37, 198–215, 294–317; IV, 10–27, 104–21, 202–19.

TBFr = *Táin Bó Fraích*
Meid, W. (1967) *Táin Bó Fraích*. Dublin, Mediaeval and Modern Irish Series 22, Dublin Institute for Advanced Studies.
Carney, James (1955) The driving of the cattle of Fráech. *Studies in Irish Literature and History*, 1–24. Dublin, Institute for Advanced Studies.

TBR = *Táin Bó Regamain*
Windisch, E. (1887) *Táin Bó Regamain. Irische Texte* ser, 2. vol. 2, 224–38. Leipzig, S. Hirzel.
Leahy, A. (1906) The raid for the cattle of Regamon. *Heroic Romances of Ireland* 2, 83–99. London, D. Nutt.

TBRa = *Táin Bó Regamna*
Windisch, E. (1887) *Táin bó Regamna. Irische Texte*, ser 2, vol. 2, 239–54. Leipzig, S. Hirzel.
Leahy, A. (1906) The apparition of the great queen to Cuchulain. *Heroic Romances of Ireland*, 2, 127–41. London, D. Nutt.

Thebaid of Statius
Mozley, J. H. (1967) *Statius*. 2 vols. Cambridge, Massachusetts and London, Harvard University and William Heinemann.

TLE = *Talland Étair*
Dobbs, M. (1949–51) *Agallamh Leborchaim. Études celtiques* 5, 154–61.

TEm = *Tochmarc Emire*
Meyer, Kuno (1890) The oldest version of Tochmarc Emire. *Revue Celtique* 11, 433–57.

TEm II = *Tochmarc Emire*
Van Hamel, A.G. (1933) Tochmarc Emire. *Compert Con Culainn and Other*

Stories, 16–68. Dublin, Medieval and Modern Irish Series 3, Institute for Advanced Studies.
Meyer, Kuno (1888) The wooing of Emer. *The Archaeological Review* I, 68–75, 150–55, 231–35, 298–307. [= Hull 55–84; CrSl 153–71].

TEt = *Tochmarc Étáine*
Bergin, O. and R. I. Best (1934–38) *Tochmarc Étáine. Ériu* 12, 137–96. [=CS 82–92].

TF = *Tochmarc Ferbe (Fís Conchobair)*
Windisch, E. (1897) Das Freien um Ferb. *Irische Texte*, ser 3, heft 2, 462–529. Leipzig, S. Hirzel.
Leahy, A. (1902) *The Courtship of Ferb* =The Irish Saga Library vol. 1. London, D. Nutt.

TL = *Tochmarc Luaine ⁊ aided Athirni*
Stokes, W. (1903) The wooing of Luaine and death of Athirne. *Revue Celtique* 24, 270–87.

Togail na Tebe
Calder, George (1922) *Togail na Tebe: the Thebaid of Statius*. Cambridge, Cambridge University Press.

Togail Troi
Stokes, Whitley (1884) The destruction of Troy, in Stokes, W. and E. Windisch (eds) *Irische Texte*, ser 2, heft 1, 1–141. Leipzig, S. Hirzel.

Topographia
O'Meara, John (1982) *Gerald of Wales. The History and Topography of Ireland*. London, Penguin.

TT = *Tochmarc Treblainne*
Meyer, Kuno (1921) Tochmarc Treblainne. *Zeitschrift für Celtische Philologie* 13, 166–75.
Jennings, Rachel (1997) A translation of the Tochmarc Treblainne. *Emania* 16, 73–78.

VS = *Verba Scáthaige*
Henry, P. (1990) *Verba Scáthaige. Celtica* 21, 101–2.

Why Mongán = Why Mongán was deprived of noble issue
Knott, Eleanor (1916) Why Mongán was deprived of noble issue. *Ériu* 8, 155–60.

Bibliography

Aitchison, N. B. (1987) The Ulster cycle: Heroic image and historical reality. *Journal of Medieval History* 13, 87–116.

Aitchison, N. B. (1994) *Armagh and the Royal Centres in Early Medieval Ireland*. Suffolk, Cruithne Press.

Arbois de Jubainville, H. d' (1903) *The Irish Mythological Cycle and Celtic Mythology* (translated Richard Irvine Best). Dublin, O'Donoghue.

Armit, Ian (2012) *Headhunting and the Body in Iron Age Europe*. Cambridge, Cambridge University.

ASCD = (1966) *Archaeological Survey of County Down*. Belfast, Her Majesty's Stationery Office.

Baillie, M. G. L. and D. Brown (2013) A chronological framework for the period from 208 BC to AD 600. *Emania* 21, 59–71.

Bauersfeld, Helmut (1933) Die Kriegsaltertumer in *Lebor na Huidre. Zeitschrift für celtische Philologie* 19, 294–345.

Bender Jørgensen, Lise (1992) *North European Textiles until AD 1000*. Aarhus, Aarhus University Press.

Bennet, John (1997) Homer and the Bronze Age, in Morris, Ian and Barry Powell (eds) *A New Companion to Homer*, 511–33, Leiden, New York, Köln, Brill.

Berschin, Walter (1982) Griechisches bei den Iren, in Löwe, Heinz (ed) *Die Iren und Europa im früheren Mittelalter*, 501–10. Stuttgart, Klett-Cotta.

Bhreathnach, Edel (2010) From *fert(ae)* to relic: mapping death in early sources, in Corlett, Christaan and Michael Potterton (eds) *Death and Burial in Early Medieval Ireland*, 23–31, Dublin, Wordwell.

Bhreathnach, Edel (2014) *Ireland in the Medieval World AD 400–1000*. Dublin, Four Courts Press.

Bøe, J. (1940) Norse antiquities in Ireland, in Shetelig, H. (ed) *Viking Antiquities in Great Britain and Ireland, Part III*. Oslo, H. Aschenoug.

Bondarenko, Grigory (2009) Oral past and written present in 'The Finding of the Táin', in Ó hUiginn, Ruairí and Ó Catháin, Brian (eds) *Ulidia 2: Proceedings of the Second International Conference on the Ulster Cycle of Tales*, 18–24. Maynooth, An Sagart.

Bone, Peter (1989) The development of Anglo-Saxon swords, in Hawkes, Sonia Chadwick (ed) *Weapons and Warfare in Anglo-Saxon England*, 63–70. Oxford, Oxford University Committee for Archaeology.

Bowra, C. M. (1970) Problems concerned with Homer and the epics, in Thomas, C. G. (ed) (1970) *Homer's History: Mycenaean or Dark Age?*, 9–16. New York, Holt, Rinehart and Winston = (1961) 'Homer's Age of Heroes', *Horizon* III, 3, 74–93.

Brady, Caroline (1979) 'Weapons' in *Beowulf*: an analysis of the nominal compounds and an evaluation of the poet's use of them. *Anglo-Saxon England* 8, 79–141.

Brown, D. M. and M. G. L. Baillie (2007) Dendrochronology and lessons learned from Irish examples, in Murphy, Eileen M. and Nicki J. Whitehouse (eds) *Environmental Archaeology in Ireland*, 18–36. Oxford, Oxbow.

Bruce-Mitford, Rupert (1983) *The Sutton Hoo Ship-Burial, vol. 3*. London, British Museum.

Bruford, Alan (1994) Why an Ulster cycle?, in Mallory, J. P. and G. Stockman (eds) *Ulidia: Proceedings of the First International Conference on the Ulster Cycle of Tales*, 23–30. Belfast, December.

Buchholz, Hans-Günter (1980) *Archaeologia Homerica: Kriegswesen, Teil 2: Angriffswaffen: Schwert, Dolch, Lanze, Speer, Keule*. Göttingen, Vandenhoeck and Ruprecht.

Butler, H. E. (2005) *The Autobiography of Gerald of Wales*. Woodbridge, Boydell Press.

Byrne, Francis John (1964) Clann Ollaman Uaisle Emna. *Studia Hibernica* 4, 59–94.

Cahill, Mary (2002) Before the Celts: Treasures in gold and bronze, in

Wallace, Patrick F. and Raghnall Ó Floinn (eds) *Treasures of the National Museum of Ireland*, 86–124. Dublin, Gill and Macmillan.

Campbell, E. (2007) *Continental and Mediterranean Imports to Atlantic Britain and Ireland, AD 400–800*. CBA Research Report 157.

Campion, Edmund (1571 [1809]) *A Historie of Ireland*. Dublin, Hibernia Press.

Carey, John (1993) *A New Introduction to Lebor Gabála Érenn*. Dublin, Irish Texts Society, Subsidiary Ser. 1.

Carey, John (1994) *The Irish National Origin-Legend: Synthetic Pseudohistory*. Cambridge, Department of Anglo-Saxon, Norse and Celtic, University of Cambridge, Quiggin Pamphlets on the Sources of Mediaeval Gaelic History 1.

Carey, John (1995) Lebor Gabála Érenn The Book of Invasions, in Koch, John T. (ed) *The Celtic Heroic Age*, 213–66. Malden, Massachusetts, Celtic Studies Publications.

Carey, John (2009) The LU copy of *Lebor Gabála*. In Carey, John (ed) *Lebor Gabála Érenn: Textual History and Pseudohistory*, 21–32. Dublin, Irish Texts Society, Subsidiary Series No. 20.

Carney, James (1966) Introduction. Knott, Eleanor and Gerard Murphy *Early Irish Literature*, 1–17. New York, Barnes and Noble.

Carney, James (2005) Language and literature to 1169, in Ó Cróinín, Dáibhí (ed) *A New History of Ireland 1 Prehistoric and Early Ireland*, 451–510. Oxford, Oxford University Press.

Carpenter, Rhys (1970) Possibly one Mycenaean relic in the poems, in Thomas, C. G. (ed) (1970) *Homer's History: Mycenaean or Dark Age?*, 41–47. New York, Holt, Rinehart and Winston = (1962) *Folk Tale, Fiction and Saga in the Homeric Epics* (Berkeley and Los Angeles, University of California Press), 26–32, 85–89.

Cessford, Craig (1995) Torcs in early historic Scotland. *Oxford Journal of Archaeology* 14, 229–42.

Charles-Edwards, T. M. (2000) *Early Christian Ireland*. Cambridge, Cambridge University Press.

Chekhonadskaya, N. Yu. (2001) Eshchë raz o Smerti Konkhobara. *Atlantika: Zapiski po istoricheskoy poetike 5*, 81–102.

Clarke, Michael (2009) An Irish Achilles and a Greek Cú Chulainn, in Ó hUiginn, Ruairí and Ó Catháin, Brian (eds) (2009) *Ulidia 2: Proceedings of the Second International Conference on the Ulster Cycle of Tales*, 238–51. Maynooth, An Sagart.

Clutterbuck, Richard (2013) Iron Age ritual and settlement at Cookstown, Co. Meath, in Corlett, Christiaan and Michael Potterton (eds) (2013) *Life and Death in Iron Age Ireland*, 35–51. Dublin, Wordwell.

Collins, A. E. P. (1957) Excavations at two standing stones in Co. Down. *Ulster Journal of Archaeology* 20, 37–42.

Commerford, Richard Vincent (2003) *Ireland*. London, Arnold.

Condit, Tom and Victor M. Buckley (1989) The 'Doon' of Drumsna – gateways to Connacht. *Emania* 6, 12–16.

Corlett, Christiaan and Michael Potterton (2011) *Settlement in Early Medieval Ireland: In the light of recent archaeological excavations*. Dublin, Wordwell.

Corthals, Johan (1989) Zur Frage des mündlichen oder schriftlichen Ursprungs der Sagenroscada, in Tranter, Stephen N. and Hildegard L. C. Tristram (eds) *Early Irish Literature – Media and Communication. Mündlichkeit und Schriftlichkeit in der frühen irischen Literatur*, 201–20. Tübingen, Gunter Narr Verlag.

Coughlan, Tim (2012) 'Follow me up to Carlow': an outline of the Iron Age sites found along the M9/N10 route from Knocktopher, Co. Kilkenny, to Powerstown, Co. Carlow, in Corlett, Christiaan and Michael Potterton (eds) (2012) *Life and Death in Iron Age Ireland*, 59–77. Dublin, Wordwell.

Cox, Richard (1689) *Hibernia anglicana, or, The history of Ireland, from the conquest thereof by the English, to this present time with an introductory discourse touching the ancient state of that kingdom and a new and exact map of the same*. London, H. Clark.

Coyle McClung, Elizabeth (2012) *A Palynological Investigation of Land-use Patterns in First Millennium AD Ireland*. PhD thesis, Queen's University Belfast.

Coyle McClung, Lisa (2013) The Late Iron Age Lull – not so Late Iron Age after all! *Emania* 21, 73–83.

Cunningham, Bernadette (2007a) The nineteenth-century legacy: publishing the Annals of the Four Masters, in Bhreathnach, Edel and Bernadette Cunningham (eds) *Writing Irish History: The Four Masters and their World*, 68–73. Dublin, Wordwell.

Cunningham, Bernadette (2007b) Writing the Annals of the Four Masters, in Bhreathnach, Edel and Bernadette Cunningham (2007) *Writing Irish History: The Four Masters and their World*, 27–30. Dublin, Wordwell.

Cunningham, Bernadette (2010) *The Annals of the Four Masters: Irish history, kingship and society in the early seventeenth century*. Dublin, Four Courts Press.

Cusack, Frances Mary (1868) *An Illustrated History of Ireland from the Earliest Period*. London, Longmans, Green and Co.

Danaher, Ed. (2013) A possible Iron Age homestead at Ballinaspig, Co. Cork, in Corlett, Christiaan and Michael Potterton (eds) (2012) *Life and Death in Iron Age Ireland*, 79–92. Dublin, Wordwell.

Davidson, Hilda Ellis (1989) The training of warriors, in Hawkes, Sonia Chadwick (ed) *Weapons and Warfare in Anglo-Saxon England*, 11–23. Oxford, Oxford University Committee for Archaeology.

Delamarre, Xavier (2003) *Dictionnaire de la langue gauloise*. Paris, Éditions Errance.

Delaney, Shane, Jim McKeon and Siobhán McNamara (2012) Two Iron Age ring-ditches in Ballyboy, Co. Galway, in Corlett, Christiaan and Michael Potterton (eds) *Life and Death in Iron Age Ireland*, 93–104. Dublin, Wordwell.

De Leeuw, Henny (2008) Chariots on high crosses: Celtic or Christian? *Journal of the Royal Society of Antiquaries of Ireland* 138, 5–25.

Dickinson, T. and H. Härke (1992) *Early Anglo-Saxon Shields*. London, Society of Antiquaries = *Archaeologia* 110.

Dillon, Myles (1994) *The Cycles of the Kings*. Dublin, Four Courts Press.

Dobbs, Margaret (1913) Some further evidence on the date of the shaping of the *Táin Bó Cúailnge*. *Journal of the Royal Society of Antiquaries of Ireland* 4, 8–12.

Dobs, Margaret (1917) *Sidelights on the Táin*. Dundalk, Tempest

Donlan, Walter (1997) The Homeric economy, in Morris, Ian and Barry Powell (eds) *A New Companion to Homer*, 649–67. Leiden, New York, Köln, Brill.

Dooley, Anne (2006) *Playing the Hero: Reading the Irish Saga Táin Bó Cúailnge*. Toronto, University of Toronto Press.

Doyle, Maureen (2015) Early medieval dress and ornament, in Kerr, Thomas R., Maureen Doyle, Matthew Seaver, Finbar McCormick and Aidan O'Sullivan *Early Medieval Crafts and Production in Ireland*, AD 400–1100: *The evidence from rural settlements*, 88–101. Oxford, BAR International Series 2707.

Dunlevy, Mairead (1989) *Dress in Ireland*. London, Batsford.

D'yakonov, M. M. (1961) *Ocherk istorii drevnego Irana*. Moscow.

Edwards, Nancy (1990) *The Archaeology of Early Medieval Ireland*. London, Batsford.

Elizabeth, Charlotte (1844) *Sketches of Irish History: Antiquities, religion, customs, and manners*. Dublin, John Robertson.

Eogan, George (1994) *The Accomplished Art: Gold and gold-working in Britain and Ireland during the Bronze Age (c. 2300–650 BC)*. Oxford, Oxbow Monograph 42.

Eogan, James (2012) An Iron Age penannular ring-ditch at Ballybronoge South, Co. Limerick, in Corlett, Christiaan and Michael Potterton (eds) (2012) *Life and Death in Iron Age Ireland*, 105–19. Dublin, Wordwell.

Fitzgerald, Maria (1997) Insular dress in medieval Ireland, in Owen-Crocker, Gale (ed) *Anglo-Saxon Texts and Contexts* = Bulletin of the John Rylands University Library at Manchester 79.3.

Fitzpatrick, Elizabeth (2004) Royal inauguration mounds in mediaeval Ireland: antique landscape and tradition, in Pantos, Aliki and Sarah Semple (eds) *Assembly Places and Practices in Medieval Europe*, 44–72. Dublin, Four Courts Press.

Foley, John Miles (1997) Oral tradition and its implications, in Morris, Ian and Barry Powell (eds) (1997) *A New*

Companion to Homer, 146–73. Leiden, New York, Köln, Brill.

Foltiny, Stephan (1980) Schwert, Dolch und Messer, in Buchholz, Hans-Günter (ed) *Archaeologia Homerica: Kriegswesen, Teil 2: Angriffswaffen: Schwert, Dolch, Lanze, Speer, Keule*, 231–74. Göttingen, Vandenhoeck and Ruprecht.

Ford, Patrick K. (2000) The Ulaid and the *Iliad*: Some considerations. *Emania* 18, 49–56.

Forester, Thomas (trans) (2000) *Geraldus Cambrensis The Topography of Ireland*. Cambridge, Ontario, In parenthesis publications. Available at http://www.yorku.ca/inpar/topography_ireland.pdf

Forester, Thomas (trans) (2001) *Geraldus Cambrensis The Conquest of Ireland*. In parenthesis publications. Available at http://www.yorku.ca/inpar/conquest_ireland.pdf

Frank, Roberta (1992) *Beowulf* and Sutton Hoo, the odd couple, in Kendall, Calvin B. and Peter S. Wells (ed) *Voyage to the Other World: The Legacy of Sutton Hoo*, 47–64. Minneapolis, University of Minnesota Press.

Frazer, William (1879–88) Description of a great sepulchral mound at Aylesburyroad, near Donnybrook, in the County of Dublin, containing human and animal remains, as well as some objects of antiquarian interest, referable to the tenth or eleventh centuries. *Proceedings of the Royal Irish Academy* 2, 29–55.

Freeman, Philip M. (1994) Elements of the Ulster Cycle in Pre-Posidonian classical literature, in Mallory, J. P. And G. Stockman (eds) *Ulidia: Proceedings of the First International Conference on the Ulster Cycle of Tales*, 207–16. Belfast, December.

Freeman, Philip (2002) *War, Women and Druids: Eyewitness reports and early accounts of the ancient Celts*. Austin, University of Texas Press.

Greene, David (1972) The chariot as described in Irish literature, in Thomas, Charles (ed) *The Iron Age in the Irish Sea Province* = C.B.A. Research Report 9, 59–73.

Halpin, Andrew (1997) Military archery in medieval Ireland: archaeology and history, in De Boe, G. and F. Verhaeghe (ed) *Military Studies in Medieval Europe-Papers of the 'Medieval Europe Brugge 1997' Conference*, vol. 2, 51–60. Zellik, Instituut voor het Archeologisch Patrimonium

Halpin, Andrew (2005) Weapons and warfare in Viking-Age Ireland, in Sheehan, John and Donnchadh Ó Corráin (eds) *The Viking Age: Ireland and the West*, 124–35. Dublin, Four Courts Press.

Halpin, Andrew (2015) The Ballinderry bow: an under-appreciated Viking weapon?, in Clarke, Howard B. and Ruth Johnson (eds) *The Vikings in Ireland and beyond before and after the Battle of Clontarf*, 151–60. Dublin, Four Courts Press.

Hamilton, J. R. C. (1968) Iron Age forts and epic literature. *Antiquity* 42, 103–8.

Hamilton-Dyer, Sheila (2007) Exploitation of birds and fish in historic Ireland: A brief review of the evidence, in Murphy, Eileen M. and Nicki J. Whitehouse (eds) *Environmental Archaeology in Ireland*, 102–18. Oxford, Oxbow.

Hammerow, Helena (2012) *Rural Settlements and Society in Anglo-Saxon England*. Oxford, Oxford University.

Hanmer, Meredith (1571[1809]) *The Chronicle of Ireland*. Dublin, Hibernia Press.

Hansbrow, G. (1835) *An Improved Topographical and Historical Hibernian Gazetteer*. Dublin, Richard Moore Tims etc.

Harrison, Stephen J. and Raghnall Ó Floinn (2015) *Viking Graves and Grave Goods in Ireland*. Dublin, National Museum of Ireland.

Haslam, Michael (1997) Homeric papyri and transmission of the text, in Morris, Ian and Barry Powell (eds) *A New Companion to Homer*, 55–100. Leiden, New York, Köln, Brill.

Hawkes, C. F. C. (1981) The wearing of the brooch: Early Iron Age dress among the Irish, in Scott, B. G. (ed) *Studies on Early Ireland: Essays in honour of M. V. Duignan*, 51–73. Belfast, Association of Young Irish Archaeologists.

Haworth, R. (1971) The horse harness of the Irish Early Iron Age. *Ulster Journal of Archaeology* 34, 26–49.

Hencken, Hugh (1938) Ballinderry crannog no. 1. *Proceedings of the Royal Irish Academy* 43C, 103–239.

Hencken, Hugh (1950–51) Lagore Crannog: an Irish royal residence of the 7th to 10th centuries AD. *Proceedings of the Royal Irish Academy* 53C, 1–247.

Henderson, I. (1967) *The Picts*. London, Thames & Hudson.

Herbert, Máire (2009) Reading Recension 1 of the *Táin*, in Ó hUiginn, Ruairí and Ó Catháin, Brian (eds) (2009) *Ulidia 2: Proceedings of the Second International Conference on the Ulster Cycle of Tales*, 208–17. Maynooth, An Sagart.

Hessen, H. (1912) Drei Palastbeschreibungen im Leabhar na h-Uidhre. *Zeitschrift für celtische Philologie* 12, 498–501.

Hicks, Ronald (2007) Dún Ailinne's role in folklore, myth, and the sacred landscape, in Johnston, Susan A. and Bernard Wailes *Dún Ailinne: Excavations at an Irish royal site 1968–1975*, 183–194. Philadelphia, University of Pennsylvania Museum of Archaeology and Anthropology.

Hill, Jacqueline R. (1988) Popery and Protestantism. Civil and religious liberty: The disputed lessons of Irish history 1690–1812. *Past and Present* 118, 96–129.

Hillers, Barbara (1996–97) *In fer fíamach fírglic*: Ulysses in medieval Irish literature. *Proceedings of the Harvard Celtic Colloquium* 16/17, 15–38.

Hines, John (1989) The military context of the *adversus* Saxonum, in Hawkes, Sonia Chadwick (ed) *Weapons and Warfare in Anglo-Saxon England*, 25–48. Oxford,

Oxford University Committee for Archaeology.

Hyde, Douglas (1899[1967]) *A Literary History of Ireland*. London, Ernest Benn Ltd.

Jackson, Kenneth (1964) *The Oldest Irish Tradition*. Cambridge, Cambridge University.

Johnston, Elva (2013) *Literacy and Identity in Early Medieval Ireland*. Woodbridge, Boydell Press.

Johnston, Susan A. and Bernard Wailes (2007) *Dún Ailinne. Excavations at an Irish Royal Site, 1968–1975*. Philadelphia, University of Pennsylvania Museum of Archaeology and Anthropology.

Jope, E. M. (1955) Chariotry and paired draught in Ireland during the Iron Age. *Ulster Journal of Archaeology* 18, 37–44.

Bender Jørgensen, Lise (1992) *North European Textiles until AD 1000*. Aarhus, Aarhus University Press.

Joyce, P. W. (1903) *A Social History of Ancient Ireland*, 2 vols. London, Longmans, Green and Co.

Karl, Raimund (2003) Iron Age chariots and medieval texts: a step too far in 'breaking down boundaries'? *E-Keltoi* 5, 1–29.

Kavanaugh, R. M. (1991) The horse in Viking Ireland, in Bradley, John (ed) *Settlement and Society in Medieval Ireland*, 89–121. Kilkenny, Boethius Press.

Keating, Geoffrey (Céitinn, Seathrún) (1902–14) *The History of Ireland*. 4 vols. London, Irish Texts Society.

Kelleher, John V. (1971) The Táin and the annals. *Eriu* 22, 107–27.

Kelly, Eamonn P. (2002) Prehistoric antiquities from the Stone Age to the end of the Middle Bronze Age, in Wallace, Patrick F. and Raghnall Ó Floinn (eds) *Treasures of the National Museum of Ireland*, 45–85. Dublin, Gill and Macmillan.

Kelly, Eamon P. (2015) The *longphort* in Viking-Age Ireland: the archaeological evidence, in Clarke, Howard B. and Ruth Johnson (eds) *The Vikings in Ireland and beyond before and after the Battle of Clontarf*, 55–92. Dublin, Four Courts Press.

Kelly, Fergus (1971) OI *claideb* and its cognates. *Ériu* 22, 192–96.

Kelly, Fergus (1997) *Early Irish Farming*. Dublin, Institute for Advanced Studies.

Knott, Eleanor and Gerard Murphy (1966) *Early Irish Literature*. New York, Barnes and Noble.

Koch, John T. (1987) *Llawr en assed (ca 932) 'The laureate hero in the war-chariot:' Some recollections of the Iron Age in the* Gododdin. *Études celtiques* 24, 253–78.

Koch, John (1994) Windows on the Iron Age: 1964–1994, in Mallory, J. P. and G. Stockman (eds) *Ulidia. Proceedings of the First International Conference on the Ulster Cycle of Tales*, 229–37. Belfast, December Publications.

Koch, John (1995) The conversion and the transition from Primitive to Old Irish *c*. 367 – *c*. 637. *Emania* 13, 39–50.

Koch, John T. (1997) *The* Gododdin *of Aneurin :text and context from Dark-Age*

North Britain : historical introduction – reconstructed text – translation – notes. Cardiff, University of Wales Press.

Laing, Lloyd (1975) *The Archaeology of Late Celtic Britain and Ireland c. 400–1200 AD*. London, Methuen.

Lakovides, Spyridon (1977) Vormykenische und mykenische Wehrbauten, in Buchholz, Hans-Günter and Joseph Wiesner (eds) *Archaeologia Homerica: Kriegswesen, Teil 1: Schutzwaffen und Wehrbauten*, 161–221. Göttingen, Vandenhoeck and Ruprecht.

Lamberton, Robert (1997) Homer in antiquity, in Morris, Ian and Barry Powell (eds) (1997) *A New Companion to Homer* 33–54. Leiden, New York, Köln, Brill.

Leaf, Walter (1892) *A Companion to the Iliad for English Readers*. London, Macmillan

Leerssen, Joep (1996) *Mere Irish and Fíor-Ghael*. Cork, Cork University Press.

Leland, Thomas (1784) *Ireland from the Earliest Authentic Accounts*. Dublin, Luke White.

Lucas, A. T. (1954) Bog wood: A study in rural economy. *Béaloideas* 23, 71–134.

Lucas, A. T. (1989) *Cattle in Ancient Ireland*. Kilkenny, Boethius Press.

Lynn, C. J. (1981) The Dorsey and other linear earthworks, in Scott, B. G. (ed) *Studies on Early Ireland*, 121–28. Belfast, Association of Young Irish Archaeologists.

Lynn, C. J. (1989) An interpretation of 'The Dorsey'. *Emania* 6, 5–10.

Lynn, C. J. (1994) Hostels, heroes and tales: Further thoughts on the Navan mound. *Emania* 12, 5–20.

Lynn, C. J. (2003) *Navan Fort: Archaeology and myth*. Dublin, Wordwell.

Lynn, C. J. and J. A. McDowell (2011) *Deer Park Farms: The Excavation of a Raised Rath in the Glenarm Valley, Co. Antrim*. Belfast, the Stationery Office.

Macalister, R. A. S. (1928) *The Archaeology of Ireland*. London, Methuen.

Macalister, R. A. S. (1941) Review of *The Chronicles of Eri. Irish Historical Studies* 2, 335–37.

Mac Cana, Proinsias (1980) *The Learned Tales of Medieval Ireland*. Dublin, Institute for Advanced Studies.

Mac Cana, Proinsias (1989) Notes on the combination of prose and verse in Early Irish narrative, in Tranter, Stephen N. and Hildegard L. C. Tristram (eds) *Early Irish Literature – Media and Communication. Mündlichkeit und Schriftlichkeit in der frühen irischen Literatur*, 125–47. Tübingen, Gunter Narr Verlag.

Mac Coitir, Niall (2010) *Ireland's Animals*. Cork, Collins Press.

Macdonald, Philip (2014a) Data Structure Report: Geophysical Survey and Excavation at the Mound of Down, County Down 2012. Belfast, Unpublished Centre for Archaeological Fieldwork report.

Macdonald, Philip (2014b) Data Structure Report: Geophysical Survey and Excavation at Dundrum Castle, County Down 2012 and 2013. Belfast,

Unpublished Centre for Archaeological Fieldwork report.

MacEoin, Gearóid (1989) Orality and literacy in some Middle-Irish King-tales, in Tranter, Stephen N. and Hildegard L. C. Tristram (eds) *Early Irish Literature – Media and Communication. Mündlichkeit und Schriftlichkeit in der frühen irischen Literatur*, 149–83. Tübingen, Gunter Narr Verlag.

Mac-Geoghegan, James (1844) *The History of Ireland, Ancient and Modern, taken from the most authentic records and dedicated to the Irish Brigade*. Trans. Patrick O'Kelly. Dublin, James Duffy.

MacKillop. Kames (1998) *Dictionary of Celtic Mythology*. Oxford, Oxford University Press.

Mac Mathúna, Liam (1976) Some words for '(man-made) ridge' in Irish, *fu(i)th(a) irbe; immaire; indra, indrad*. Bulletin of the Board of Celtic Studies 26, 445–49.

MacNeill, T. E. (1983) The stone castles of northern County Antrim. *Ulster Journal of Archaeology* 46, 101–28.

MacWhite, Eoin (1945) Early Irish board games. *Éigse* 5, 25–35.

Mäder, S. (1995–96) *Der keltische Streitwagen im Spiegel archäologischer und literarischer Quellen*. Unpublished MA thesis, Albert-Ludwigs-Universität zu Freiburg im Breisgau.

Maguire, Rena (2014) The Y-piece: function, production, typology and possible origins. *Emania* 22, 77–98.

Mahr, Adolph and Joseph Raftery (1932–41) *Christian Art in Ireland*. Dublin, The Stationery Office.

Mallory, J. P. (1981) The sword of the Ulster cycle, in B. G. Scott (ed) *Studies on Early Ireland: Essays in honour of M. V. Duignan*, 99–114. Belfast, Association of Young Irish Archaeologists.

Mallory, J. P. (1984) The Long Stone, Ballybeen, Dundonald, County Down. *Ulster Journal of Archaeology* 47, 1–4.

Mallory, J. P. (1986) Silver in the Ulster Cycle of tales. *Proceedings of the Seventh International Congress of Celtic Studies, Oxford*, 31–78.

Mallory, J. P. (1988) A provisional checklist of Crúachain in the annals. *Emania* 5, 24–26.

Mallory, J. P. (1992) The world of CúChulainn: The archaeology of the *Táin Bó Cuailgne*, in Mallory, J. P. (ed) *Aspects of the Táin*, 103–59. Belfast, December.

Mallory, J. P. (1994) The fort of the Ulster tales. *Emania* 12, 28–38.

Mallory, J. P. (1995) The archaeology of the Irish Dreamtime. *Proceedings of the Harvard Celtic Colloquium* 13 (1993), 1–24.

Mallory, J. P. (1997) Emain Macha and Navan Fort, in Waterman, D. M. (and Lynn, C. J., ed.) *Excavations at Navan Fort 1961–71*, 197–207. Belfast, The Stationery Office.

Mallory, J. P. (1998) The Old Irish chariot in Jasanoff, J., H. C. Melchert and L. Olivier (eds) *Mír Curad: Studies in honor of Calvert Watkins*, 451–64. Innsbruck, Innsbrücker Beiträge zur Sprachwissenschaft.

Mallory, J. P. (2009) The conundrum of Iron Age ceramics: the evidence of language, in Cooney, Gabriel, Katharina Becker, John Coles, Michael Ryan and Susanne Sievers (eds) *Relics of Old Decency: Archaeological studies in later prehistory. Festschrift for Barry Raftery*, 181–92. Dublin, Wordwell.

Mallory, J. P. (2013) *The Origins of the Irish*. London, Thames & Hudson.

Mallory, J. P. and D. Q. Adams (2006) *The Oxford Introduction to Proto-Indo-European and the Proto-Indo-European World*. Oxford, Oxford University.

Mallory, J. P. and M. G. L. Baillie (1988) *Tech ndaruch*: The fall of the house of oak. *Emania* 5, 27–33.

Mallory, J. P. and M. G. L. Baillie (1999) Dating Navan Fort. *Antiquity* 73, 427–31.

Mallory, J. P. and Ruairí Ó hUiginn (1994) The Ulster cycle: A checklist of translations, in Mallory, J. P. and G. Stockman (eds) *Ulidia: Proceedings of the First International Conference on the Ulster Cycle of Tales*, 291–303. Belfast, December.

Matasović, Ranko (2009) *Etymological Dictionary of Proto-Celtic*. Leiden, Brill.

Matasović, Ranko (2009) Descriptions in the Ulster Cycle, in Ó hUiginn, Ruairí and Brian Ó Catháin (eds) *Ulidia 2: Proceedings of the Second International Conference on the Ulster Cycle of Tales*, 95–105. Maynooth, An Sagart.

McCarthy, Daniel P. (2008) *The Irish Annals: Their genesis, evolution and history*. Dublin, Four Courts.

McCone, Kim (1984) Aided Cheltchair Maic Uithechair: Hounds, heroes and hospitallers in Early Irish myth and story. *Ériu* 35, 1–30.

McCone, Kim (1987) Hund, Wolf und Krieger bei den Indogermanen, in Meid, W. (ed) *Studien zum indogermanischen Wortschatz*, 101–54. Innsbruck, Institut für Sprachwissenschaft der Universität.

McCone, Kim (1990) *Pagan Past and Christian Present*. Maynooth, An Sagart.

McCormick, Finbar (1988) The domesticated cat in early Christian and medieval Ireland, in Mac Niocaill, G. and P. Wallace (eds) *Keimelia: Studies in Medieval Archaeology and History in Memory of Tom Delaney*, 218–28. Galway, Galway University Press.

McCormick, Finbar (1991) The animal bones from Haughey's Fort: Second report. *Emania* 8, 27–33.

McCormick, Finbar (1992) Early faunal evidence for dairying. *Oxford Journal of Archaeology* 11, 201–11.

McCormick, Finbar (1995) Cows, ringforts and the origins of Early Christian Ireland. *Emania* 13, 33–37.

McCormick, Finbar (1999) Early evidence for wild animals in Ireland, in Benecke, Norbert (ed) *The Holocene History of the European Vertebrate Fauna, Modern Aspects of Research*, 355–71. Berlin, Verlag Marie Leidorf.

McCormick, Finbar (2002) Appendix 2: The animal bones from Tara. *Discovery Programme Reports, No. 6*, 103–16. Dublin, Royal Irish Academy.

McCormick, Finbar (2008) The decline of the cow: agricultural and settlement change in Early Medieval Ireland. *Peritia* 20, 210–25.

McCormick, Finbar, G. Cribbin, M. E. Robinson, D. W. Shimwell and E. Murphy (1995) A Pagan-Christian transitional burial at Kiltullagh. *Emania* 13, 89–98.

McCormick, Finbar and Emily Murray (2007) *Knowth and the Zooarchaeology of Early Christian Ireland*. Dublin, Royal Irish Academy.

McErlean, Tom (2013) The archaeology of the Ulster cycle on the North Coast, in Toner, Gregory and Séamus Mac Mathúna (eds) *Ulidia 3: Proceedings of the Third International Conference on the Ulster Cycle of Tales*, 1–16. Berlin, Curach Bhán.

McGarry, Tiernan (2010) Late pagan and Early Christian burials in Ireland: some issues and potential explanations, in Corlett, Christaan and Michael Potterton (eds) *Death and Burial in Early Medieval Ireland*, 173–85, Dublin, Wordwell.

McKay, Patrick (1999) *A Dictionary of Ulster Place-names*. Belfast, Queen's University Belfast.

McManus, Damien (1983) A chronology of the Latin loan-words in early Irish. *Ériu* 34, 21–71.

McManus, Damien (1991) *A Guide to Ogam*. Maynooth, An Sagart.

McSparron, Cormac (in press) Pots and peoples: Identity and ceramic technology in medieval Ulster 700–1600 AD, in Hornung, Audrey and Elizabeth Fitzpatrick (eds) *Becoming and Belonging*.

Meyer, Kuno (1895) *The Voyage of Bran Son of Febal to the Land of the Living*. 2 vols. London, David Nutt.

Miles, Brent (2011) *Heroic Saga and Classical Epic in Medieval Ireland*. Cambridge, D. S. Brewer.

Moffat, Alistair (2005) *Before Scotland*. London, Thames & Hudson.

Mooney, Thomas (1845) *History of Ireland, from its first settlement to the present time*. Boston, The Author.

Moore, Sam (2012) *The Archaeology of Slieve Donard*. Downpatrick, Down County Museum.

Morris, Sarah (1997) Homer and the Near East, in Morris, Ian and Barry Powell (eds) (1997) *A New Companion to Homer*, 599–623. Leiden, New York, Köln, Brill.

Muhr, Kay (1996). *Place-Names of Northern Ireland, Vol. 6: County Down IV, North-West Down/Iveagh*. Belfast, Queen's University.

Muhr, Kay (2009) Where did the Brown Bull die: An hypothesis from Ireland's epic *Táin Bó Cúailnge* version I, in Ó hUiginn, Ruairí and Ó Catháin, Brian (eds) *Ulidia 2: Proceedings of the Second International Conference on the Ulster Cycle of Tales*, 121–39. Maynooth, An Sagart.

Murphy, Gerard (1956) *Early Irish Lyrics*. Oxford, Clarendon Press.

Mytum, H. (1992) *The Origins of Early Christian Ireland*. London and New York, Routledge.

Neill, M. E. (2011) The use of woodland in the construction of the houses, in Lynn, C. J. and J. A. McDowell (eds) *Deer Park Farms: The Excavation of a Raised Rath in the Glenarm Valley, Co. Antrim*, 448–68. Belfast, the Stationery Office.

Newman, Conor (1997) *Tara: An Archaeological Survey*. Discovery Programme Monograph 2. Dublin.

Ní Bhrolcháin, Muireann (2009) *An Introduction to Early Irish Literature*. Dublin, Four Courts Press.

Ní Chatháin, Próinséas (1991) Traces of the cult of the horse in Early Irish sources. *Journal of Indo-European Studies* 19, 123–31.

Niehues, Jan (2011) All the king's men? On Celtic board games and their identification, in Bock, Franziska, Dagmar Bronner and Dagmar Schlüter (eds) *Allerlei Keltisches: Studien zu Ehren von Erich Poppe*, 45–60. Berlin, Curach Bhán.

Ní Mhaonaigh, Máire (2005) The literature of medieval Ireland, 800–1200: from the Vikings to the Normans, in Kelleher, Margaret and O'Leary, Philip (eds) *The Cambridge History of Irish Literature*, 32–73. Cambridge, Cambridge University Press.

Ó Béarra, Fergal (2009) The Otherworld realm of *Tír Scáith*, in Hemprich, Gisbert (ed) *Festgabe für Hildegard L. C. Tristram*, 81–100. Berlin, Curach Bhán.

O'Brien, E. (1992a) Pagan and Christian burial in Ireland during the first millennium AD, in Edwards, N. and A. Lane (eds) *The Early Church in Wales and the West*, 130–37, Oxford, Oxbow.

O'Brien, E. (1992b) A re-assessment of the 'Great Sepulchral Mound' containing a Viking burial at Donnybrook, Dublin. *Medieval Archaeology* 36, 170–73.

O'Brien, E. (1993) Contacts between Ireland and Anglo-Saxon England in the Seventh Century. Filmer-Sankey, W. (ed) *Anglo-Saxon Studies in Archaeology and History*, 93–102, Oxford, Oxford University Committee for Archaeology.

O'Brien, E. (1999) *Post-Roman Britain to Anglo-Saxon England: Burial Practices Reviewed*. Oxford, BAR British Series 289.

O'Brien, E. (2008a) Literary insights into the basis of some burial practices in Ireland and Anglo-Saxon England in the seventh and eighth centuries, in Catherine E. Karkov and Helen Damico (eds) *Aedificia Nova: Studies in Honor of Rosemary Cramp* 283–299. Kalamazoo, Medieval Institute Publications.

O'Brien, E. (2008b) Early Medieval sentinel warrior burials. *Peritia* 20, 323–30.

O'Brien, E. (2009) Pagan or Christian? Burial in Ireland during the 5th to 8th centuries AD. Edwards, N. (ed) *The Archaeology of the Early Medieval Celtic Churches*, 135–54. Society for Medieval Archaeology Monograph 29.

O'Brien, E and Bhreathnach, E. (2011) Irish boundary *ferta*, their physical manifestation and historical context, in Edmonds, F. and P. Russell (eds), *Tome: Studies in Medieval Celtic History and Law in Honour of Thomas Charles-Edwards*, 53–64 (Studies in Celtic Histories 31), Woodbridge, The Boydell Press.

O'Brien, Steven (1976) Indo-European eschatology: A model. *Journal of Indo-European Studies* 4, 295–320.

Ó Cathasaigh, Tomás (2006) The literature of medieval Ireland to *c.* 800: St. Patrick to the Vikings, in Kelleher, Margaret and O'Leary, Philip (eds) *The Cambridge History of Irish Literature*, 9–31. Cambridge, Cambridge University Press.

O'Connell, Aidan (2013) *Harvesting the Stars: A Pagan Temple at Lismullin, Co. Meath.* Dublin, National Roads Authority.

O'Connor, Ralph (2013) *The Destruction of Da Derga's Hostel: Kingship and Narrative Artistry in a Mediaeval Irish Saga.* Oxford, Oxford University Press.

O'Connor, Roger (1822–23) *Chronicles of Eri; being the History of the Gaal Sciot Iber: or, the Irish People; translated from the original manuscripts in the Phoenician dialect of the Scythian language.* 2 vols. London, Sir Richard Phillips and Co.

Ó Cróinín, D. (1995) *Early Medieval Ireland 400–1200.* Harlow, Longmans.

O'Curry, Eugene (1861) *Lectures on the Manuscript Materials of Ancient Irish History.* Dublin, James Duffy.

O'Curry, Eugene (1873) *On the Manners and Customs of the Ancient Irish.* 3 vols. Reprinted New York, Lemma, 1971.

O'Flaherty, Roderic (1684 [1793]) *Ogygia, or, a chronological account of Irish Events.* Translated by James Hely. Dublin, M'kenzie.

Ó Floinn, Raghnall (1995) Recent research into Irish bog bodies, in Turner, R. C. and R. G. Scaife (eds) *Bog Bodies: New Discoveries and New Perspectives*, 137–45. London, British Museum Press.

O'Halloran, Clare (2004) *Golden Ages and Barbarous Nations.* Cork, Cork University Press.

Ó hÓgain, Dáithí (1996) Chapter 9. The road and the literature, in Raftery, Barry, *Trackway Excavations in the Mountdillon Bogs, Co. Longford, 1985–1991*, 359–66. Dublin, Crannóg Publication.

Ó hUiginn, Ruairí (1988) Crúachu, Connachta, and the Ulster cycle. *Emania* 5, 19–23.

Olmsted, Garrett (1976) The Gundestrup version of *Táin Bó Cúailnge. Antiquity* 50, 95–103.

Olmsted, Garrett (1992) The earliest narrative version of the *Táin*: Seventh-century poetic references to *Táin Bó Cúailnge. Emania* 10, 5–17.

Ó Maolfabhail, Art (1973) *Camán: Two Thousand Years of Hurling in Ireland.* Dundalk, Dundalgan Press.

Ó Néill, Pádraig (1999) The Latin colophon to the 'Táin Bó Cúailnge' in the Book of Leinster: A critical view of Old Irish literature. *Celtica* 23, 269–75.

O'Nolan, Kevin (1968) Homer and the Irish hero tale. *Studia Hibernica* 8, 7–20.

O'Rahilly, Thomas (1946) *Early Irish History and Mythology.* Dublin, Dublin Institute for Advanced Studies.

O'Sullivan, Aidan and Colin Breen (2007) *Maritime Ireland: An Archaeology of Coastal Communities.* Stroud, Tempus.

O'Sullivan, Aidan and L. Harney (2008) *Early Medieval Archaeology Project: Investigating the character of early medieval archaeological excavations, 1970–2002.* Dublin, the Heritage Council and UCD.

O'Sullivan, Aidan, McCormick, F., Kerr, T.R., and Harney, L. (2014) *Early Medieval Ireland, AD 400–1100. The evidence from archaeological excavations.* Dublin: Royal Irish Academy.

Owen-Crocker, Gale R. (2004) *Dress in Anglo-Saxon England.* Woodbridge, Boydell Press.

Page, Denys L. (1959) *History and the Homeric Iliad.* Berkeley and Los Angeles, University of California Press.

Pflug-Harttung, J. (1892) Les cycles épiques d'Irlande: leur date et leur charactere. *Revue celtique* 13, 170–86.

Plowden, Francis (1831) *The History of Ireland from its Invasion under Henry II to its Union with Great Britain.* 2 vols. London, Wm. Eusebius Andrews.

Plunkett, Gill (2008) Land-use patterns and cultural change in the Middle to Late Bronze Age in Ireland: Inferences from pollen records. *Vegetational History Archaeobotany* 18, 273–95.

Pokorny, Julius (1918) Beiträge zur ältesten Geschichte Irlands. *Zeitschrift für celtische Philologie* 12, 195–231.

Powell, T. G. E. (1950) The Celtic settlement of Ireland, in Fox, C. and B. Dickens (eds) *The Early Cultures of North-west Europe*, 173–95. Cambridge, Cambridge University.

Raaflaub, Kurt A. (1997) Homeric society, in Morris, Ian and Barry Powell (eds) (1997) *A New Companion to Homer*, 624–48. Leiden, New York, Köln, Brill.

Raftery, B. (1981) Iron Age burials in Ireland, in D. Ó Corráin (ed) *Irish Antiquity: Essays and Studies presented to Professor M. J. O'Kelly*, 173–204. Cork, Tower Books.

Raftery, B. (1983) *A Catalogue of Irish Iron Age Antiquities.* Marburg, Veröffentlichung des vorgeschichtlichen Seminars Marburg.

Raftery, B. (1984) *La Tène in Ireland.* Marburg, Veröffentlichung des vorgeschichtlichen Seminars Marburg.

Raftery, B. (1993) Fahren und Reiten in Irland in der Eisenzeit: Die archäologischen Belege, in Tristram, Hildegard L. C. (ed) *Studien zur Táin Bó Cuailnge*, 173–91. Tübingen, Gunter Narr Verlag.

Raftery, B. (1994) *Pagan Celtic Ireland.* London, Thames & Hudson.

Raftery, B. (1995) The conundrum of Irish Iron Age pottery, in Raftery, B., V. Megaw and V. Rigby (eds.), *Sites and Sights of the Iron Age: Essays on Fieldwork and Museum Research presented to Ian Mathieson Stead*, 149–56. Oxbow Monograph 56. Oxford.

Raftery, B. (1996) *Trackway Excavations in the Mountdillon Bogs, Co. Longford,*

1985–1991, 359–66. Dublin, Crannóg Publication.

Rau, W. (1983) *Zur vedischen Altertumskunde.* Wiesbaden.

Riddler, Ian and Nicola Trzaska-Nartowski (2009) Appendix 13: Bone objects, in O'Hara, R. (ed) *Report on the Archaeological Excavation of Collierstown 1, Co. Meath.* Unpublished report at www.m3motorway.ie

Ridgeway, William (1905–6) The date of the first shaping of the Cuchulainn saga. *Proceedings of the British Academy 1905–06*, 135–68.

Roche, Helen (2002) Excavations at Ráith na Ríg, Tara, Co. Meath, 1997. *Discovery Programme Reports* 6, 19–165.

Roosevelt, Theodore (1924) The ancient Irish sagas, *The Works of Theodore Roosevelt, Memorial Edition, vol. 14*, 384–401 (originally published in the *Century Magazine*, January, 1907).

Russell, I., M. Mossops and E. Corcoran (2002) Claristown 2: a cemetery and later cairn. *Ríocht na Midhe* 13, 23–31.

Russell, I., M. Mossops and E. Corcoran (2012) The excavation of an Iron Age site at Claristown, Co. Meath, in Corlett, Christiaan and Michael Potterton (eds) (2012) *Life and Death in Iron Age Ireland*, 267–72. Dublin, Wordwell.

Ryan, Michael (1981) Some archaeological comments on the occurrence and use of silver in pre-Viking Ireland, B. G. Scott (ed) *Studies on Early Ireland: Essays in Honour of M. V. Duignan*, 45–50. Belfast, Association of Young Irish Archaeologists.

Rynne, Etienne (1981) A classification of pre-Viking Irish iron swords, in B. G. Scott (ed) *Studies on Early Ireland: Essays in Honour of M. V. Duignan*, 93–97. Belfast.

Sandberg-McGowan, Astrid (1996) Viking influence on Irish weaponry and dress?, in Ahlqvist, Anders et al. (eds) *Celtica Helsingiensia: Proceedings from a Symposium on Celtic Studies*, 215–31. Helsinki (= *Commentationes Humanarum Litterarum* 107).

Sayers, William (1981) Three charioteering gifts in Táin Bó Cúailnge and Mesca Ulad: *immorchor ndelend, foscul ndíruch, léim dar boild. Ériu* 32, 163–67.

Sayers, William (1984) Old Irish *fert* 'tie-pole', *fertas* 'swingle-tree', and the seeress Fedelm. *Études celtiques* 21, 171–83.

Sayers, William (1991) Textual notes on descriptions of the Old Irish chariot and team. *Studia Celtica Japonica* 4, 15–35.

Sayers, William (1994) Conventional descriptions of the horse in the Ulster cycle. *Études celtiques* 30, 233–49.

Sayers, William (1996) Homeric echoes in Táin Bó Cúailnge? *Emania* 14, 65–73.

Sayers, William (2014) Fantastic technology in early Irish literature. *Études celtiques* 40, 85–98.

Schlüter, Dagmar (2009) A contradiction in terms? A short note on *Do Fhaillsigud Tána Bó Cúailnge*, in Ó hUiginn, Ruairí and Ó Catháin, Brian (eds) *Ulidia 2: Proceedings of the Second International Conference on the Ulster Cycle of Tales*, 25–30. Maynooth, An Sagart.

Schlüter, Dagmar (2010) *History or Fable? The Book of Leinster as a Document of Cultural Memory in Twelfth-century Ireland*. Munster, Nodus Publikationen.

Scowcroft, Mark (2009) Mediaeval recensions of the *Lebor Gabála*, in Carey, John (ed) *Lebor Gabála Érenn: Textual History and Pseudohistory*, 1–20. Dublin, Irish Texts Society, Subsidiary Series No. 20.

Sherratt, E. S. (1990) 'Reading the texts': Archaeology and the Homeric question. *Antiquity* 64, 807–24.

Siewers, Alfred K. (2009) Nature as Otherworld: Landscape as centre in *Táin Bó Cúailnge*, in Ó hUiginn, Ruairí and Ó Catháin, Brian (eds) *Ulidia 2: Proceedings of the Second International Conference on the Ulster Cycle of Tales*, 81–94. Maynooth, An Sagart.

Singh, Sarva Daman (1965) *Ancient Indian Warfare with Special Reference to the Vedic Period*. Leiden, Brill.

Slavin, Michael (2005) *The Ancient Books of Ireland*. Dublin, Wolfhound Press.

Smith, Roland M. (1958) Meredith Hanmer and the Cesair myth. *Journal of Celtic Studies* 2, 207–13.

Smyth, Jessica and Richard P. Evershed (2015) Milking the megafauna: Using organic residue analysis to understand early farming practice. *Environmental Archaeology*, available at http://www.maneyonline.com/doi/full/10.1179/1749631414Y.0000000045

Spenser, Edmund (1633) *A View of the State of Ireland*. Available at http://www.ucc.ie/celt/published/E500000-001/

Stanford, W. B. (1970) Towards a history of classical influences in Ireland. *Proceedings of the Royal Irish Academy* 70C, 13–91.

Stevenson, R. and J. Emery (1963–64) The Gaulcross hoard of Pictish silver. *Proceedings of the Society of Antiquaries of Scotland* 97, 206–11.

Stifter, David (2009) The Old Irish chariot and its technology: A case of creative transmission in medieval Irish literature, in Zimmer, Stefan (ed) *Kelten am Rhein*, 279–89. Mainz, Verlag Philipp von Zabern.

Stout, Matthew (2000) *The Irish Ringfort*. Dublin, Four Courts Press.

Stubbings, Frank H. (1962) Arms and armour, in Alan J. B. Wace (ed) *A Companion to Homer*, 504–22. London, Macmillan.

Sweetman, P. D. (1982–83) Reconstruction and partial excavation of a burial mound at Ninch, Co. Meath. *Ríocht na Midhe* 7, 42–57.

Swift, Catherine (1997) *Ogam Stones and the Earliest Irish Christians*. Maynooth Monographs, Series Minor 2. Maynooth.

Swift, Catherine (2015) Celtic berserkrs and feeble steersmen: Hiberno-Scandinavian military culture in Middle Irish literature, in Clarke, Howard B. and Ruth Johnson (eds) *The Vikings in Ireland and beyond before and after the Battle of Clontarf*, 451–69. Dublin, Four Courts Press.

Thomas, C. G. (ed.) (1970) *Homer's History: Mycenaean or Dark Age?* New York, Holt, Rinehart and Winston.

Thurneysen, Rudolf (1921) *Die irische Helden- und Königsage bis zum 17. Jahrhundert*. Halle, Max Niemeyer.

Tierney, J. J. (1959–60) The Celtic ethnography of Poseidonius. *Proceedings of the Royal Irish Academy* 60C, 189–275.

Toner, Gregory (2000) The Ulster cycle: historiography or fiction? *Cambrian Medieval Celtic Studies* 40, 1–20.

Toner, Gregory (2009) Scribe and text in *Lebor na hUidre*: H's intentions and methodology, in Ó hUiginn, Ruairí and Ó Catháin, Brian (eds) *Ulidia 2: Proceedings of the Second International Conference on the Ulster Cycle of Tales*, 106–20. Maynooth, An Sagart.

Tranter, S. (1989) Marginal problems, in Tranter, Stephen N. and Hildegard L. C. Tristram (eds) *Early Irish Literature – Media and Communication*, 221–40. Tübingen, Gunter Narr Verlag.

Tristram, Hildegard L. C. (1988) Aspects of tradition and innovation in the *Táin Bó Cuailnge*, in Matthews, Richard and Joachim Schmole-Rostosky (1988) *Papers on Language and Mediaeval Studies Presented to Alfred Schopf*, 19–38. Frankfurth, Peter Lang.

Tristram, Hildegard L. C. (1989) Einleitung, in Tranter, Stephen N. and Hildegard L. C. Tristram (eds) *Early Irish Literature – Media and Communication*, 13–38. Tübingen, Gunter Narr Verlag.

Tsvetoukhina, Maria, Tatyana Mikhailovka and Grigory Bondarenko (2013) The Ulster cycle in Russia. *Emania* 21, 5–13.

Turner, Frank M. (1997) The Homeric question, in Morris, Ian and Barry Powell (eds) *A New Companion to Homer*, 123–45. Leiden, New York, Köln, Brill.

Vansina, Jan (1961) *Oral Tradition: A Study in Historical Methodology*. London, Routledge and Kegan Paul.

van Wees, Hans (1997) Homeric warfare, in Morris, Ian and Barry Powell (eds) *A New Companion to Homer*, 668–93. Leiden, New York, Köln, Brill.

Van Wijngaarden-Bakker, Louise H. (1989) Faunal remains and the Irish Mesolithic, in Bonsall, Clive (ed) *The Mesolithic in Europe*, 125–33. Edinburgh, John Donald.

Waddell, John (2005) *Foundation Myths: The Beginnings of Irish Archaeology*. Dublin, Wordwell.

Waddell, John (2014) *Archaeology and Celtic Myth*. Dublin, Four Courts Press.

Waddell, John, Fenwick, Joseph and Barton, Kevin (2009) *Rathcroghan: Archaeological and Geophysical Survey in a Ritual Landscape*. Dublin, Wordwell.

Walsh, Aidan (1987) Excavating the Black Pig's Dyke. *Emania* 3, 5–11.

Walter, H. (1969) *Die 'Collectanea rerum memorabilum' des C. Iulius Solinus: Ihre Entstehung und die Echtheit ihrer Zweitfassung (= Hermes Einzelschriften Heft 22)*. Wiesbaden.

Warner, R. (1985) The Mountsandel area in later prehistoric and historic times, in Woodman, Peter, *Excavations at Mountsandel 1973–77*, 193–95. Belfast, Stationary Office.

Warner, R. B. (1988) Loch Cirr/Cúl Chíre. *Emania* 4, 36.

Warner, R. (1990) The 'prehistoric' Irish annals. *Archaeology Ireland* 4, 1, 30–33.

Warner, R. B. (1994) The 'Ernean house'. *Emania* 12, 21–27.

Warner, R. B. (2000) Keeping out the Otherworld: The internal ditch at Navan and the other 'hengiform' enclosures. *Emania* 18, 39–44.

Warner, R. B. (2004) Notes on the inception and early development of the royal mound in Ireland, in Pantos, Aliki and Sarah Semple (eds) *Assembly Places and Practices in Medieval Europe*, 27–43. Dublin, Four Courts Press.

Warner, R. B. (2014) The gold fragments from Haughey's Fort, Co. Armagh: Description and XRF analysis. *Emania* 22, 69–76.

Warner, R. (in press) The Navan temple, the tech midchúarta and Fiachna's fatal round-house.

Waterman, D. M. and C. J. Lynn (eds) (1997) *Excavations at Navan Fort 1961–71*. Belfast, The Stationery Office.

Watkins, Calvert (1963) Indo-European metrics and archaic Irish verse. *Celtica* 6, 194–249.

West, Máire (2013) Weavers' beams, weaving rods and the Prophetess Fedelm, in Ó Baoill, Dónall, Donncha Ó hAodha and Nollaig Ó Muraile (eds), *Saltair Saíochta, Sanasaíochta agus Seanchais: A Festschrift for Gearóid Mac Eoin*, 463–74. Dublin, Four Courts Press.

Whitfield, Niamh (2004) More thoughts on the wearing of brooches in early medieval Ireland, in Hourihane, Colum (ed) *Irish Art Historical Studies in Honour of Peter Harbison*, 70–108. Princeton, Princeton University.

Whitfield, Niamh (2006) Dress and accessories in the early Irish tale 'The wooing of Becfhola', in Netherton, Robin and Gale R. Owen-Crocker (eds) *Medieval Clothing and Textiles*, 1–34. Woodbridge, Boydell.

Whitty, Yvonne (2012) A Iron Age ring-ditch complex at Holdenstown 1, Co. Kilkenny, in Corlett, Christiaan and Michael Potterton (eds) *Life and Death in Iron Age Ireland*, 313–26. Dublin, Wordwell.

Williams, Fionnuala (1987) The Black Pig and linear earthworks. *Emania* 3, 12–19.

Wilson, Jacqueline, Christopher Standish and Elizabeth O'Brien (2012) Investigating mobility and migration in the later Irish Iron Age, in Wilson, Jacqueline, Ger Dowling, Michael Bevivino and Philippa Barry (eds) *Late Iron Age and 'Roman' Ireland (Discovery Programme Reports 8)*, 127–49. Dublin, Wordwell.

Wolf, Mark J. P. (2012) *Building Imaginary Worlds: The Theory and History of Subcreation*. New York and London, Routledge.

Wright, Thomas (1905) *The Historical Works of Giraldus Cambrensis*. London, Bell.

Sources of Illustrations

Unless otherwise credited, illustrations are courtesy the author.

1.1 after frontispiece Yeats, W. B (1925) *A Vision*. London, T. Werner Laurie; 1.2 after O'Meara 1982, 71; 1.3 after O'Meara 1982, 85; 1.4 Trinity College Library, Dublin; 1.5 after O'Curry 1873, vol. 1, ccccxl, fig. 23; 4.2 after O'Curry 1873, vol. 1, ccccxxxviii-iv, figs 14 and 15; 4.3 after Mallory 2013, 132, fig. 5.1; 4.4 after Eogan, George (1983) *Hoards of the Irish Later Bronze Age*. Dublin, University College, 259, fig. 2; 4.5 after Eogan 1983, 241, fig. A3; 4.6 after Eogan 1983, 228, fig. A; 4.7 courtesy Mike Baillie; 6.2 after Raftery 1996, 259, fig. 381, E310:37 and E310:34; 6.4 after Jope, Martyn (ed.) (1966) *An Archaeological Survey of County Down*. Belfast, Her Majesty's Stationery Office, 150, fig. 89; 6.5 © Crown copyright. Reproduced with the permission of the Controller of Her Majesty's Stationery Office; 6.6 after Mallory 1992, 127, fig. 7; 6.7 Knockaulin and Navan after Mallory 2013, 166, fig. 6.5; Deer Park after Lynn and McDowell 2011, 134, fig. 7.5; 6.8 © Crown copyright. Reproduced with the permission of the Controller of Her Majesty's Stationery Office; 6.9 after Mallory, J. P. and T. E. MacNeill (1991)

The Archaeology of Ulster. Belfast, Institute of Irish Studies, 151, fig. 5-8; 6.10 after Mallory, J. P. and T. E. MacNeill (1991) *The Archaeology of Ulster*. Belfast, Institute of Irish Studies, 153, fig. 5-11; 6.12 courtesy Barrie Hartwell; 6.14 after Mallory 2013, 167, fig. 6.6a; 6.15 after Mallory 2013, 167, fig. 6.6b; 6.16 courtesy John Waddell; 6.17 after O'Connell 2013, 151; 6.18 courtesy Richard Warner, reconstructions drawn by Deirdre Crone; 7.1 after Mallory 1981, 105, fig. 1; 7.2 after Raftery 1983, fig. 111, 263; 7.3 after Mallory 1992, 142, fig. 11; 7.4 after Mallory 1981, fig. 2; 7.5 after O'Curry 1873, ccccxlvii, fig. 31; 7.6 after Raftery 1983, fig. 115, 283; 7.7 after Raftery 1983, fig. 119, 310; 7.8a (after Sliney, Will (2013) *Celtic Warrior The Legend of Cú Chulainn*. Dublin, O' Brien Press, cover; 7.8b Brown, Patrick (2014) *The Cattle Raid of Cooley* = The Ulster Cycle, Issue 8, 25, Belfast, Patrick Brown; 7.8c Gary Hamilton, 1989 comic *Cúchulainn: Champion of Ulster*, written by Michael Hall; 7.9 after Hines 1989, 31, fig. 3.3; 7.10 after O'Meara 1982, 107; 7.11 after Raftery 1983, fig. 113, 279; 7.12 courtesy Barrie Hartwell and Libby Mulqueeny; 8.1 after Raftery 1983, fig. 98, 236b; 8.2 after Raftery 1983, fig. 99, 235; 8.3 after Raftery 1994, 107, fig. 57c; 8.4 after Raftery

1983, fig. 99, 237; 8.5 after Raftery 1983, fig. 89, 215; 8.7 after Greene 1972, 65, fig. 16; 8.8 after Karl 2003, 20, fig. 12; 8.9 after Raftery 1983, fig. 4, 8; 8.10 after Raftery 1994, 100, fig. 51; 8.11 courtesy Valerie Hall; 8.12 after Raftery 1983, fig. 231, 834; 9.1 after Hawkes 1981, 69, pl. 3; 9.2 after Raftery 1993, fig. 130, 383; 9.3 after Laing, Lloyd (1975) *Late Celtic Britain and Ireland*, 318, fig. 119. London, Methuen; 9.4 after Raftery 1993, fig. 219, 820; 9.5 © Crown copyright. Reproduced with the permission of the Controller of Her Majesty's Stationery Office; 9.6 after Bruce-Mitford, Rupert (1983) *The Sutton Hoo Ship-Burial*. London, British Museum, Vol. 3, 631 (f 447), 682 (f496-harp) and 706 (f 511-Taplow); 9.7 after Raftery 1994, 123, fig. 73; 10.1 courtesy Finbar McCormick; 10.2 after Mytum 1992, 32, fig. 2:3.

PLATES

II Noel Ross; V John Waddell; IX, X By permission of the Royal Irish Academy © RIA; XI Trinity College Library, Dublin; XII © Rik Hamilton/Alamy Stock Photo; XIII © Design Pics Inc/Alamy Stock Photo; XV © Tibor Bognar/Alamy Stock Photo; XVI Central Bank of Ireland; XVII © Design Pics Inc/Alamy Stock Photo; XVIII, XIX National Museum of Ireland, Dublin.

Index